Language, Discourse and Literature

Also available from Unwin Hyman

Vocabulary
Applied Linguistic Perspectives
Ronald Carter

Reading Children's Writing
A Linguistic View
Edited by John Harris and Jeff Wilkinson

Rhetoric of Everyday English Texts
Michael P. Jordan

On the Surface of Discourse
Michael Hoey

Language and Literature
An Introductory Reader in Stylistics
Edited by Ronald Carter

Towards a Contextual Grammar of English
Eugene Winter

Psychology in Foreign Language Teaching
Second Edition
Steven H. McDonough

Variety in Contemporary English
W. R. O'Donnell, Loreto Todd

Language Planning and Language Education
Edited by Chris Kennedy

Language, Discourse and Literature

An Introductory Reader in Discourse Stylistics

Edited by
RONALD CARTER
Department of English Studies, University of Nottingham

and

PAUL SIMPSON
Department of English Language and Literature, University of Liverpool

London
UNWIN HYMAN
Boston   Sydney   Wellington

Published by the Academic Division of
Unwin Hyman Ltd
15/17 Broadwick Street, London W1V 1FP

Unwin Hyman Inc.
8 Winchester Place, Winchester, Mass. 01890, USA

Allen & Unwin (Australia) Ltd
8 Napier Street, North Sydney, NSW 2060, Australia

Allen & Unwin (New Zealand) Ltd in association with the
Port Nicholson Press Ltd
60 Cambridge Terrace, Wellington, New Zealand

First published in 1989

British Library Cataloguing in Publication Data

Language, discourse and literature; an introductory reader in
discourse stylistics.
1. English language. Discourse. Analysis
I. Carter, Ronald, 1947–   II. Simpson, Paul
425
ISBN 0–04–445007–9
ISBN 0–04–445006–0 Pbk

Library of Congress Cataloging-in-Publication Data
Language, discourse and literature.
Includes index.
1. English literature – History and criticism.
2. Discourse analysis, Literary. I. Carter, Ronald. II. Simpson, Paul.
PR65.D57L36   1988   809   88–5678
ISBN 0–04–445007–9 (alk. paper)
ISBN 0–04–445006–0 (pbk. : alk. paper)

Set in 10 on 11 point Times by Phoenix Photosetting, Chatham
and printed in Great Britain by
Billing and Sons, London and Worcester

Contents

Editors' Preface

The introduction which follows tries to say a lot about the subject of stylistics within a limited number of words. We also presume a general acquaintance with the aims and methods of stylistics and with the kinds of controversies and disputes which surround its academic practice either in separate language and literature departments or, more controversially, as an integrating discipline within departments of English studies. The introduction to the book also assumes some understanding of developments in contemporary linguistics; in particular, it is important to grasp why analysis of grammar only takes us some of the way in accounting for textual meaning and why this needs to be supplemented by analysis 'beyond the sentence' or beyond grammar, i.e. in the domain which is termed text or discourse. We also have to presume that readers recognize that linguistic-stylistic analysis does not proceed without theoretical assumptions and that it is important that these should be made explicit. In this respect developments in modern literary theory are especially important and we make no apology for dealing with these developments; neither do we feel the need to point out recognizable self-evident positions: for example, that there is no such thing as an innocent, theory-free reading of a text.

The introduction which follows may therefore appear rather dense in some places for some readers. In part, this is because the volume of essays collected here 'follows on' from the companion volume *Language and Literature: An Introductory Reader in Stylistics* (Carter, 1982), in which considerable space is devoted to discussion of basic concepts in stylistics, language study and literary theory. In part, it is because several books now exist which provide an appropriate introduction to key concepts and theories. Apart from the introduction to the companion volume, other useful introductory discussions of these issues occur in Widdowson's *Stylistics and the Teaching of Literature* (Widdowson, 1975), Belsey's *Critical Practice* (Belsey, 1980), and Leech and Short's *Style in Fiction* (especially ch. 10) (Leech and Short, 1981). Readers may wish to undertake preliminary reading in these areas prior to embarking on our 'introduction'.

RONALD CARTER
University of Nottingham

PAUL SIMPSON
University of Liverpool

Acknowledgements

The editors wish to thank the following for making the production of this volume possible: the contributors for their hard work, co-operation and patience in dealing with many unsolicited comments and queries from the editors; Cathy Rees, Tina Benson, Sue Drury and Ann Collins for their assistance in typing the manuscript and pointing out inconsistencies of presentation and spelling; Jane Harris-Matthews of Unwin Hyman for her hard work, efficiency and high level of support and encouragement; colleagues at the Universities of Nottingham and Liverpool, especially Margaret Berry, Reader in Modern English Language at Nottingham, for many enlightening conversations about text and discourse analysis; Professor John Sinclair for advice on the design of the earlier volume in a series he edited on which this book is largely modelled.

Acknowledgement is also due to the following journals and publishers for allowing us to reprint articles and chapters which originally appeared under their imprint. (In all cases, however, the chapters published here have been revised, extended, or re-edited, in some cases extensively, in order to fit the pedagogical design of the volume.) For Chapter 2, Trinity College Press, Dublin in J. Harris, D. Little and D. Singleton (eds), *Perspectives on the English Language in Ireland* (1986); for Chapter 3, *Language and Style* (1983); for Chapter 4, Vision Press, London, in R. Giddings (ed.), *The Changing World of Charles Dickens* (1983); for Chapter 7, *Lacus Forum* (1981); For Chapter 8, *Language and Style* (1981); for Chapter 10, *Poetics Today* (1987); for Chapter 11, *Lingua e Stile* (1987); for Chapter 13, Singapore University Press, in Hyland, P. (ed.) *Discharging the Canon: Cross-Cultural Readings in Literature* (1986).

Acknowledgement is due to the copyright holders for their kind permission to reprint the following extracts: The Bernard Shaw Estate for the extract from *Major Barbara*; Faber and Faber Ltd for 'O Where Are You Going?' from *Collected Poems* by W. H. Auden (acknowledgement also due to Random House, Inc., USA); Methuen London for 'Trouble in the Works' from *A Slight Ache and Other Plays* by Harold Pinter (acknowledgement also due to Grove Press, Inc., USA); Rex Collings for 'Book Ends' from *The School of Eloquence and Other Poems* by Tony Harrison; Jonathan Cape Ltd, for the extract from *Portrait of the Artist as a Young Man* also reprinted with the permission of Viking Penguin Inc., USA and the Estate of James Joyce; Edwin Thumboo for 'Steel', 'May, 1954' and 'Fifteen Years After' by Edwin Thumboo; and the English Folk Dance and Song Society for 'Salisbury Plain' from *The Penguin Book of English Folk Songs*.

Notes on Contributors

RONALD CARTER (editor) is senior lecturer in English studies and director of the Centre for English Language Education at the University of Nottingham. He has written and edited numerous books and articles in the fields of applied linguistics, language education, and literary studies. He is currently working on a book on language and literature in education.

PAUL SIMPSON (editor) is lecturer in English language in the Department of English Language and Literature, University of Liverpool, where he teaches courses in sociolinguistics, the history of English and stylistics. He has recently contributed a section on stylistics to *The Year's Work in English Studies* (1987) and papers to international symposia on the writings of Flann O'Brien. He is preparing a book on sociolinguistic approaches to narrative.

DAVID BIRCH lectures in the Department of Human Communication, Murdoch University, Western Australia. He is the author of numerous articles in stylistics, literary and cultural theory, and drama studies, as well as editor of two collections of papers on stylistics and discourse. His book *Language, Literature and Critical Practice* is shortly to be published by Routledge.

WINIFRED CROMBIE is principal lecturer in linguistics at the Hatfield Polytechnic. She has published widely on applied linguistic topics, with particular reference to syllabus design. Her most recent book, *Free Verse and Prose Style*, was published by Croom Helm in 1987. She is currently interested in approaches to teaching English as a mother tongue.

ROGER FOWLER is Professor of English and Linguistics at the University of East Anglia. He has written twelve books on linguistics and literature. His most recent was *Linguistic Criticism* (Oxford University Press). He is currently working further on the theory and practice of a critical linguistics.

JOHN HAYNES is reader in English at the Ahmadu Bello University in Zaria, Nigeria. He has published articles on the teaching of stylistics, systemic linguistics, and literatures in English in Africa. His book *African Poetry and the English Language* (Macmillan) was published in 1987. A further book, *Introducing Stylistics*, is to be published in 1988 by Hutchinson.

VIMALA HERMAN lectures in the Department of English, University of Lancaster. She has published widely on stylistics and literary theory, pragmatics, and nineteenth- and twentieth-century literature. She is currently engaged in writing a book on metaphor.

MICHAEL HOEY lectures in the Department of English Language and Literature, University of Birmingham, where he teaches stylistics, discourse analysis, and modern English language. His research interests are in written discourse studies, and he has published widely in this field. He is currently working on an introduction to discourse analysis, a book on narrative organization and an extensive study of lexis in text.

WALTER NASH is Professor of Modern English Language, University of Nottingham. He has published numerous articles and books on literary style, English usage, and the language of texts. His current work includes a study of *Style in Popular Fiction*, an edited collection of papers on *Academic Writing* and a book on rhetoric.

MICK SHORT is senior lecturer and Head of Department of Linguistics and Modern English Language, University of Lancaster. He has published extensively in the field of stylistics and pedagogies of language and literature and is the co-author (with G. N. Leech) of *Style in Fiction* (Longman, 1981). A collection of essays edited by Mick Short entitled *Reading, Analyzing and Teaching Literature* (Longman) is to be published in 1988. He is working on a new introduction to stylistics.

MICHAEL TOOLAN is lecturer in the Department of English, University of Washington, Seattle. He has published extensively on literary dialogue, stylistics, and literary theory. His book *Narrative: A Critical Linguistic Introduction* is to be published in 1988 by Routledge. He is currently working on a book on the language of William Faulkner.

JEAN JACQUES WEBER lectures at the University of Trier, West Germany, and at colleges in Luxemburg, where he is also resident. He has published several articles on stylistics and discourse and a widely used teaching bibliography on linguistic stylistics (PALA). He is currently working on a book on the language of George Eliot's fiction.

Language, Discourse and Literature

Introduction

I The Growth of Stylistics 1960–1980

In a paper published in 1960 Roman Jakobson made a statement about the relationship between linguistics and literary studies which has been cited in almost every subsequent book on the subject. This book is no exception:

> If there are some critics who still doubt the competence of linguistics to embrace the field of poetics, I privately believe that the poetic incompetence of some bigoted linguists has been mistaken for an inadequacy of the linguistic science itself. All of us here, however, definitely realize that a linguist deaf to the poetic function of language and a literary scholar indifferent to linguistic problems and unconversant with linguistic methods are equally flagrant anachronisms. (Jakobson, 1960: 377)

In the intervening years Jakobson's call has echoed in roughly the same form in many communities of linguists and literary critics. Many chose not to heed the call or, indeed, chose not to listen in the first place; and at times the decision of the non-listeners looks to have been a wise one, for the relationship between these two disciplines has been uneasy and is still fraught with all kinds of theoretical and practical difficulties. An introduction such as this cannot be the place to chart such difficulties in any real detail, but it does help to put the present volume in context if we attempt to review some of the main landmarks in the field of stylistics during the past twenty-five years or so. In so doing, we cannot avoid exploring the nature of the interface between linguistics and literature.

Jakobson's 'concluding statement' – the title of his paper presented to the Indiana Style Conference in 1958, from which the above extract is taken – was published in the first of a number of landmark volumes of papers devoted to the subject of stylistics. In fact, a sense of the main movements in the field can be obtained from an examination of three collections of essays, in particular, published one at the beginning of each of the last three decades – in 1960, 1970 and 1981.

In 1960 the newly developing field of stylistics was dominated by attempts to define *style* and to isolate the particular properties of authorial, period, or group *styles*. An interesting feature of the work in stylistics represented by the Indiana Style Conference was that it was not wholly intrinsic to linguistics; the impetus to definition was provided by literary critics, anthropologists and psychologists as well as linguists. The specifically linguistic investigations undertaken at that time were devoted mainly to syntax and phonology, especially the latter, which is seen in the relatively large number of articles devoted to metrics and sound patterning in poetry. There was also considerable interest in the psychological properties of style, particularly in readers' responses to style and in style as a psycholinguistic and cognitive phenomenon.

The eclectic, interdisciplinary nature of the work indicates an open-mindedness characteristic of new fields of research which are in the process of defining their own epistemologies and methodologies. At the interface with literary criticism, however, it is worth noting that at this stage there was some measure of absorption of stylistics into the dominant critical paradigm at that time, the approach which was termed New Criticism and which was characterized by a close verbal analysis of texts.

By 1970 the map had been partly redrawn. During the 1960s a rapid expansion took place, with the dominant influences in linguistics those of Chomsky's work on transformational grammar together with Chomsky-inspired work in generative phonology. The transformational–generative approach to stylistic analysis is represented in Ohmann (1964, 1966), Levin (1971) and Thorne (1969), and lucidly surveyed in Messing (1971). Stylisticians within this period sought to demonstrate the differences between a poet's grammar and underlying grammatical norms, which are usually seen to be simple kernel sentences in a basic declarative form. A writer's style was thus described in terms of the particular transformational options selected by the writer from the underlying base.

The character of this work was largely formalist, and the decade also saw a return to a fuller consideration of the work of Russian formalists and their Prague School descendants, such as Jakobson, Mukarovsky and Havranek, whose essays from the 1930s received a timely reprint in the volume edited by Donald Freeman entitled *Linguistics and Literary Style* (Freeman, 1970), which is especially representative of work in stylistics in the 1960s. Another aspect of the formalism of these years was that the impulse to explain continued. Linguistics was used for its explanatory potential and to enable basic questions such as 'What *is* style?' to be addressed in a thorough and fundamental manner. There was less emphasis on describing the language of individual texts and on interpreting them; correspondingly, there was now a predominant awareness that style could be more fully accounted for by text-immanent linguistic explanation and less effectively by means of interdisciplinary approaches.

Given the nature of stylistics, which is a discipline that will necessarily be dependent on the nature of advances within the field of linguistics, it is not surprising that the 1970s saw the increasing influence of what within linguistics can be termed *functionalism*. In the second of Donald Freeman's decade-marking volumes, published in 1981 and entitled *Essays in Modern Stylistics*, formalist- and functionalist-inspired papers sit alongside one another (see Freeman, 1981).

Functionalism in linguistics grew up in the 1970s under the influence of Michael Halliday's approach to language analysis, which is more strictly termed *systemic-functional* linguistics (see Halliday, 1978). Functionalism is, however, often defined by contrasting it with formalism, particularly with linguistic formalism of the kind most directly associated with Chomsky. The functionalist position is that the language system and the forms which make it up are inescapably determined by the *uses* or functions which they serve. For the formalists, a language system is independent of the uses to which it is put: these are merely surface operations. For them, the forms of language are in principle independent of use and function and in a strong sense actually pre-exist them. Formalism is thus more naturally inclined to cognitive explanations of examples of language, and often resorts to innatism by arguing that the brain is genetically pre-programmed to acquire an esssentially unchanging linguistic order of things. The data on which functionalism depends is, by contrast, less introspective or mind-dependent, but rather consists of naturally occurring texts in social contexts where the operation of linguistic forms can only be described with reference to the context. The forms are socially constituted and contextually determined and their meaning cannot be construed in isolation from such a social semiotic. Functionalists argue that their models of language are better suited to the description of literature since literary styles are an integral part of what are essentially naturally occurring texts.

Another volume published at the beginning of the 1980s, which has a more pedagogic orientation, is likewise marked by functionalist and sociolinguistic influences. *Linguistics for Students of Literature*, by Elizabeth Traugott and Mary Louise Pratt, explores not only the relevance of pragmatics and speech act theory to the study of literary texts but also the functions of different social varieties of language in the organization of texts. There is also discussion of speech representation and dialogue and of the contribution of analysis at such levels to the description of stylistic effects (see Traugott and Pratt, 1980). Much of the work in discourse analysis, pragmatics and text linguistics, which is reviewed in detail in section III below and which forms the analytical basis for many of the articles in this book, derives its main impetus from socially based functional models for the description of language.

It is a particular argument underlying this book that too narrow a focus on linguistic forms does not release what is essentially of interest in the study of literary texts: the effects which arise when linguistic forms implicate aspects of context or when they signal, directly or indirectly, the many functions they can be made to perform. This is not to say that grammatical or phonological forms of literary texts are not of interest. It is to say that they involve micro-structural aspects of text, which is one reason why so much stylistic analysis in the 1960s and early 1970s focuses on short lyric poems rather than on the larger macro-structural units beyond the sentence which are more within the realm of discourse stylistics. A focus on language functions is also more enabling for purposes of describing the structural patterning of literary texts.

II Literary and Linguistic Stylistics

In several respects, *linguistic stylistics* is the purest form of stylistics, in that its practitioners attempt to derive from the study of style and language a refinement of models for the analysis of language and thus to contribute to the development of linguistic theory. Work in linguistic stylistics is generally less accommodating to the aims of non-linguistic disciplines and is thus, when applied, most likely to provoke reservations about its relevance. Linguistic stylisticians believe that in the analysis of language there are dangers in compromising the rigour and systematicity of analysis of stylistic effects, and that practitioners in related disciplines are unwilling to accept the kind of standards of principled description of language necessary to a genuinely mutual integration of interests. In literary studies such debate appears interminable (see, for example, Knight, 1982; Ferrar, 1984) and still bears traces of the Fowler–Bateson controversy at the end of the 1960s (see Fowler, 1971). The most recent studies in linguistic stylistics have tended to focus on application of studies in discourse analysis and narrative organization to the study of literary text.

Two of the most prominent recent examples of linguistic stylistics are Burton's study of drama dialogue (Burton, 1980) and Banfield's study of narrative discourse (Banfield, 1982). Banfield's book is an ambitious attempt to undermine much current narrative theory and to resettle it on the foundations provided by a generative grammar of narrative sentences. Banfield categorizes and catalogues the communicative and expressive functions of language in narrative and then argues that narrative sentences are those which are neither communicative nor expressive and which are therefore, by virtue of excluding the subjective and discoursal acts of the narrator, those sentences which signal the 'true', unmarked propositions of the narrative. There is not space to discuss Banfield's proposals in detail here (though see

McHale, 1983, for an extensive critique) but her efforts to provide the reader of her study with detailed, explicit recognition criteria for the narrative language phenomena she discerns should be noted alongside a rather more extravagant claim that a universal grammar of linguistic representation in narration can be set up.

Burton's study likewise proposes models of analysis which aim to account for as much of the available data as possible. Here Burton offers a modified version of Sinclair and Coulthard's (1975) model for the analysis of classroom discourse, applying it to examples of modern drama dialogue, mostly from the plays of Harold Pinter. The textual analysis she undertakes – in an area of language use not traditionally covered in stylistics – goes some considerable way towards systematically accounting for the 'alienated' structure of the dialogues, in which numerous silences, *non sequiturs*, breaking of rules for turn-taking, etc. serve to underscore the kinds of power relations which obtain in the dramatized conversations. Particularly innovative and useful are her proposals for challenging and supporting 'moves' (extending the necessarily asymmetrical design features inherent in classroom discourse models) and for a limitation of classes of 'act' to no more than twenty-two separate realizations.

The studies of both Banfield and Burton serve to highlight the strengths and weaknesses inherent in linguistic stylistics. The strengths are that, first, a descriptive framework is supplied which is sufficiently detailed to allow the analysts' decisions to be retrieved and checked against our own analysis. There is thus a systematic basis provided for agreement and disagreement. Few stylisticians and very few literary critics meet such standards of explicitness or provide such clear criteria for their descriptive decisions. Secondly, in a related way, the use of models enables work to proceed in a suitable 'scientific' manner. In Popperian terms at least, we can take Burton's model as a hypothesis concerning key structural features of conversational interaction, apply it to data, examine the implications for the model of confirmatory or counter-examples and revise or extend the model as necessary. And it has sufficient predictive power to accommodate this. Thirdly, in keeping with an aim of linguistic stylistics expressed in several sources (for example, Sinclair, 1966; Pearce, 1977), there is no compromise made in the goals of linguistic descriptive adequacy in order to accommodate a dominant literary paradigm of analysis. The aforementioned studies in linguistic stylistics make contributions to *linguistic* theory and *linguistic* description and imply that there should be no reason why literary texts cannot be 'used' for the purposes of extending and redefining models of linguistic description. Although linguistic stylisticians have to recognize that literary critics may want to do different things with their models, such a methodology can ensure that identity is preserved for the linguistic side of stylistics and that due caution is exercised in terms of the sometimes undue semanticization of linguistic features for literary interpretative purposes pointed out by Pearce (1977).

But it is in this kind of conjunction that some problems of linguistic-stylistic models become manifest. Disadvantages, both potential and actual, must be recognized accordingly. It is, in fact, in the area of interpretation that problems appear to surface most markedly.

First, it is naive to pretend that any application of linguistic knowledge, whether modelled or otherwise, and however dedicatedly and rigorously formalized the model, can result in an 'objective', value-free interpretation of data. The system will inevitably be partial (in both senses of the word) and so, accordingly, will be the interpretation.

Second, as Taylor and Toolan (1984) point out, models such as those described here do not of themselves indicate what in the language of the interaction or the narrative is relevant to an interpretation of the text, but only how this *might* be textually realized. The assignment of meaning or stylistic function to a formal category in the language remains an interpretative act and thus cannot transcend the individual human subject who originates the interpretation. Thus, while the recognition of specific formal features can in most cases be attested within the terms of the system, the analyst has to be taken on trust in his or her interpretative assignment. It is a perennial problem, or even dilemma, in stylistics that no reliable criteria can be generated whereby specific functions or effects can be unambiguously attributed to specific formal features of the language system. In this respect stylisticians have still to answer satisfactorily charges made by Fish (1973) and, more recently, Thurley (1983). Thirdly, any description is only as good as the model or system of analysis used. And there is always a related danger that the analyst will reduce everything to the terms supplied by that system. Consistency may thus be achieved but interpretation will again be revealed as partial. The partiality of Banfield's model has, for example, been strongly criticized by McHale (1983) in that it operates with what is for McHale a static, decontextualized and essentialist model of language (the fate to some extent of most models) and does not therefore take sufficient account of textual or, more seriously for literary study, historical context. Even the decision to formalize on the part of linguistic stylisticians, and the extent to which many do proceed with formalization, commits them to a belief that literary language use *can* be formalized in linguistic terms (a position to which many literary critics feel compelled to address themselves, and in stronger and more explicit terms than most linguists: see Knight, 1982).

Finally, but perhaps less obviously, any resolution to describe the data rather than interpret it constitutes an interpretation. It is an interpretation of the way literary study can or should be approached and analyses of it conducted. Moving 'beyond interpretation', as Jonathan Culler progressively advocates (see Culler, 1981: ch. 2) is only a substitution of one kind of interpretative activity by another, albeit a less traditional, less institutionally authorized kind. The advocacy of this position in Carter and Simpson (1982) stands thus indicted for a relative innocence and theoretical naivety.

Not all of these questions and issues are addressed by linguistic stylisticians. However well motivated their studies, whatever their contribution to linguistic theory, whatever is decided to be 'done' with explicit, analytical, retrievable and 'scientific' procedures, such stylisticians should at least acknowledge that they are acquiescing in some silences between their lines.

A distinguishing feature of work in *literary stylistics* is the provision of a basis for fuller understanding, appreciation and interpretation of avowedly literary and author-centred texts. The general impulse will be to draw eclectically on linguistic insights and to use them in the service of what is generally claimed to be fuller interpretation of language effects than is possible without the benefit of linguistics. In general, analysis will be multi-levelled and not confined to the kind of single-level rigours exemplified by much work in linguistic stylistics. Indeed, it is argued that style itself results from a simultaneous convergence of effects at a number of levels of language organization.

Although the precision of analysis made available by linguistic methods offers a challenge to established procedures of 'close reading' or practical criticism, the general aims and techniques of literary stylistics remain closely associated with those of practical or New Criticism. In spite of the aforementioned sociolinguistic trends, most literary-stylistic analysis still sees referential, text-immanent language as a primary constituent of the text and as a locus for author-initiated effects and responses to those effects. The existence of an extra-textual world of social, political, psychological, or historical forces is often discounted as being beyond the analytical remit of stylistics. Such forces are also felt to have little influence on the language of the texts as 'language artefacts' which have survived historical change and whose only relevant context is a linguistic one.

A potentially self-consuming circularity characterizes this argument and serves also to insulate the interpretative procedures involved. Thus protected, stylisticians can focus on texts which are, whether consciously or not, interpreted as existing in an ahistorical, almost timeless vacuum; and analysis can proceed for the most part untroubled by awkward questions about semantic change or the ontological status of language itself as a medium for the transmission of meanings. For if questions were to be raised about the relationship between language and the world, and an assumedly unproblematic 'referential' fit between words and meanings were problematized, then analysis would have to confront issues such as the arbitrariness of the sign, the fit between language, representation and cultural relativity, as well as the sorts of theories of language advanced by post-structuralists and by deconstructionism. (See much recent work in deconstruction theory. For introductory accounts, Norris, 1982; Belsey, 1980: ch. 1). If such were the case, then the attempts of most literary stylisticians to narrow down meaning options would be subverted or deconstructed from within by the plurality of signification made available by alternative theoretical perspectives. (See Eagleton, 1983: ch. 3, for extended discussion along these lines.)

For the most part, literary stylisticians have proceeded along the kinds of lines advocated by practical or New Criticism, but have provided pedagogical defences for their implicit 'interpretation', or theory of language, arguing particularly for the basis of familiarity to literature students which such modes of operation provide (see particularly Carter, 1982a). Some, such as Leech and Short (1981), have proceeded cautiously, modestly and eclectically; others, such as Cluysenaar (1976) and Cummins and Simmons (1983), rather more incautiously, the latter being particularly insistent in their view of the transparency of language and of an equation between linguistic forms and literary meanings which is predicated on an assumption of the kind of one-to-one correlation or iconicity between words and meanings to which 'neutral' and 'objective' linguistic description can 'attest', For further discussion, see pp. 66–70 and 259ff. below.

Burton (1982), implicitly recognizing some limitations in her earlier position, explicitly politicizes this failure on the part of stylisticians to interpret their own interpretations and is one of very few to attempt to answer charges of theoretical shortsightedness. For Burton, no analysis can be anything other than ideologically committed. Stylistic analysis is a political activity. Neutrality and objectivity are not possible in a language game where what and how we interpret the data of a literary work is inextricably connected with our beliefs. A goal of neutral, value-free literary-stylistic analysis embodies, for Burton, an ideologically reactionary adherence to keeping things the way they are. It is an argument which runs close to that of Fowler (1981) examined in section IV below.

III   Developments in Discourse Analysis

The term discourse analysis is a contested one. Various groups of linguists, literary and film theoreticians, cultural historians and semioticians all argue that their work is centrally concerned with the analysis of discourse. In this section particular attention is given to work by linguists in the field of discourse analysis.

According to the subtitle of a recent book, discourse analysis is 'the sociolinguistic analysis of natural language' (Stubbs, 1983). The definition requires a little unpacking. It is, first of all, sociolinguistic in orientation because it is concerned with describing instances of language use in context. The context in which language use is studied should be a *real* one, according to discourse analysts. By real is meant that the examples of language studied should be genuine samples of actual data collected by or provided for the analyst rather than made up by the analyst in the artificial environment of his own armchair with only his own intuitions to verify whether the example is a real one or not. In this crucial respect, the data examined by discourse analysts will not be introspective; they will be 'natural' language, i.e. naturally occurring language in a social context of actual language use.

Data collected in such contexts will not be as neat or manageable as introspective data. They will also have to be more than just happenstantial or eccentric and be genuinely representative of a significant patterning between language and context. They will inevitably be messy for the analyst to describe, especially if they are spoken; and they will invariably be *stretches of text*, for the interaction of language and social context cannot be adequately illustrated by samples of language which occur only within the limits of a single clause or sentence.

As we have seen, the concern of formalist linguistics has been to describe systematically the operations of language below the level of the clause, and the result has been much rigorous and sophisticatedly tooled definition of the workings of individual words, morphemes and phonemes, as well as of syntactic patterns. For formalists of a transformational–generative persuasion this was, as we have seen, linked to a desire to *explain* the nature of a genetically endowed competence to construct what all ideal speaker/hearers *know* about the structure of their language. Of course, single words and sentences can also be used to perform discoursal acts, and sometimes more than one act simultaneously. For example, a single sentence, 'Isn't it time you went to bed?', spoken by a parent to a child can chain together three speech acts – a request, a command and a threat – the interpretation of which depends on more than knowledge simply of the internal interrogative form of the sentence. Similarly, interrogatives can be used, and often are in densely patterned texts such as literary texts, to assert a proposition rhetorically. However, discourse analysis is generally concerned not with isolated decontextualized sentences but with uncovering the patterns and regularities which occur between and across sentences or conversational turns as they are *used* in real contexts of language.

We have so far introduced a number of potentially confusing or at least overlapping terms. In a field, particularly a new field such as discourse analysis, in which there are always likely to be a number of contesting orientations it would be unlikely for there to be an agreed metalanguage. But it is necessary to offer some clarification before proceeding, not least since later sections examine the nature of discourse stylistics, and some theoretical groundwork should be laid at this stage. In particular, it is necessary to attempt to distinguish the following:

(1) grammar
(2) text linguistics
(3) pragmatics
(4) discourse analysis

and in so doing to discuss the complex relationship between *spoken* and *written* discourse in so far as the distinction affects the goals underlying the collection of essays which makes up this book.

In a recent book devoted to discourse analysis Willis Edmondson has offered a 'componential' description of what he takes to be the different features of each domain in relation to grammar: (see Edmondson, 1981: 3–4)

Field of Study			Delimiting Linguistic Unit
Grammar	[−suprasentential]	[−use]	sentence
Text linguistics	[+suprasentential]	[−use]	text
Pragmatics	[−suprasentential]	[+use]	utterance
Discourse analysis	[+suprasentential]	[+use]	discourse

Of course such a componential account oversimplifies. It suggests that these fields of study are all more distinct than they are; it also suggests that they are well-defined disciplines – when the last three are in fact all nascent disciplines. Also not all text linguists would accept that they were not concerned with language use. However, the diagram does indicate the importance in discourse analysis of language use in naturally occurring contexts and the significance of the upper limit of the stretches of language which each field takes to be its normal analytical remit.

Additionally, it is important to recognize here that Edmonson's model tends to blur distinctions between spoken and written discourse and, in a related way, offers no clear way of disambiguating utterance from text. For most purposes, linguists do not consider it essential to differentiate *text* from *discourse* and do not assume that discourse analysis is exclusively concerned with spoken discourse (see Stubbs, 1983; Brown and Yule, 1983). However, the use of the term 'utterance' suggests, as does the phrase 'conversation analysis', a rather more direct relation with spontaneous, unrehearsed language produced in a context and between participants. What is perhaps more significant is the length of text which is normally studied. Within pragmatics and the ethnomethodological tradition of conversation analysis, one is normally concerned with no more than one contribution to a conversation or discourse. Within discourse or text analysis the orientation is more markedly towards *intra*-sentential relations (as opposed to *supra*-sentential) and towards sequences of conversational contributions *across* pairs of individual speaking turns.

The essays in this collection illustrate some of these main trends in discourse analysis. All the writers take literary texts as occurrences of naturally occurring communication and view analysis of discourse organization as a set of methods which lays a basis for the analysis of *larger* units or stretches of text than has conventionally been the case in literary and linguistic stylistics. There is a shared recognition that analysis at the level of discourse allows insights into the semantic structures of whole texts and how such structures produce textual meanings. In particular, analysis is made of dialogue. This includes dialogue between characters in novels, plays and poems as well as dialogic interaction between authors, narrators, implied readers and actual readers.

The essays do not represent any exclusive model of analysis. They draw on different traditions in discourse analysis, including Birmingham School analysis of spoken discourse, pragmatics (especially speech act theory and the roles of phatic communion and politeness phenomena) and text linguistics (including models of clause-relational analysis developed by Eugene Winter, and Hallidayan functional models of language). Two essays draw on the work of the Russian literary linguist Mikhail Bakhtin, especially his analysis of language as *dialogic*, relating it to more recent work on the modalities of interpersonal language use. And, finally, two essays explore the role of interpretation of discourse in relation to social ideologies and the ideology of personal interpretation, and examine critically recent work in stylistics in relation to literary-theoretical accounts of the nature of discourse as a socio-political entity. The particular orientations of the umbrella term of *discourse stylistics* under which these essays may be arranged is discussed in greater detail in the last section of this introduction; the point to be underlined here is that the collection does not foreclose on the many different kinds of discourse analysis available.

IV Literature as Social Discourse

This section points us towards another sense of the word *discourse*. The term differs from the senses discussed in the previous section under the heading of 'discourse analysis'. The title to this section is taken from a seminal book published by Roger Fowler (who is a contributor to this collection of essays), which, since its publication in 1981, has influenced both the practice of stylistics and the nature of the intersection between linguistics and literary theory.

Fowler's approach in *Literature as Social Discourse* (Fowler, 1981) stresses the interpersonal dimension of literature. From within a broadly sociolinguistic framework he examines writers' uses of language in so far as linguistic choices reflect and influence relations with society. Following theories outlined in Halliday (1978), Fowler gives attention to the sociolinguistic varieties or registers of language and examines how they crystallize in a range of literary texts in response to the social, economic, technological and theoretical needs of the cultures concerned. A particular focus emerges, too, on the linguistic relations produced by the text between authors and readers; these will in turn encode, according to Fowler, the determining socio-economic structures of particular historical contexts.

There is a dialectical interrelationship between language and social structure: the varieties of linguistic usage are both *products* of socio-economic forces and institutions – reflexes of such factors as power relations, occupation roles, social stratifications, etc., and *practices* which are instrumental in forming and legitimating these same social forces and institutions. The New Critics and the Formalists vehemently denied that 'literature' had social determinants and social consequences, but a sociolinguistic theory . . . will show that *all* discourse is part of social structure and enters into . . . effected and effecting relationships . . . (Fowler, 1981: 21)

Discourse is also used by Fowler in another related but quite distinct sense. He refers to literature itself as a discourse. Here the meaning is rather more that of an institutionalized category. Literature is seen by Fowler as a discourse which is in varying degrees defined and controlled by the social institutions within which it is embedded. The urge here is to prevent literature from becoming a body of texts institutionally authorized by the academy, examination boards and publishers as possessing the qualities necessary for 'literature'. Fowler is anxious to demonstrate the truth of Roland Barthes's statement that 'literature is what gets taught' and that claims for the universal validity of literary values are specious. What is valued as literature changes from one society, or culture within a society, to another and cannot be validated outside a study of the discourses which a society produces and lives by. Even the term 'literature' itself changes, for in the eighteenth century it was used to mean writing in the broadest sense of the word and not necessarily in the sense of creative, imaginatively marked production which it has come to have under the influence of culturally powerful figures such as Matthew Arnold and F. R. Leavis.

In terms of linguistic properties, too, Fowler, argues that there is no special variety of language use which is distinctively or exclusively literary:

> Some of the varieties used in the constitution of a specific 'literary' text may tend to occur regularly in some, but not all, other 'literary' texts but they are not restricted to 'literary' texts (rhyme and alliteration are found in advertisements); and 'literary' texts also draw upon patterns which tend to occur in 'non -literary' texts (conversation, news report). This stylistic overlapping and the absence of any necessary and sufficient linguistic criterion for the 'literary' text, is well known though often ignored. My suggestion is that stylistics and literary studies must take sociolinguistic variety theory and methodology seriously as a way of accounting for the specific linguistic properties of the texts concerned. (Fowler, 1981: 21)

Formalist theories of literary language may attempt to isolate 'literary' language, but such language use can be found in social *discourses* which are not institutionally defined as literary. And this, for Fowler, would be further evidence of the paradoxes inherent in not seeing literature as social discourse.

Notwithstanding the emphasis in this book on works commonly designated 'literary', there is an assumption throughout that the techniques of analysis demonstrated may be used in an interpretative way on any use of language in any kind of text. There is no automatic restriction either to established, canonical authors or to exclusively perceived canons of British and American literature. As the essay by David Birch demonstrates, literature in English has wider cultural and ideological parameters. Many of the essays in this book bear traces of the influence of Roger Fowler's view of literature as social discourse.

V Towards a Theory of Discourse Stylistics

> Stylistics . . . may be regarded simply as the variety of discourse analysis dealing with literary discourse. (Leech, 1983: 151)

As stated in a previous section, the essays brought together in this volume represent a number of diverse approaches to discourse analysis and to stylistics. It would be incautious to suggest that they form anything other than a basis for a fuller development of discourse stylistics. And we shall later suggest orientations *not* represented here which we believe are also necessary for such development in both theory and practice. But it is probably helpful to state at the outset the underlying factors which in our view give the essays in this collection a unified and coherent character.

First, each of the contributors to the volume argues a case, either explicitly or implicitly, for the stylistic analysis of texts to occupy territory beyond the level of the sentence or the single conversational exchange, and to examine those broader contextual properties of texts which affect their description and interpretation. In its varied forms, discourse analysis is that branch of linguistics most directly concerned with the ways in which texts create contexts, with their organization at this suprasentential level and with their operation as part of a dynamic process between participants. The contributors demonstrate that developments in recent years in the field of discourse analysis allow this to be done in a systematic and rigorous manner.

Secondly, the analyses undertaken in the book aim to be sufficiently detailed, explicit and *retrievable* for other analysts, working on the same texts, to check or retrieve the original analytical decisions and procedures. These other readers may not indeed share the writers' intuitions, and this may lead them to their own different interpretations of the texts; but it is regarded as essential that they should be able to follow the steps by which particular analyses are made. And because the analysis is systematic and according to clearly defined models or procedures, such readers are in a position to argue against the positions adopted in each chapter, should they wish to do so. Also, as Ronald Carter points out in Chapter 3, although such methods of analysis do not, of course, guarantee a single meaning or the only possible reading of a text, they do have an added *pedagogical* advantage. One of the problems with traditional methods of close reading is that the procedures of analysis and interpretation are not made particularly explicit, with the result that learning to read in this way takes place, if it takes place at all, by a kind of osmosis. (For more extensive discussion, see Carter, 1982a: 4–8; 1982b.) Although no contributor would claim that the skills demonstrated here were other than basic and preparatory to fuller interpretation, it is especially appropriate to a textbook in stylistics that such initial procedures should not be so hidden between the lines that only a few students can gain access to them.

Thirdly, a number of the chapters contain references to specific models. Here the use of the term *model* requires some explanation, lest it should be thought that we are suggesting that a particular model represents the one and only way in which particular discoursal or interactive properties of texts can be accounted for. In fact, the use of the term model has a more specialized sense. It means a particular analytical scheme developed and applied, basically in the form of a *hypothesis*, to the text(s) concerned. The models which are employed aim to be as explicit and enabling as possible. But all models need to be continually adapted and developed as they are tested against new kinds of data in the form of different kinds of texts. Analysis at this level of discourse is complex, and discourse analysis is in many respects still at a formative stage of development; similarly, literary discourse is complexly patterned and necessarily invokes contextual properties which are non-linguistic as well as linguistic. The models of analysis proposed in these chapters are designed to help readers to undertake discourse analysis of the language organization of texts; but it would be naive to suppose or to suggest that this was the *only* way it could or should be done.

Finally, the use of models and the commitment to systematic, retrievable analysis means that there is an orientation in the book towards the role of *linguistic* rather than literary stylistics (see section II above), though there are, of course, no neat dividing lines between such orientations and there are thus several points of overlap. This final main unifying characteristic of the book requires further discussion, for it clearly underscores an impulse in many of the chapters for stylistic analysis to retain its identity as a discipline grounded in linguistics. The increasing emphasis on contextualization and on the wider parameters of discourse, particularly on factors which are not amenable to linguistic description, poses the question of whether discourse stylistics can exist in productive integration with other descriptive frameworks and essentially non-linguistic goals. For example, how compatible with systematic linguistic textual description is an account of the role of gender, class and ideological position in the interpretation of texts, however essential it may be for discourse stylisticians *not* to ignore such factors and *not* to assume that somehow description of texts is neutral and value-free? The main problem here is that such goals can push language description to limits where analytical procedures from other disciplines have to be conjoined. It is at such points that the relative discreteness of linguistic description may be compromised. Of course, compromise is a necessary feature of interdisciplinary work, but whether compromise on standards of descriptive systematicity can be entertained must be a matter for individual stylisticians to resolve. Our own view would be that without the 'scientific' procedures, and without the development of 'models' with predictive power, it becomes difficult to undertake analysis which is sufficiently principled to promote linguistic descriptive progress, and to prevent the kind of integration with other disciplines which is absorption rather than mutually productive support. (But for a volume in which several important steps are taken in this direction, see Birch and O'Toole, 1987, especially papers by Fairclough and Threadgold.)

However, we must also examine the extent to which discourse analysts can accommodate work in the analysis of literature in which the notion of discourse is viewed with different theoretical assumptions, and from different analytical perspectives. The question is a particularly acute one as far as analysis of discourse as a social and political phenomenon is concerned, for discourse analysis of both spoken and written texts in the tradition represented in this volume is concerned with language as a social semiotic. Issues of class, gender, socio-political determination and ideology can never be very far away from analysis of the words on the page. Discourse analysis should, it might be argued, be concerned not simply with the micro-contexts of the effects of words across sentences or conversational turns but also with the macro-contexts of larger social patterns. Most of the papers collected here focus on micro-contexts; some touch upon macro-contextual issues. One question is: how far can we go and still retain for our analysis a character which is linguistic? Another is: how far should we take into account the 'position' of the analyst and the ideologies of both analysis and analyst, which are invariably and unavoidably embedded in discourse? In our use of the term discourse here we are moving in a direction common in much contemporary literary theory. Reasons of space as well as the overall remit of the volume allow no more than a cursory inspection of such questions here.

Work within alternative traditions of discourse thus takes us beyond the traditional concern of stylistics with aesthetic values towards concern with the social and political ideologies encoded in texts. The starting point for such concerns in literary–linguistic studies can be traced to Voloshinov and Bakhtin writing in the Soviet Union in the late 1920s and early 1930s:

> Existence reflected in the sign is not merely reflected but refracted. How is this refraction of existence in the ideological sign determined? By an intersecting of differently oriented social interests in every ideological sign. Sign becomes an arena of class struggle. This social multi-accentuality of the ideological sign is a very crucial aspect. (Voloshinov, 1930: 23)

In other words, language does not mediate 'reality' in any simple or 'common-sense' way. There is no easy one-to-one or uni-accentual correspondence between words and what they refer to 'objectively' in the world. Intead, users of language or 'subjects' are positioned at the intersection of various discourses which are inherently unequal and the site of struggle. A crucial contribution to analysis of such multi-accentuality or 'heteroglossia' is Michel Foucault's argument that discourses are historically determinate. Foucault, whose influence as a critic of culture on much contemporary literary theory has been powerful, argues that there is no single right way to see things. Our knowledge and beliefs are *discursively* produced; they are not universal but social-semiotic in origin, and function and depend on power-based cultural shaping processes in a society (Foucault, 1972). However much dominant ideologies may work to reinforce stability and resist alternative orders, any speaker of the language is a part of an ongoing struggle in which different interests are embedded. How we see things depends on where we see them from, and where we see them from is a socio-historical, culturally shaped position. The language we use does not reflect; it refracts a world which we are in but which we can contest and change. Literary discourse analysis should seek to demonstrate the determining positions available within texts, and show how 'meanings' and 'interpretations of meanings' are always and inevitably discursively produced. This is one of the main arguments to emerge from the final chapter in this book, and the challenge posed by David Birch is one which stylisticians will have to take up if they wish their analyses of texts to become genuine studies in literature as social discourse. At the risk of overgeneralization and oversimplification, we might say that if the 1960s was a decade of formalism in stylistics, the 1970s a decade of functionalism and the 1980s a decade of discourse stylistics, then the 1990s could well become the decade in which socio-historical and socio-cultural stylistic studies are a main preoccupation. The chapters in this book by Birch, Fowler and Haynes offer particular pointers in this direction. For further reading see Macdonell (1986), and for a social-semiotic account of discourse and drama text Elam (1981). The whole argument for a siting of text analysis in relation to socio-political ideologies and their attendant discourses is carried further in Birch (forthcoming).

VI Using This Book: A Reader's Guide

This book follows the same format as the previous volume, *Language and Literature: An Introductory Reader in Stylistics* (Carter, 1982a). The essays are organized in such a way as to serve as a progressive introductory course in stylistics for group or individual study. It is designed to complement the first volume, and to be studied either in parallel with it or subsequently to it. We do not, of course, discount the possibility of this volume being studied in its own right, and hope that it is sufficiently self-contained to allow this. However, we should point out again that references to syntax and related formal properties of language do presuppose at least some general acquaintance with the kind of material explored in the first volume. In other respects, we have tried to adhere to the following guiding principles in the organization of the book:

(1) There is a reference list at the end of each chapter which may be used as a starting point for further reading in the specific area dealt with, as well as for the purpose of following up particular references.
(2) A glossary is provided at the back of the book in which key terms

used in the book are explained with examples and suggestions for further reading.

(3)   Together with the authors, the editors have attempted to grade the essays in terms of linguistic-analytical difficulty. As a general rule, chapters later in the book are designed to be studied after earlier ones. However, each chapter is also self-standing. It can be read as directed by a tutor, according to the specific purposes of a course, or according to an individual reader's requirements and interests.

(4)   Each chapter has exercises appended to it. As far as possible, we have tried to ensure that these are progressively sequenced, although it is inevitable that some students will find some exercises more complex than the sequence might suggest. The aim of these exercises or 'suggestions for further work' is to extend competence in the use of the particular descriptive framework outlined in the chapter, to provide opportunities for cross-reference to texts and analytical systems used in other chapters, to guide further theoretical and practical work in discourse stylistics, and to give opportunities for interpretation of other texts which compare or contrast revealingly with the key text adopted for analysis in each chapter. There are also places where students are encourged to engage with theoretical issues in the analysis of texts. These exercises are designed to provide an integrated and developmental study programme.

Finally, we reiterate our recognition of the importance of language in literary studies. Language is the literary medium; the more that students are able to understand and describe effects produced by language, the stronger the position they will be in when attempting to account systematically for their intuitions, and to build the base for a fuller interpretation of the text. We hope this book demonstrates the particular importance of language as discourse, and provides a starting point for the development of discourse stylistics. It is, in our view, an essential step in the progress of work at the interface of language and literature, and in the more extensive integration of their treatment in the classroom.

References: Introduction

Banfield, A. (1982), *Unspeakable Sentences: Narration and Representation in the Language of Fiction* (Boston and London: Routledge & Kegan Paul).

Belsey, C. (1980), *Critical Practice* (London: Methuen).

Birch, D. (forthcoming), *Language, Literature and Critical Practice* (London: Routledge & Kegan Paul).

Birch, D., and O'Toole, L. M. (eds) (1987), *Functions of Style* (London: Frances Pinter).

Brown, G., and Yule, G. (1983), *Discourse Analysis* (Cambridge: Cambridge University Press).

Burton, D. (1980), *Dialogue and Discourse: A Sociolinguistic Approach to Modern Drama Dialogue and Naturally Occurring Conversation* (London: Routledge & Kegan Paul).

Burton, D. (1982), 'Through Glass Darkly: Through Dark Glasses', in Carter (1982a), pp. 195–214.

Carter, R. (ed.) (1982a), *Language and Literature: An Introductory Reader in Stylistics* (London: Allen & Unwin).

Carter, R. (1982b), 'Responses to Language in Poetry', in Carter R. and D. Burton (eds), *Literary Text and Language Study* (London: Edward Arnold), pp 28–57.

Carter, R., and Simpson, P. (1982), 'The Sociolinguistic Analysis of Narrative', *Belfast Working Papers in Language and Linguistics*, vol. 6, pp. 123–52.

Cluysenaar, A. (1976), *Introduction to Literary Stylistics* (London: Batsford).

Culler, J. (1981), *The Pursuit of Signs* (London: Routledge & Kegan Paul).

Cummins, M., and Simmons, R. (1983), *The Language of Literature* (London: Pergamon Press).

Eagleton, T. (1983), *Literary Theory: An Introduction* (Oxford: Blackwell).

Edmondson, W. (1981), *Spoken Discourse* (London: Longman).

Elam, K. (1981), *The Semiotics of Theatre and Drama* (London: Methuen).

Ferrar, M. (1984), 'Linguistics and Literary Text', *Use of English* vol. 35, no. 2, pp. 33–40.

Fish, S. (1973) 'What Is Stylistics And Why Are They Saying Such Terrible Things About It?', in S. Chatman (ed.) *Approaches to Poetics* (New York: Columbia University Press). Repr. in Fish, S. *Is there a Text in this Class?* (Cambridge, Mass., Harvard University Press).

Foucault, M. (1972), *The Archaeology of Knowledge* (London: Tavistock).

Fowler, R. (1971), *The Languages of Literature* (London: Routledge & Kegan Paul).

Fowler, R. (1981), *Literature as Social Discourse* (London: Batsford).

Freeman, D. C. (ed.) (1970), *Linguistics and Literary Style* (New York; Holt, Rinehart & Winston).

Freeman, D. C. (ed.) (1981), *Essays in Modern Stylistics* (London: Methuen).

Halliday, M. A. K. (1978), *Language as Social Semiotic* (London: Edward Arnold).

Jakobson, R. (1960), 'Linguistics and Poetics', in T. Sebeok (ed.), *Style in Language* (Cambridge, Mass: Massachusetts Institute of Technology Press), pp. 350–77.

Knight, R. (1982), 'Literature and the Language of Linguists', *Use of English* vol. 33, no. 3, pp. 58–67.

Leech, G. N. (1983), 'Pragmatics Discourse Analysis, Stylistics and "The Celebrated Letter"', *Prose Studies*, vol. 6, no. 2, pp. 142–58.

Leech, G. N., and Short, M. H. (1981), *Style in Fiction* (London: Longman).

Levin, S. (1971), 'The Analysis of Compression in Poetry', *Foundations of Language*, vol. 7, pp.38–55.

Macdonell, D. (1986), *Theories of Discourse: An Introduction* (Oxford: Basil Blackwell).

McHale, B. (1983), 'Unspeakable Sentences, Unnatural Acts: Linguistics and Poetics Revisited', *Poetics Today* vol. 4, no. 1, pp. 17–45.

Messing, G. M. (1971), 'The Impact of Transformational Grammar upon Stylistics and Literary Analysis', *Linguistics*, vol. 66, pp. 56–73.

Norris, C. (1982), *Deconstruction: Theory and Practice* (London: Methuen).

Ohmann, R. (1964), 'Generative Grammars and the Concept of Literary Style', *Word* vol. 20, pp. 423–39.

Ohmann, R. (1966), 'Literature as Sentences', *Collective English*, vol. 27, no. 4, pp. 261–7.

Pearce, R. (1977), *Literary Texts*, University of Birmingham: English Language Research.

Sinclair, J. M. (1966), 'Taking a Poem to Pieces', in R. Fowler, (ed.), *Essays on Style and Language* (London: Routledge & Kegan Paul), pp. 68–81.

Sinclair, J. M., and Coulthard, R. M. (1975), *Towards an Analysis of Discourse: The English Used by Teachers and Pupils* (London: Oxford University Press).

Stubbs, M. (1983), *Discourse Analysis: The Sociolinguistic Analysis of Natural Language* (Oxford: Blackwell).

Taylor, T., and Toolan, M. (1984), 'Recent Trends in Stylistics', *Journal of Llterary Semantics*, vol. 13, no. 1, pp. 57–79.

Thorne, J. P. (1969), 'Poetry, Stylistics and Imaginary Grammars', *Journal of Linguistics*, vol. 5, pp. 147–50.

Thurley, G. (1983), *Counter-Modernism in Current Critical Theory* (London: Macmillan).

Traugott, E., and Pratt, M. L. (1980), *Linguistics for Students of Literature* (New York: Harcourt Brace Jovanovich).

Voloshinov, V. (1930), *Marxism and the Philosophy of Language*, trans. L. Matejka and I. R. Titunik (London: Seminar Press, 1973).

Widdowson, H. G. (1975), *Stylistics and the Teaching of Literature* (London: Longman).

Introduction to Chapter 1

Walter Nash examines a very familiar piece of text, the opening of *Hamlet*, using three complementary methods of presentation. The first of these is paraphrase; the second, commentary, or line-by-line exposition; and the third, a synopsis couched in terms of pragmatics and discourse analysis. Nash presents a brief study of the transactional structure of the dialogue, of its component discourse acts, and of its evidences of power and deference in the management of language in formal situations. From this study he concludes that the three methods – paraphrase, commentary and analytical synopsis – support each other; further, that discourse analysis in quite simple forms may actually enhance the interpretation of a text by bringing into sharp focus elements in the literary pattern not so clearly defined by other methods. What is thus revealed about the 'microtext', he suggests, may have particular relevance to the interpretation of the 'macrotext' – i.e. the scene, the act, or even the whole play. The chapter ends with some suggestions for further exploration.

1 Changing the Guard at Elsinore

WALTER NASH

I   A Paraphrase

(A fortification. On a parapet, a sentry is keeping guard. His name is Frank. It is evidently a very cold night, or Frank is ill at ease, or both; as he paces back and forth he stamps, shivers, whistles under his breath. Presently another soldier, Bernie, is dimly seen on the stairs that climb to the parapet. As Frank comes towards him, he starts nervously.)

Bernie: Who's there?

Frank: *(startled and affronted.)* Eh? Oh no you don't! *(Then remembering the drill, issues the formal challenge.)* Halt! Who goes there?

Bernie: *(Trying to get the password right.)* Long live the king!

Frank: *(Uncertain.)* Bernie?

Bernie: Yes, it's me.

Frank: Here on the dot, aren't you?

Bernie: It's gone twelve. Time you were in bed.

Frank: I won't say no. It's freezing cold, and I've got the shakes.

Bernie: *(Intensely casual.)* Anything to report?

Frank: No. Dead quiet.

Bernie: Off you go, then. If you run into Harry and Mark, tell them to get a move on, will you?

Frank: *(He has been moving away from Bernie, and now stands at the head of the parapet stair.)* Here they are now, I can hear them. *(As the newcomers emerge into view, he slips into his 'sentry' routine, forgetting, perhaps, that Bernie has now assumed the duty.)* Halt! Who goes there?

Harry: *(Who is not a soldier, but perceives the need to say something reassuring.)* We're on your side.

Mark: *(Who is, and who can therefore hastily produce a password not unlike the one already given by Bernie.)* Soldiers of the king.

Frank: *(Evidently satisfied with this response.)* Good-night, then.

Mark: *(A little surprised at this abrupt departure of the 'sentry' who has just challenged them.)* Oh! Cheerio, old son! Who's relieved you?

Frank:	Bernie just took over from me. I'll say goodnight.
Mark:	Hey there, Bernie!
Bernie:	Over here. Say, is Harry with you?
Harry:	*(Whimsical.)* Some of him is.
Bernie:	Hello, Harry. Mark, I'm glad you're here.
Mark:	*(With a stifled eagerness.)* Why – has – you know what – paid us a visit?
Bernie:	*(Cautiously, watching Harry.)* Not that I know of.

This is how *Hamlet* opens; not in so many words, it is true, but in so many interactions or exchanges between professional soldiers who are frightened and excited and behave, on the whole, rather unprofessionally. The paraphrase of their conversation may reduce to modern banality the sharp impact of Shakespeare's dramatic language, but it has one advantage. The commonplace phrasing, unsanctified by time and literary reputation, presents a direct reading of motives, a reading here freely supported by the interpolation of explanatory directions. This means, of course, that the paraphrase is not simply a translation of the scene into modern colloquial English, but also an interpretation, or more precisely a close sequence of interpretations, from sentence to sentence, emphasis to emphasis, inflection to inflection. The paraphrase simply does what any producer of a play has to do. It reflects decisions about context and motive, which lead to decisions about language, about underlying meanings, about the stylistic cohesion of the scene. But any reader of a drama is a producer of the drama, for an audience of one. To read is to construct mentally an image of performance, and the mental image is reflected in paraphrase.

II   A Commentary

To explain, and if need be justify, that mental image calls for a retracing, step by step, of the paths of meaning laid out in the original text. The first point for commentary is the obvious one, that Hamlet begins with an abortive exchange: a sentry is challenged by an intruder. Shakespeare put it thus:

Bernardo:	Who's there?
Francisco:	Nay, answer me; stand, and unfold yourself.[1]

In the theatre, the onlooker must become instantly aware of the irregularity of Bernardo's behaviour. It is Francisco who is in charge, and who insists, correctively, on his authority; the actor playing him must surely stress the pronoun *me*. His first words are indignant and alarmed, but he then proceeds by the book, making the formal challenge his duty prescribes. In response, Bernardo produces what is evidently a password. Yet still there is a hint of abnormality in the conventional exchange:

Bernardo: Long live the king!
Francisco: Bernardo?
Bernardo: He.

We have the impression that Francisco is not altogether certain of the newcomer's identity. It is in any case not the 'password' that reassures him; it is Bernardo's homely and laconic 'He' (= 'It's me'). It is a minor and possibly irrelevant detail, but it seems none the less that there is a momentary flaw in the formal exchange, a stutter, as it were, that is to be recalled a few lines further on, when the question of the correct password is again highlighted.

Francisco comments with surprise (or possibly gratitude, or even irony) on Bernardo's apparent punctuality:

Francisco: You come most carefully upon your hour.

Sentries are not in the habit of arriving at their posts a moment earlier than the duty roster demands. Francisco's remark thus draws attention to a further oddity in Bernardo's conduct. He is a professional soldier, but tonight he is so inept that he challenges the man he is supposed to be relieving, gives a dubious password, and, most significantly, is nervously eager to come on duty. As to this matter, however, he is quick to disclaim punctuality, alleging that he is in fact *late:*

Bernardo: 'Tis now struck twelve; get thee to bed, Francisco.

Late or early, Francisco is relieved to be relieved; so relieved, indeed that he openly confesses his relief:

Francisco: For this relief, much thanks; 'tis bitter cold
And I am sick at heart.

'I am sick at heart' has the ring of a significant announcement, though as yet the significance is obscure. Does he simply mean 'I am frozen to the marrow' (because of the 'bitter cold'), or is he complaining of something else, a psychic chill, a nameless glacial dread?[2] Bernardo's next remark could be a response to the hidden implication, though on the face of it it seems non-commital:

Bernardo: Have you had quiet guard?

This may be the conventional inquiry, the customary speech act of the relieving sentry ('Everything OK?' 'Anything to report?'), or it may be taken as an oblique reference to something no one dares name on this dark night in this cold and lonely place. The words appear to carry a message beyond their commonplace significance, and Francisco's reply has the same air of coded cliché:

Francisco: Not a mouse stirring.

We are at this point no more than ten lines into the play, and its language is already touched by tremors of ambiguity and covert meaning. Bernardo's 'quiet' (in 'Have you had quiet guard') and Francisco's 'stirring' are suspect words, referring indirectly to some knowledge shared by the characters and as yet hidden from the audience.

These oblique references yield, for the moment, to the ordinary business of changing guard:

Bernardo: Well, good-night.
If you do meet Horatio and Marcellus,
The rivals of my watch, bid them make haste.

Either Bernardo is understandably anxious not to be left alone (it is, incidentally, a matter for puzzlement that Francisco has been allowed to stand solitary guard, without 'rivals'), or he is keen for some reason to have witnesses at hand. Francisco announces their advent:

Francisco: I think I hear them – Stand, ho! Who's there?

We are back to the business of challenging – and still it is a challenge from the wrong quarter, for Francisco has now been relieved and the sentinel's authority is properly invested in Bernardo. Once again, the military convention is violated, in a moment of excited apprehension. Horatio and Marcellus emerge from the darkness to reply to the challenge:

Horatio: Friends to this ground.
Marcellus: And liegemen to the Dane.

But what is Horatio doing, answering the challenge? As we are presently to learn, he is not a soldier, and his 'Friends to this ground' does not quite have the air of a soldierly response. It is apparently left to Marcellus, the professional, to redeem Horatio's civilian incompetence with a formula ('liegemen to the Dane') having the ring of a real password and bearing, as it happens, some resemblance to the earlier 'Long live the king!' Francisco admits the incomers without further ado:

Francisco: Give you good-night.

Yet why should Francisco be so obviously satisfied with 'liegemen to the Dane' when earlier he has apparently been so cautious about 'long live the king'? Which is the correct password? Are there two passwords? Is the 'password' simply a brief expression of the appropriate sentiment, a variable form of loyal words? Surely not. A plausible explanation is that 'Long live the king!' is an approximation to the correct password, a fumbled attempt produced by Bernardo in his excitement. Given such a doubtful or approximate password, Francisco might well question the identity of the intruder; whereas, when the password convinces him, he has no more to say.

And now Marcellus is understandably a little surprised at being challenged by a man so obviously about to quit the scene:

Marcellus: O, farewell, honest soldier:
               Who hath reliev'd you?

Here is yet another piece of confusion. It is barely a moment since Bernardo has identified Marcellus as one of his 'rivals', and yet Marcellus apparently does not know the identity of the person he is about to join. Francisco obligingly reminds him:

Francisco: Bernardo has my place.
               Give you good-night.

That word 'place' is of some consequence. Earlier, *in* his 'place', Francisco has rightly insisted, 'Nay, answer *me*'; but it is not his 'place' to challenge Horatio and Marcellus, and he knows it. His exit speech serves merely to emphasize what we already know, that the usual drills are at sixes and sevens, and that nothing is being done properly or routinely on this strange night.

The subsequent exchanges between Marcellus, Bernardo and Horatio ask us to envisage a spacious darkness, an isolating expanse not easily represented on a small stage, Thus, the interlocutors are first within.earshot, yet cannot see each other clearly:

Marcellus: Holla! Bernardo!
Bernardo: Say,
               What, is Horatio there?

Thus attention is drawn to Horatio, whose presence is evidently of some importance. He responds, speaking up on his own behalf:

Horatio: A piece of him.

The response is laconic and ironic, a humorous utterance that marks out the speaker as a different sort of animal from those around him. It is, to be sure, a very cold night, and people are behaving rather oddly, and Horatio may well be wondering why he is out at this hour with the superstitious soldiery when he might be tucked up in a warm place. Bernardo greets him and his companion:

Bernardo: Welcome, Horatio; welcome good Marcellus.

These 'welcome's seem a little out of the ordinary. Is 'welcome' a conventional salutation from one soldier on duty to another, or is Bernardo perhaps a little effusive, and do his words once agan reveal an unwonted nervousness? Marcellus's next remark reads, indeed, like a response to some suppressed agitation in Bernardo's manner; or possibly Marcellus himself is so excited that he plunges straight into the matter that concerns him most, cutting short the exchange of civilities:

Marcellus: What! has this thing appear'd again to-night?

And now we are very close – with 'this thing' – to discovering just what it is that has put these disciplined men into such disarray. Yet Bernardo still shies away from open discussion:

Bernardo: I have seen nothing.

Taken at its face value, this is a baffling remark. Marcellus's question can be broadly supposed to mean 'have you – has Francisco – has *anybody* – seen "this thing" tonight?'; to which Bernardo replies, 'I have seen nothing.' But since it is not five minutes since he came on watch, who would expect him to have seen anything? Perhaps, then, we are to stress *I*, and paraphrase: 'I don't know about anyone else, but *I've* seen nothing.' Yet even this is a questionable assumption. We know that Bernardo has questioned Francisco about his 'quiet guard', and has received the assurance 'not a mouse stirring'. The stress on *I* would then be misleading, because it would imply that someone other than Bernardo might have seen *this thing* tonight – and Bernardo is aware that this is not the case. Whatever intonation or stress pattern we attribute to the utterance it remains a kind of lie, because it ostensibly allows Marcellus to draw the wrong inferences. This is obviously unsatisfactory; why would Shakespeare make a very minor character perpetrate such a stupid conversational cheat? One plausible conjecture is that Bernardo is passing a coded message, indicating his wariness of the outsider, Horatio. What is Horatio's attitude? The soldiers who keep the night watches on these grim, vast, dark battlements all know about 'this thing', whatever it is, but Horatio is not a soldier. He is a scholar, and as such may be inclined to pour rational scorn on the sentries' experience.

This is confirmed by Marcellus's next speech (not included in our paraphrase) and Horatio's subsequent comment:

> *Marcellus:* Horatio says 'tis but our fantasy,
> And will not let belief take hold of him
> Touching this dreaded sight, twice seen of us:
> Therefore have I entreated him along
> With us, to watch the minutes of this night;
> That, if again this apparition come,
> He may approve our eyes, and speak to it.
> *Horatio:* Tush, tush, 'twill not appear.

'This thing' is now 'this dreaded sight', 'this apparation' – in short, this ghost; and we may now fairly guess at the motive underlying Bernardo's 'I have seen nothing'. He is being cautious in the presence of the newcomer, the known sceptic, the educated fellow who has been brought along to bear corroborative witness, and, if necessary, to 'speak to' the phantom.

The speech of Marcellus quoted above is the real beginning of the play. From this point onwards, it is relevant to note, the dramatic discourse settles regularly into blank verse. In the speeches that precede it, from the first 'Who's there?' down to 'I have seen nothing', the prosodic impulse is sporadic, fragmented, as irregular as the exchanges themselves. The discourse is unsettled and holds no more than tenuously to predictable rules; people speak out of turn, with odd implications and unexpected responses. As a military exercise, this changing of the guard at Elsinore is a scrambling makeshift. It amounts to something not far short of panic, or at least close to the bounds of a controlled fear. It establishes, indeed, the mood of the play, which throughout is confused and full of apprehension.

III An Analysis

(i) The Structure of the Discourse

Paraphrase and commentary are ways of *experiencing* literary discourse; and now comes the task of *analysing* the experience.[3] The procedures supporting such an analysis can be freely drawn from sociolinguistics and pragmatics. These studies are conveniently oriented to the description of literary works in which dialogue figures prominently, and can often throw light on the dual function of such dialogue, on the one hand as a reflex of 'ordinary' conversation, and on the other as a literary artifice, an aesthetic structure with no more than superficial claims to naturalistic status.

The first task of the discourse analyst describing patterns of conversation is to determine their structure as a complex of exchanges minimally represented as I(nitiation) and R(esponse). In some descriptions (see, for example, Burton, 1980; Carter and Burton, 1982) the IR structure is related to a hierarchy in which the comprehensive unit is the *interaction*, comprising *transactions* between certain speakers on certain topics, realized in *exchanges* governing the phasing of the topic, the exchanges being worked out in *moves*, for example, opening moves, supporting moves, challenging moves, expounded by specific verbal *acts*, of eliciting, directing, informing, commenting, acknowledging and so forth. This hierarchical model echoes the taxonomy of forms propounded by systemic grammarians (Sentence–Clause–Group–Word–Morpheme), and has the same advantage of allowing access, for the purposes of 'coarse' or 'delicate' analysis, at different levels in the scheme.

A rigorous analysis of the first twenty-nine lines of *Hamlet* would thus account for the transaction structure, plot the exchanges and specify the component acts. Some of this activity, however, might well prove redundant. The necessary first step is to begin at the general level of the *transaction*, and to ask how many of these are involved in the represented interaction, i.e. in the passage beginning with 'Who's there?' and concluding in 'I have seen nothing'. It appears that there are two distinct transactions. The first reads thus:

Bernardo:	Who's there?	1
Francisco:	Nay, answer me; stand and unfold yourself.	2
Bernardo:	Long live the king!	3
Francisco:	Bernardo?	4
Bernardo:	He.	5
Francisco:	You come most carefully upon your hour.	6
Bernardo:	'Tis now struck twelve; get thee to bed, Francisco.	7
Francisco:	For this relief much thanks; 'tis bitter cold	8
	And I am sick at heart.	9
Bernardo:	Have you had quiet guard?	10
Francisco:	Not a mouse stirring.	11
Bernardo:	Well, good-night.	12
	If you do meet Horatio and Marcellus,	13
	The rivals of my watch, bid them make haste.	14
Francisco:	I think I hear them . . .	15

And the second continues:

Francisco:	Stand, ho! Who's there?	15
Horatio:	Friends to this ground.	16
Marcellus:	And liegemen to the Dane	17

Francisco:	Give you good-night.	18
Marcellus:	O, farewell, honest soldier:	19
	Who hath reliev'd you?	20
Francisco:	Bernardo has my place.	21
	Give-you good-night.	22
Marcellus:	Holla! Bernardo:	23
Bernardo:	Say,	24
	What, is Horatio there?	25
Horatio:	A piece of him.	26
Bernardo:	Welcome, Horatio; welcome good Marcellus.	27
Marcellus:	What! has this thing appear'd again to-night?	28
Bernardo:	I have seen nothing.	29

Line 15 thus marks the closure of one set of exchanges and the transition to another set which is in some places quite closely mimetic of the first. The mimicry appears almost obviously in the parallel challenge routines of 2–3 and 15–17, but lines 2–7 and 15–22 are generally comparable. The utterances of 2–7 are concerned successively with challenging, with recognizing someone, with raising a query about the guard-changing routine, and with leavetaking. Lines 15–22 are correspondingly devoted to challenging, to recognition, to a question about the guard and to leavetaking. The verbal forms, however, are not directly correspondent. There are parallels, contrasts, comparables, thus:

Lines 2–7	*Lines 15–22*	
Stand, and unfold yourself.	Stand, ho! Who's there?	*Challenging*
Long live the king!	Friends to this ground.	
	And liegemen to the Dane	
Bernardo?	Give you good-night.	*Identifying,*
He.	O, farewell, honest soldier:	*recognizing*
You come most carefully	Who hath reliev'd you?	*Questioning,*
upon your hour.		*seeking to clarify*
'Tis now struck twelve:	Bernardo has my place.	*situation*
Get thee to bed, Francisco.	Give you good-night.	*Leavetaking*

These topical *correspondences*, whether clear or muted, are perhaps not altogether surprising; the conventional conduct of the military occasion might be assumed to produce broadly similar speech acts.[4] When the participants are briefly released from the dictates of convention and speak impulsively, as in lines 8–9 and 23–6, the parallels lapse. But only briefly; for in lines 10–11 and 28–9 we have what is clearly the most significant pair of correspondent exchanges:

Lines 10–11	*Lines 28–9*
Have you had quiet guard?	What! has this thing appear'd again to-night?
Not a mouse stirring.	I have seen nothing.

The earlier exchange patently foreshadows the later, but where the earlier is general and oblique the later is specific and direct. A diffuse question ('Everything all right?') is matched by a pointed question ('Has the ghost appeared?'), and an impersonal answer ('Nothing has happened') is echoed by one that emphasizes personal agency ('I have seen nothing'). What is also apparent, however, is that the elements of the earlier exchange *imply* the formulations of the later. *Have you had quiet guard?* contains the meaning 'Has this thing appeared?', and *Not a mouse stirring* involves 'I have seen nothing'.

It seems that the general situational and verbal parallels of lines 1–7 and 15–22 function as discursive tracks, leading us towards the important waymarks of lines 10–11 and 28–9; and that 28–9 in particular is a piece of text brought into prominence by the carefully constructed perspective of the exchange patterns. Thus the scene which, at the level of dramatic representation, presents confusion, shiftiness, indiscipline, is at the level of textual design a minor artifice, thoughtfully and almost symmetrically ordered.

(ii) Speech Acts and Implicatures

The patterning of the interaction accommodates a play of utterances which, on the whole, are not statements or descriptions but have other functions in the discursive process. We know that the framing of propositions and the conveying of 'messages' is far from being the sole function of language, and that discourse, particularly spoken discourse, operates to a very great extent through verbal acts which are tokens of social relationship, ritual performances, conversational signposts, *pragmatic* indicators pointing to a result, an action, a response, rather than a 'message' in the propositional sense. A propositional (statement, description) can be declared true or false, but that is not the case with utterances that in some way affect the shape and management of discourse (for example, questions, directives, signals of continuation, interruption, resumption, closure), or with so-called *illocutions*, i.e. forms of words marking a performance, an announcement, an agreement, a promise, a contract, a verdict and so on. There is a distinction to be drawn between 'discourse acts' and 'speech acts' in the illocutionary sense (see Stubbs, 1983: 148), but the common property of these interactional strategies is that they are functionally different from propositions, and express or imply different kinds of meaning.

The opening of *Hamlet* is short on information and long on interaction. In the first twenty-nine lines of the play there are some twenty-three discourse acts, i.e. questions, challenges, nominations, acknowledgements, directives, expressions of courtesy, greetings, leavetakings. They are:

(Bernardo)	Who's there?	(challenges)	1
(Francisco)	Nay, answer me;	(aborts, redirects)	2
(Francisco)	stand and unfold yourself.	(challenges)	2
(Bernardo)	Long live the king!	(password)	3
(Francisco)	Bernardo?	(nominates (?))	4
(Bernardo)	He.	(acknowledges (?))	5
(Bernardo)	get thee to bed, Francisco.	(directs)	7
(Francisco)	For this relief much thanks;	(thanks)	8
(Bernardo)	Have you had quiet guard?	(questions)	10
(Bernardo)	Well, good-night.	(leavetaking)	12
(Bernardo)	If you do meet Horatio and Marcellus,		
	The rivals of my watch, bid them make haste.		
		(directs)	13–14
(Francisco)	Stand, ho!	(directs)	15
(Francisco)	Who's there?	(challenges)	15
(Horatio)	Friends to this ground.	(password)	16
(Marcellus)	And liegemen to the Dane.	(password)	17
(Francisco)	Give you good-night.	(leavetaking)	18
(Marcellus)	O, farewell, honest soldier:		
		(greeting/leavetaking)	19
(Marcellus)	Who hath reliev'd you?	(questions)	20
(Francisco)	Give you good-night.	(leavetaking)	22
(Marcellus)	Holla! Bernardo!	(greets/nominates)	23
(Bernardo)	Say, What, is Horatio there?	(questions)	24–5
(Bernardo)	Welcome, Horatio; welcome good Marcellus.		
		(greets)	27
(Marcellus)	What! has this thing appear'd again to-night?		
		(questions)	28

Of the items listed here, four come under the heading of 'questions', and four are directives, leaving no less than fifteen in the remaining categories of 'challenge', 'password', 'nominate', 'acknowledge', 'thank', 'greet', 'take leave'. This is an instructive index to the general character of the scene as a complex of nervous interactive gestures, implying much yet conveying little.[5] To interpret lines 4–5 as nomination and acknowledgement is perhaps questionable, and yet it makes good interactive sense to read Bernardo's 'He' pragmatically, as a verbal gesture tantamount to 'Yes' or 'Here'. Almost certainly the speaker does not intend the proposition 'My name is Bernardo'. Horatio's 'Friends to this ground' in line 16 is discursively ambivalent by comparison with 'liegemen to the Dane'. The latter reads straightforwardly as a password, but Horatio's speech might be interpreted as compromise between a password and a proposition, for example, 'We are your friends'. It is Horatio's first utterance, and its ambivalent status – the very fact that we do not know whether he is attempting a password or answering a civil question – marks him out.

In contrast to this plenitude of discourse acts, there are no more than nine utterances that can be interpreted as propositional, i.e.:

(*Francisco*)	You come most carefully upon your hour.	6
(*Bernardo*)	'Tis now struck twelve.	7
(*Francisco*)	'tis bitter cold	8
(*Francisco*)	And I am sick at heart.	9
(*Francisco*)	Not a mouse stirring.	11
(*Francisco*)	I think I hear them.	15
(*Francisco*)	Bernardo has my place.	21
(*Horatio*)	A piece of him.	(?) 26
(*Bernardo*)	I have seen nothing.	29

There are one or two dubious instances here. Francisco's 'I think I hear them' (line 15) is uncertainly poised between proposition (i.e. as statement) and performative (i.e. the act of announcing).[6] Further, it may seem odd to read Horatio's 'A piece of him' (line 16) propositionally, especially if we regard Bernardo's 'He' in line 5 as an 'acknowledging' act in response to a nomination. Lines 25–6 (Bernardo's question and Horatio's response) arguably present a parallel case. But the oddity of Horatio's reply again marks him as a personality somewhat out of the ordinary. The ruefully ironic impression he succeeds in conveying here seems to rise from a humorous confusion of speech functions. Bernardo's question in effect 'nominates' Horatio, and requires no more than 'Yes' or 'Here' in token of acknowledgement. Instead, Horatio chooses to respond as though the exchange demanded the implementation of a propositional reply ('Yes, Horatio is present to some extent'). This is Horatio's second utterance; by the time we reach his third ('Tush, tush, 'twill not appear'), his identity as a brisk, good-humoured sceptic is established.

Apart from this one remark of Horatio's, the whole propositional content of the scene, all the information we can glean, indirectly and uncertainly, about what is going on, is supplied by Francisco (who is 'sick at heart' and wants to get out as soon as he can) and Bernardo (who is a little less than outspoken). What is interesting about the statements they make is not so much their verifiability – though of course we are concerned with what is true or false – as the masking of meanings darkly glimpsed beneath the surface of language. Their sayings both conceal and convey *implicatures* (see Grice, 1975). 'You come most carefully upon your hour' involves the meaning 'You don't usually come so promptly', and hence is a kind of discourse act, 'Why are you so punctual?'; similarly, ''Tis now struck twelve' involves 'I should have been here before now', 'I'm not all that punctual', and interpreted thus is the corrective response to a question. When Francisco says 'Not a mouse stirring' (line 11), his reply implicates the possible stirring of something rather more consequential than a mouse. And when Bernardo declares 'I have seen nothing', he frames a proposition that is strictly true, with implicatures that are perversely misleading.

Bernardo's brief role is a curious one, and subtler than we may at first be disposed to think. He focuses the soldier's clannishness and dark anxiety, just as Horatio focuses the outsider's breezy scepticism. It is Bernardo who is so anxious to come on duty; Bernardo who (ineffectually) pumps Francisco for information; Bernardo who, having taken Francisco's 'place', welcomes the advent of colleagues, and who, in Horatio's incredulous presence, manages to imply that there *is* something to be seen, although *he* has not seen it. His 'I have seen nothing' puts him, oddly enough, into the position of the man who knows.

(iii) 'Face' and Situational Power

At this point in the play, indeed, Bernardo enjoys the temporary privilege of being in charge of the situation. (And in fact he remains in charge of it – until the ghost appears, making him redundant.) He has a kind of power which may be defined in terms of *territory, status* and *competence*. The battlements are for the time being his territory, over which he disposes (as the teacher disposes over his classroom, the cook over her kitchen, the policeman over his 'patch'); the change of guard has endowed him with the status of officer-in-charge, a status he will keep until a superior comes along, or until he relinquishes it at the end of his stint of duty; and he is competent in a dual sense, both as a soldier with a knowledge of military routines (a sphere in which Horatio, for example, is manifestly incompetent), and as someone evidently quali-fied to speak about 'this thing'. Territory, status and competence are the three requisites of power or control in formal situations. If one of these is removed or diminished, whether by accident or design, the power is compromised and (in the absence of any gestures of apology or condolence) there is some loss of 'face'. Bernardo would lose face to some extent if he were to say anything other than 'I have seen nothing'. More candid formulations – 'Francisco saw nothing', 'I can't say' – would put his competence into question, and erode the power he has been busily acquiring from the opening exchange (when his erroneous challenge is a face-threatening act[7] to Francisco), down to the moment when Francisco says 'Bernardo has my place'. The play of *Hamlet* opens with a little power game – a power playlet – from which Bernardo emerges in brief authority. The guard being finally changed, 'Sit down awhile,' Bernardo instructs Horatio; and so the narrative begins to unfold.

IV Interpretation: Three grades

Close reading of a literary text is not without hazards of absurdity; there is always the risk that the interpreter's micro-analysis will ponderously discover significances hardly envisaged by the author and contemptuously resisted by the intelligent reader. For this reason alone, it is useful to grade the interpretative process, beginning with the plausible conjectures of common sense (or sensible sensibility) and gradually refining the mesh, so to speak, in order to discover how much of 'common sense' remains in the last analysis. The 'grading' here proposed, as a method amenable to this particular passage, is first to rehearse the text by paraphrasing it; then to assess the paraphrase by attempting to describe in greater elaboration the cumulative psychological impact of the passage; and finally to assess paraphrase and commentary in the light of some theoretical principles of discourse. Paraphrase is a 'coarse' method, a direct engagement with language, a sort of translation, which in this case, however, carries its own interpretative notes in the form of the 'stage directions' that offer a perception of motives lurking beneath the verbal surface. Paraphrase is 'warm'; or 'direct'; or any other word that may serve to express the notion of explaining a scene by making a scene. Commentary distances itself or, rather, displaces the engagement a little. It does not attempt to re-create the text; only to explain the perceptions that might underlie such a re-creation. Yet it, too, is a 'warmish' method – in its descriptive language, which implies no theory, uses no technical terms, follows the order of the text, dismantles nothing. Analysis brings us into a cooler climate; here a theoretical overview is proposed, language is viewed through the terms of a metalanguage, the text is stripped down to its component details. This may seem to lead us away from warm common sense and possibly set us on the road to cold lunacy, yet the analytical process, prudently managed, has at least two prizes to offer. One is that it may actually confirm, with additional emphasis and a sharpening of focus, the findings of common sense; the other is that it may prove to be heuristic, providing us with some way of perceiving what our distracted attentions have initially overlooked.

As far as the opening of *Hamlet* is concerned, theoretical analysis indeed tends to support the ordinary intuitions of paraphrase and commentary. Over and above that, it brings to the fore things that are blurred in the paraphrase and all but missed in the step-by-step proceeding of the commentary. It tells us, for example, that discourse acts outnumber propositions in a proportion of nearly three to one – and this is not merely a statistic but a matter of serious interpretative relevance. It also sets a particular exchange (line 28–9) in clear prominence on three counts – as an element in discourse structure, as a propositional highlight and as an index to situational power and 'face'; and in doing these things it points to the importance of a very minor character, Bernardo, as the person who effectively introduces the story, the narrative agent who brings us out of the eerie prelude and into the main action. It is strange, ridiculous even, to think of

Bernardo as an indispensable character, but indeed he is. What if Shakespeare had elected to do without him? What if there had been no changing of the guard at Elsinore? Suppose the play had begun with Francisco on guard, Horatio and Marcellus breezily entering – 'What! has this thing appear'd again to-night?' – and Francisco replying, 'I have seen nothing' – what then? We should have lost the dramatic tension, the controlled ascent of horror, from the nameless dread to the naming of 'this thing', then 'this apparition', then the actual appearance of the ghost. Bernardo is the talker who gives us time for gooseflesh. And something else we should have lost – the significance of the scene as a paradigm of a larger motif. Bernardo assumes – is eager to assume – Francisco's 'place'; and throughout the play 'place taking' and 'place seeking' in one form or another are important themes. The chief 'place taker' is, of course, Claudius, as perceived by Hamlet.

It is a common experience that close analysis of short passages will often afford interesting insights into the text at large. The theme in its breadth lies outside the scope of this essay, but one small point is worth noting. *Hamlet* begins with a military speech act, a sentry's challenge; it also ends with one, a general's command, 'Go bid the soldiers shoot'. In issuing that command – which of course lies within his competence – Fortinbras assumes an overlord's status and lays claim to a territory, that is, to Denmark itself. The great power play is complete. The guard is conclusively changed at Elsinore.

Suggestions for Further Work: Chapter 1

1   *Hamlet: the scope of paraphrase.* Paraphrase is a difficult, sometimes self-defeating exercise. However skilfully we go about it, there will come a point when it will cease to throw light on the meaning of dialogue, unless it is supplemented by some sort of commentary. Consider the passage III, i, 90–123, which begins with Ophelia's words 'Good my lord,/How does your honour for this many a day?' and ends with 'I was the more deceived'. Rhetorical tangles and the meanings of certain words (for example *honest*) must somewhat obscure the reader's/onlooker's view of the interaction. Can any paraphrase convincingly 'translate' this stylized colloquy? More than that, can a paraphrase throw light on the *attitudes* of the interlocutors? What happens to make Hamlet suddenly abusive ('Ha, ha! are you honest?')? Is Ophelia's attitude generally submissive, or is she more spirited than stage representations often lead us to believe? For example, what is the inner sense – the affective purport – of 'I was the more deceived'? For an exercise, attempt a 'bare' paraphrase of the speeches; then add

'stage directions' (i.e. notes on reactions and motives); then write a commentary, explaining the motivational process from exchange to exchange.

2   *Hamlet: the co-operative principle and the politeness principle.* In the passage III, ii, 312–411, which begins with Guildenstern's 'Good my lord, vouchsafe me a word with you' and ends with Hamlet's 'By and by is easily said', Hamlet wilfully rejects the courtesies that should sustain transactions between a social superior and his subordinates; he refuses to play the politeness game. This passage provides material for a short dissertation on 'The Rudest Man in Elsinore'. The co-operative principle expressed in the maxims of Grice (1975) is repeatedly violated; the principles of politeness and tact formulated, for example, by Leech (1983) are mocked; face-threatening acts (see Brown and Levinson, 1978) are perceived and ruthlessly performed. To write our dissertation, we might begin with a commentary on this scene, expounding Hamlet's successive breaches of politeness and failures to co-operate. This may occasionally necessitate paraphrase with modern equivalents (for example, 'Can I have a word?' – 'You can have an encyclopaedia if you like'). But perhaps we should aim at the definition of a further principle, the inversion of the principles of co-operation and politeness: *the defensive principle.* Hamlet is the rudest man in Elsinore, we may argue, because he is talking for his life. What are the *maxims of defence?* (For 'co-operative principle', see also Glossary, and for more about face-threatening acts see Chapter 9.)

3   *Hamlet: speech acts and propositions.* Consider the text of the duel episode from the final scene of the play, which opens with the king's 'Come begin;/And you, the judges, bear a wary eye' (V, ii, 292–3) and closes with Hamlet's 'I am dead, Horatio. Wretched queen, adieu!' (V, ii, 347). Note, in this passage, the occurrences (*i*) of discourse acts and illocutions, and (*ii*) of propositions. Accounted for in detail, these contrasting types will be found to be interestingly related to the pattern and dramatic evolution of the scene. The theme is 'Fighting to a Finish'; and the method is to examine how, and with what effect, the 'propositional' types mesh with, or counterpoint, or cut across the 'speech act' types, as the characters are dispatched and the action is brought to a close.

4   *And now for something almost different: territories and faces.* Wonderland is a long way from Elsinore, but the rules of discourse hold (or are broken) in both environments. Here are two of Alice's attempts to manage unmanageable conversations.

(a)   [*Alice approaches the Duchess' house; the Footman at the door is a frog.*]
Alice went timidly up to the door and knocked.

'There's no sort of use in knocking', said the Footman, 'and that for two reasons. First, because I'm on the same side of the door as you are. Secondly, because they're making such a noise inside, no one could possibly hear you.' And certainly there was a most extraordinary noise going on within — a constant howling and sneezing, and every now and then a great crash, as if a dish or a kettle had been broken to pieces.

'Please, then,' said Alice, 'how am I to get in?'

'There might be some sense in your knocking,' the Footman went on, without attending to her, 'if we had the door between us. For instance, if you were *inside*, you might knock, and I could let you out, you know.' He was looking up to the sky all the time he was speaking, and this Alice thought decidedly uncivil. 'But perhaps he can't help it,' she said to herself; 'his eyes are so *very* nearly at the top of his head. But at any rate he might answer questions. — 'How am I to get in?' she repeated,

'I shall sit here,' the Footman remarked, 'till to-morrow — '

At this moment the door of the house opened, and a large plate came skimming out, straight at the Footman's head: it just grazed his nose, and broke to pieces against one of the trees behind him.

' — or next day, maybe,' the Footman continued in the same tone, exactly as if nothing had happened.

'How am I to get in?' asked Alice again, in a louder tone.

'*Are* you to get in at all?' said the Footman. 'That's the first question you know.'

It was, no doubt: only Alice did not like to be told so. 'It's really dreadful,' she muttered to herself, 'the way all the creatures argue. It's enough to drive one crazy!'

The Footman seemed to think this a good opportunity for repeating his remark, with variations. 'I shall sit here,' he said, 'on and off, for days and days.'

'But what am *I* to do?' said Alice.

'Anything you like,' said the Footman, and began whistling.

'Oh, there's no use in talking to him,' said Alice desperately: 'he's perfectly idiotic!' And she opened the door and went in.

(b) [*Alice approaches the March Hare's house. The Hare, the Mad Hatter and the Dormouse are having tea in the garden.*]

The table was a large one, but the three were all crowded together at one corner of it. 'No room! No room!' they cried out when they saw Alice coming. 'There's *plenty* of room!' said Alice indignantly, and she sat down in a large armchair at one end of the table.

'Have some wine,' the March Hare said in an encouraging tone.

Alice looked all round the table, but there was nothing on it but tea. 'I don't see any wine,' she remarked.

'There isn't any,' said the March Hare.

'Then it wasn't very civil of you to offer it,' said Alice angrily.

> 'It wasn't very civil of you to sit down without being invited,' said the March Hare.
> 'I didn't know it was *your* table,' said Alice; 'it's laid for a great many more than three.'
> 'Your hair wants cutting,' said the Hatter. He had been looking at Alice for some time with great curiosity, and this was his first speech.
> 'You should learn not to make personal remarks,' Alice said with some severity. 'It's very rude.'
> The Hatter opened his eyes very wide on hearing this, but all he *said* was 'Why is a raven like a writing-desk?'
> 'Come, we shall have some fun now!' thought Alice. 'I'm glad they've begun asking riddles, – I believe I can guess that,' she added aloud.
> 'Do you mean that you think you can find out the answer to it?' said the March Hare.
> 'Exactly so,' said Alice.
> 'Then you should say what you mean,' the March Hare went on.[8]

In each of these passages Alice is represented as an incomer encroaching on someone else's territory (a recurrent situation throughout the *Alice* books). The Wonderlanders are apparently very uncooperative and impolite; the Footman and the March Hare go for different reasons to the bottom of the Gricean class, and the Hatter's raven–writing-desk riddle is as unmeaningful as Hamlet's camel–whale–weasel cloud. (But there is method in the Hatter's madness, as there is in Hamlet's.) Alice constantly passes comment, mental or spoken, on the rudeness of the Wonderlanders, without apparently realizing that *they* often see *her* as a discourteous and irrelevant intruder, whose assumptions about their society constitute a repeated threat to 'face'. (Her manners sometimes suggest the upper-middle class style with servants and shopkeepers.) So how do they defend their territory, save face and make the intruder keep her distance – for it is the essence of the book that she is *in* Wonderland, but never *of* it?

Notes: Chapter 1

1   Quotations are from Shakespeare, *Complete Works*, ed. W. J. Craig (London: Oxford University Press, 1945).
2   Francisco's words are echoed by Laertes in IV, vii, 54–6. 'It warms the very sickness in my heart/That I shall live and tell him to his teeth,/"Thus diddest thou".' This chilly sickness is obviously figurative – as Francisco's surely is.
3   Discourse analysis, even when its object is so-called 'naturally occurring speech', is largely concerned with the *perception* of how words work; this is

emphatically and unavoidably the case when the object is a literary text. In the last analysis, literary experience remains subjective.

4 On the face of it, the least plausible correspondence here is between the pair of exchanges labelled *identifying, recognizing*. 'Give you good night' and 'O, farewell, honest soldier' are forms of greeting and leavetaking, not strictly matching the nominate/acknowledge patterns of 'Bernardo?' and 'He'. But Marcellus exclamation (the 'O' is a tell-tale) *implies* recognition of the departing sentry, whom he does not see clearly until this moment.

5 Information is occasionally 'conveyed' through the discourse act in which it is embedded. Thus from Bernardo's speech in lines 13–14 we can in fact retrieve a proposition, 'Horatio and Marcellus are the rivals of my watch'. Though such embeddings can certainly occur in questions and directives ('Who was that lady I saw you with last night?', 'Hand me that book with the yellow cover'), we are here concerned with questioning and directing primarily as transactional operators.

6 Had Francisco said, 'I can hear them,' the case would be clearer. The verb *think* slightly complicates the issue, from its potential affinity with verbs like *believe, declare*, which would tend to give Francisco's words the colouring of an illocutionary act.

7 The notion of 'face-threatening act' will be expanded more fully in Chapter 9 of this book.

8 From Lewis Carroll, *Alice's Adventures in Wonderland* (Macmillan miniature edn, London, 1935) chs 6, 7.

References: Chapter 1

Brown, P., and Levinson, S. (1978), 'Universals in Language Usage: Politeness 'Phenomena'. in E. N. Goody (ed.), *Questions and Politeness: Strategies in Social Interaction* (Cambridge: Cambridge University Press), pp. 56–289.

Burton, D. (1980), *Dialogue and Discourse: A Sociolinguistic Approach to Modern Drama Dialogue and Naturally Occurring Conversation* (London: Routledge & Kegan Paul).

Carter, R., and Burton, D. (eds) (1982), *Literary Text and Language Study*. (London: Edward Arnold).

Grice, H. P. (1975), 'Logic and Conversation', in P. Cole and J. Morgan (eds), *Syntax and Semantics*, vol. 3 *Speech Acts* (New York: Academic Press), pp. 41–58.

Leech, G. N. (1983), *Principles of Pragmatics* (London: Longman).

Stubbs, M. (1983), *Discourse Analysis: The Sociolinguistic Analysis of Natural Language* (Oxford: Blackwell).

Introduction to Chapter 2

In Paul Simpson's chapter, a commonplace feature of naturally occurring conversation provides the starting point for his stylistic analysis. This routine aspect of interaction is known as *phatic communion* and it refers to the stereotypical remarks that speakers make at the beginnings and endings of conversations.

For the purposes of his analysis, Simpson draws specifically on John Laver's research on the communicative functions of phatic communion. Laver has proposed that the kinds of comments – or 'tokens' – that speakers use in phatic exchanges can be classified under three headings:

(1) *neutral tokens* – comments relating to the immediate context of interaction which are not personal to either the speaker or the hearer;
(2) *self-oriented tokens* – comments on factors that are personal to the speaker;
(3) *other-oriented tokens* – comments on factors that are personal to the hearer.

The selection of a particular type of token, it is argued, is influenced by important contextual constraints – not least of which is the relative social status of the interactants.

Simpson goes on to incorporate this framework into his analysis of some conversational openings in the dialogue of Flann O'Brien's novel *The Third Policeman*. Through this, he seeks to explain, in a systematic way, the underlying comic structure of this fictional dialogue. His conclusion to the chapter is contrastive in orientation. He argues that the examples of 'foregrounded' conversation in a literary text provide one means of highlighting the familiarized patterns that are there all the time in the language of everyday social encounters.

2 Phatic Communion and Fictional Dialogue

PAUL SIMPSON

I General Framework

This chapter will concentrate on a feature of linguistic behaviour which is common to many everyday social encounters: *phatic communion*. The main body of data for the analysis will be provided by the fictional dialogue in Flann O'Brien's novel *The Third Policeman*. In the course of the chapter, it is intended that three broad theoretical issues should be developed.

First, the investigation will draw on a sociolinguistic framework designed for the analysis of naturally occurring conversation. This framework will be applied to the rather unusual dialogue which takes place between the characters in O'Brien's novel. It is hoped that such an analysis will highlight the ways in which the conventions of 'normal' talk can be manipulated by a writer for special effect, and thereby explain the comic impact of this fictional dialogue. In this respect, the analysis can be regarded as an exercise in *discourse stylistics*.

Secondly, by contrast, it is intended that the following analysis of literary dialogue will have some implications for the study of naturally occurring conversation. Oddly enough, by examining strikingly unusual interactions in a literary text, we may alert ourselves to the discourse patterns in everyday interaction. The principle here is in keeping with Burton (1980) in that we often only recognize norms once they are broken. Put another way, as native speakers our expectations about talk are often highlighted when these expectations are withheld.

The investigation has a more tentative third aim, which is to offer some reasonably systematic comments on the principles which make dialogue *absurd*. This is clearly not the place to undertake a detailed review of existing literature on absurdism. In any case, strict working definitions of the term are difficult to find. For example, Abrams, in his glossary of literary terms, describes absurdism in the following way:

The name is applied to a number of works in drama and prose fiction which have in common the sense that the human condition is essentially and ineradicably absurd, and that this condition can be adequately represented only in works of literature that are themselves absurd. (Abrams 1981: 1)

Interesting though this comment may be, it still does not actually define what is meant by the term *absurd*. Without explaining the important principles involved, it simply tells us that *absurd* texts exist – thereby offering no criteria for the recognition of such a text. Although the focus of this chapter is narrow (in so far as only *phatic* exchanges will be examined), it is hoped that the linguistic analysis will at least provide evidence upon which an exploratory definition of the *absurd* can be based. Moreover, this is particularly pertinent to the present study, as the label *absurd* is applied to *The Third Policeman* with depressing regularity.

II The Notion of Phatic Communion: Background Remarks

In general, *phatic communion* is taken to mean the kind of ritualistic linguistic behaviour which characterizes the beginnings and endings of conversations. This normally includes the formulaic gambits of greet-ing and parting (for example, 'Hello', 'Good morning'), along with a set of stereotypical remarks concerning the weather. Malinowski, who actually coined the term in the 1920s, defined phatic communion as 'a type of speech in which ties of union are created by a mere exchange of words' (Malinowski, 1972: 151). Furthermore, he stresses that in a phatic exchange the actual words used

fulfil a social function and that is their principal aim, but they are neither the result of intellectual reflection, nor do they necessarily arouse interest in the listener. (Malinowski 1972: 151)

In this respect, the information imparted between interactants in a phatic exchange can be said to be *indexical*, rather than *cognitive*. (See Laver and Hutcheson, 1972: 11.)

Other linguists have commented on phatic communion. Fowler (1981: 84) defines it as the 'routine vacuities' that people perform in verbal interaction. Lyons, on the other hand, comments on phatic communion in the following way:

This felicitous expression . . . emphasizes the notion of fellowship and participation in common social rituals: hence 'communion' rather than 'communication'. (Lyons 1981: 143)

It is important to reiterate Malinowski's comment that phatic communion has an important *social* function. Amongst other things, this 'small talk' helps avoid uncomfortable silences at the beginnings and endings of conversations. This is particularly relevant to encounters with new acquaintances. However, the kinds of topics chosen for phatic exchanges are not normally referentially significant. That is to say, such remarks are not intended to convey important or 'newsworthy' information; nor are they to be interpreted as such by an interlocutor. This explains the apparent incongruity (and perhaps humour) of the following example. This exchange took place between myself and an acquaintance who is more than a little keen on meteorology:

PS: It's right'n changeable today.
JS: Ah . . . well . . . that's probably because of the south-westerly coming in with the North Atlantic Drift . . . that would bring in an occluded front, you know. . . .

This unusual exchange, which raises some issues which will be relevant to the analysis of fictional dialogue in section IV, seems to derive from an idiosyncratic interpretation of the communicative function of the phatic opening. Other examples of 'marked' phatic behaviour are provided by Bauman (1983: 44) in his study of the language of seventeenth-century Quakers. He notes that one particular Quaker practice which caused affront to those with whom Quakers came into contact was their refusal to use greetings and leavetakings, such as 'Good morning', 'Good evening', 'Good morrow' and 'Farewell'. They believed that these forms constituted unnecessary talk, and thereby led one into the sinful trap of 'idle words'. Not surprisingly, this practice was often interpreted by non-Quakers as a serious lack of civil courtesy.

III   A Framework for the Analysis of Phatic Communion

I now wish to draw upon John Laver's important research on phatic communion. In a paper entitled 'Communicative Functions of Phatic Communion' (Laver, 1975) he offers a useful description of the kind of strategies that speakers use in the opening and closing phases of conversation.

In this study, Laver draws upon his personal observations of linguistic behaviour in the initial and final stages of encounters. Moreover, these observations are supported by over a hundred student projects, which examine phatic communion in a wide variety of interactions. Although he concedes that much of this work is still exploratory, he still asserts that his methodological procedure produces a wide measure of agreement about the behavioural phenomena involved. Many of Laver's findings tie in neatly with the discussion above. For instance, he notices how, particularly in the initial phase of a conversation, speakers often make supremely obvious comments to one another. These comments – or *tokens* – do have a communicative function in that they serve to break any uncomfortable silence as well as laying the foundation for further interaction. In this respect, phatic tokens are used to make the transition from non-interaction to interaction smooth.

Laver develops his theory in the following way. He proposes a three-way typology, which is intended to account for the literal reference of the phatic tokens. The first category is *neutral tokens*. These comprise references to factors concerning the context of situation, which are not personal to either the speaker or hearer. In English, such tokens are frequently comments on the weather. There are, however, other kinds of neutral tokens. Laver provides some examples of variations on this theme: 'Great view' (to a fellow tourist) or 'About time these trains were cleaned' (to a fellow passenger). Clearly, in all cases neutral tokens have relevance to factors affecting both participants equally.

The remaining two categories are *self-oriented tokens* and *other-oriented tokens*. Self-oriented tokens refer to factors personal to the *speaker*, whilst other-oriented tokens refer to factors personal to the *listener*. Examples of the former category would be 'Hot work, this' or 'My legs weren't made for these hills'; whilst examples of the latter category would be 'How's life?' or 'Do you come here often?'

Laver takes the discussion further, by asserting that the choice of category is constrained by the relative social status of the interactant. It is worth quoting his formulation at length:

> The NEUTRAL category remains available to a speaker of any relative social status, but the conventional choice between the SELF-ORIENTED and the OTHER-ORIENTED category is normally governed by the status differential between the two speakers. In an 'upwards' interaction, where a nonsolidary inferior speaks first to an acknowledged superior, he may choose the self-oriented category, but not the other-oriented category. In a 'downwards' interaction, where a nonsolidary superior speaks first to an acknowledged inferior, he may choose the other-oriented category, but not the self-oriented category. (Laver, 1975: 224)

Thus, if a superior were to initiate the phatic exchange, he would use an other-oriented token (such as 'That looks like hard work'). Whereas, if the inferior were to initiate, he would use a self-oriented token (such as 'Hard work, this'). A more extreme example will emphasize this point. Imagine that one wished to initiate a phatic exchange with a member of the British Royal family. The selection of an other-oriented token which, say, commented on the physical disposition or demeanour of the interlocutor, would be unlikely to be the best choice that one might make.

IV The Analysis

The Laver framework (as outlined above) will now be applied to some short sequences of phatic communion in Irish fiction. All the examples are taken from Flann O'Brien's novel *The Third Policeman*.[1] In order to place these examples firmly in context, it is necessary to say a few words on the plot of the novel – even at the expense of spoiling the story of those yet unfamiliar with the text.

The rather bizarre plot of *The Third Policeman* centres on an unnamed first-person narrator. Early in the novel, this protagonist forms a partnership with a rascal named Divney. Together they murder an old man and rob him of his mysterious black box, in which is contained apparently infinite riches. However, a short time later, the protagonist is in turn murdered by his partner in crime. After his death, which is somewhere in the second chapter of the book, he tells of his strange adventures in a nightmarish world where he encounters a pair of excessively obese policemen named Sergeant Pluck and Policeman MacCruiskeen. So peculiar is this world that eternity is realized as an accessible place which can be reached simply by means of an escalator. What is really disconcerting, however, is that we don't *know* that the main character has been dead during all this – we only discover it in the final chapter of the novel. In this respect, the novel actually has an *in medias res* ending – if that is possible – as it concludes with a sudden switch back in time to a scene from eight chapters earlier. There is the implication that the strange events of the novel will unfold again and again, in an infinite cycle. Example (*a*) below occurs in the seventh chapter of the novel. At this stage the protagonist has been arrested for an obscure murder which is actually unrelated to the one he himself has committed. As he has the misfortune to be close at hand when the news of the murder reaches the police barracks, he is arrested and summarily sentenced to death. During the subsequent period of remarkably lax incarceration, the following exchange takes place:

(*a*) MacCruiskeen was not gone for long but I was lonely during that diminutive meantime. When he came in again he gave me a cigarette which was warm and wrinkled from his pocket.
'I believe they are going to stretch you,' he said pleasantly.
I replied with nods. (p. 90)

In this example, Policeman MacCruiskeen initiates a very unusual phatic exchange. Several points concerning this phatic token merit discussion. First of all, it is clear that MacCruiskeen selects an *other-oriented* token: he refers to a matter which is personal to the addressee. This is interesting as an encounter between a policeman and a prisoner would normally be considered a 'downwards' interaction, with the former holding superior interactive rights. In this respect, Mac-Cruiskeen's phatic token is in keeping with the formula proposed by Laver.

Furthermore, it is significant that the policeman's remark is about an *AB event*, as defined by Labov and Fanshel (1977: 100). In a dyadic interaction, AB-events concern information which is known to both speakers. In this case, MacCruiskeen (speaker A) is referring to an AB-event – which is the question of the protagonist's impending execution. The protagonist (speaker B) is already aware of this information – it is part of the *shared knowledge* of the interactants. Such AB-events play an important part in phatic communion. As they represent knowledge that is already known to both participants, they are not referentially important in themselves. Rather, references to AB-events are used in a social-solidary sense. By focusing on mutually shared knowledge, they provide a kind of 'safe' conversational token which allows further referentially significant transactions to take place. (For a further discussion of AB-events and shared knowledge, see the following chapter of this book.)

It is also worth noting the overall *propitiatory* nature of Mac-Cruiskeen's phatic initiation. For instance, the token is accompanied by the gift of a cigarette. Moreover, the authorial clue 'pleasantly' in the reporting clause emphasizes the friendly intention behind the utterance. There is also a suggestion of informality with the lexical selection of 'stretch' – which serves as a casual (and somewhat grisly) euphemism for 'hang'. It is interesting that the phatic purpose of the utterance is discerned by the interlocutor, who responds with an affirmatory non-verbal surrogate.

In fact, the discussion of example (*a*) provides an appropriate place at which to introduce another of Laver's observations on phatic communion. This concerns the physical movement and positioning of interlocutors during a phatic exchange. Laver proposes the following formula:

> When one participant is static in space, and the other is moving towards him, in whatever type of physical locale, then . . . there seems to be a strong tendency . . . for the 'incomer' to initiate the exchange of phatic communion. (Laver, 1975: 226)

This formula is certainly adhered to, as MacCruiskeen, the 'incomer', offers the phatic token to the protagonist, who is static in space.

However, with regard to naturally occurring conversation, my informal observations on this particular aspect of phatic communion have not produced any significant support for this hypothesis. Furthermore, the reasons which Laver himself provides as to *why* the incomer should initiate the phatic exchange seem a little speculative:

> The speaker recognizes that in some sense the static listener is in a closer psychological relationship with the immediate territory than he is, and that in a way the listener can be regarded as the owner of the territory. (Laver, 1975: 226)

This is clearly not the case with respect to example (*a*). Here, the static listener is positioned squarely within the territory of his interlocutor and, as he is also under arrest, he is hardly likely to be in a close 'psychological relationship' with this territory. Nevertheless, having said this, the incomer still does initiate – regardless of Laver's suggestions concerning the psychological basis for such initiation. Moreover, the same pattern of 'incomer initiation' is repeated in all of the phatic exchanges in the novel – as further examples will show. Indeed, the novel in this respect sets up its own *intra-textual norm*, although whether this feature is of any thematic significance is another matter.

I wish to consider one final aspect of example (*a*). This relates to Laver's observations on the motivation which prompts speakers to make phatic initiations. In fact, this final aspect is crucial in so far as it helps to explain the absurdity of MacCruiskeen's utterance.

It is important to remember that perhaps the most important motivation behind phatic initiation is that the speaker wants to declare that his intentions are pacific. As Laver points out, the speaker 'asserts a claim to sociolinguistic solidarity with the listener' (Laver 1975: 226). However, as in this initial conversational phase the pyschological comfort of the co-participants is most at risk, the topic of the phatic tokens should be *emotionally uncontroversial* material – and it is this particular notion which finally penetrates the 'absurdity' of the policeman's utterance. His 'token' – if it can even be called that – could hardly be said to 'facilitate the comfortable initiation, free from tension and hostility, of the interaction's' (Laver 1975: 227). In fact, the converse is true. If it were not for the policeman's choice of phatic topic, the utterance would faithfully follow the formula set down by Laver. But glib talk of the listener's impending death hardly consolidates the relationship of the participants – nor does it ease the transition to and from interaction. It is perhaps because MacCruiskeen follows meticulously all Laver's other formulas, yet departs so drastically on his choice of topic, that the utterance derives much of its comic effect.

I would suggest that the impact of example (*a*) is heightened by its relationship to other phatic tokens in *The Third Policeman*. To

illustrate this, a second example of phatic communion will be introduced. This example is more typical of the general pattern of phatic
exchanges in the novel, and in this respect it will provide a useful
contrast to (*a*). The following exchange takes place between the protagonist and a second policeman, Sergeant Pluck, who is evidently no
less corpulent than his colleague:

> (*b*) It soon turned out that the hammering was the work of Sergeant
> Pluck. He was standing smiling at me from the doorway and he
> looked large and lifelike and surprisingly full of breakfast. Over
> the tight collar of his tunic he wore a red ring of fat that looked
> fresh and decorative as if it had come directly from the laundry.
> His moustache was damp from drinking milk . . .
>   'Good morning to you in the morning-time,' the Sergeant said
> pleasantly.
>   I answered him in a civil way. . . . (p. 104)

Several interesting things happen in this exchange. First, as in example
(*a*), the incomer initiates the phatic exchange. Secondly, again like
example (*a*), the propitiatory aspect of the token is strengthened by
contextual clues. For instance, the adverbial clue 'pleasantly' appears
in the reporting clause – identical, in fact, to the previous example. It
is also interesting that the protagonist acknowledges the phatic purpose by answering his interlocutor in a 'civil way'.

Of course, where this example differs significantly from (*a*) is in the
choice of topic for the phatic token. Here, the material *is* emotionally
uncontroversial, as the Sergeant chooses a more conventional formula
for this greeting.

It might be appropriate at this stage to focus on a third example of
phatic communion in *The Third Policeman*. The following exchange –
again between the Sergeant and the protagonist – occurs in the tenth
chapter:

> (c) The Sergeant knocked very delicately at the door, came in with
> great courtesy and bade me good morning. (p. 132)

It should be noted that this phatic exchange differs significantly from
the previous two examples in its actual textual realization. Following
the suggestion of Leech and Short (1981: 322–4), example (*c*) can be
coded as a Narrative Report of Speech Act (NRSA). In this case, the
Sergeant's utterance is deeply embedded in the central narrative structure. The previous two examples, on the other hand, employ direct
speech forms with external reporting clauses. Nevertheless it should be
clear that (*c*) exhibits a pattern very similar to that of (*b*). Thus, we may
leave aside (*c*) for the moment and move on to consider one final
example from *The Third Policeman*.

Example (*d*), below, requires some explanation. In the final stages of the novel, the protagonist escapes from the police barracks. The word 'escape' is perhaps rather strong, as he simply gets on a bicycle and casually rides away! It is during this nocturnal flight that the incident in (*d*) occurs. This confrontation is, in fact, with the 'third policeman' alluded to in the title of the novel. However, we have not previously encountered this mysterious figure, even though he overshadows the entire story. It should be stressed that the suspense here is considerable, as the huge policeman approaches in the darkness – making this arguably the climactic scene of the novel:

(*d*) The steps suddenly clattered out on the roadway not six yards away, came up behind me and then stopped. It is no joke to say that my heart nearly stopped also. Every part of me that was behind me – neck, ears, back and head – shrank and quailed painfully before the presence confronting them, each expecting an onslaught of indescribable ferocity. Then I heard the words.
'This is a brave night!'
I swung round in amazement. (p. 156)

In this example, a very subtle mismatch is achieved. The narrative detail which precedes the policeman's utterance predicts an 'onslaught of indescribably ferocity'. However, instead of this expected onslaught, the policeman simply provides an affable, relaxed phatic token. Indeed, this is a *neutral* token, realized, in this case, by a commonplace remark on the weather. It is difficult to imagine a 'safer', more mundane initiation to a conversation.

The very banality of this phatic token creates its own kind of deviation here. The mismatch between the expected and the realized form is striking – indeed, striking to the extent that the protagonist (as the subsequent narrative reveals) is too shocked even to reply.

To follow this discussion through, I would suggest that phatic tokens can be regarded as a subset of the *politeness strategies* that are available to speakers. In relation to this point, Brown and Levinson (1978) – whose work will receive greater attention in Chapter 9 of this book – contend that politeness may be abandoned under certain conditions. These conditions are normally emergencies, where politeness strategies are foregone in the interests of urgency and efficiency. With regard to example (*d*), an emergency certainly prevails. However, the politeness strategy which is realized in the form of a phatic token is quite unexpected. It is worth reiterating that an 'onslaught of indescribable ferocity' is predicted: what is offered is a mild, solidary, neutral phatic token.

V Conclusion

This concluding subsection will be devoted to a brief discussion of the results of the analysis. It will also consider some of the theoretical implications of these results.

In order to bring the various strands of discussion together, a Token Realization Matrix (see Table 2.1) has been developed. Although this matrix is not based on strictly quantifiable data, it nevertheless provides a convenient way of looking at the important features of each example. It should also highlight, to a certain extent, some of the significant 'deviations'.

Table 2.1   *Token Realization Matrix*

Example	Position opening phase	Incomer initiates	Material emotionally uncontroversial	Positive acknowledgement by addressee
a	√	√	×	√
b	√	√	√	√
c	√	√	√	√
d	√	√	√	×

With regard to the first column of the matrix, all the phatic exchanges studied are clearly positioned in the *opening* (as opposed to *closing*) phase of interaction. The second column shows that in all cases the incoming participant initiates the phatic exchange. The tendencies displayed by the remaining two columns are more complex, and are best explained by commenting on each of the examples across the matrix.

By looking across the matrix, it is clear that examples (*b*) and (*c*) realize all four features. In fact these examples represent the general form of phatic initiation in *The Third Policeman* – the phatic exchanges which have not been covered in this chapter exhibit the same basic tendency. Thus examples (*b*) and (*c*) reflect the *intra-textual norm* for phatic initiation in the novel.

There are problems in accounting for the absurd feel of example (*d*) on this kind of matrix. One may recall that, given the circumstances of the exchange, the phatic token itself is startling. In fact, the deviation here is because the speaker actually selects neutral, emotionally uncontroversial material in an emergency. To highlight this kind of deviation, an additional component which accounted for, say, the extra-linguistic context of the exchange would have to be built into the matrix. There is no acknowledgement in this example also because the addressee is simply too terrified to reply to the phatic token.

A final comment is necessary on example (*a*). The absurd effect of this example is achieved quite clearly through the choice of material for the phatic token. This is the only token analysed which does *not* select emotionally uncontroversial material. Bearing this in mind, it might therefore be argued that example (*a*) is *foregrounded*. If this is the case, it is a particularly interesting example of foregrounding, as it appears to operate on two distinct levels. First, it is foregrounded by its relationship to naturally occurring conversation. A phatic initiation which amicably introduces the topic of the interlocutor's imminent execution is surely deviant!

Secondly, example (*a*) is foregrounded by its relationship to the patterns of interaction set up in the novel. Examples (*b*), (*c*) and (*d*) provide a statistical basis for this claim. This particular kind of foregrounding might be more appropriately termed *internal deviation* (see Leech and Short, 1981: 55–6).

It is interesting that in the case of example (*a*) only one of the four features displaying along the top of the matrix is withheld. Nevertheless, considerable effect is achieved by this simple manipulation. In fact, this is a general paradigm for the style of O'Brien's fictional dialogue. His 'absurd' touches do not derive from stringing together unrelated sequences of utterances. Nor do they emanate from complete breakdowns in discourse coherence. Instead, they are produced from careful manipulations, here and there, of the strategies of verbal interaction. In effect, we are now moving towards a consideration of the writer as conversationalist and member of a speech community – a theme that will recur in some of the subsequent chapters of this book. In the case of O'Brien, the linguistic routines of everyday social encounters provide a set of conventions which can be exploited through the dialogue he assigns to his fictional characters.

Suggestions for Further Work: Chapter 2

1 Consider the following conversational opening from Lewis Carroll's *Alice's Adventures in Wonderland*.

> She stretched herself up on tiptoe and peeped over the edge of the mushroom, and her eyes immediately met those of a large blue caterpillar, that was sitting on the top with its arms folded, quietly smoking a long hookah, and taking not the smallest notice of her or of anything else.
> The Caterpillar and Alice looked at each other for some time in silence: at last the Caterpillar took the hookah out of its mouth, and addressed her in a languid, sleepy voice.
> 'Who are *you*?' said the Caterpillar.
> This was not an encouraging opening for a conversation.[2]

In the light of the comments made in section II on the function of phatic communion, can you explain *why* this is not 'an encouraging opening for a conversation'?

2 The following extract is taken from Patrick Kavanagh's auto-biographical novel *The Green Fool*.

> Further on the road I passed MacEntaggart's house. Old Mac, as he was called, was an ex-schoolmaster. He taught in the same school that I had attended. He was dismissed for drink. My father spent one day at MacEntaggart's school and thought one day too long. Old Mac was a rough schoolmaster. He was one of the most inquisitive men you could know.
> 'Good morning, young man,' he addressed me.
> 'Good morning,' I returned.
> 'Lovely morning,' he said.
> 'Not too bad,' I agreed.
> 'How's your father, and your mother?'
> 'They're very well.'
> 'Have you many pigs?'
> 'Twelve,' I lied.
> 'Ahem, ahem,' he coughed. 'Did you see John MacCaffrey as you came along?'
> 'Damn to the sight or sight.'
> 'Where are you going?'
> 'To a turf bog.'
> 'Who are you going to work for?'
> 'Oul' Quinn.'
> 'Can you spell Antitrinitarians?'
> 'I must be moving,' I explained.
> I moved off and though I didn't look back I could feel his school-master-quizzical eyes on the small of my back like indigestion.[3]

Following the framework proposed by Laver, can you:

(i) identify the types of tokens used in the dialogue between the characters;
(ii) assess how the dialogue progresses *as a conversation*;
(iii) explain the evident discomfort that the narrator feels towards the end of the interaction?

3 It was stressed in the course of this chapter that the information imparted in phatic exchanges is not normally referentially signifi-cant. With regard to literary text data, one novel which might be useful in developing this point further is George Orwell's *Burmese Days*. The central character of this novel, the weak and vulnerable Flory, finds himself part of a British imperial system to which he does not wish to conform. His alienation and sense of frustration with his expatriate colleagues is underlined by his repeated attempts to initiate 'real' conversations with them. This is nowhere more manifest than in his failures with Elizabeth Lackersteen – a shallow conventional woman whom Flory is in love with but who is bored by

his sensitivity. The following passage takes place after Flory has made several unsuccessful attempts to interest Elizabeth in, amongst other things, oriental affairs, Burmese culture and the political consequences of imperialism.

They walked up the road, he to the left of her and a little behind. He watched her averted cheek and the tiny gold hairs on her nape beneath the brim of her Terai hat. How he loved her, how he loved her! It was as though he had never truly loved her till this moment, when he walked behind her in disgrace, not even daring to show his disfigured face. He made to speak several times, and stopped himself. His voice was not quite steady, and he did not know what he could say that did not risk offending her somehow. At last he said, flatly, with a feeble pretence that nothing was the matter:

'It's getting beastly hot, isn't it?'

With the temperature at 90 degrees in the shade it was not a brilliant remark. To his surprise she seized on it with a kind of eagerness. She turned to face him, and she was smiling again.

'Isn't it simply baking!'

With that they were at peace. The silly, banal remark, bringing with it the reassuring atmosphere of Club-chatter, had soothed her like a charm. Flo, who had lagged behind, came puffing up to them dribbling saliva; in an instant they were talking, quite as usual, about dogs. They talked about dogs for the rest of the way home, almost without a pause. Dogs are an inexhaustible subject. Dogs, dogs! thought Flory as they climbed the hot hillside, with the mounting sun scorching their shoulders through their thin clothes, like the breath of a fire – were they never to talk of anything except dogs? Or failing dogs, gramophone records and tennis racquets? And yet, when they kept to trash like this, how easily, how amicably they could talk![4]

What can you say about this passage in the light of your knowledge of:

(i)   phatic communion;
(ii) shared knowledge;
(iii) the function of referentially insignificant information in conversation?

4 Students interested in the relationship of phatic communion to naturally occurring conversation might wish to construct an informal experiment along the following lines:

(i)   Collect (by noting down or recording) as many conversational openings and closings as you can over the period of a day. Try to ensure that your monitoring does not affect the linguistic behaviour of those you observe.

(ii) Attempt to categorize the examples you collect in terms of the framework outlined in section III of this chapter. Are there any modifications or suggestions which, in the light of your results, you would wish to make concerning this framework? For instance, does the incoming (or moving) participant always initiate the phatic exchange? In a perceived asymmetrical interaction, does the higher-status participant always use an other-oriented token, and the lower-status participant a self-oriented token?

(iii) Try to account for any 'noticeable absences' or 'marked' exchanges that you may have collected.

(iv) How do your examples from naturally occurring conversation compare with the literary text data provided in the course of this chapter?

Notes: Chapter 2

1 Picador edn (London, 1974). The novel was first published in 1967.
2 Macmillan miniature edn (London, 1935), chs 4, 5.
3 Martin Brian & O'Keeffe edn (London, 1971), p. 92. The novel was first published in 1938.
4 Penguin edn (Harmondsworth, 1984), pp. 126–7. First published 1934.

References: Chapter 2

Abrams, M. H. (1981), *A Glossary of Literary Terms* (New York: Holt Rinehart & Winston, 4th edn).

Bauman, R. (1983), *Let Your Words Be Few* (Cambridge: Cambridge University Press).

Brown, P., and Levinson, S. (1978), 'Universals in Language Usage: Politeness Phenomena', in E. N. Goody (ed.), *Questions and Politeness: Strategies in Social Interaction* (Cambridge: Cambridge University Press), pp. 56–289.

Burton, D. (1980), *Dialogue and Discourse: A Sociolinguistic Approach to Modern Drama Dialogue and Naturally Occurring Conversation* (London: Routledge & Kegan Paul).

Fowler, R. (1981), *Literature as Social Discourse* (London: Batsford).

Labov, W., and Fanshel, D. (1977), *Therapeutic Discourse* (New York: Academic Press).

Laver, J. (1975), 'Communicative Functions of Phatic Communion', in A. Kendon, R. M. Harris and M. R. Key (eds), *Organisation of Behaviour in Face to Face Interaction* (The Hague: Mouton), pp. 215–40.

Laver, J., and Hutcheson, S. (eds) (1972), *Communication in Face to Face Interaction* (Harmondsworth: Penguin).

Leech, G. N., and Short, M. H. (1981), *Style in Fiction* (London: Longman).

Lyons, J. (1981), *Language and Linguistics* (Cambridge: Cambridge University Press).

Malinowski, B. (1972), 'Phatic Communion', in Laver and Hutcheson (1972), pp. 146–52 (first published in 1923).

Introduction to Chapter 3

Poetry is a genre which, on the surface at least, does not appear to lend itself to a discourse-based approach. In this chapter it is Ron Carter's main concern to show the relevance of discourse analysis to the interpretation of poetry, especially in respect of those forms, such as ballads, which are often overtly dialogic in structure. Here he takes a well known poem by W. H. Auden and argues that analysis of the patterns of interaction between *personae* in the poem is quite crucial to its interpretation, and that some previous literary-critical accounts of this poem have either not understood such interaction or have given only rather vague, impressionistic descriptions of relevant patterns.

Carter argues that reference to the notion of *shared knowledge* enables clearer discrimination between what is said and what is actually done with the words. Application of rule-governed frameworks suggested by Labov provides a basis for interpreting how an atmosphere of fear and strangeness is communicated in the poem, and how the two main personae exploit such unease in the course of their 'dialogue' with each other. The chapter also discusses the general nature of the communication situation in poetic texts, particularly in relation to the positions of authors and readers; and the overall analysis is augmented by an examination of more conventional features of poetry such as rhythm and rhyme, but with a focus on how such features overlay the main discoursal interactive properties of the particular ballad. The chapter concludes with an examination of the roles of intuition and interpretation in stylistic analysis.

3 Poetry and Conversation: An Essay in Discourse Analysis

RONALD CARTER

I From Intuitions to Analysis

My main aim is to explore some of the possibilities available within a framework of discourse analysis for explaining effects produced by conversation in poetry. The text I wish to devote particular attention to is a dialogue by W. H. Auden, entitled 'Song V' in *Collected Shorter Poems* (London: Faber, 1966), but more widely known as 'From Reader to Rider'. It will, I hope, be an interesting exercise, since this is the kind of poem to which stylistic analysis is not normally applied. In performing this analysis the following subsidiary purposes may be fulfilled: first, I want to suggest, that, in tackling such poems, grammatical analysis is not always particularly useful; second, I hope to make out a case for all poems being in varying degrees interactive, and to suggest that analysis should therefore acknowledge appropriate contextualizations for the literary message.

After introducing the text, I include an account of my intuitions concerning the effects of the poem. This means that analysis starts from a subjective base of hunches about the text. I feel that this is only right and proper, and even though analysis is limited to and by those intuitions it is at least preferable to exhaustive and unfocused unravelling of the text. As a poem, 'Song V' is both short and neat, and works in a specific tradition. Comments on its particular literary context will also be conjoined with the purely linguistic analysis.

Song V

'O where are you going?' said reader to rider,
'That valley is fatal when furnaces burn,
Yonder's the midden whose odours will madden,
That gap is the grave where the tall return.'

> 'O do you imagine,' said fearer to farer,   5
> 'That dusk will delay on your path to the pass,
> That diligent looking discover the lacking
> Your footsteps feel from granite to grass?'
>
> 'O what was that bird,' said horror to hearer,
> 'Did you see that shape in the twisted trees?   10
> Behind you swiftly the figure comes softly,
> The spot on your skin is a shocking disease.'
>
> 'Out of this house' – said rider to reader,
> 'Yours never will' – said farer to fearer,
> They're looking for you' – said hearer to horror,   15
> As he left them there, as he left them there.

My intuitions about this poem are as follows. It is distinctly a conversation poem, with at least two speakers interacting within an inner context or micro-conversation (though we should not forget that there is also a macro-conversation or outer context operating between Auden and the reader). Within this exchange I feel the tone of the dialogue is markedly fearful and unsettling. The response in each case sounds aggressive and threatening while the questioner seems somehow uncertain of his ground. Even though the exchange is short, I sense too a struggle between the speakers for dominance. As someone overhearing the conversation, as it were, I am also unsettled by the lack of referential clarity; the speakers seem to know what is being referred to, but to me the object of their talk is ambiguous. My intutions are to some extent corroborated by a number of literary critics writing on the text. For example, Richard Hoggart (1951: 56) concludes that an important effect of the poem is that the reader should learn that 'the first positive step . . . is not to give in to fear'; Monroe K. Spears (1963: 57) sees the poem as 'a refusal to compromise and a call to action'; while Samuel Hynes (1976: 94) infers that the poem offers the alternatives of 'a fearful action' or a 'frightened sick passiveness'. However, such impressions need to be converted into harder currency.

Analysis of the poem's grammar reveals that as far as sentence and clause structure are concerned 'grammetrics' play a significant part. Indeed, the congruence of sentence and stanza structure is matched only by that of clause and line. In three of the four stanzas each line introduces a new main clause (and a new proposition), while in the remaining one (st. 3) the whole stanza is taken up with one main clause. In grammatical mood there is a similarly neat pattern, in the almost equal division between interrogatives and declaratives, with the final stanza containing what appear to be replies to the interrogative. For example:

'O where are you going?' said reader to rider, (st. 1)
Out of this house' said rider to reader, (st. 4)

It might be worth recording here that at these levels, at least, the neatness of fit does not seem to go with the unevenness of the interaction.

However, the verbal groups in the poem have a much more hetero-geneous pattern. Most notable are the switches in tense between present (lines 1–2, 4), future (line 3), present (line 5), future (lines 6–8), past (lines 9–10) and present (lines 11–12), leading to, in the final stanza, a present tense followed in the final line by a simple past tense item ('as he left them there') that suggests an action completed, yet also curiously suspended in time. The 'reader', 'fearer', 'horror' figure(s) perceive(s) an unknown threat in the immediate environment (I am here taking lines 9–10 to refer to a very recent past) that will somehow affect future action. The shuttling between future, a conti-nuous present, a more 'permanent' or modal present (for example, line 12), a simple past, and a past tense in the final line that seems to frame a perpetually frozen action lends some objective linguistic support to the confusion and uncertainty the poem communicates. This kind of feeling may be explained further by recognizing that within nominal group structure the deictics here are mostly exophoric, thus forcing the reader to construct imaginatively a situation for the action. Yet when it is seen that only minimal adverbial/prepositional information is provided concerning the time, manner (line 11), or place (line 3) of these occurrences, then it is clear that no real context for the referents is disclosed. In fact, it could be said that the ques-tioner fears things but does not know how or why or where these fears will materialize. For the reader in the outer context, at one further remove from the action, the nature of the discourse is even more puzzling.

One feature of the poem, foregrounded by repetition, that has not been discussed so far but may contribute to some of the effects described above is the manner of notation for the participants, i.e. 'reader'/'rider', 'fearer'/'farer', 'horror'/'hearer'. The absence of either modification or qualification of those key functional headwords, together with a suppression of articles, works to isolate these parti-cipants in two main expressive ways. First, the self-standing nature of the headwords suggests a collective or generic (rather than indi-viduated) speaker, representing perhaps a wider group and/or some universal characterizing feature. As a result, Auden might be seen to be polarizing moral or psychological positions in a process of formal disputation – a feature also characteristic of the ballad tradition.[1] More immediately striking is a second meaning that each stanza may contain a different interlocutor (i.e. the 'reader' changes to 'fearer' and then to 'horror'), which raises the question of whether the nature of the interaction is changed in consequence. A solution to this may be to assume that only *two* participants are engaged in the exchange and that in the course of, and probably as a result of, the ensuing dialogue, the identity of the interlocutors is constantly shifting – almost as if two types in a community or, more extremely, two parts of the same personality were represented. In the ensuing discourse analysis of the text I shall thus presume a two-party conversation and, for convenience, refer to the interlocutors as questioner (Q) and respondent (R), although the particular notions proposed by such tags may well prove to be inappropriate.

A grammar of the poem – here necessarily somewhat truncated – helps to explain some things but it does not get very near to accounting for the kind of intuitions developed. To name but a single problematic feature: to what extent do the neatly balanced interrogatives and declaratives actually communicate questions and statements? If the interaction is perceived to be unsettling or is felt to contain tones of threat and assertion, then linguistic analysis has to go beyond the mere form of such features.

One of the most important functions of discourse analysis is to help us distinguish what is said from what is *done*, i.e. from the actions performed with the words. It is worth quoting in this respect from an article by William Labov in which he attempts to formulate rules that explain our ability to connect utterances in sequence by the functions they have. This may be particularly apposite in the case of 'Song V' since, although it has been remarked that the poem contains a sequence of questions and answers/replies, this does not in fact, account for the sense of threat and strangeness. Labov outlines the problem as follows:

> A *statement* follows a *question*; the question is a *request for information*; but in what way does the statement form an *answer* to that request? . . . In answering A's request for information Q-S_1 with a superficially unrelated statement S_2, B is in fact asserting that there is a proposition known to both A and B that connects this with S_1. (Labov, 1972: 134)

This is developed by Labov into the concept of 'shared knowledge':

> Given any two-party conversation, there exists an understanding that there are events that A knows about, but B does not; and events that B knows about but A does not; and AB events that are known to both. We can then state simply the rules of interpretation:
>
> If A makes a statement about a B event, it is heard as a request for confirmation.

That is, if A talks about an A event it is not heard as a request; if A talks about a B event it is a request for confirmation; if A talks about an AB event a 'shared knowledge' is being drawn on. (Labov, 1972: 138)

To return to 'Song V' the main problem is in explicating how the answers of the respondent (R) might follow in some rule-governed way from the questions put by Q. For example, the question from 'fearer' to 'farer':

> 'O do you imagine . . .
> That diligent looking [will] discover the lacking
> Your footsteps feel from granite to grass?'

is answered by:

> 'Yours never will'.

The latter is a statement that, except limitedly via the second-person pronoun, does not in any real sense pick up cues from the questioner and use them in the formulation of an answer. In fact, the expected response to questions containing 'you' and 'your' would be those that preface the requested information with a personal 'I'. Here the propositions are, as it were, returned to the questioner in what may intuitively be felt to be a clipped and assertive manner. According to the framework suggested by Labov for connecting the actions being performed with words in initiation/response sequences, it is possible to account for this kind of interchange in terms of them being something known to both interlocutors. In other words, there is a 'shared knowledge' of (an) AB event(s) known to R and Q which explains R's statements as sequential and coherent responses to Q's propositions. Thus, to take a related example, the reply 'They're looking for you' (line 15) – particularly since there is no reference for the third-person plural pronoun – would appear to be an unconnected answer except in terms of discourse rules allowing reference to some knowledge shared by both participants.

However, there still remains the problem of our intuition that R returns Q's question in such a way that, whatever their shared knowledge, it can be felt to be threatening. One way of attempting to account for this is to concentrate attention on the 'questions' posed by Q. The term is placed in quotation marks because, although addressed to R, the propositions put forward do not always seem to function directly as questions. First, some questions (lines 1 and 11) are not so much 'why' questions requesting information as closed questions requiring only a 'yes'/'no', or single-phrase reply, or, from another view-point, function rather as regulators of behaviour than as elicitations. If, as rereading of the poem confirms, Q does not want R to leave, then the opening 'question' is more likely to be construed as an attempt to control the action or behaviour of R. Second, Q appears to answer his own questions and to allow no space for R to reply. This is brought about primarily by the structure of the poem and its particular folksong conventions, but the effect is to reinforce the position of authority clearly claimed for himself by Q. By allowing no turns to R until the end of the sequence, 'reader' puts himself in an authority structure and forces us to see his 'questions' as a series of power moves that enable him to hold the floor for as long as he requires.

How, then, might this handling of discourse structure be interpreted, particularly by R? If viewed in the context of the utterance preceding or subsequent to them, Q's questions would be felt to function more as declarations or assertions to which counter-assertion might be the only appropriate response. In themselves, particularly given Q's control of the exchange structure of the discourse, the questions would appear to be threats or particularly assertive challenges to R. Furthermore, if a shared knowledge of referents is assumed (note the repetition of 'that' with its deictic pointing to what might be taken to be recognizable to both participants[2]), then the questions become, as it were, requests for confirmation. Requests for confirmation or questions about what is already known suggest an initially dominant role for Q, but they also progressively reveal (it is a pattern characteristic of teachers talking to pupils, cf. Sinclair and Coulthard, 1975) a parallel tone of unsettledness or uncertainty surrounding Q's actions.

The effect of this on R is to produce what are largely interpretable as counter-assertions. The force of R's replies is given particular prominence on three main counts. First, when R finally holds the floor he makes three separate utterances, allowing no turn to Q. Three such statements in sequence can be felt to take on the function of a threat or, at the least, a challenge.[3] Secondly, the increasing independence of R's successive replies needs to be noted. In other words, R's first reply, 'Out of this house', is in more or less strict sequence with the opening question (and in one sense provides an assertive counter to any connotations of control of behaviour contained in the question). But the second and final replies, as noted previously, return the propositions to Q without any modification being advanced. Finally, and perhaps most significantly, Q is allowed no re-initiation of the discourse. In any exchange structure there is, as shown by Harvey Sacks, an accepted norm of the floor being returned to the questioner after the interlocutor has answered.[4] This is broken here by R's action ('as he left them there'). It lends further support to the view of R gaining increasing ascendancy in the discourse over an increasingly uncertain Q – as well as providing some linguistic explanation for what has been described loosely as his assertive tone.

This characterization of the participants is confirmed as the discourse proceeds, since the lexical items describing the 'reader' become more powerfully associated with fear ('fearer', 'horror') while those connected with R or the 'rider' remain more consistent lexically. The alternation between confident assertion and increasing tentativeness in the interaction/discourse structure is reflected formally, too, by the alternating stressed and unstressed syllables of the end-rhymes (the latter with its falling last syllable suggesting tentativeness); by the shifting identity of the speakers (especially Q); by the rhythmic organization of the poem between rising and falling movement divided by a consistently placed caesura:

> Behind you swiftly/the figure comes softly,
> The spot on your skin/ is a shocking
> disease

and, finally, by a pattern of lexical incongruity consisting of archaisms juxtaposed with contemporary usages and dialectisms that, together with the switches in the poem's tense patterns, reinforces a sense of our not quite knowing what kind of order we are in. The impression of division, of a confused condition and of alternating viewpoints may also be compounded by the phonological similarities in the designation of the two speakers ('fearer'/'farer', 'horror'/'hearer'), suggesting almost two aspects or slightly shifting parts of the same personality (hence the reference made by R to 'them').[5]

The final word here seems to be left with R, the rider who, in interaction with Q, is dominant in controlling and exploiting the rules of discourse to gain the ascendancy and issue something in the nature of a challenge to Q as he moves on. It is a feature of the interaction resources of the poem that, together with other similar effects, can only be explicated by analysis at the suprasentential level, although it is one that still requires greater refinements in discourse analysis to explain its total effect.

I hope to have shown here that it is difficult to speak of the style employed by Auden in this poem without drawing on work undertaken within discourse analysis. The framework of discourse analysis used here is neither strongly defined nor broad enough to categorize all aspects of the poem's structure. But it will be clear that, by drawing on the work of analysts such as Labov and Sacks, we can begin to substantiate impressions that resist explanation within the grammatical model, such as tone and the style of the conversational interchange. Of course, it can be pointed out that such overtly 'dialogue' poems are rare occurrences. None the less, linguistic analysis has so far resisted the challenge offered by such poems; in fact, with the exception of

Burton (1980) and several of the chapters of this book, I know of no consistent attempt to undertake stylistic analysis of dialogue. Yet I do not want such an analysis to be restricted only to poems with this kind of overtly dialogic structure. It is my contention that all texts, to the extent that they are interactive, require analysis from within a dimension of discourse. To make this point, I want to extend further the notion of contextualization for the text, and adopt Henry Widdowson's productive suggestions concerning the nature of the communication situation in literary artefacts (Widdowson 1975: 51).

Widdowson proposes the following 'dual-focus situation' as appropriate to literary discourse:

| I_1 | I_2 | II_2 | II_1 |
| Sender | Addresser | Addressee | Receiver |

He argues that in normal communication sender and addresser, and addressee and receiver, are identical, whereas in literary communication the two poles are separable. This is certainly borne out in the case of 'Song V', where Q and R inhabit an inner context of I_2/II_2, whose discourse is the subject of communication between Auden I_1 and the reader II_1.

This adds an extra dimension to the nature of conversation in a literary context. However direct and naturalistic the exchanges in the inner context may be, it should not be forgotten that this forms only a part of the total message Auden communicates to his reader. The competent reader overhears this conversation and can perceive the challenges issued to Q, but he must be at the same time alert to the speech acts transmitted indirectly by the author himself. Much work has still to be done in this area of overlap between direct and indirect speech acts in literature – and I am here concentrating largely on the former – but such analysis might, for example, reveal that a challenge in the inner context may constitute a threat in the outer context, or it may, for example, provide a basis for analysing authorial irony.

There is a further aspect to literary conversation. This embraces the 'negotiation' a text can have with its antecedents and it is a feature that is particularly marked in the case of this poem (see note 5). Although there is not the space here for such exploration, full discoursal analysis should recognize the literary tradition a text works in and any alterations the author may make to the form or content of the original(s).

II Beyond Intuitions: Ideology, Interpretation and Discourse

The starting point for this chapter was a set of *intuitions* about the effects produced by the Auden poem. The conclusion has involved some initial speculation concerning the nature of the contexts in which the poem is embedded. In between, an interpretation of the text has been proffered which, by reference to certain linguistic properties of the poem, has been argued as to some extent corroborating the original set of intuitions; at the same time it has been recognized that the nature of the *literary* context of the poem can be significant in a fuller interpretation of the poem. Readers would be entitled in the light of these procedures to ask what the status of the proffered interpretation was. Students working through a textbook on language, discourse and literature may also want to ask what exactly can be learned from this essay in discourse stylistics, and how it relates to the book as a whole. This final section attempts to answer some of these questions with reference both to underlying theories and to practices of stylistic analysis.

(i) Intuitions

First, it is important to recognize that the main intuitions recorded about 'From Reader to Rider' are *limiting*. They are those of one individual commentator only and may not be shared by others.

Secondly, the analysis and interpretation of the poem so far has been guided by those intuitions and again limited by them. It would be incautious to claim too great a validity for the interpretation.

Thirdly, it should be noted, however, that intuitions concerning a balance between the speakers of fear and aggression were *shared* with a number of literary critics who have commented on the text. There is a measure of inter-subjective agreement. Inter-subjective intuitions are more reliable than purely subjective ones.

But, fourthly, intuitions about a text cannot be neutral in quite the way that the term inter-subjective suggests. Intuitions about texts depend on their 'familiarity' to the commentators, and the commentators' acquaintance with such texts depends in turn on the kinds of access to literary texts which their education has allowed. The educational background of the commentators is a matter of social class; thus, 'intuitions' will depend on the different ways in which the reader of a text is positioned socially and ideologically (see pp. 15–17 above). Intuitions are not neutral in any simple or value-free way.

(ii) Language Analysis

A strong position here is that the intuitions concerning the poem are primarily produced by the linguistic choices of the writer. Language is not simply a medium beyond which exists the content or subject matter of the text. This chapter takes as a starting point that the content is constituted by the language.

Secondly, stylistic analysis aims to link intuitions about meaning (whatever their unavoidable limitations) with the language patterns of the text. At any one level the analysis should be detailed and explicit, so that readers can retrieve the interpretation by checking it against the original intuitions. This does not give exclusive validity to the interpretation; but it is better to account for an interpretation than not to account for it. It also makes a particular interpretation more open to genuine debate. Subjecting the language of the text to detailed analysis does not, of course, automatically lead to an interpretation, for stylistics is not a mechanical discovery procedure. The aim is to provide a reasonable and convincing interpretation which is tied to and tries to account for intuitions and hunches about meanings by a systematic, rigorous and replicable analysis of the language of the text. It is the strong view of most stylisticians that it is at best naive to assume that the patterns and structures of language play no significant part in the interpretive process.

Thirdly, by learning techniques of stylistic analysis *students* of literature can have equipment available which helps them to begin to account for intuitions and build towards interpretation in an especially systematic and principled way.

Fourthly, however, it would be equally naive to claim that a coincidence between intuitions and interpretation of language effects had validity when the analysis was restricted to only *one* linguistic level. In this chapter, analysis has concentrated on the level of discourse.

The underlying argument of this book is that analysis of patterns beyond the level of the sentence is necessary if richer, more inclusive stylistic analysis is to be produced. This cannot, however, be taken to mean that the meaning of texts reside wholly at this level. In the case of 'From Reader to Rider' the fit between intuitions and language patterns at the level of discourse needs to be checked further against fuller analysis at the levels of grammar and phonology, for example. Only then can a fuller interpretation begin to emerge. In the section at the end of this chapter devoted to suggestions for further work, readers are directed to an essay in the companion volume to this book by Alex Rodger (1982). The essay contains a detailed *grammatical* analysis of Auden's poem. The more points of interpretive similarity that are accumulated by this comparison, the more firmly the stylistic interpretation of the poem might be said to be based. A further naivety would be to claim, however, that there was ever any one single meaning of a text which could be unravelled. The proffered interpretations here must always remain provisional.

(iii)   Discourse

As was pointed out in the introduction to this volume, the term discourse is polyvalent. It is used here to refer to a level of language analysis (*discourse analysis*) and to the *context* in which all texts are invariably embedded. In this chapter context has three main reference points:

(1) *the inner and outer context* of the relations between speakers internal to the text and between author and reader external to the text;
(2) *the intertextual context* – it has been pointed out how 'From Reader to Rider' exists in a literary tradition of dialogic ballad poetry and has antecedents to which it alludes by analogues of structural, metrical and formal organization;
(3) *the historical context* of the 1930s in which Auden was situated – in this regard, the poem has to be seen in the context of the dominant discourses of that decade, that is, in relation to its prevailing ideologies.

The poem cannot be fully interpreted only by reference to the *linguistic* context of discourse. This would suggest that the meanings of the text were wholly intrinsic to the language of the text. To the linguistic analysis must be conjoined an analysis of the poem which attends systematically to the networks the text contracts as part of its place within socio-historical and cultural discourses. This network includes other texts produced at the same historical juncture as well as the poem's antecedents within a literary tradition.

To enable such networking to assist fuller interpretation, the suggestions for further work refer readers to another ballad poem 'O What is that Sound?' written by Auden within the same period. Readers are invited to examine the two poems with reference to the level of discourse and to the controlling discourses of the period such as the rise of Fascism and Fascist thinking, policies of appeasement and the stance adopted to 'alternative' communist ideologies by the upper-middle class intellectuals of the Auden group. Useful starting points are provided in Hynes (1976) and Carter (ed.) (1984: esp. pp. 25–92). In this examination the ideological positioning of the interpreter him/herself will be crucial in the formulation of an interpretation.

III Conclusion: Pedagogical Aims

This chapter and the two preceding ones by Walter Nash and Paul Simpson have been concerned to demonstrate a systematic explication of intuitive responses to texts by means of a process of rigorous discourse-stylistic analysis. The empirical, practical-analytical orientation of this chapter has a particular pedagogic end. As with all the chapters in this book, a main pedagogical aim is to foster skills of interpretation by demonstrating that interpretive skills should be developed in relation to a capacity to analyse the language organization of texts. Such a method has roots in the history of twentieth-century critical practice, especially in the movements known as New Criticism or Practical Criticism, which actively encourage close reading of the verbal particularities of texts.

Discourse stylistic analysis aims to be both more rigorous and linguistically detailed and more inclusive than Practical Criticism in the kind of textual features it examines; and its procedures offer, I would argue, at least an *initial method* for undertaking analysis and interpretation. As a method it also provides a way of reading which has the pedagogic advantage of being an established and widely practised means of assisting students with entry to literary text analysis. However, it is also a pedagogic aim of this chapter to provoke self-awareness and introspection about the processes and procedures of stylistics-based interpretive activities. Some of the limitations of this practice have been outlined in this final section, and certainly nothing is to be gained from assuming that this is a wholly unproblematic means of reading texts. But the pedagogical priority has been to encourage a measure of competence *in* the practice before deconstructing it *as* a practice. In other words, too self-critical a problematizing of the role of language analysis in the interpretation of literary texts can hinder the development of skills, and without these skills students will lack a base from which theoretical awareness and critical perspective can grow.

In this chapter I have aimed to do no more than suggest starting points and offer directions for further research. I have tried to demonstrate that there are strengths *and* limitations in this kind of introductory discourse stylistics. But a final parting thought from rider to reader might be that we can only talk of texts such as this in so far as we learn to talk about and with the language, ideologies and discourses which produce them. It is a process carried further in several subsequent chapters in the book, especially those by John Haynes and David Birch and the one by Roger Fowler which immediately follows.

Suggestions for Further Work: Chapter 3

1   Another poem by Auden that is also a dialogic ballad and also lends itself to treatment with reference to Labov's 'rules of interpretation' and 'shared knowledge' is 'O What is that Sound?' (which appears in most collections of Auden's poetry). In the case of the exchanges in this poem, it is interesting to explore the extent to which the approach and then incursion of the soldiers is an AB

event, known to both parties, and the extent to which it is unexpected to the first speaker (Q) and the second speaker (R). We also need to observe that Q does not make statements but asks questions. If the questions are about AB events then there would appear to be something irregular and unexpected in those events which Q registers with increasing uncertainty and fear. If the questions are about B events then they can be heard as requests for action in the manner of the following exchange:

> Q: Were there any handouts at last week's lecture?
> R: Yes, here you are.
> (*Yes, there were.)

If this is the case, how does R respond to these requests for action?

2   There seems to be evidence to support the view that R knows more than Q. For example, R knows the colour of the soldier's tunics when Q can only hear them (st. 1). Their 'manoeuvres' (st. 3) are 'usual' and hence familiar to R (though, maybe, also to Q). And in the fifth stanza R knows that none of them is wounded (even from a considerable distance) and refers to them as '*these* forces' – a deictic which expresses greater closeness and familiarity than, say, '*those* forces'.

3   Even if Q does know of the soldiers' 'usual' movements the questions appear to convey a need for reassurance, especially since Auden uses ballad-like repetition as a device to suggest anxiety and insistence. At first R appears reassuring: '*Only* the scarlet soldiers dear' ('only' repeated three times); and even though 'perhaps' introduces greater uncertainty, the replies in stanzas 3 and 4 and the exclamatory 'why' in stanza 5 could be interpreted as dismissing Q's anxieties. The definite replies (beginning with 'No' – st. 6) in the remaining stanzas, culminating in 'But I must be leaving' indicate, however, no concession of any kind to Q. Furthermore the progressive aspect of 'I must be leaving' does not necessarily commit Q to physical removal from the scene. It only signals intention. And that opens up an intriguing and even more insidious possibility that R stays to watch the soldiers arrive for Q, and as a concluding move in the 'deception', speaks the last two lines just as has happened in every other stanza of the poem.

4   Note also that R is the only one to use the term of endearment 'dear'. Does this deepen the deception and cynicism of R's moves or does it, rather more charitably, allow us to read greater kindness and support into the exchanges? What is the role of rhyme in this respect, too? 'Dear' is a pivotal rhyming word. How consistent and

full are the rhymes and how do they function in relation to the developing tones and meanings across all the stanzas of the poem?

5   Continue to think about the poem and to challenge these interpretations by pointing to counter-examples in the language data of the text. Don't forget that language analysis provides a firm basis from which to work but that it has to be supplemented for more extensive interpretations. For example, what does your knowledge of Europe and armies on the move in the 1930s contribute to your interpretation of the juxtaposition of private and public worlds in the lives of the two speakers?

6   One classic piece of stylistic analysis with particular reference to shared knowledge is Deirdre Burton's (1980) discussion of Harold Pinter's sketch *Last to Go*. Examine the ways in which the conversation between the man and the barman in this sketch is different from the dialogue between 'reader' and 'rider' in Auden's poem.

7   An interesting extension to work on shared knowledge would be to apply the rules of interpretation to the following exchange from Shakespeare's *Macbeth* in which Macbeth realizes the horror and the possible consequences of his action in murdering the king. But Lady Macbeth does not allow him to lose his original purpose (to become king himself). In this regard, the sequence, pattern and function of questions, statements and imperatives (as well as their relative distribution between Macbeth and Lady Macbeth) also require closer examination.

Macbeth:	*looks at his hands.* This is a sorry sight.	20
Lady:	A foolish thought, to say a sorry sight.	
Macbeth:	There's one did laugh in's sleep, and one cried 'Murder!'	
	That they did wake each other. I stood and heard them;	
	But they did say their prayers and addressed them	
	Again to sleep.	
Lady:	There are two lodged together.	25
Macbeth:	One cried 'God bless us' and 'Amen' the other,	
	As they had seen me with these hangman's hands.	
	Listening their fear I could not say 'Amen'	
	When they did say 'God bless us.'	
Lady:	Consider it not so deeply.	30
Macbeth:	But wherefore could not I pronounce 'Amen'?	
	I had most need of blessing, and 'Amen'	
	Stuck in my throat.	
Lady:	These deeds must not be thought	
	After these ways; so, it will make us mad.	
Macbeth:	Methought I heard a voice cry, 'Sleep no more!	35
	Macbeth does murder sleep – the innocent sleep,	

```
            Sleep that knits up the ravelled sleave of care,
            The death of each day's life, sore labour's bath,
            Balm of hurt minds, great nature's second course,
            Chief nourisher in life's feast.'
    Lady:   What do you mean?                                    40
    Macbeth: Still it cried 'Sleep no more' to all the house;
            'Glamis hath murdered sleep, and therefore Cawdor
            Shall sleep no more, Macbeth shall sleep no more.'
    Lady:   Who was it that thus cried? Why, worthy thane,
            You do unbend your noble strength, to think        45
            So brain-sickly of things. Go, get some water,
            And wash this filthy witness from your hand.
            Why did you bring these daggers from the place?
            They must lie there. Go, carry them and smear
            The sleepy grooms with blood. (II, ii, 20–50)       50
```

8   Compare the analysis of discourse structure in 'From Reader to Rider' with the analysis of the poem's grammar by Alex Rodger in the companion volume (Rodger, 1982), What are the differences and similarities in the respective interpretations of the poem?

Notes: Chapter 3

1   For example, the folksong 'The Cutty Wren'. An original version of the poem was printed in *New Verse*, vol. 7 (1935), a journal to which Auden contributed regularly.

2   In line 10 the insertion of 'that' for 'a' in the question 'Did you see *that* shape in the twisted trees?' might have the effect of increasing the tension of the utterance by asking a question about what is presumably known.

3   Though no reliable rules have as yet been established within discourse analysis to account for this, John Searle (1969: 65) in several respects provides a most useful starting point via his analysis of the speech act of promising.

4   Sacks (1972: 343) argues that '– a person who has asked a question has . . . a reserved right to talk again, after the one to whom he has addressed the question speaks. *And* in using this reserved right he can ask a question.' However, Sacks, Schegloff and Jefferson (1974) contend that questions and answers are chained over a long sequence. Malcolm Coulthard (1977: 71) notes that such sequences are typical of doctor–patient interviews or courtroom cross-examination. Both these facts suggest further possible interpretative lines: for example, a substantiation of impressions concerning the poem's tone of formal disputation; or support in the structure of the exchanges for the references in the poem to illness, for example, line 12. A further point of interest here (which for reasons of space cannot be developed) is Sinclair and Coulthard's (1975: 130) notion of orientation. It is significant in this exchange that the respondent asserts his independence

of the questioner by not allowing in his own discourse any convergence of linguistic items that appear in the questioner's initiations.
5 Further discussion and interpretation of such features may be found in Spears (1963: 57–8, 73). Spears pays particular attention to the balladic tradition in which 'From Reader to Rider' is placed.

References: Chapter 3

Burton, D. (1980), *Dialogue and Discourse: A Sociolinguistic Approach to Modern Drama Dialogue and Naturally Occurring Conversation* (London: Routledge & Kegan Paul).

Carter, R. (ed.) (1984), *Thirties Poets: The Auden Group* (London: Macmillan).

Coulthard, R. M. (1977), *An Introduction to Discourse Analysis* (London: Longman).

Hoggart, R. (1951), *Auden: An Introductory Essay* (London: Chatto & Windus).

Hynes, S. (1976), *The Auden Generation* (London: Bodley Head).

Labov, W. (1972), 'Rules for Ritual Insults', in D. Sudnow (ed.), *Studies in Social Interaction* (New York: Free Press), pp. 120–69.

Rodger, A. (1982), '"O Where Are You Going?": A Suggested Experiment in Classroom Stylistics', in R. Carter (ed.), *Language and Literature: An Introductory Reader in Stylistics* (London: Allen & Unwin), pp. 123–61.

Sacks, H. (1972), 'On the Analyzability of Stories by Children', in J. J. Gumperz and D. Hymes (eds), *Directions in Sociolinguistics* (New York: Holt, Rinehart & Winston), pp. 325–45.

Sacks, H., Schegloff, E. A., and Jefferson, G. (1974), 'A Simplest Systematics for the Organization of Turn-Taking for Conversations', *Language*, vol. 50, no. 4, pp. 696–735.

Searle, J. R. (1969), *Speech Acts: An Essay in the Philosophy of Language* (London: Cambridge University Press).

Sinclair, J. M., and Coulthard, M. (1975), *Towards an Analysis of Discourse: The English Used by Teachers and Pupils* (London: Oxford University Press).

Spears, M. K. (1963), *The Poetry of W. H. Auden* (New York: Oxford University Press).

Widdowson, H. G. (1975), *Stylistics and the Teaching of Literature*, (London: Longman).

Introduction to Chapter 4

Roger Fowler begins his chapter with a short review of the literary-critical background to Dicken's *Hard Times*. He suggests that the polarization of critical response is some evidence of the complexity and peculiarity of the novel's form and he points out that a stylistic analysis may resolve the problematic status of critical reception of the book.

The theoretical model which Fowler selects for his analysis is drawn from the work of the influential Russian critic Mikhail Bakhtin. Bakhtin has proposed that there are two basic modes of representational fiction. These are:

(1) *monologic mode* – characterized by a single, unified ideology voiced by the author;
(2) *dialogic or polyphonic mode* – the former characterized by unresolved, opposing voices within a text, the latter by a plurality of independent and unmerged voices and consciousnesses.

Fowler reinterprets Bakhtin's theory in the light of some recent work in linguistics and goes on to provide a stylistic analysis of *Hard Times* within this framework. His analysis is directed towards three main areas: *idiolect, sociolect* and *dialogue*.

Fowler argues that *Hard Times* is essentially a polyphonic novel. He examines the contrasts in the speech styles of major characters and shows how the multiple voices in the novel interact with one another. These voices are revealed as discordant and fluctuating in terms of the views they express. Fowler concludes that a discordant polyphony is created in *Hard Times* which is some indication of the problematic nature of the social and theoretical issues with which Dickens deals.

4   Polyphony in *Hard Times*

ROGER FOWLER

The polarization of critical response to *Hard Times* is familiar enough to make detailed reporting unnecessary, but since this polarization is a fact relevant to my argument I will recapitulate it briefly.

Popular reception of the novel has been largely antagonistic or uninterested. The character of the earlier novels has led to the formation of a cheerful and sentimental 'Dickensian' response which finds *Hard Times* (1854), like the other later novels, cold and uncomfortable, lacking in the innocent jollity, sentimentality and grotesquery of the earlier writings. When Dickens's anniversary was mentioned on television on 7 February 1983, the novelist was identified through a list of his works which totally excluded the later 'social' novels.

In other circles, there has been a keenly appreciative response to *Hard Times*: in some quarters more academic, and in some quarters more socialist. Committedly positive evaluation is found as early as 1860 in Ruskin and then in this century in Shaw (1912), whose appreciation of the book as 'serious social history' initiated a line of evaluation more recently reflected in, for example, Raymond Williams (1968) and David Craig (1969). Then there is a famous and extravagant essay by Leavis:

> Of all Dickens's works it is one that has all the strength of his genius, together with a strength no other of them can show – that of a completely serious work of art. (Leavis 1967: 249)

If Leavis was overenthusiastic, others – some, such as John Holloway (1962) and David M. Hirsch (1964), provoked by Leavis's surplus of commendation – have insisted on faults in the novel both as art and as social history. Even that majority of modern academic critics who accept and praise *Hard Times* concede some faults. Among the flaws cited by both camps are the following. A failure of a documentary kind is the presentation of the demagogue Slackbridge – 'a mere figment of the middle-class imagination. No such man would be listened to by a meeting of English factory hands' (Shaw, 1912). Similarly, the use of a professional circus to represent Fancy as opposed to Fact has been faulted on the ground that Dickens might have found Fancy in the native recreations of working people (Craig, 1969). A more 'ideological' criticism would allege that Dickens's *concept* of Fancy was, judging from the symbols by which he represented it, too trivial to weigh effectively against the Fact of Utilitarian economic theory and philosophy of education (Holloway, 1962; Lodge, 1966). Other critics have admitted faults of characterization – the girl Sissy is sentimentally presented and emerges as inadequate: her childhood attributes do not ground her later strength on Louisa's behalf. Again, Stephen and Rachael are said to be too good to be true: Stephen's martyrdom to a drunken wife is a cliché; his refusal to join the union is not motivated and therefore puts him into a weak, contradictory position in relation to his fellow workers. Now these allegations of faults of construction are not naive, 'Dickensian' complaints. There is real evidence that many things are not quite right with the book, for whatever reason: because of the unfamiliar constraints of small-scale writing for weekly parts: Because of the second-hand nature of Dickens's experience?

Since *Hard Times* has gained a very positive reputation in this century, we should beware of condemning it by totting up 'faults'. Perhaps the yardstick which we unconsciously apply, the tradition of the humanistic novel already well established by 1850, is not entirely relevant. It might be preferable to revise our conception of what type of novel this is, or at least to suspend preconception. *Hard Times* is problematic for the critics, a response which is itself perhaps evidence of peculiarities of form. And what we know about the genesis of the novel suggests that it was problematic for Dickens, too, involving him in compositional innovations. By this I do not refer merely to the structural consequences of weekly serialization (a discipline he had experienced only once before, in writing *Barnaby Rudge* (1841)), though this mode undoubtedly imposed constraints on episodic and thematic structure, and demanded compression. I mean by 'compositional innovations' new and defamiliarizing dispositions of language in response to new themes and unprecedented *and unresolved* ideological complexity.

A possible model for the structure of *Hard Times* is provided by Mikhail Bakhtin's theory of the 'polyphonic' novel; a theory which has the great benefit, for my purpose, of being interpretable in linguistic terms (see Bakhtin, 1973). In a complex argument, partly theoretical and partly historical, Bakhtin proposes that there have existed modes of representational fiction: monologic on the one hand and polyphonic or dialogic on the other. The monologic novel, which he claims has been the dominant traditional form, is authoritarian in essence: the author insists on the particular ideology which he voices, and the characters are 'objectified', dependent on the authorial position, and evaluated from the point of view of that position. In the polyphonic novel, on the other hand, the characters (or the 'hero', according to Bakhtin) are more liberated: they achieve voices, and points of view, which challenge the validity of the authorial position. The musical metaphor of polyphony refers to the co-presence of independent but interconnected voices. 'Dialogue' means implicit dialogue, not turn-by-turn speeches: it refers to the fact that one person's speech-forms reflect consciousness of the actual or potential response of an interlocutor, orientation towards a second act of speech. But there is a stronger meaning which Bakhtin seems to have in mind for 'dialogic', and that is 'dialectical'. The dialogic relationship confronts unresolved contrary ideologies, opposing voices in which conflicting world-views resist submersion or cancellation. The dialectical nature of Bakhtin's aesthetic can best be seen in his discussion of *carnival*, which was in his view the medieval forerunner of the polyphonic novel (Bakhtin, 1968). Carnival, with its boy kings and other multifarious travesties, mediates opposites, associates them while preserving their autonomous identities. It rejoices in extremes, negation, inversion, subversion, antithesis. The rhetorical figures generated by the logic of carnival are clear: they include prominently hyperbole, litotes, negation, syntactic inversions, paradox, contradiction. In social terms, the carnivalistic dialectic is the tension between mutually supportive but antithetical partners such as ruler and subject, employer and worker, teacher and pupil, husband and wife. And we would expect these differences of role, and antagonisms, to be articulated in the language of carnivalistic structures.

At a superficial level, the application of these ideas to *Hard Times* seems well justified. Three of the role clashes just mentioned (employer/worker, teacher/pupil, husband/wife) figure directly and importantly in the plot. Then the novel contains a large number of diverse characters and groups of characters of very different social origins and affiliations, putting forward many and clashing points of view. The circus performers are an almost literal case of carnival: their diversity and deviance are strongly emphasized, as is their challenge to the authority of Gradgrind and Bounderby (bk 1, ch. 6). But polyphonic or dialogic structure is by no means limited to these circus artistes: it exists in the ensemble of numerous voices of opinion and conflict – Slackbridge, Bounderby, Stephen Blackpool, Harthouse, Louisa, Sissy etc. The task for the analyst who wishes to make sense of this medley of voices is two-fold. First, it is necessary to show in detail the linguistic and semiotic characteristics of the various voices (including the narrating voice) which participate in the dialogic structure. Secondly, the polyphonic structure, the multiplicity of voices, needs to be interpreted in terms of the author's ideology. A plurality of voices does not in itself mean a non-authoritarian narrative stance.

Turning to language itself, Bakhtin does not give a very clear guide as to how the structure of language contributes to the dialogic aesthetic. In fact, he appears to be quite negative on the dialogic value of stylistic variety. But this caution is strategic. He has to concede that Dostoyevsky, his main subject, is stylistically flat, but he must claim, of course, that his thesis works even in this linguistically undifferentiated case. He observes that marked linguistic individuation of fictional characters may lead to an impression of closure, a feeling that the author has definitively analysed a character and placed a boundary around its imaginative or moral potential: 'characters' linguistic differentiation and clear-cut 'characteristics of speech' have the greatest significance precisely for the creation of objectivized, finalized images of people. This seems to me not so much a limitation as an illumination, specifically an insight into our response to Dicken's grotesques: Peggotty, Micawber, Mrs Gamp, and here, Slackbridge. All such characters seem to be clearly delineated, completely known, striking but uncomplicated. But we also need Bakhtin's more positive concession concerning the dialogic potential of speech styles; this potential is effective under certain conditions:

> the point is not the mere presence of specific styles, social dialects, etc., . . . the point is the dialogical *angle* at which they . . . are juxtaposed or counterposed in the work . . .

and

> dialogical relationships are possible among linguistic styles, social dialects, etc., if those phenomena are perceived as semantic positions, as a sort of linguistic *Weltanschauung*. (Bakhtin, 1981)

That is to say, speech styles need not be just caricaturing oddities, but to transcend caricature they must encode characters' world-views as dialectical alternatives to the world-view of the author and/or, I would suggest, other characters. Thus we might investigate whether, say, Stephen Blackpool's speech, or Bounderby's, encodes in its specific linguistic form a world-view, a set of attitudes; and how the two attitudes relate – in this case, antithetically. Similarly, and perhaps easier to demonstrate, we can look at the dialogic relationships between Gradgrind and Sleary on the one hand, and Gradgrind and the author on the other.

How to proceed in this project? The examples just mentioned are merely striking instances of many, perhaps dozens, of semiotically significant stylistic oppositions which permeate *Hard Times*. To provide a full account would require a book, not a chapter. As essential as space, however, is analytic methodology. Bakhtin provides no tools for analysing linguistic structure, but there is one linguistic theory which explicitly covers Bakhtin's condition that speech styles should be treated as embodying world-views: M. A. K. Halliday's 'functional' theory of language. I must send my readers elsewhere for details[1], but Halliday's main premiss is that linguistic varieties within a community, or 'registers', encode different kinds of meaning, different orientations on experience. Halliday offers a number of analytic systems, such as 'transitivity', 'mood', 'cohesion', 'information structure', which I and others have found very valuable in analysing texts for the world-views which they embody.[2] I shall use some of these categories below, but my analysis is constrained by space to be largely untechnical.

A list of distinct speech styles in the novel would show that there is an exceptional range of clearly differentiated voices: Sissy, Sleary, Slackbridge, Harthouse, Childers, Bounderby, Stephen, Gradgrind etc. The length and diversity of the list are of less importance than the specific meanings of the voices and their significance for the notion of polyphony. It could be argued merely on the basis of the multiplicity and variousness of voices and people that *Hard Times* makes a prima-facie claim to be a polyphonic novel. The case would be putative as a global observation, more concrete and demonstrable in relation to specific sections which are explicitly carnivalistic in conduct. The best instance of the latter is the scene at the Pegasus's Arms in book 1, chapter 6, when Gradgrind and Bounderby, in search of Sissy's father, are confronted by the members of the circus troupe, who speak 'in a variety of voices' (p. 82)[3] and who are combative and subversive in their address to these gentlemen. This scene, which is both challenging and farcical, threatens an anarchic overriding of utility and authority, and touches on antitheses which are more thoroughly debated elsewhere in the book.

I shall now look more closely at how the multiple languages of *Hard Times* signify and intersect by examining samples under three headings: *idiolect, sociolect* and *dialogue*.

An idiolect is the characteristic speech style of an individual. Like dialect, it is a set of background features of language, supposedly constant and permanent characteristics which distinguish a person linguistically. In its most sophisticated realization it is the complex of features, mostly phonetic, by which we recognize our acquaintances' voices on the telephone. Now idiolects apply to literature in two ways. First, the elusive 'style of an author' might be thought of as an idiolect. I mention this only to observe that *Hard Times* has no consistent authorial idiolect (unlike, to cite a comparable example, Mrs Gaskell's *North and South*). Secondly, in fiction foregrounding of idiolect produces caricature; and although caricature is a fixing, objectifying process, as Bakhtin has indicated, it is a device for making statements, and that is something we are looking for in *Hard Times*. The two sharp instances in the novel are the union demagogue Slackbridge and the circus master Sleary. Each has a mode of speech which is quite idiosyncratic (with a qualification in the case of Sleary, below) and absolutely self-consistent.

Slackbridge conducts himself with a violent, biblical rhetoric:

> Oh my friends, the down-trodden operatives of Coketown! Oh my friends and fellow countrymen, the slaves of an iron-handed and a grinding despotism! Oh my friends and fellow-sufferers, and fellow-workmen, and fellow-men! I tell you that the hour is come, when we must rally round one another as One united power, and crumble into dust the oppressors that too long have battened upon the plunder of our families, upon the sweat of our brows, upon the labour of our hands, upon the strength of our sinews, upon the God-created glorious rights of Humanity, and upon the holy and eternal privileges of Brotherhood!

It has been objected that no trade unionist of the time would have spoken like that (although, apparently, this is not beyond question). But fidelity to the language of the delegates' platform is only part of the issue. The point is that Dickens does not represent *any* social role in a focused way. He has created a symbolic language for his conception of 'Slackbridges'; but this language signifies nothing precise: it is a generalized bombast which might inhabit the pulpit, the House of Lords, or any kind of political or public meeting. Conventionally, of course, this sort of language connotes vacuousness and insincerity, and presumably it does so here; but Slackbridge's appearance is an intervention in a complex moral dilemma (Stephen's refusal to 'combine', and his subsequent ostracism by the workmates who know and respect him) and the signification of his speech style is inadequate to the situation. So Dickens is forced to comment directly on what Slackbridge represents:

> He was not so honest [as the assembled workmen], he was not so manly, he was not so good-humoured; he substituted cunning for their simplicity, and passion for their safe solid sense.

These judgments cannot be read off from the language in which Slackbridge is presented. His role remains puzzling and, since he is dramatically foregrounded as the main speaker against Stephen in this scene, the troubling nature of the scene (stemming largely from the unclarity of Stephen's motives and therefore of his relations with others at the meeting) remains provocatively unresolved.

Sleary is the second linguistic grotesque in the novel. Whereas Slackbridge's language is dominated by a bombastic rhetoric, Sleary's speech is submerged under brandy-and-water. Sibilants are drowned: [s, z, t ʃ , ʃ , dʒ , ts] all reduce to a sound spelled *th*:

> Tho be it, my dear. (You thee how it ith, Thquire!) Farewell, Thethilia! My latht wordth to you ith thith, Thtick to the termth of your engagement, be obedient to the Thquire and forget uth. But if, when you're grown up and married and well off, you come upon any hortheriding ever, don't be hard upon it, don't be croth with it, give it a Bethspeak if you can, and think you might do wurth. People mutht be amuthed, Thquire, thomehow, . . . they can't be alwayth a working, nor yet they can't be alwayth a learning. Make the betht of uth; not the wortht.

But Sleary's function in the plot and in the thematic structure of the novel make him more than a comic drunk. In his first appearance (bk 1, ch. 6), he is a firm leader of the circus people in their challenge to the bullying of Gradgrind and Bounderby, and effectively presides over the passage of Sissy into the care of Gradgrind. At the end of the novel, he has been harbouring Gradgrind's criminal son Tom, and (carnivalistically, through the good offices of a dancing horse) manages Tom's flight from apprehension. He is then given virtually the last word, an almost verbatim repetition of the sentiment just quoted. His interventions in the story are directly implicated in Gradgrind's fortunes, and he is the philsophical antithesis to Gradgrind's utilitarian educational thesis: Sleary's Horse-riding stands for Fancy. This notion of Fancy may well be too trivial for Dickens's purpose, as has been conceded; but at least Sleary is so constituted as to demand attention. The idiolect is insistently defamiliarizing: it 'make[s] forms difficult . . . increases the difficulty and length of perception', as Shklovsky (1965: 12) puts it. It takes effort to determine what Sleary is saying, because of the completeness and the whimsicality of the phonological transformation which has been applied to his speech. The reader is compelled to decipher a radical, and not entirely consistent, code which deforms everyday English words into momentarily unrecognizable spellings: *bitterth, prentitht*. These difficulties do not guarantee that what Sleary says is of any great interest; but the fact that Dickens has placed these difficulties in our way indicates that Sleary is *meant* to be listened to, that he is designed as a significant voice against Gradgrindism in the polyphonic structure of the book.

There is another interesting aspect of Sleary's speech, and one which further distinguishes his discourse from that of Slackbridge. Beneath the idiolect there are markers which suggest a social dialect, or sociolect. Dickens builds into Sleary's speech hints of working-class morphology and lexis – *eathy* (easily), *ath* (who), *wouldn't . . . no more, took* (taken), *plain* (plainly), *winder, lyin'* etc. (plus some odd spellings which suggest deviance from the middle-class code, but obscurely – *natur, fortun, wurthst, conwenienth*); and slang and oaths – *morrithed* (morrissed, 'fled'), *cut it short, damned, mith'd your tip* (missed your tip, 'jumped short'), *cackler, pound* ('wager') etc. These characteristics link Sleary with the working class – in this novel, the interests of the 'Hands' – and with the circus fraternity, the spokespeople for Fancy. These links not only 'naturalize' Sleary by providing him with social affiliations but also broaden the basis of opposition to the Utilitarian philosophies embodied in Gradgrind (whom Sleary first meets in a confrontation).

The novel contains many other contrasts of speech style, and on the whole they can be explained sociolectally rather than idiolectally: Dickens seems to have accepted the principle that now provides the theoretical basis for Hallidayan linguistics, namely that registers of language characterize social groups and encode their values. Consider, for example, the contrasting speech of Harthouse and Stephen Blackpool. The former is first introduced as an idle waster ('carelessly lounging') with a languid, verb-less, fragmented speech (bk 2, ch. 1). When he is established in Louisa's favours, however, this affection is replaced by the syntax of 'elaborated code':

> Mrs. Bounderby, though a graceless person, of the world worldly, I feel the utmost interest, I assure you, in what you tell me. I cannot possibly be hard upon your brother. I understand and share the wise consideration with which you regard his errors. With all possible respect both for Mr. Gradgrind and for Mr. Bounderby, I think I perceive that he has not been fortunate in his training. Bred at a disadvantage towards the society in which he has to play, he rushes into these extremes for himself, from opposite extremes that have long been forced – with the very best intentions we have no doubt – upon him. Mr. Bounderby's fine bluff English independence, though a most charming characteristic, does not – as we have agreed – invite confidence. If I might venture to remark that it is the least in the world deficient in that delicacy to which a youth mistaken, a character misconceived, and abilities misdirected, would turn for relief and guidance, I should express what it presents to my view.

Hypotaxis – the use of multiple subordinate clauses – dominates the syntax, which is further complicated by parenthetical clauses such as '– as we have agreed –'. Main clauses are delayed by preposed adjective clauses ('Bred at a disadvantage . . .') and by suspect protestations of diffidence or sincerity ('If I might venture . . .'). Nouns are liberally modified by adjectives, many of them evaluative and evocative of extremes (*graceless, worldly, utmost, wise, opposite, very best* etc). Modals are also prominent, emphasizing the speaker's claim to epistemic and deontic involvement in what he says: *cannot possibly, all possible, very best, no doubt, most, least.* Touches of rhetoric of more identifiable origin than Slackbridge's are present: 'a youth mistaken, a character misconceived, and abilities misdirected' is a literary, educated form associated with writing, not oratory – the key to this literariness being the inverted structure N + Adjective (there is only one inversion, Verb + Subject, in all of Slackbridge's speeches (p. 173)). Harthouse's speech in this episode is marked as middle-class, elaborated, evasive.[4]

At the other pole, socio-economically and linguistically, is Stephen Blackpool. There is a detailed effort to make Stephen's language indicate his representativeness of a class. A number of different features of his language combine to make the language suggest the regional, uneducated and oral properties of the language of the Hands. He is first shown in an intimate conversation with Rachael, an introduction which makes an immediate point that his speech style is shared, not idiosyncratic. I must quote a sizeable extract, including some commentary by the narrator which offers a clear contrast of style:

> 'Ah, lad! 'Tis thou?' When she had said this, with a smile which would have been quite expressed, though nothing of her had been seen but her pleasant eyes, she replaced her hood again, and they went on together.
> 'I thought thou wast ahind me, Rachael?'
> 'No.'
> 'Early t'night, lass?'
> ''Times I'm a little early, Stephen; 'times a little late. I'm never to be counted on, going home.'
> 'Nor going t'other way, neither, t'seems to me, Rachael?'
> 'No, Stephen.'
> He looked at her with some disappointment in his face, but with a respect and patient conviction that she must be right in whatever she did. The expression was not lost upon her; she laid her hand lightly on his arm a moment, as if to thank him for it.
> 'We are such true friends, lad, and such old friends, and getting to be such old folk, now.'
> 'No, Rachael, thou'rt as young as ever thou wast.'
> 'One of us would be puzzled how to get old, Stephen, without t'other getting so too, both being alive,' she answered, laughing; 'but, any ways, we're such old friends, that t'hide a word of honest truth fro' one another would be a sin and a pity. 'Tis better not to walk too much together. 'Times, yes! 'Twould be hard, indeed, if 'twas not to be at all,' she said, with a cheerfulness she sought to communicate to him.
> ''Tis hard, anyways, Rachael.'
> 'Try to think not; and 'twill seem better.'
> 'I've tried a long time, and 'ta'nt got better. But thou'rt right; 'tmight mak fok talk, even of thee. Thou has been that to me, through so many year: thou hast done me so much good, and heartened of me in that cheering way, that thy word is a law to me. Ah lass, and a bright good law! Better than some real ones.'

'Never fret about them, Stephen,' she answered quickly, and not without an anxious glance at his face. 'Let the laws be.'

'Yes,' he said, with a slow nod or two. 'Let 'em be. Let everything be. Let all sorts alone. 'Tis a muddle, and that's aw.'

A minimum of deviant spellings here serves to hint at the vowel sounds and the elisions of a northern accent. Elsewhere, Dickens indicates the accent by a more radical set of orthographic, lexical and morphological peculiarities:

'My friends,' Stephen began, in the midst of a dead calm; 'I ha'hed what's been spok'n o' me, and 'tis lickly that I shan't mend it. But I'd liefer you'd hearn the truth concernin myseln, fro my lips than fro onny other man's, though I never cud'n speak afore so monny, wi'out bein moydert and muddled.'

Detailed analyses of these dialect notations are unnecessary. Different novelists (for example, Mrs Gaskell, Emily Bronte) use different notational devices: some use more archaisms, others more 'non-standard' morphology, and there is variation in the spelling conventions for vowels. There are two simple points to grasp in all such cases. First, these are not to be judged as realistic transcriptions where fidelity might be an issue – they are simply conventional signals of sociolinguistic difference. Second, only a very slight deviance, as in the conversation between Stephen and Rachael, is needed to persuade middle-class readers that they are in the presence of a social group below their own.

More significant is the syntax, which is in sharp contrast to Harthouse's elaborated forms. Halliday (1976: ch. 12) maintains that speech and writing have different information structures, and therefore different modes of syntactic organization. Writing, which can be scanned and re-scanned for complexities and qualifications of meaning, is a medium which can accommodate the kinds of indirections which we noted in Harthouse's language. Speech, according to Halliday, is more straighforwardly linear, and it releases its meanings in a sequence of short chunks or 'information units'; these units are segmented off by intonation patterns, rises and falls in the pitch of the voice. Syntactically, they need not be complete clauses, but are often phrases or single words, and often loosely linked by apposition or concatenation. The overall style is not, strictly speaking, paratactic, because the conjoined constituents are not clauses of equal weight; but in its avoidance of clause subordination it is much more like parataxis than hypotaxis.

Once the existence of this mode of speech has been pointed out, it takes no great analytic expertise to recognize that the description fits the conversation of Stephen and Rachael. The point is that Dickens has – in *writing* of course – deliberately constructed a very *oral* model of language for these two humble characters, contrasting with the formal, written model used for some unsympathetic middle-class speakers, such as Harthouse. I think there is a contrast of values intended here: solidarity and naturalness on the one hand, deviousness and insincerity on the other. I cannot prove this by reference to the language alone; I simply suggest that Dickens is using speech style stereotypes to which his readers, on the basis of their sociolinguistic competence and of their knowledge of the novel's plot, assign conventional significances.

So far I have offered examples of significant individual voices, and of speech styles which seem to take the imprint of social values ('social semiotic' in Halliday's (1978) term). Other examples could be discussed; together they would assemble a picture of a text articulated in a multitude of voices. These voices are, overall, discordant and fluctuating in the kaleidoscope of views they express. Furthermore, the opposing points of view do not neatly align. Though Sleary confronts Gradgrind directly, so that the symbols of Fancy and Fact are in direct opposition, Harthouse and Stephen are not immediately opposed, nor are many other significant antitheses of voices. Dickens's intellectual scheme for the book does not seem to have been symmetrical: his sociolinguistic symbols embodied in characters do not relate diagrammatically, and so the relationships between theoretical issues such as factual education, exploitative capitalism, statistics, social reform, play etc. are not dramatized neatly in the linguistic or narrative relationships between the characters. The story and the language figure the ideological debates in an unsettled, troubled way. I think this raggedness is a strength. But, before commenting on it directly, I want to refer to other areas of linguistic instability, different from the 'unpatternedness' of the global canvas. These areas involve dialogue, explicit or implicit, and involve shifting organization in the style of the voice.

Stephen Blackpool visits Bounderby's house on two occasions and each time finds himself in a stand-up argument. The debates start with each speaker using his characteristic speech style. Bounderby is blustery and bullying, his speech packed with commands and demands:

Well Stephen, what's this I hear? What have these pests of the earth being doing to *you*? Come in, and speak up . . . Now, speak up! . . . Speak up like a man . . .

Bounderby continues in this register (which is his constant idiolect, or a major part of it), while Stephen's responses begin quiet and polite, in a language heavily marked for the dialectal phonology and based on the short information units noticed earlier:

'What were it, sir, as yo' were pleased to want wi' me?'
'Wi' yor pardon, sir, I ha' nowt to sen about it.'
'I sed as I had nowt to sen, sir; not as I was fearfo' o' openin' my lips.'
'I'm as sooary as yo, sir, when the people's leaders is bad. They taks
such as offers. Haply 'tis na' the sma'est o' their misfortuns when they
can get no better.'

Pressed to state how he would solve the troubles of the weaving
industry, Stephen moves into a sequence of five long speeches; their
sheer length is a sign of departure from character, against the norm of
his conversation with Rachael. The spelling peculiarities are main-
tained to a large degree, as is the syntax of spoken information. This is
from the third long speech:

> Look round town – so rich as 'tis – and see the numbers of people as
> has been broughten into bein heer, fur to weave, an to card, an to piece
> out a livin', aw the same one way, somehows, twixt their cradles and
> their graves.

The fifth of these speeches has Stephen, under intense provocation,
voicing sentiments of 'man' against 'master' which on independent
evidence, as well as the evidence of the novel, can be associated with
Dickens's own humanitarian point of view. Stephen cannot say what
will right the world, but he can say what will not: the strong hand of the
masters, *laissez-faire*, lack of regard for the humanity of the mill
workers and so on. When Stephen gives voice to these sentiments, the
overall structure of his language changes to the parallelistic rhetoric of
a public speech: a succession of balanced sentences, steadily increasing
in length, is used to enumerate his arguments. Here are two of them:

> Not drawin' nigh to fok, wi' kindness and patience an cheery ways, that
> so draws nigh to one another in their monny troubles and so cherishes
> one another in their distresses wi' what they need themseln – like, I
> humbly believe, as no people the genelman ha seen in aw his travels
> can beat – will never do't till th'Sun turns t'ice. Most of aw, ratin 'em as
> so much Power, and reg'latin 'em as if they was figures in a soom, or
> machines: wi'out loves and likeins, wi'out memories and inclinations,
> wi'out souls to weary and souls to hope – when aw goes quiet, draggin
> on wi' 'em as if they'd nowt o' th'kind, an when aw goes onquiet,
> reproachin 'e, for their want o' sitch humanly feelins in their dealins wi'
> you – this will never do't, sir, till God's work is onmade.

Some of the elaborated syntax noticed in Harthouse's language can be
found here in the internal structure of clauses, in the qualifications and
self-interruptions. And the overall format of repetitive structure
recalls the insistent harangue of the book's opening scene, in the
schoolroom.

When Stephen engages with the moral issues which concern Dickens centrally, then his language deviates sharply from what has earlier been offered as his own characteristic sociolinguistic style. I point this out not as an inconsistency of characterization but as an application of the dialogic principle in the language through which Stephen is constituted. The stylistic shift shows strain in Dickens's use of a voice to express an ideological position that has become problematic through being assigned to that speaker. Stephen as originally set up by Dickens is inadequate to occupy the place in debate in which he has become situated: his language strains towards the rhetoric of a more public form of disputation than his social role warrants.

Surprising shifts of register occur in the speech of other characters, although none so remarkable as the transformation from tongue-tied weaver to articulate orator. I have no space to demonstrate any more of these changes; nor, most regrettably, can I show any selection of the range of styles of the narrative voice. Dickens ranges from subversive parody (bk 1, ch. 1, on Gradgrind on Fact), to complex animating and de-animating metaphors (bk 1, ch. 5, the superb evocation of Coketown) to pathos, and to simple direct judgment ('He was a good powerloom weaver, and a man of perfect integrity'). David Lodge has analysed some varieties of the narrative rhetoric of *Hard Times* in an excellent chapter (Lodge, 1966) analysis which readers can consult to fill out this gap in my account. Lodge also relates these variations to uncertainties in Dickens's own position, as I do. But his judgement is essentially based on a monologic norm: '*Hard Times* succeeds where its rhetoric succeeds and fails where its rhetoric fails.' Generally, Lodge argues, this rhetoric is successful when Dickens is being antagonistic or ironic, but fails when he is trying to celebrate his fictional positives.

But it is more complex than that. The various styles are not just 'successful' or 'failed', but transcend a two-term set of values: it is the plurality of codes, their inconstancy and their frequent stridency which all together constitute a fruitful and discordant poplyphony. Any account of Dickens's 'argument' in this novel is bound to come to the conclusion that he attacks an unmanageably large and miscellaneous range of evils (Utilitarianism in education and economics, industrial capitalism, abuse of unions, statistics, bad marriage, selfishness etc.); that he mostly oversimplifies them (for example, fails to see the beneficial relationship between some fact-gathering activities and real social reforms); that he is unclear on what evil causes what other evil. On the other side, his proposed palliatives are feeble, misconceived in terms of purely individual initiatives and responsibilities, and sentimentally formulated. Most of this conceptual muddle stems from the crucial inadequacy of Dickens's idealized solution of tolerant *rapprochement* of the two parties to the industrial situation:

'I believe,' said I, 'that into the relations between employers and employed, as into all the relations of this life, there must enter something of feeling and sentiment; something of mutual explanation, forbearance, and consideration; something which is not to be found in Mr. McCulloch's dictionary, and is not exactly stateable in figures; otherwise those relations are wrong and rotten at the core and will never bear sound fruit.'[5]

Translation of all Dickens's insecurely based theses and antitheses into elements and structural relationships of this novel's form has produced the asymmetries and dissonances which my stylistic analysis has begun to display. But few people today would condemn *Hard Times* as a ragged failure. The inconsistencies and discords are an indication of the problematic status of the social and theoretical crisis in question for a great imagination like Dickens, who would not articulate unequivocally in fiction the facile solutions which were consciously available to him as theory. The novel's lack of monologic authority fits Bakhtin's description, I believe; and the stylistic polyphony is provocative and creative, compelling the reader to grapple uneasily with the tangle of issues that Dickens problematizes.

Suggestions for Further Work: Chapter 4

1   The following passage is from Dickens's novel *Bleak House* (1853). The chapter from which the passage is taken is narrated in the present tense by a third person narrator, and deals with the inquest into the death of Nemo. The coroner, as will be seen, rather hastily reaches a verdict of accidental death, but not before he has interrogated the young crossing sweeper, Jo.

Says the Coroner, is that boy here? Says the beadle, no, sir, he is not here. Says the Coroner, go and fetch him then. In the absence of the active and intelligent, the Coroner converses with Mr. Tulkinghorn.

O! Here's the boy, gentlemen!

Here he is, very muddy, very hoarse, very ragged. Now, boy! – But stop a minute. Caution. This boy must be put through a few preliminary paces.

Name, Jo. Nothing else that he knows on. Don't know that everybody has two names. Never heerd of sich a think. Don't know that Jo is short for a longer name. Thinks it long enough for him. He don't find no fault with it. Spell it? No. He can't spell it. No father, no mother, no friends. Never been to school. What's home? Knows a broom's a broom, and knows it's wicked to tell a lie. Don't recollect who told him about the broom, or about the lie, but knows both. Can't exactly say what'll be done to him arter he's dead if he tells a lie to the gentlemen here, but believes it'll be something wery bad to punish him, and serve him right – and so he'll tell the truth.

'This won't do, gentlemen!' says the Coroner, with a melancholy shake of the head.

'Don't you think you can receive his evidence, sir?' asks an attentive Juryman.

'Out of the question', says the Coroner. 'You have heard the boy. "Can't exactly say" won't do, you know. We can't take *that*, in a Court of Justice, gentlemen. It's terrible depravity. Put the boy aside.'

Boy put aside; to the great edification of the audience; – especially of Little Swills, the Comic Vocalist.

Now. Is there any other witness? No other witness.

Very well, gentlemen! Here's a man unknown, proved to have been in a habit of taking opium. If you think you have any evidence to lead you to the conclusion that he committed suicide, you will come to that conclusion. If you think it is a case of accidental death, you will find a Verdict accordingly.

Verdict accordingly. Accidental death. No doubt. Gentlemen, you are discharged. Good afternoon.[6]

Drawing on the concepts of *polyphonic* and *dialogic* structure, examine the contrasts in values, attitudes and world-views that are encoded in the speech styles of the characters in the passage. To what extent does the language of the different voices reflect differing power relationships? The following comment from Bakhtin might be usefully integrated into your discussion:

The novel can be defined as a diversity of social speech types (sometimes even diversity of languages) and a diversity of individual voices, artistically organized. The internal stratification of any single national language into social dialects, characteristic group behaviour, professional jargons ... languages of the authorities, of various circles and of passing fashions, languages that serve the specific sociopolitical purposes of the day ... – this internal stratification present in every language at any given moment of its historical existence is the indispensable prerequisite for the novel as a genre. (Bakhtin, 1981: 262–3)

2   *Stylistic analyses of Dickens: further reading.* A book devoted to the language of the characters in Dickens's novels is Robert Golding's *Idiolects in Dickens* (London: Macmillan, 1985). Golding examines the fictional idiolects of these characters and assesses the techniques Dickens uses to represent oratorial language, occupational registers and social and regional dialects. The following additional studies may also be of interest: G. L. Brook, *The Language of Dickens* (London: Deutsch, 1970); R. Quirk 'Charles Dickens and Appropriate Language', in S. Wall (ed.), *Charles*

Dickens, Penguin Critical Anthology (Harmondsworth: Penguin, 1970); R. J. Watts *The Pragmalinguistic Analysis of Narrative Texts: Narrative Co-operation in Charles Dickens's 'Hard Times'* (Tubingen: Gunter Nar Verlag, 1981).

Notes: Chapter 4

1   See, for example, Halliday (1978, 1985); Kress (1976). Most of the works cited in note 2 below give accounts of relevant aspects of Halliday's theory.
2   A seminal literary application by Halliday is his paper Halliday (1971). Relevant applications by others include Fowler (1981), especially ch. 8; Fowler (1977); Kennedy (1982); Burton (1982).
3   Quotations from *Hard Times* follow the Penguin edition (Harmondsworth, 1969), edited by David Craig, with a very few minor apparent printing errors corrected.
4   The theory of 'elaborated' and 'restricted' codes has been proposed by the sociologist Basil Bernstein (1971). However, this theory has come under considerable attack from sociolinguists: a notable example is Labov (1972).
5   Reprinted in Ford and Monod (1966).
6   Penguin edn (Harmondsworth, 1978), pp. 199–200 (bk 4, ch. 11).

References: Chapter 4

Bakhtin, M. (1968), *Rabelais and his World*, trans. H. Iswolsky (Cambridge Mass.: Massachusetts Institute of Technology Press).
Bakhtin, M. (1973), *Problems of Dostoyevsky's Poetics*, trans. R. W. Rotsel (Ann Arbor: Ardis).
Bakhtin, M. (1981), *The Dialogic Imagination: Four Essays*, trans. C. Emerson and M. Holquist (Austin, Texas, and London: University of Texas Press).
Bernstein, B. (1971), *Class, Codes and Control* (London: Routledge & Kegan Paul).
Burton, D. (1982), 'Through Glass Darkly: Through Dark Glasses', in R. Carter (ed.), *Language and Literature: An Introductory Reader in Stylistics* (London: Allen & Unwin), pp. 195–214.
Craig, D. (1969) Introduction to *Hard Times* (Harmondsworth: Penguin).
Ford, G., and Monod, S. (eds) (1966), *Hard Times* (New York: W. W. Norton and Co.),
Fowler, R. (1977), *Linguistics and the Novel* (London: Methuen).
Fowler, R. (1981), *Literature as Social Discourse* (London: Batsford).
Halliday, M. A. K. (1971), 'Linguistic Function and Literary Style', in S. Chatman (ed.), *Literary Style: A Symposium* (New York and London: Oxford University Press).
Halliday, M. A. K. (1976), *System and Function in Language* (New York and London: Oxford University Press).
Halliday, M. A. K. (1978), *Language as Social Semiotic* (London: Edward Arnold).

Halliday, M. A. K. (1985), *An Introduction to Functional Grammar* (London: Edward Arnold).

Hirsch, D. (1964), '*Hard Times* and F. R. Leavis', *Criticism*, vol. 4, pp. 1–16.

Holloway, J. (1962), '*Hard Times*: A History and a Criticism', in J. Grass and G. Pearson (eds), *Dickens and the Twentieth Century* (London: Routledge & Kegan Paul), reprinted in Ford and Monod (1966), pp. 361–6.

Kennedy, C. (1982), 'Systemic Grammar and its Use in Literary Analysis', in R. Carter (ed.), *Language and Literature: An Introductory Reader in Stylistics* (London: Allen & Unwin), pp. 83–99.

Kress, G. (ed.) (1976), *Halliday: System and Function in Language* (London: Oxford University Press).

Labov, W. (1972), 'The Logic of Non-standard English', in P. P. Giglioli (ed.), *Language and Social Context* (Harmondsworth: Penguin), pp. 179–215.

Leavis, F. R. (1967), *The Great Tradition* (Harmondsworth: Penguin).

Lodge, D. (1966), *Language of Fiction* (London: Routledge & Kegan Paul).

Ruskin, J. (1860), 'A note on *Hard Times*', *Cornhill Magazine*, vol. 2, reprinted in Ford and Monod (1966), pp. 331–2.

Shaw, G. B. (1912), *Introduction to Hard Times* (London: Waverley), extract reprinted in Ford and Monod (1966), pp. 332–9.

Shklovsky, V. (1965), 'Art as Technique', in L. T. Lemon and M. J. Reis (eds and trans), *Russian Formalist Criticism* (Lincoln, Nebr.: University of Nebraska Press), pp. 5–24.

Williams, R. (1968), *Culture and Society 1780–1950* (Harmondsworth: Penguin).

Introduction to Chapter 5

Jean Jacques Weber's chapter forms a useful link with Roger Fowler's in several ways. First of all, it reviews some of the work in 'critical linguistics' pioneered by Roger Fowler and his associates. This is an approach to language study which uses linguistic techniques to investigate the ideologies (value-systems and sets of beliefs) which underlie texts.

Weber then proposes that, in the ideological analysis of literary texts, greater attention should be paid to linguistic *modality*. Modality is that function of language which concerns the speaker's or writer's attitude to, and commitment to, the content of what he says. Weber thus sets out to combine the approach adopted by Fowler with an analysis of narrative modality and, like Fowler, he selects Dickens's *Hard Times* as a primary text.

In the course of his analysis, Weber demonstrates that a particular type of modality is foregrounded in the speech of each of the major characters in the novel. He isolates the following types:

(1) *Low-value modalities* for Bounderby – exemplified in constructions of 'uncertainty', such as 'I don't know', 'I suppose' etc.;

(2) *high-value modalities* for Sissy, Stephen and Rachael – exemplified in constructions of 'certainty', such as 'I am quite sure', 'I know' etc.;

(3) *high-value modulations* for Gradgrind – exemplified in expressions indicating a high degree of obligation, such as 'mustn't do this', 'they are not to do that' etc.

Drawing on Dolezel's work on narrative semantics, Weber then shows how these modals construct different types of narrative worlds: a world of 'constriction' for Gradgrind, a world of 'turbulence' for Bounderby and worlds of moral values for Sissy, Stephen and Rachael. He concludes that a modal analysis of narrative universes highlights the tension between the narrator's explicitly stated ideology and his implicit radical ideology.

5 Dickens's Social Semiotic: the Modal Analysis of Ideological Structure

JEAN JACQUES WEBER

Over the last ten years, Roger Fowler has been a consistent advocate of the ideological analysis of literary (and non-literary) texts: in other words, an analysis of the systems of values and beliefs underlying the texts.[1] In the preceding chapter, he follows the Russian theorist Bakhtin, and maintains that opposing voices in a text embody conflicting world-views or ideologies. At the same time he has reinterpreted Bakhtin's findings in a stricter way within Halliday's social-semiotic framework. This has led to the development of Fowler's sociolinguistic functionalism, his 'theory of literature as social discourse' or simply, to quote the title of his recent book (Fowler, 1986), 'linguistic criticism'. Its practitioner studies a literary text as a communicative event, not as an autonomous verbal artefact. He is interested in the relationships between author, narrator, characters and reader: hence, he is particularly interested in interpersonal features of language (Fowler 1981: 175). And the most important interpersonal feature of language is *modality*, which is defined in a broad sense as follows:

> Modality covers all those features of discourse which concern a speaker's or writer's attitude to, or commitment to, the value of applicability of the propositional content of an utterance, and concomitantly, his relationship with whoever he directs the speech act to. (Fowler 1977: 13).

or

> Modality is the grammar of explicit comment, the means by which people express their degree of commitment to the truth of the propositions they utter, and their views on the desirability or otherwise of the states of affairs referred to. (Fowler 1982: 216)

Ideological analysis consists of two steps: one descriptive and the other interpretative. In relation to this, it is worth reintroducing some of the observations which Fowler makes in the previous chapter:

> First, it is necessary to show in detail the linguistic and semiotic characteristics of the various voices (including the narrating voice) which participate in the dialogic structure. Secondly, the polyphonic structure, the multiplicity of voices, needs to be interpreted in terms of the author's ideology. (p. 79)

In many of his analyses in this area, Fowler pays particular attention to step 1, the analysis of sociolinguistic registers, rather than step 2, the analysis of the ideologies involved. This chapter is therefore an attempt to develop this work, by combining Fowler's linguistic approach with an analysis of the narrative universes in *Hard Times*, an analysis based on the pioneering work in narrative semantics undertaken by Dolezel (1976) and Ryan (1985).

Fowler further contends that there are two privileged areas of linguistic structure in ideological analysis. These are:

(a)   a variety of modal structures which make 'explicit (though sometimes ironic) announcements of beliefs';
(b)   a number of other structures which, 'indirectly but nevertheless convincingly, may be symptomatic of world-view'. (Fowler 1986: 132)

The features under (b) include lexical structure, Halliday's 'transitivity structure' (1970: 327), and certain syntactic structures. Thus systematic syntactic or lexical choices can throw a certain slant upon the presentation of 'reality', and hence be indicative of ideology. Fowler has explored the ideological implications of the lexical structure of Anthony Burgess's *A Clockwork Orange* and William Burroughs's *The Naked Lunch* in Fowler (1981: 42–61). Transitivity structure is dealt with *passim* (for example, Fowler, 1977: 103–113; Fowler, 1986: 156–67). And the ideological functions of syntactic transformations are discussed most extensively in Fowler *et al.* (1979) through a comparative study of various newspaper styles.

As for the constructions mentioned under (a) above, they include: modal auxiliaries (*may, might, should, would* etc.); modal and sentence adverbs (*certainly, possibly, perhaps, probably* etc.); evaluative adjectives and adverbs (*luckily, fortunate, regrettably, awfully* etc.); verbs of knowledge, prediction, evaluation (*believe, guess, approve, dislike* etc.); and generic sentences (generalized sentences which proclaim universal truths) (Fowler, 1986: 131–2). Generics (especially in George Eliot) are studied in Fowler (1981: 96–128). And finally, concerning modality proper (in the traditional, linguistic sense), Fowler has repeatedly stressed the importance of its study in ideological analysis. He has shown how a narrator can use 'modal words of estrangement' to create distance from a character (for example, Fowler, 1977: 94–5, on Bounderby in *Hard Times* and Fowler, 1982: 232–3, on Flay and Swelter in *Titus Groan*). However, the direct ideological repercussions of systematic modal choices have largely been ignored. The present chapter will thus attempt to redress the balance and will set out to show, using *Hard Times* as a primary text, how a study of linguistic modality can reveal the exact nature of ideological structure.

However, before we turn to Dickens's novel, let me briefly review some of the relevant literature. There have been surprisingly few linguistic analyses of modality in literary texts. In addition to my own analysis of modal distance in Graham Greene's *The Honorary Consul* (Weber, 1984), I would cite only five articles of related interest. Kress (1978) studies the modal function of tense in Donne's 'Nocturnall'. Halliday (1982) shows how modality and modulation in both grammatical and lexical structure actualize the themes of time and social obligations in Priestley's *An Inspector Calls*. Both Taylor (1978) and Lee (1982) analyse the modal structure of Jane Austen's *Emma*. And Ruthrof (1984) applies his interesting and potentially useful, though slightly vague, notion of 'modal inference' to Joyce's short story 'The Sisters'.

The vagueness of Ruthrof's analysis is due to the fact that he almost totally ignores the linguistic aspects of modality categorized above. For example, he claims that the boy protagonist of 'The Sisters' 'emerges at the end of the narrative as a more independent personality than any of the other presented personae' (Ruthrof 1984: 104), but he does not mention that the growth of the boy is reflected in Joyce's distribution of modal verbs: indeed it consists in his acquisition of factivity. At the beginning of the story, the boy 'thinks' for himself, but 'knows' through the priest only:

> If he was dead, *I thought*, I would see the reflection of candles on the darkened blind for *I knew* that two candles *must* be set at the head of a corpse. He had often said to me: 'I am not long for this world', and *I had thought* his words idle. *Now I knew* they were true. (p. 7)[2]

The boy's knowledge is clearly derived from the priest, whose infallible beliefs are contrasted with the boy's fallible beliefs. But his dream of the priest, and the latter's death, lead the boy towards 'liberation' or emancipation. And so, at the end of the story, it is the other people who 'think', but the boy 'knows' for himself:

> I knew that the old priest was lying still in his coffin as we had seen him, solemn and truculent in death, an idle chalice on his breast.

Eliza resumed:
– Wide awake and laughing-like to himself . . . So then, of course,
when they saw that, that made *them think* that there was something
gone wrong with him . . . (p. 15)

Beyond this, very few interpretative clues are offered to the reader.
The boy seems obsessed with a number of highly charged key-words
such as *simony, paralysis, gnomon, truculent, chalice*. But how exactly
these relate to each other and to the ideological structure of the story is
left to the reader to reconstruct. Many causal connections are possible,
as shown by the many different interpretations that have been given of
this story. That is why I call its ideological structure implicit and
unstable.

On the other hand, a good example of a narrative with an explicit
and stable ideological structure is Jane Austen's *Emma*. Lee's (1982)
analysis of modality in the opening pages of *Emma* focuses on positive
and negative evaluations of Emma in the narrative voice, which, he
claims, prepare the reader for 'the appearance of Mr Knightley, whose
judgment of Emma reconciles the perception of her flaws with the
appreciation of her qualities' (Lee 1982: 109). His concern is thus with
how the norm ideology, the ideology of both the narrative voice and of
Mr Knightley, is set up in the very first pages of the book. Taylor's
(1978) analysis is a useful complement: she shows how Emma's use of
must (and some other modals) changes from being an endeavour to
make the world fit in with her own wishes at the beginning of the novel
to the inverse attempt to make her wishes fit in with the world towards
the end of the novel. This changing modal pattern is then seen as the
'linguistic embodiment of (Emma's) social–moral growth' (Taylor
1978: 368). The two analyses thus present a mutually reinforcing
picture of how the novel moves from initial divergence between the
norm ideology and the conflicting ideology of the young Emma to final
convergence between the norm ideology and the ideology of the
mature Emma, with the norm ideology itself being both explicit and
stable throughout the book.

How does *Hard Times* fit into this scheme? I hope to show that its
ideological structure has the rather more unusual characteristics of
being explicit yet unstable.[3] Its norm ideology is in fact subverted from
within by a conflicting ideology. This second level of conflict is super-
imposed upon the normal and ubiquitous contradictions existing
between norm ideology and the ideologies of characters such as
Gradgrind and Bounderby. In *Hard Times*, the norm ideology itself
suffers from an inner split; its ideological structure is deconstructive,
self-subversive.

We have now reached the point where we can start to investigate the
linguistic realization of these ideologies. In the previous chapter,

Fowler makes an astute observation about what might be called Dickens's social semiotic:

> Dickens seems to have accepted the principle that now provides the theoretical basis for Hallidayan linguistics, namely that registers of language characterize social groups and encode their values. (p. 84)

Moreover, the different sociolects and idiolects in *Hard Times* are, of course, distinguished from each other by the foregrounded use of certain linguistic constructions, and in particular (I shall claim) of certain types of modals. Before embarking on the analysis of these constructions, I just want to add two more caveats. First, the analysis will be largely restricted to a small number of selected passages, namely those which introduce the main characters: book 1, chapters 1 and 2 for Gradgrind, chapter 4 for Bounderby and chapter 10 for Stephen and Rachael. Secondly, the analysis will briefly touch upon generic sentences and syntactic structure, then we will move into a discussion of modal expressions, and we will finish by looking at one aspect of the transitivity structure of *Hard Times*.

If we now turn to the opening pages of Dicken's novel, we are immediately struck by the overwhelming weight and power of fact which is to crush the children (Dickens calls it 'murdering the innocents'). A large range of linguistic constructions support this 'emphasis'. For example, Lodge (1966: 149–50), in his discussion of the narrator's rhetoric, mentions the dehumanizing commercial and geometric language of chapter 1, and also the narrator's repetition of the passive clause, 'The emphasis was helped by . . .'. The authoritarian emphasis is also helped by the sheer universality of Gradgrind's claims, which are often couched in the form of generic sentences:

> 'Facts alone are wanted in life. Plant nothing else, and root out everything else. You can only form the minds of reasoning animals upon Facts: nothing else will ever be of any service to them . . . in this life, we want nothing but Facts, sir; nothing but Facts!' (p. 47; bk 1, ch 1)[4]

The nominalizing tendency of this authoritarian discourse (evidenced by the repeated use of 'emphasis') is further developed by the series of complex noun phrases which introduce both Gradgrind and Bounderby – they have the effect of freezing the world into a heap of brute facts designed to smother both children and reader:

> Thomas Gradgrind, sir. A man of realities. A man of fact and calculations. A man who proceeds upon the principle that two and two are four, and nothing over, and who is not to be talked into allowing for anything over. Thomas Gradgrind, sir – peremptorily Thomas – Thomas Gradgrind. (p. 58; bk 1, ch. 2)

With Bounderby, the list of noun phrases is even longer, their complexity even greater and their effect even more crushing:

> A big, loud man, with a stare and metallic laugh. A man made out of a coarse material, which seemed to have been stretched to make so much out of him. A man with a great puffed head and forehead, swelled veins in his temples, and such a strained skin to his face that it seemed to hold his eyes open and lift his eyebrows up. A man with a pervading appearance on him of being inflated like a balloon, and ready to start. A man who could never sufficiently vaunt himself a self-made man. A man who was always proclaiming, through that brassy speaking-trumpet of a voice of his, his old ignorance and his old poverty. A man who was the Bully of humility. (p. 58; bk 1, ch. 4)

In his discussion of the latter passage, Fowler (1977: 94–5) shows how the narrator uses modal words of estrangement such as 'seemed' and 'appearance' to distance or alienate the reader from Bounderby, thus presenting him from an external perspective. (Indeed, Bounderby himself frequently contributes to the establishment of this external perspective through his habit of referring to himself in the third person as 'Josiah Bounderby of Coketown'.) But the vocabulary of seeming also sets up Bounderby as the man of appearances, who has lost all contact with reality – an ironic characterization of this hard-facts man which will be confirmed by the revelation of the totally imaginary nature of his past.

I believe that the modal expressions associated with Gradgrind and Bounderby reflect both themes identified above: the authoritarian nature of Gradgrind's views and the theme of appearance v. reality. In the identification of modals, I rely on Halliday's model, which distinguishes between the two basic systems of modality and modulation: 'modality is the speaker's judgment of probability, modulation is the speaker's assessment of obligation' (Halliday 1982: 140). Within either system, three values can be distinguished:

Value	Probability	Obligation
HIGH	certain	required
MEDIAN	probable	supposed
LOW	possible	allowed

Halliday (1985: 337) also notes that, with the outer values, a reversal of polarity entails a reversal of values: thus, for example, *not allowed* has the value HIGH and *not required* the value of LOW. In what follows, I have reduced Halliday's three-value function to a two-value function, distinguishing between high-value and non-high (or low-value) modals. Such a binary distinction suffices to account for the modal structure of *Hard Times*, while at the same time considerably simplifying the description of it.

The first theme, the authoritarian nature of Gradgrind's views, is emphasized by the foregrounded repetition of high-value modulations. In book 1, chapters 1 and 2, Gradgrind and his acolytes (Mr M'Choakumchild and especially the other 'gentleman') use an impressive number of these bullying modulations in their efforts to mould and coerce the children: the children *mustn't* do this, they *are not to* do that. Out of a total of thirty-two modals used by Gradgrind and the gentleman, no less than fourteen belong to this group. Even the narrator ironically mimics Gradgrind's modulations:

> Thomas Gradgrind, sir. A man of realities. A man of fact and calculations. A man who proceeds upon the principle that two and two are four, and nothing over, and who *is not to* be talked into allowing for anything over ... In such terms, no doubt, substituting the words 'boys and girls', for 'sir', Thomas Gradgrind now presented Thomas Gradgrind to the little pitchers before him, who *were to* be filled so full of facts. Indeed, as he eagerly sparkled at them from the cellarage before mentioned, he seemed a kind of cannon loaded to the muzzle with facts, and prepared to blow them clean out of the regions of childhood at one discharge. He seemed a galvanizing apparatus, too, charged with a grim mechanical substitute for the tender young imaginations that *were to* be stormed away. (p. 48; bk 1, ch. 2)[5]

As Halliday (1982: 141) points out, the use of such modulations implies an external source of obligation. Moreover, the fact that both Gradgrind and the gentlemen use the same modulations shows us that they are part of a larger system. This system, which has a restrictive, imprisoning effect, is of course Utilitarianism. At the same time, however, this points to the possibility that, once the external source of obligation has been removed, Gradgrind should theoretically be open to change.

If we apply Ryan's (1985: 728) classification of possible worlds according to modality, we could say that Gradgrind's narrative universe is an 'obligation world', a deontic world of regulative principles which affect every aspect of life. Its collapse throws Gradgrind into an epistemic crisis. Indeed, the large majority of his modals after the collapse of his deontic world are low-value modalities, which reflect his newly found humility. And the constructive *was to* modulation is now ironically turned against Gradgrind in his confrontation with Bitzer:

> 'I really wonder, sir,' rejoined the old pupil in an argumentative manner, 'to find you taking a position so untenable. My schooling was paid for; it was a bargain; and when I came away, the bargain ended.'
> It was a fundamental principle of the Gradgrind philosophy, that

everything *was* to be paid for. Nobody *was ever on any account to* give anybody anything, or render anybody help without purchase. Gratitude *was to* be abolished, and the virtues springing from it *were not to* be. Every inch of the existence of mankind, from birth to death, *was to* be a bargain across a counter. (p. 304; bk 3, ch. 8)

Bounderby also uses the *was to* modulation, but in his case it is qualified by explicitly subjective modalities:

'I *was to* pull through it *I suppose*, Mrs Gradgrind. Whether I *was to* do it or not, ma'am, I did it.' (p. 60; bk 1, ch. 4)

The subordination of the *was to* modulation to the *I suppose* modality shows us that, in Bounderby's case, the external source of obligation has been internalized into the 'balloon' of his personality. Hence it should be very difficult, or even impossible, for Bounderby to change; otherwise his 'balloon' would burst (even though the 'balloon' will be badly damaged – in the scene with his mother).

The frequent occurrence of low-value modalities of the *I suppose* type is an unexpected feature of this bully's speech:

'How I fought through it, *I don't know*,' said Bounderby. 'I was determined, *I suppose*. I have been a determined character in later life, and *I suppose* I was then.' (p. 59; bk 1, ch. 4)

It is true that they constantly alternate with expressions of blustering assertiveness; but at the same time they seem to reflect an attitude of modesty on the part of a man who is in a position of epistemic superiority, being the only one to know all the gruesome details of his childhood. However, after the scene with his mother (bk 3, ch. 5), the reader has to reinterpret Bounderby's modals: he realizes that, far from being in a position of epistemic superiority, Bounderby has in fact been pushing back alethic frontiers and creating a world of fantasy, an 'alternate universe', in Ryan's (1985: 730) terminology.

But Bounderby himself is totally unaffected by this revelation; the double pattern of his modals never changes throughout the book. And so, in the very last chapter, we still find Bounderby indulging in veiled threats which, though hidden under the guise of his false obsequiousness, are just as bullying as his open aggressiveness:

'A female may be highly connected, but she can't be permitted to bother and badger a man in my position, and I am not going to put up with it . . . Mrs Sparsit, ma'am, I rather think you are cramped here, do you know? It appears to me, that, under my humble roof, there's hardly opening enough for a lady of your genius in other people's affairs. . . . it appears to my poor judgement . . . It appears to me, ma'am, I say, that a different sort of establishment altogether, would bring out a lady of your powers . . . I really ought to apologize to you – being only Josiah Bounderby of Coketown – for having stood in your light so long.' (pp. 310–11; bk 3, ch. 9)

Our analysis of modal expressions in Gradgrind's and Bounderby's speech, however brief and superficial, will have achieved its purpose if it has brought out the clear distinction between the two protagonists. Watts (1981: 140) defines this opposition between Gradgrind and Bounderby as the opposition between 'square' and 'round'; Sonstroem (1969: 524) calls it the opposition between 'constriction' and 'turbulence'. But at the same time Gradgrind and Bounderby as the representatives of the world of Fact are opposed to the people of Fancy, mainly Sissy, Stephen and Rachael, with the first representing the circus people and the other two the working class.

Sissy's, Stephen's and Rachael's speech contains a marked incidence of high-value modalities, at least in passages where they vouch for the integrity of some trusted individual (Louisa, Stephen) or group of individuals (his co-workers, in Stephen's case). After her initial diffidence at school (bk 1, ch. 2), Sissy rises to an attitude of supreme confidence in her dealings with Harthouse, as reflected by the fourfold repetition of 'I am quite sure' (p. 255). Stephen's assurance, when he faces Bounderby, is not only expressed by high-value modalities such as 'I know' (p. 179 three times, p. 182) and 'I am sure' (pp. 180, 181); it is also lexicalized by the narrator ('with the quiet confidence of absolute certainty' p. 181) and underlined by Stephen's sevenfold repetition of '[x] will never do it' (p. 182) or his repetition here and *passim* of the categoricality ' 'tis a muddle'. (Categoricalities, as Halliday (1985: 340) points out, are even stronger than expressions of certainty such as 'it must be a muddle'.) And Rachael gives everybody a '*sure and certain* promise' that Stephen will be back within two days: '*I know* with pride that he will come back to shame it!' (p. 271). Thus, these characters have a clear awareness of the distinction between what is good and what is bad. In Ryan's (1985: 728) terminology, their narrative universes are 'worlds of moral values' or worlds with an axiological dimension.

Support for such an interpretation can be gained by looking at the transitivity structure of *Hard Times*, which, according to Fowler (1986: 132), is 'symptomatic of world view' I shall limit my comments to part of the longer passage from *Hard Times* which Fowler examines in the previous chapter. It is an extract from book 1, chapter 10, in which the reader meets Stephen and Rachael for the first time. Fowler suggests that the reader tends to associate the informal, non-hypotactic syntax with values such as 'solidarity and naturalness'. In fact, the short, paratactic-like units used by Stephen and Rachael consist largely of what Halliday (1985: 112) called 'relational processes of being'. These relational processes express Stephen's and Rachael's concern with what is good and what is bad, not for themselves, but in a more universal moral sense:

> 'We are such true friends, lad, and such old friends, and getting to be such old folk, now.'
> 'No, Rachael, thou'rt as young as ever thou wast.'
> '. . . we're such old friends, that t'hide a word of honest truth fro' one another would be a sin and a pity. 'Tis better not to walk too much together. 'Times, yes! 'Twould be hard, indeed, if 'twas not to be at all,' . . .
> ''Tis hard, anyways, Rachael.'
> 'Try to think not; and 'twill seem better.'
> 'I've tried a long time, and 'ta'nt got better. But thou'rt right. . . . Thou hast been that to me, . . . thy word is a law to me. Ah lass, and a bright good law! Better than some real ones.'. . .
> '. . . 'Tis a muddle, and that's aw.' (pp. 104–5; bk 1, ch. 10)

This passage thus provides further evidence for the above contention that Stephen's and Rachael's narrative universes are worlds of moral values, worlds with an axiological dimension, the lack of which makes most other narrative worlds in *Hard Times* so sadly and so tragically deficient.

Indeed, Gradgrind's deontic world of constriction is a world which almost by definition denies the validity of all non-factual, moral, or axiological statements. Bounderby's speech, on the other hand, does contain a high density of relational processes in such passages as:

> 'For years, ma'am, I was one of the most miserable little wretches ever seen. I was so sickly, that I was always moaning and groaning. I was so ragged and dirty, that you wouldn't have touched me with a pair of tongs . . . She kept a chandler's shop,' pursued Bounderby, 'and kept me in an eggbox. That was the cot of my infancy; an old egg-box. As soon as I was big enough to run away, of course I ran away. Then I became a young vagabond; and instead of one old woman knocking me about and starving me, everybody of all ages knocked me about and starved me. They were right; they had no business to do anything else. I was a nuisance, an incumbrance and a pest.' (pp. 59–60; bk 1, ch. 4)

Could this reflect an awareness on Bounderby's part of what is morally right and wrong? Of course not, since all the above relational processes are concerned with his imaginary past. Hence, any seeming awareness of a moral dimension in Bounderby's speech turns out to be mere pretence, used for the sole purpose of self-aggrandizement.

We now begin to see that the basic opposition in *Hard Times* is not the antithesis between Fact and Fancy, as has been claimed by Lodge (1966: 157) and many other critics.[6] It is rather a distinction between the narrative worlds of Stephen, Rachael and Sissy, which incorporate a moral or axiological dimension, and narrative worlds lacking such a dimension – Gradgrind's deontic world of 'constriction' and Bounderby's alethic world of 'turbulence.' These different types of narrative worlds are symbolically encoded in the narrator's descriptions of his characters' hair (with the grotesque metaphors of the first two again distancing the reader from the characters being described):

(*Gradgrind*) The emphasis was helped by the speaker's hair, which bristled on the skirts of his bald head, a plantation of firs to keep the wind from its shining surface, all covered with knobs, like the crust of a plum pie, as if the head had scarcely warehouse-room for the hard facts stored inside. (p. 47; bk 1, ch. 1)

(*Bounderby*) He had not much hair. One might have fancied he had talked it all off; and that what was left, all standing up in disorder, was in that condition from being constantly blown about by his own windy boastfulness. (p. 59; bk. 1, ch. 4)

(*Stephen*) A rather stooping man, with a knitted brow, a pondering expression of face, and a hard-looking head sufficiently capacious, on which his iron-grey hair lay long and thin . . . (p. 103; bk 1, ch. 10)

(*Rachael*) She turned, being then in the brightness of a lamp; and raising her hood a little, showed a quiet oval face, dark and rather delicate, irradiated by a pair of very gentle eyes, and further set off by the perfect order of her shining black hair. (p. 104; bk 1, ch. 10)

The implication seems to be that constriction and turbulence, what Stephen calls the 'muddle' of the Utilitarian worlds, can be transformed into 'order' by adding a moral or axiological dimension. This is the narrator's covert message, a revolutionary message, since adding an axiological dimension would necessarily amount to a negation of the established system.

As such the narrator's covert message contrasts sharply with his overt ideological stance:

Is it possible, I wonder, that there was any analogy between the case of the Coketown population and the case of the little Gradgrinds? Surely, none of us in our sober senses and acquainted with figures, are to be told at this time of day, that one of the foremost elements in the existence of the Coketown working people had been for scores of years, deliberately set at nought? That there was any Fancy in them demanding to be brought into healthy existence instead of struggling on in convulsions? That exactly in the ratio as they worked long and

monotonously, the craving grew within them for some physical relief
– some relaxation, encouraging good humour and good spirits, and
giving them a vent – some recognized holiday, though it were for an
honest dance to a stirring band of music – some occasional light pie in
which even M'Choakumchild had no finger – which craving *must and
would* be satisfied aright, or *must and would* inevitably go wrong, until
the laws of the Creation were repealed? (pp. 67–8; bk 1, ch. 5)

The modulation here is endorsed by the narrator ('must and would'),
who seems to suggest that the best way of keeping the social status quo
is to add an imaginative dimension to the workers' lives. It is this
panem-et-circenses type of argument, along with the narrator's rejection of the trade-union movement, which has been objected to by
many critics (see, for example, Lodge 1966: 159). However, these
critics may have rejected *Hard Times* prematurely: they have only seen
its narrator's overt ideology, but have remained unaware of the covert
ideology of *Hard Times*. I believe that what ensures the lasting appeal
of *Hard Times*, in spite of all its major inconsistencies, is precisely the
existence of ideological difference, the tension between the narrator's
explicitly stated ideology and his implicit radical ideology, as revealed
by a modal analysis of the narrative universes in *Hard Times*.[7]

Suggestions for Further Work: Chapter 5

1   Follow-up Exercises on *Hard Times*. If we accept that ideologies
    involve relationships of power and solidarity, which are encoded in
    language, then Fig. 5.1 could be seen as a diagrammatic represen-
    tation of the arguments presented in this chapter:

    (i)   Study the Slackbridge, Sleary and Harthouse passages
          quoted in Roger Fowler's chapter (pp. 82–4 above) and see
          how these characters fit into the above scheme. You could
          also go through *Hard Times* and study the modals in the
          speech of these and/or other characters, e.g. Mrs Sparsit.
    (ii) In the light of your analyses, try to decide whether (or to what
          extent) such a generalizing scheme based on a few key pas-
          sages can be justified.
2   'Cat in the Rain' and 'Two Gallants'. Read the two stories by
    Hemingway and Joyce and try to determine which character in
    each story most of the modals are associated with. Can you attach
    any ideological or thematic significance to your linguistic observa-
    tion? What have the two stories, and more precisely the two sets of
    characters, got in common. How do they differ? ('Cat in the Rain'
    is published in Ernest Hemingway, *In Our Time* (New York:
    Scribner, 1970); 'Two Gallants' in *The Essential James Joyce*, ed.

DISCOURSE IDEOLOGY	LANGUAGE OF POWER		LANGUAGE OF SOLIDARITY	
	Repression	*Hypocrisy*	*Moral* *awareness*	*Subversion*
FOREGROUNDED MODAL STRUCTURE	high-value modulations (nominalization etc.)	low-value modalities	processes of being	high-value modalities
CHARACTER	Gradgrind (in bks 1, 2) Bounderby	Bounderby	Stephen Rachael Sissy	

Figure 5.1

H. Levin (Harmondsworth: Penguin, 1969)). Read Dolezel's, (1976) paper: his classification of stories in four categories – alethic, deontic, axiological, epistemic – will help you to answer some of the above questions.

3   Henry James's *The Turn of the Screw*. Study the following passage and show by what means the narrator tries to impose her (biased?) view of the world upon the reader. The governess is looking out of the window at a figure on the lawn below her who she fears might be one of the ghosts.

> The moon made the night extraordinarily penetrable and showed me on the lawn a person, diminished by distance, who stood there motionless and as if fascinated, looking up to where I had appeared – looking, that is, not so much straight at me as at something that was apparently above me. There was clearly another person above me – there was a person on the tower; but the presence on the lawn was not in the least what I had conceived and had confidently hurried to meet. The presence on the lawn – I felt sick as I made it out – was poor little Miles himself.[8]

4   Jane Austen's *Emma*. One aspect of modality highly relevant for ideological analysis but not dealt with in this paper is lexical modality. Fillmore (1971) was the first to point out the 'evaluative' implications of lexical items such as *accuse, criticise, praise*. Thus, for example, the sentence:

The teacher accused Linda of copying

implies that the teacher thinks that copying is bad.

(i)   Study the modal and lexical choices of the narrator in the sentences below, taken from the first page of *Emma*, in order to determine the exact nature of the narrator's evaluation of her heroine.

(ii) Compare your results with Lee's (1982) analysis of the same passage.

> Emma Woodhouse, handsome, clever, and rich, with a comfortable home and a happy disposition, seemed to unite some of the best blessings of existence; and had lived nearly twenty-one years in the world with very little to distress or vex her.
> She was the youngest of the two daughters of a most affectionate, indulgent father . . .
> The real evils indeed of Emma's situation were the power of having rather too much her own way, and a disposition to think a little too well of herself; these were the disadvantages which threatened alloy to her many enjoyments.[9]

5   'The Bucket and the Rope'. In this strange story by T. F. Powys, a bucket and a rope, presented as almost human (or at least highly articulate) servants of Mr Dendy, a farmer, review the latter's life in order to find a reason for his final act of committing suicide. In the first extract below, the bucket remembers the day when Mr Dendy bought them, 'which happened to be the very day before Mr Dendy was married'.

> 'He married, as you know, a woman, a creature to ease a man of the heavy burden of desire, a burden as troublesome to carry as a kicking ass.'
> 'And who also,' observed the rope, 'was intended to cook and prepare a man's food, to rear his children and to clean his house.'
> 'That should certainly be so,' said the other . . .
> 'While [Mrs Dendy] toyed with me,' said the rope, 'I had the chance to look at her the more narrowly. She seemed just the creature to delight any man with her sweetness and eagerness for love . . . She showed her good nature to a young man, the son of the lawyer, who happened to pass her in a by-street when Mr Dendy slipped into a small inn. The lawyer's son looked unhappy and she allowed him to kiss her, while Mr Dendy was out of the way.'
> 'She had a little foot,' observed the bucket, 'and a winning gait, and had Mr Dendy peeped through the dingy bar-window, when he was having a merry jest with Farmer Pardy, he should have

been glad to see that the lawyer's son thought her as nice as he did.'

'A rope would have fancied so,' said the other dryly . . .

'Only once,' observed the bucket, 'did I notice Mr Dendy act in a way that was not usual for a village man. He was bearing me, full, along a path from a small cottage where he bought swill. On each side of the path there were flowers, both white and yellow. Mr Dendy set me down, a rotten orange bobbed up on my surface. Mr Dendy rested by the path, plucked some of the flowers, and seemed to take delight in holding them in his hand.'

'What did he do next?' asked the rope.

'He carried the flowers home to his wife,' replied the bucket . . .

'The summer pleased Mr Dendy, and so did the winter,' said the rope . . .

'His wife made him [happy],' said the rope, 'and feeling her success with him she naturally wished to make another happy too.'

'What could be more proper?' said the bucket.

One evening Mrs Dendy had arranged a secret meeting with the lawyer's son in the shed, while Mr Dendy was supposed to be at church; but in fact Mr Dendy had hidden himself in the shed:

'For the pleasure of witnessing the kindness of his wife, I suppose,' said the bucket.

'One would have thought so,' replied the rope, 'but the look upon Mr Dendy's face when he saw what was going on did not warrant such a supposition.'

'Perhaps he thought,' reasoned the bucket, 'that Betty should have remained at home and warmed the rabbit pie for his supper; . . . it is natural that a man should wish the woman that he keeps to prepare food for him, even though she may prefer to be loving and kind to another man.'

'You should have heard Mr Dendy,' said the rope; 'he gnashed his teeth and moaned horribly, and when his wife's friend seemed to be altogether forgetting his sorrow, being come, as the lyric poet says, "Where comfort is –" Mr Dendy crept out of the bundle and hid in the lane, snarling like a bitten dog.'

'His hunger, I suppose, had gone beyond the proper bounds,' suggested the bucket.

'It is difficult,' said the rope, after a few minutes silence, as the body swung to and fro, 'for us to decide what could have troubled this good man. No one had robbed him. No one had beaten or hurt him, and never once since they had been married had Betty refused his embraces.'

'It must have been that nosegay,' exclaimed the bucket.[10]

If possible read the whole story, but even from these extracts you should be able to infer that the narrative universe of the bucket and the rope is epistemically deficient, in the sense that it is only a subset of the narrator's (and the reader's) universe of discourse. Thus there is a relation of one-way accessibility between the two universes: the reader understands where the bucket and the rope have gone wrong, and to what extent they are right, but *not* the other way around!

(i)   What is the 'knowledge base' of the bucket and the rope deficient in? To what extent is their interpretation of events nevertheless right?

(ii)   In order to elucidate the bucket's and the rope's ideology, analyse their modals. Comment on their use of such modal items as *seemed, proper, natural(ly)*. Also analyse the presuppositions and other implicit assumptions hidden in their speech.

(iii)   Compare their ideology with Gradgrind's and Bounderby's.

(iv)   Are the ideologies in 'The Bucket and the Rope' and *Hard Times* constructed by the same (linguistic) means? Do the differences reflect the authors' divergent aims?

Notes: Chapter 5

1   This approach to textual analysis is often referred to as 'critical linguistics'. See Chapter 13 for a further discussion.

2   This extract and the following one are taken from Joyce, *The Dubliners* (Granada edn, 1981); my emphasis here and *passim*.

3   The final case of implicit and stable ideological structure can be attested, too; it can be found, for instance, in many spy novels, which take for granted the ideological partitioning of 'West equals good' v. 'East equals bad'.

4   Quotations are from the Penguin edition (Harmondsworth, 1969), edited by David Craig.

5   Note that the narrator also uses an external perspective ('Thomas Gradgrind now presented Thomas Gradgrind') and modal words of estrangement (especially 'seemed' twice) in the presentation of Gradgrind. This may well contradict Gradgrind's own assessment of himself as a 'man of realities' and suggest that he too, just like Bounderby, lives in a world of illusions.

6   Critics such as D. Sonstroem have in fact shown that the Fact v. Fancy antithesis does not stand up to closer scrutiny. Sonstroem (1969: 527) comments on the lack of Fancy – in the sense of imaginative play – 'on the part of the virtuous, compassionate characters: Stephen, Rachael, Louisa, the circus fold, and especially Sissy Jupe. They show up very badly against the villainous characters: Bounderby, with his magnificent imaginative reconstruction of his past'. Readers may like to consult Sell (1986) for further discussion and demonstration of 'pragmalinguistic' approaches.

7   I should like to thank Willie Van Peer for his most helpful comments on an earlier version of this chapter.

8   Penguin edn (Harmondsworth, 1969), p. 64.
9   Penguin edn (Harmondsworth, 1972), p. 37.
10 T. F. Powys, *God's Eyes A-Twinkle* (London: Chatto & Windus, 1947), pp. 174–9, 179–80.

References: Chapter 5

Dolezel, L. (1976), 'Narrative Modalities' *Journal of Literary Semantics*, vol. 5, pp. 5–14.

Fillmore, C. J. (1971), 'Verbs of Judging: An Exercise in Linguistic Description', in Fillmore and D. T. Langendoen (eds.) *Studies in Linguistic Semantics* (New York: Holt Rinehart & Winston), pp. 273–89.

Fowler, R. (1977), *Linguistics and the Novel* (London: Methuen).

Fowler, R. (1981), *Literature as Social Discourse* (London: Batsford).

Fowler, R. (1982), 'How to See through Language: Perspective in Fiction', *Poetics*, vol. 11, no. 2, pp. 213–35.

Fowler, R. (1986), *Linguistic Criticism* (Oxford: Oxford University Press).

Fowler, R., *et al.* (1979), *Language and Control* (London: Routledge & Kegan Paul).

Halliday, M. A. K. (1970), 'Functional Diversity in Language as Seen from a Consideration of Modality and Mood in English', *Foundations of Language*, vol. 6, pp. 322–61.

Halliday, M. A. K. (1982), 'The De-automatization of Grammar: From Priestley's "An Inspector Calls"', in J. Anderson (ed.), *Language Form and Linguistic Variation* (Amsterdam: Benjamins), pp. 129–59.

Halliday, M. A. K. (1985), *An Introduction to Functional Grammar* (London: Edward Arnold).

Kress, G. (1978), 'Poetry as Anti-Language: A Reconstruction of Donne's "Nocturnal upon S. Lucies Day"', *PTL*, vol. 3, pp. 327–44.

Lee, D. A. (1982), 'Modality, Perspective and the Concept of Objective Narrative', *Journal of Literary Semantics*, vol. 11, pp. 104–11.

Lodge, D. (1966), *Language of Fiction* (London: Routledge & Kegan Paul).

Ruthrof, H. (1984), 'The Problem of Inferred Modality in Narrative', *Journal of Literary Semantics,* vol. 13, pp. 97–108.

Ryan, M. L. (1985), 'The Modal Structure of Narrative Universes', *Poetics Today*, vol. 6, pp. 717–55.

Sell, R. (1986) 'The Drama of Fictionalized Author and Reader: A Formalist Obstacle to Literary Pragmatics', *REAL: The Yearbook of Research in English and American literature IV.*

Sonstroem, D. (1969), 'Fettered Fancy in Hard Times', *PMLA*, vol. 84, pp. 520–9.

Taylor, M. V. (1978), 'The Grammar of Conduct: Speech Act Theory and the Education of Emma Woodhouse', *Style*, vol. 12, pp. 357–71.

Watts, R. J. (1981), *The Pragmalinguistic Analysis of Narrative Texts: Narrative Cooperation in Charles Dickens's Hard Times* (Tübingen; Narr).

Weber, J. J. (1984), 'Deontic, Axiological and Epistemic Distance in Graham Greene's "The Honorary Consul"', *Nottingham Linguistic Circular*, vol. 13, pp. 146–56.

Introduction to Chapter 6

This is the first of two chapters which concentrate on the structure of written discourse. Here, Winifred Crombie examines a section of Milton's *Areopagitica* in terms of the various types of relationships that exist between discourse segments. She argues that the persuasive, argumentative structure of *Areopagitica* depends for its effect not on immediately obvious rhetorical techniques or exact structural balance but upon an underlying semantic relational rhetoric. This underlying rhetoric is realized chiefly by the interaction between different types of semantic relation. Crombie isolates two major categories of semantic relations:

(1) *logico-deductive relations* – cause-effect relations;
(2) *associative relations* – relations based on comparison and contrast.

She goes on to demonstrate how Milton's argument gathers force through the use of various subtypes of logico-deductive and associative semantic relations and she concludes that the examination of written discourses in semantic relational terms should have a place in discourse stylistics.

6 Semantic Relational Structuring in Milton's *Areopagitica*

WINIFRED CROMBIE

My aim in this chapter is to examine a section of Milton's *Areopagitica* in terms of some of the ways in which discourse segments may be related to one another and to determine the extent to which these relationships may be regarded as stylistically significant.

Milton was opposed to the use of rhetorical techniques which served merely as embellishment, to eloquence for its own sake. In *An Apology for Smectymnuus*, he writes: 'true eloquence I find to be none, but the serious and hearty love of truth.'[1] Indeed, Milton's *Areopagitica*, in recalling the *Areopagiticus* of Isocrates, recalls also Isocrates' concern that eloquence should serve wisdom.[2] The persuasive, argumentative structure of *Areopagitica* depends for its effect not on immediately obvious rhetorical embellishment but upon its underlying semantic relational rhetoric – its closely woven pattern of discoursal relationships in which *logico-deductive semantic relations* (i.e. cause–effect relations) and *associative semantic relations* (i.e. relations based on comparison and contrast) between discourse segments interact and reinforce one another.

Robert E. Longacre (1972) has claimed that there are a finite number of ways of combining clauses in inter-clausal relations in the deep structure of discourse which encode into the surface grammar of languages. What is particularly interesting for our purposes here, however, is that from this finite means a whole range of different rhetorical possibilities emerge.

Semantic relations between discourse segments underlie *all* coherent stretches of language. However, the ways in which they co-occur and interrelate and the frequency with which certain types of relations occur varies from writer to writer and from discourse to discourse. Whereas, for example, Lancelot Andrewes relies heavily in his so-called 'metaphysical' prose on logico-deductive argumentation, there is in the 'baroque' prose of John Donne a marked preference for associative progression – a preference which appears to reflect a belief in the greater persuasive power of the presentation of a particular point of view through the imaginative apprehension of similarities and differences.[3]

Although different classificatory schemes are used by different researchers, I believe that a division of semantic relations into three main types is particularly useful in literary studies. These three types are the *logico-deductive*, the *associative* and the *tempero-contigual*.[4] The last of these, which involves relations such as *chronological sequence* (i.e. events following one another in time) and *temporal overlap* (i.e. events overlapping in time) will not be referred to in the following discussion. Those specific semantic relations which belong to the other two categories and which will be referred to are the following:

(1)   *Associative relations:*

   (i)   simple contrast – e.g. The one was a soldier, the other a priest.
   (ii) comparative similarity – e.g. The princes were afraid and so were their followers.
   (iii) statement–affirmation – e.g. He said that the terrorists should be punished and I agree.
   (iv) statement–denial – e.g. A: The Greeks won. B: They lost.
   (v)   concession–contraexpectation – e.g. Although they intended to attack, they defended.

(2)   *Logico-deductive relations:*

   (i)   reason–result – e.g. Because he wanted to be independent, he left home.
   (ii) grounds–conclusion – e.g. He's wearing a crown, so he must be the king.
   (iii) condition–consequence – e.g. If you don't understand, ask.

The following extract from *Areopagitica* is examined in terms of these semantic relations.

I deny not, but that it is of greatest concernment in the	1
Church and Commonwealth, to have a vigilant eye how Books	2
demean themselves as well as men; and thereafter to confine,	3
imprison and do sharpest justice on them as malefactors:	4
For Books are not absolutely dead things, but do contain	5
a potency of life in them to be as active as that soul	6
whose progeny they are; nay they do preserve as in a	7
vial the purest efficacy and extraction of that living	8
intellect that bred them. I know they are as lively,	9

and as vigorously productive, as those fabulous Dragon's	10
teeth; and being sewn up and down may chance to spring	11
up armed men. And yet on the other hand unless wariness	12
be used, as good almost kill a Man as kill a good	13
Book; who kills a man kills a reasonable creature, God's	14
Image; but he who destroys a good Book, kills reason	15
itself, kills the Image of God, as it were in the eye.	16
Many a man lives a burden to the Earth; but a good	17
Book is the precious life-blood of a master spirit,	18
embalmed and treasured up on purpose to a life beyond	19
life. 'Tis true, no age can restore a life, whereof	20
perhaps there is no great loss; and revolutions of ages	21
do not oft recover the loss of a rejected truth, for	22
the want of which whole Nations fare the worse. We should	23
be wary therefore what persecution we raise against the	24
living labours of public men, how we spill that seasoned	25
life of man preserved and stored up in Books; since we see	26
a kind of homicide may be thus committed, sometimes a	27
martyrdom, and if it extend to the whole impression, a	28
kind of massacre, whereof the execution ends not in the	29
slaying of an elemental life, but strikes at that	30
ethereal and fifth essence, the breath of reason itself,	31
slays an immortality rather than a life.[5]	32

In the section lines 1–12, Milton introduces the idea that books, in representing the spirit of their authors, are in some sense alive and potentially dangerous. This section begins with an inverted *reason–result* (deductive) relation:

> I deny not, but that it is of greatest concernment in the
> church and Commonwealth, to have a vigilant eye how Books
> demean themselves as well as men/ (*result*)
> For Books are not absolutely dead things/ (*reason*)

The *result* also acts as a denial which forms the first member of a *denial–correction* (associative) relation in which 'Books are not absolutely dead things' is replaced by 'but do contain a potency of life in them'.

There follow two *comparative similarity* relations, the first in lines 6–7, the second in lines 9–11. In the first of these two comparisons, books and their authors are seen to be equally active; in the second, Milton goes further metaphorically in his acceptance of the potential danger of books.

In this first section (lines 1–12), Milton expresses agreement with those who argue that books are harmful. In the remainder of the extract, however, he argues that the indiscriminate destruction or suppression of books can be more injurious than the retention of potentially harmful ones. This second section begins in line 12 with 'And yet on the other hand', which signals an associative relation of *concession–contraexpectation* between it and the preceding section. Here, there is a very heavy reliance on associative relations of various types, although the first relation we encounter – *condition–consequence* is actually a logico-deductive one:

> unless wariness be used/ (negative *condition*)
> as good almost kill a Man as kill a good Book/ (*consequence*)

The second member of this relation takes the form of an associative relation of *comparative similarity* which is itself immediately followed by a further associative relation of *simple contrast*:

> as good as almost kill a Man/ as kill a good Book/ (*comparative similarity*)
>
> Who kills a Man kills a reasonable creature, God's Image/
> but he who destroys a good Book, kills reason itself/ (*simple contrast*)

Milton has moved here from comparison to contrast. He began by claiming that the killing of a man is almost comparable to the killing of a good book, the comparison being made to appear more reasonable by the equation of 'a man' (i.e. *any* man) with 'a *good* book', and by the inclusion of 'almost'. The comparison having been thus presented in a form which makes assent likely, Milton moves immediately, using the comparison as a basis, to a relation of contrast so that the two things – a man and a good book – are no longer compared but contrasted. This move from comparison to contrast takes place within the framework of a deductive relation – inverted *grounds–conclusion* – in which the relation of *contrast* forms the *grounds* for the previously stated *conclusion*, which is made up of the two parts of the *comparative similarity* relation in lines 14–16. Thus:

> as good almost kill a Man as kill a good Book (*conclusion*)
>
> who kills a Man kills a reasonable creature; God's Image;
> but he who destroys a good Book, kills reason itself (*grounds*)

The interaction of relations here makes the argument more credible, the establishment of the *comparative similarity* relation preparing the way for, and giving more credibility to, the *simple contrast*. In turn, the *simple contrast* relation, providing as it does the *grounds* for the reinterpretation of the *comparative similarity* relation as a *conclusion* gives, in the provision of a deductive framework, more weight to the initial comparison. In arguing that a man is a 'reasonable creature' but a book 'reason itself', and in placing this within a contrastive framework, Milton is, it could be argued, now claiming that a good book is *more* valuable than a person.

> Many a man lives a burden to the earth;/
> but a good Book is the precious life-blood of a master spirit

Once again, the comparison is *not* between like and like – between a good book and a good man – but between a good book and a man 'who may live a burden to the earth'. The imbalance of this comparison is reinforced by the addition in the second member of the relation of a comment clause which elevates good books even further:

> a good Book is the precious life-blood of a master spirit,
> *embalmed and treasured up on purpose to a life beyond life*

Milton then offers, in line 20, a further justification for his argument in the form of an *affirmation* whose purpose seems to be entirely rhetorical in that it is immediately undercut in the following comment clause:

> 'Tis true, no age can restore a life, *whereof perhaps there is no great loss*

This argument is placed within the framework of an associative relation of *comparative similarity* in which 'a life' is compared with 'a rejected truth':

> 'Tis true, no age can restore a life, whereof perhaps there is no great loss/
> and revolutions of ages do not oft recover a rejected truth, for the want of which whole Nations fare the worse

What we *appear* to have here is a *comparison* of things within a comparative similarity framework; what we *actually* have is a *contrast*, which is contained within the overall comparative similarity framework. It is within the two comment clauses that the contrast occurs:

> a life, *whereof perhaps there is no great loss*/
> a rejected truth, for the want of which whole Nations fare the worse

It is upon the contained contrast that the emphasis actually falls. However, the fact that the loss of a life is seen as *less* significant than the loss of a truth is less stark, and therefore probably less likely to be rejected by Milton's readers, precisely because it is placed within a comparative similarity framework.

Having established his argument using a series of associative relations involving comparison and contrast, Milton goes on to discuss further the consequences of the destruction of a good book, beginning in line 24 with a *conclusion* signalled by 'therefore'. The *grounds* member of this relation follows in lines 26–32. Milton then proceeds to an associative relation of *denial–correction* signalled by 'not . . . but' in lines 29–31. Here, the contrast first established in lines 14–16 is restated:

> whereof the execution ends not in the slaying of an elemental life/
> but strikes at the ethereal and fifth essence, the breath of reason
> itself

This section ends with a *simple contrast* relation which serves as the final justification for the argument presented here – a justification arrived at largely through the medium of metaphor and conveyed throughout the extract largely in associative relational terms:

> The execution slays an immortality/
> rather than a life

A good book is no longer compared, as it was in lines 12–14, with a man. The two are now directly contrasted. Of course, the contrast which Milton originally established was not between the life of *any* man and the preservation of a good book, but between the life of a man 'who may live a burden to the earth' and a good book. The contrast is now a starker one: it is a simple contrast between a book, 'an immortality', and a life.

It seems that an examination of *Areopagitica* in terms of its semantic relations helps explain the effect noted by C. A. Patrides – an effect which seems, at the very least, odd in view of the conclusions that Milton reaches:

> *Areopagitica* advances cumulatively in a series of waves, until the gathered force of argument and rhetorical patterns overwhelms our reservations and commands our assent. (Patrides, 1974: 29)

Suggestions for Further Work: Chapter 6

1   Attempt, by rewriting the following extract from *Areopagitica*, to clarify the main lines of Milton's argument. What sections are most difficult to rewrite and why? When you have rewritten the extract, compare your version with the original and try to work out, using the semantic relational framework provided here, what rhetorical

devices Milton uses in order to support the conclusions he reaches in this section:

> Besides another inconvenience, if learned men be the first receivers out of books, and dispreaders both of vice and error, how shall the licencers themselves be confided in, unless we can confer on them, or they assume to themselves above all others in the Land, the grace of infallibility, and uncorruptedness? And again, if it be true, that a wise man like a good refiner can gather gold out of the drossiest volume, and that a fool will be a fool with the best book, yea, or without book, there is no reason that we should deprive a wise man of any advantage to his wisdom, while we seek to restrain from a fool, that which being restrained will be a hindrance to his folly. For if there should be so much exactness always used to keep that from him which is unfit for his reading, we should in the judgment of Aristotle not only, but of Solomon, and of our Saviour, not vouchsafe him good precepts, and by consequence not willingly admit him to good books; as being certain that a wise man will make better use of an idle pamphlet, than a fool will do of a sacred Scripture. 'Tis next alleged we must not expose ourselves to temptations without necessity, and next to that, not employ our time in vain things. To both these objections one answer will serve, out of the grounds already laid, that to all men such books are not temptations, nor vanities; but useful drugs and materials wherewith to temper and compose effective and strong medicines which man's life cannot want. The rest, as children and childish men, who have not the art to qualify and prepare these working minerals, well may be exhorted to forbear, but hindered forceably they cannot be by all the licensing that Sainted Inquisition could ever yet contrive . . . For if they fell upon one kind of strictness, unless their care were equal to regulate all other things of like aptness to corrupt the mind, that single endeavour they knew would be but a fond labour.

2   Concentrating on the use of associative and logico-deductive relations, compare the types of argumentation used in the following two extracts. The first is from Lancelot Andrewes's *Sermon of the Nativity* (1610), the second from John Donne's *Second Prebend Sermon* (1625). In both, spelling has been regularized.

> (a) Here comes an Angel with news from Heaven: what news he brings we know not, and therefore we fear, because we know not, which shows, all is not well between Heaven and us; that upon every coming of an Angel, we promise ourselves no better news from thence; but are still afraid of the messages and messengers that come from that place.

That the message may proceed; this fear must be removed. In a troubled water, no face will well be seen: nor by a troubled mind, no message received, till it be settled.[6]

(b)   He that was called the beloved Son of God, and made partner of the glory of heaven, in this world, in his Transfiguration is made now the Sewer of all the corruption, of all the sins of this world, as no Son of God, but a mere man, as no man, but a contemptible worm. As though the greatest weakness in this world, were man, and the greatest fault in man were to be good, man is more miserable than other creatures, and good men more miserable than any other men.[7]

Notes: Chapter 6

1   *The Works of John Milton*, ed. F. A. Patterson (New York: Columbia University Press, 1931–40), vol. 3, p. 362. The *Apology* was first published in 1642.
2   The title *Areopagitica* is an allusion to the areopagus – the seat of the Athenian Council of State – which became a judicial tribunal in the seventh and sixth centuries BC and for whose resuscitation the Athenian orator Isocrates pleaded in 355 BC in his *Areopagiticus*. Milton's *Areopagitica* was published in 1644.
3   The distinction between 'baroque' and 'metaphysical' prose is discussed in Crombie (1987). Although Donne's prose style is referred to as 'baroque', his poems are, of course, generally described as being 'metaphysical' in style.
4   I have discussed these semantic relations in detail in a number of places, in particular, Crombie (1985, 1987).
5   *Works of John Milton*, ed. Patterson, vol. 4, pp.297–8. The spelling has been regularized throughout this extract.
6   *Lancelot Andrewes: Sermons*, ed. G. M. Story (Oxford: Clarendon Press, 1967), p. 26.
7   *The Sermons of John Donne*, ed. T. A. Gill (New York: Meridian, 1958), p. 121.

References: Chapter 6

Crombie, W. (1985), *Process and Relation in Discourse and Language Learning* (Oxford: Oxford University Press).
Crombie, W. (1987), *Free Verse and Prose Style: An Operational Definition and Description* (London: Croom Helm).
Longacre, R. E. (1972), *Hierarchy and Universality of Discourse Constituents in New Guinea Languages: Discussion* (Washington D.C.: Georgetown University Press).
Patrides, C. A. (1974), *John Milton: Selected Prose* (Harmondsworth: Penguin).

Introduction to Chapter 7

Michael Hoey's chapter complements that of Winifred Crombie in that it offers additional insights into the nature of written discourse. Hoey proposes that a useful interpretation of a literary work can be reached by an analysis of the text's organization as discourse. He seeks to demonstrate this through his analysis of John Donne's poem 'A Hymne to God the Father'.

For his analysis, Hoey draws on a descriptive system developed by himself and his associates. This system accounts for the types of relations that exist between elements in a discourse. Certain patterns of discourse organization are regarded as particularly important. These include:

(1) *problem–solution patterns* – these have three essential components:

   (*a*) a statement of a problem
   (*b*) a response (whether suggested or carried out)
   (*c*) an evaluation of the effectiveness of the response;

(2) *matching relation patterns* – these are created by devices of various kinds, including systematic repetition, which may signal relations of compatibility and contrast.

Hoey uses the analytic system as a way of accounting for the numerous processes that are at work in the Donne poem. He contends that the poem realizes several layers of discourse organization simultaneously. These are:

   (i)   a series of problem–solution patterns;
   (ii) a dialogue between 'Donne' and God the Father;
   (iii) a network of cohesive devices setting up ambiguous readings;
   (iv) a dialogue between the discourse and the reader;
   (v)   a series of matching relation patterns.

Hoey explores each of these layers in turn, but also supplements his analysis by making use of non-linguistic knowledge. He concludes his chapter by arguing that a discourse-centred stylistic analysis has an important input into both discourse analysis and literary criticism. For discourse analysts, such an analysis provides a testing ground for the models and systems they develop; for literary critics, it produces a variety of useful readings which can lead to a fuller interpretation of the text.

7   Discourse-Centred Stylistics: a Way Forward?

MICHAEL HOEY

The study of literary language by linguists has always promised two types of insight. The first is insight into the individuality of a writer's style; indeed the very name 'stylistics' reflects that concern. Milic (1967) on Swift, and Ohmann (1962, 1964) on Shaw and Faulkner, represent early successes in this area. The second is as a tool for the interpretation of individual works; here successes have perhaps been more sporadic and have been more dependent on the individual than on the development of useful techniques of analysis, with literary critics having at times justification for their oft-voiced suspicion of linguists' interference in their discipline. One reason for this has been that systems of analysis centring on the sentence have only been revealing about eccentric works. Those many works whose individuality does not rest in any syntactic deviance have for the most part not been illuminated by sentential analysis. The burgeoning research in discourse analysis over the past decade offers, however, the possibility of approaching these works in a new and more productive way. If every discourse has a unique organization, then it follows that one way of identifying the individuality of a work is by analysing its organization as discourse. In Hoey and Winter (1981), based on an earlier unpublished paper by Winter, we attempted to show how a new interpretation of *Julius Caesar* grew naturally out of the detailed analyses of the speeches of Brutus and Mark Antony at Caesar's funeral. In this essay I seek to demonstrate that the discourse analysis of a poem by John Donne results in a greater number of readings for the poem and a synthesis of those readings; at the same time it serves to test and challenge the descriptive system used.

A detailed account of the descriptive system to be employed on the poem would be out of place here. A short account must however be attempted. The approach described is derived from the work of Winter (particularly 1974, 1977, 1979) and his associates (particularly Jordan, 1978, 1980, 1984; and Hoey, 1979, 1983). Certain basic asumptions are made about the nature of written discourses based on years of detailed analyses of short discourses. First, it is assumed that every clause in a discourse is in at least one semantic relation with at least one other clause or group of clauses in that discourse. Secondly, it is assumed that out of a finite number of such clause relations an infinite number of patterns of organization may be built. Every discourse has therefore a potentially unique organization. Thirdly, it is assumed that the clause relations in a discourse may be between clauses, groups of clauses, or parts of clauses; in other words the relation is no respecter of syntactic boundaries, though its realization is necessarily rooted in the grammar of the clause. Fourthly, it is assumed that certain patterns of organization have become culturally dominant, of which the problem–solution pattern is a particularly good example. This has three essential parts – a statement of an aspect of the situation requiring a response (or problem), a response (whether suggested or carried out), and an evaluation of the effectiveness of that response (see Winter, 1976; Hoey, 1979; Jordan, 1980.) If the evaluation is negative, then the problem is deemed unsolved and further responses are expected by the reader to follow. Fifthly, it is assumed that clause relations are an abstraction of connections readers make between the parts of a discourse as part of the effort of understanding the discourse; those connections are aptly and more precisely represented as questions asked of the discourse. What this means is that every reader is engaged in a dialogue with the discourse being read. Sixthly, lastly, and most importantly, it is assumed that the clause relations and the patterns of organization which they form are indentifiable by means of signalling devices of various kinds, including subordination, conjuncts and lexical signals, and by projecting the discourse into question-and-answer dialogue. Signals of clause relations also include systematic repetition, which may signal matching relations of, for example, compatibility and contrast; examples will be considered in the poem to be analysed.

All the assumptions listed have been defended elsewhere (see Winter, 1974, 1979, 1983; Hoey, 1979, 1983; Hoey and Winter, 1981). Brevity prevents a repetition of that defence here. The extent to which they are able to account for the fact of the particular discourse we shall be considering will however serve as some sort of test of their validity.

One extra assumption needs to be added when the object of study is a literary discourse, namely that the implied writer (i.e. the writer required to understand the discourse, who may or may not tally with the real writer) may also be in dialogue with an implied reader (who may well be different from the actual reader). Thus in the poem that follows the implied writer is a repentant sinner who is in dialogue with an implied reader who is God the Father.

The approach to be used involves analysing the poem in the light of all these assumptions; out of the understanding of the poem thereby achieved, readings of the poem are created and checked against non-linguistic evidence. Donne's 'Hymne to God the Father' (1633) was chosen because it seemed prima facie to have an organization worth explaining.

A Hymne to God the Father

Wilt thou forgive that sinne where I begunne,
  Which was my sin, though it were done before?
Wilt thou forgive that sinne; through which I runne,
  And do run still: though still I do deplore?
    When thou hast done, thou hast not done,
      For, I have more.

Wilt thou forgive that sinne which I have wonne
  Others to sinne? and, made my sinne their doore?
Wilt thou forgive that sinne which I did shunne
  A yeare, or two: but wallowed in, a score?
    When thou hast done, thou hast not done,
      For, I have more.

I have a sinne of feare, that when I have spunne
  My last thred, I shall perish on the shore;
But sweare by thy selfe, that at my death thy sonne
  Shall shine as he shines now, and heretofore;
    And, having done that, Thou hast done,
      I feare no more.[1]

There are a number of ways of viewing this poem, all of them overlapping with each other. These are as a series of problem–solution patterns, as a dialogue between 'Donne' and God the Father, as a network of cohesive devices setting up ambiguous readings, as a dialogue between the discourse and the reader, and as a series of matching patterns. Wherever we begin we shall need the others, so we might as well begin with the poem as problem–solution pattern.

The first verse has the pattern:

that sinne where I begunne, which was my sin, though it were done before (*problem*)
Wilt thou forgive. . . ? (*possible response*)
that sinne; through which I runne, and do run still: though still I do deplore (*another problem*)
Wilt thou forgive. . . ? (*same possible response*)
When thou has done, thou hast not done (*negative evaluation of possible response (which reinstates the problems)*)
For, I have more (*reason for negative evaluation*)

The second verse has an identical pattern. The third verse offers, however, a variant, whereby the first two lines are *problem*, lines 3–4 are *possible response*, line 5 is *positive evaluation of possible response* (thereby closing the pattern) and line 6 is *either* the reason for *or* the result of the positive evaluation.

Apart from this last aberrant line, which we will return to, the poem appears to be organized according to the normal problem–solution pattern. Consideration of the poem as dialogue between 'Donne' and 'God' serves to make the pattern more complex. To begin with, we must ask what status the possible response has. We may read the interrogative 'Wilt thou forgive. . . ?' in verses 1 and 2 in three ways. First, it may be read as an example of the discourse act *informative* (all discourse act terms are taken from Sinclair and Coulthard, 1975), i.e. as a rhetorical question. In this reading it is equivalent to saying 'Thou wilt forgive' or perhaps 'Thou sayst thou wilt forgive'. Interpreted this way the response may be read as actual response and the 'when thou has done' clause becomes simply a time-sequencing clause with no conditional meaning.

Secondly, 'Wilt thou forgive. . . ?' may be read as an example of the discourse act *elicitation*, i.e. as a real question. In this reading it is equivalent to saying 'Tell me whether thou wilt forgive'. Interpreted this way, the response can only be a possible response, not a certain one. If, however, it is an elicitation, a reply has to be given or assumed given if the discourse is to continue. The most natural way of reading the 'when thou hast done' clause in such circumstances is to assume that the answer 'yes' has been given. Even so certainty is not as complete as in the first case, and *when* carries with it the slight possibility of a conditional meaning.

Thirdly, 'Wilt thou forgive. . . ?' may be read as an example of an act akin to *directive*, namely a request. In this reading, it is equivalent to saying 'I request that thou wilt forgive' or, more naturally, 'I pray that thou wilt forgive'. As with the elicitation reading, the response can be only a possible response. There is no need to assume that an answer need be given to the request before the discourse can continue. Although in my experience petitions in prayer are usually answered, part of the conventions of a prayer is that one does not wait for the fulfilment of a petition before continuing. Since there is no assumed assent to the request, the 'when thou hast done' clause can only be read as conditional, i.e. 'when and if thou hast done'. Depending therefore on the act that 'Wilt thou forgive. . . ?' is interpreted as performing, we arrive at different conclusions as to whether or not the sins are forgiven. This uncertainty is important, because it will affect our reading of the last verse.

Looking now at the poem as a network of cohesive devices, we encounter further complications. In the penultimate lines of verses 1 and 2, 'thou hast . . . done' can be interpreted in three different ways. First, with stress on *hast*, it can mean 'thou hast forgiven the sin', where *done* is acting as a pro-form for 'forgiven the sin'. Secondly, with stress on *done*, it can mean 'thou hast finished', *done* here functioning as a full verb. Thirdly, with stress on both *hast* and *done*, it can mean 'thou possessest the poet Donne' in true metaphysical punning fashion. This gives us at least three good uncontradictory readings for the line, as follows:

(1) When you have forgiven these sins, you haven't finished
(2) When you have forgiven these sins, you still don't possess me
(3) When you have finished forgiving me, you still don't possess me

and three contradictory ones:

(1) When you have finished, you haven't finished after all
(2) When you possess me, you still don't possess me after all

and, most strikingly, the apparently blasphemous

(3) When you have forgiven these sins, you haven't forgiven them after all.

Whichever reading is taken, 'For, I have more' is offered as the reason for the failure, and this too is interpretable in several ways. The ellipsis after *more* is irresolvable; *more* may refer to 'more sins', 'more to forgive', or 'more to say', the last reading being possible if we interpret 'Wilt thou forgive. . . ?' as prayer. All of these readings will suffice to explain why God has not finished forgiving Donne, but none of them is adequate to explain the apparently blasphemous reading that God's forgiveness still leaves the poet unforgiven. Either we must abandon this reading as unacceptable or we must seek another explanation in the discourse organization.

The poem is to be seen not only as a dialogue with God but, according to the descriptive system outlined earlier, also as a dialogue with the reader. Much of the dialogue within the verses between the poem and the reader has already been indirectly spelt out in our analysis so far. What has not been spelt out is the relationship *between* the verses. After 'For, I have more' in verse 1, there is only one question a reader can reasonably ask of the poem, namely 'What is your more?', in which case verse 2 will be seen as supplying the answer. Likewise verse 3 will be seen as supplying the answer to the same question raised by the end of verse 2. This makes sense of the contradictory readings of the penultimate lines of verses 1 and 2. It is obviously true that God has not finished forgiving Donne's sins if he has more to confess. On the other hand, if we take the apparently blasphemous reading, we are still left with the uncomfortable argument that the reason why the sins in the first verse cannot be forgiven is because of the sins in the second, and the reason why the sins in the second cannot be forgiven is because of the sin named in the third. On the face of it this argument appears to make no sense. Here, however, we can no longer operate as discourse analysts without reference to non-linguistic real-world knowledge. For the rules of the confession box are that if you consciously withhold any sins from the confession, the confession is invalid. Until the confession is complete, therefore, the first sins remain unforgiven. Only when the last sin is confessed does the forgiveness become operative.

That is a satisfactory solution as far as it goes, but it can only be the full solution if we abandon the informative and elicitative readings of 'Wilt thou forgive. . . ?'. Must we then lose these readings? Let us consider the relationship between verses 1 and 2 from another point of view. The repetition within them and between them shows that they are organized by a number of *matching relations* in addition to the relations we have already mentioned. To begin with the matching within them, lines 1–2 are matched with lines 3–4 in verse 1. If we set them out in table fashion (Fig. 7.1) we find that they are matched for similarity. Likewise lines 1–2 are matched with lines 3–4 in verse 2, though less closely (see Fig. 7.2).

In addition to the matching within each verse there is matching between them as well, but the matching is for difference rather than similarity, the difference lying in the contrast between verse 1's mitigating circumstances and verse 2's aggravating circumstances. It will be noticed that this not only supports the confessional reading as a valid reading but goes some way to supporting the other readings as well, *more* taking on the meaning of *worse*. This however would have the effect of making verse 3's sin the worst sin of all, discourse organization normally demanding that a progression of *bad* and *worse* be followed by *worst*. We look then to verse 3 to resolve our difficulties.

Verse 3 is different in a number of respects. To begin with, lines 3–4

	Wilt thou forgive that sinne	where I begunne,	Which was my sin,	though it were done before?
	Wilt thou forgive that sinne;	through which I runne,	And do run still:	though still I do deplore?
Shared feature	repetition	I sin	I sin	mitigating circumstance
Difference		past v. present	past v. present	nature of circumstances

Figure 7.1

	Wilt thou forgive that sinne		which I have wonne others to sinne? and, made my sinne their doore?
	Wilt thou forgive that sinne	Which I did shunne a yeare, or two:	but wallowed in, a score?
Shared feature	repetition		aggravating circumstance
Difference		mitigating circumstance	nature of circumstances

Figure 7.2

are couched in the form of a request. The readings of certainty (rhetorical question) or probability (real question) are not therefore available for the response element of the problem–solution pattern in this verse. Secondly, 'having done that' does not allow the multiple readings available for 'when thou hast done'; it can only mean 'having sworn that'. This then leads to three readings for line 5 of this verse:

(1) Having sworn that, thou hast finished forgiving me
(2) Having sworn that, thou hast forgiven me

and

(3) Having sworn that, thou possessest the poet Donne.

Thirdly, 'I feare no more', as was remarked earlier, can be read either as a reason for 'thou hast done' or as the result and positive evaluation of it. If we consider the dialogue between reader and discourse, it answers equally well the reader's question 'Why?' or 'What is the result of this?' On the face of it, it makes no sense and we would appear to have to reject one of these readings. Once again we must call on our non-linguistic knowledge to rescue us from our discourse-analytical impasse. It is fundamental to Christian belief that to receive God's forgiveness we must first put our trust in Christ; this is expressed in Acts 26:18; for example, in Christ's reported words 'by trust in me they may obtain forgiveness of sins'.[2] This pulls all the discourse readings and the problems arising out of them into a harmonious whole.

If our sins are forgiven if we trust in Christ, then lack of trust means that our sins are unforgiven. Thus the sin of fear potentially means that the other sins are not forgiven. Our first difficulty is thereby overcome.

Our contradictory and blasphemous readings are neither contradictory nor blasphemous: we can keep them. Our second difficulty is
also overcome. We are not dependent on 'Wilt thou forgive. . . ?'
being read as prayer for our interpretation of 'thou hast not done': we
can keep the rhetorical question and real question readings. One
difficulty only remains, can we know whether the response is actual or
not? In other words, does 'Donne' get forgiven? The ambiguity of
function of the last line of verse 3 resolves the difficulty.

If the last line of the poem is both reason and result, we have an
unbreakable circle, in which fearing no more leads to forgiveness and
forgiveness leads to fearing no more. Everything then depends on
God's swearing, which precedes both forgiveness and fearing no more,
whichever comes first. If He swears, 'Donne's' only block to forgiveness is removed because that will give 'Donne' the grounds he
needs for trust. If he does not swear, then nothing is forgiven.

This uncertainty is central to the poem; everything is dependent on
whether God answers the final petition which, as it is not a rhetorical or
real question, does not presuppose an answer within the poem. Three
features however lead us to believe that 'Donne's' problem is success-
fully solved:

(1)   'I feare no more' is ambiguous in its time reference; it may refer
      to a hypothetical future or to an actual present. If it is read as the
      latter, the circle is broken.
(2)   The act of asking for forgiveness of the sin of the lack of trust is
      itself an act of trust. Once again then the circle is broken.
(3)   God is asked to swear 'by thy selfe'. In other words 'Donne' is
      willing to take God's authority as a basis on which to believe what
      He swears. This is an act of trust. This too therefore breaks the
      vicious circle. We may take it that the problem is successfully
      solved; 'Donne's' sins are forgiven.

The analysis just completed seems to have several implications for
work in discourse analysis and stylistics. First, the use of a system of
discourse analysis can produce a variety of useful readings of a literary
discourse and supply literary critics with precisely defined problems for
them to solve. Secondly, the success of such an approach in producing
useful readings indirectly reflects favourably on the discourse assumptions made at the beginning. Thirdly, only an approach that allows for
multiple simultaneous relations between the parts of a discourse is
adequate to account for the complexity of a poetic discourse. Fourthly
and finally, there must be allowances made in any system of discourse
analysis for non-linguistic data.

To sum up, the study of discourse stylistics promises discourse
analysts a useful testing ground for their hypotheses about discourses

and literary critics a useful tool for illuminating literary works and highlighting matters within them requiring explanation. It would therefore appear to offer a fruitful way forward for both discourse analysis and stylistics, and is, after all, a natural development from both.

Suggestions for Further Work: Chapter 7

1 Analyse the following poem by William Blake in terms of its problem–solution pattern:

A Poison Tree

I was angry with my friend:
I told my wrath, my wrath did end.
I was angry with my foe:
I told it not, my wrath did grow.

And I watered it in fears,
Night and morning with my tears;
And I sunned it with smiles,
And with soft deceitful wiles.

And it grew both day and night,
Till it bore an apple bright;
And my foe beheld it shine,
And he knew that it was mine.

And into my garden stole
When the night had veiled the pole
In the morning glad I see
My foe outstretched beneath the tree.[3]

What difficulties do you encounter in your analysis? How might observation of the *matching relations* in the first verse help you in interpreting the poem? Similarly, how might observation of the cause–consequence relations in verses 2 and 3 help? To what extent is the problem the narrator responds to in the case of the foe different from the one the narrator responds to in the case of the friend? What are the moral implications of the contrast between the two matching patterns?

2 Identify and analyse the *matching relations* in the following poem by John Keats. What are the dominant patterns?

La Belle Dame Sans Merci

O, what can ail thee, knight-at-arms,
Alone and palely loitering?
The sedge has withered from the lake,
And no birds sing.

O, what can ail thee, knight-at-arms,
So haggard and so woe-begone?
The squirrel's granary is full.
And the harvest's done.

I see a lily on thy brow,
With anguish moist and fever dew;
And on thy cheeks a fading rose
Fast withereth too.

I met a lady in the meads,
Full beautiful – a faery's child,
Her hair was long, her foot was light,
And her eyes were wild.

I made a garland for her head,
And bracelets too, and fragrant zone,
She looked at me as she did love,
And made sweet moan.

I set her on my pacing steed,
And nothing else saw all day long;
For sidelong would she bend, and sing
A faery's song.

She found me roots of relish sweet,
And honey wild, and manna dew,
And sure in language strange she said –
'I love thee true'.

She took me to her elfin grot,
And there she wept and sighed full sore,
And there I shut her wild wild eyes
With kisses four.

And there she lulled me asleep
And there I dreamed – Ah! woe betide!
The latest dream I ever dreamed
On the cold hill side.

I saw pale kings and princes too,
Pale warriors, death-pale were they all;
They cried – 'La Belle Dame sans Merci
Hath thee in thrall!'

I saw their starved lips in the gloam,
With horrid warning gaped wide,
And I awoke and found me here,
On the cold hill's side.

And this is why I sojourn here
Alone and palely loitering,
Though the sedge has withered from the lake,
And no birds sing.[4]

Discuss the function and effect of those stanzas in which and between which the matching relations are different from the predominant pattern? The ballad develops through two different periods of time and is set in two different places. To what extent are these differences marked by matching relations? Is there any correspondence between the design and distribution of matching relations in the poem and an expression of intensity of love? Finally, explore the poetic structure of the poem as a ballad. How is the patterning of the dialogues here different from Auden's dialogic ballad 'Song V', discussed in Chapter 3. After working through the exercises for Chapter 12 devoted to the relationship between metre and discourse, examine the role of metre in this poem in conveying its messages.

3   Analyse the following poem by William Wordsworth in terms of the interaction between the speakers, and relate your analysis to the *matching relations* both within and between the speakers' utterances:

We are Seven

– A simple Child,
That lightly draws its breath,
And feels its life in every limb,
What should it know of death?

I met a little cottage Girl;
She was eight years old, she said;
Her hair was thick with many a curl
That clustered round her head.

She had a rustic, woodland air,
And she was wildly clad;
Her eyes were fair, and very fair;
– Her beauty made me glad.

'Sisters and brothers, little Maid,
how many may you be?'
'How many? Seven in all,' she said,
And wondering looked at me.

'And where are they? I pray you tell.'
She answered, 'Seven are we;
And two of us at Conway dwell,
And two are gone to sea.

'Two of us in the churchyard lie,
My sister and my brother;
And, in the churchyard cottage, I
Dwell near them with my mother.'

'You say that two at Conway dwell,
And two are gone to sea,
Yet ye are seven! – I pray you tell,
Sweet Maid, how this may be.'

Then did the little Maid reply
'Seven boys and girls are we;
Two of us in the churchyard lie,
Beneath the churchyard tree.'

'You run about, my little Maid,
Your limbs they are alive;
If two are in the churchyard laid,
Then ye are only five.'

'Their graves are green, they may be
seen,'
The Little Maid replied,
'Twelve steps or more from my mother's
door,
And they are side by side.

'My stockings there I often knit
My kerchief there I hem;
And there upon the ground I sit,
And sing a song to them.

'And often after sunset, Sir,
When it is light and fair,
I take my little porringer,
And eat my supper there.

'The first that died was sister Jane;
In bed she moaning lay,
Till God released her of her pain;
And then she went away.

'So in the churchyard she was laid;
And, when the grass was dry,
Together round her grave we played,
My brother John and I.

'And when the ground was white with
snow,
And I could run and slide,
My brother John was forced to go,
And he lies by her side.'

'How many are you then?' said I,
'If they two are in heaven!'
Quick was the little Maid's reply,
'O Master! we are seven.'

'But they are dead; those two are dead!
Their spirits are in heaven!'
'Twas throwing words away; for still
The little Maid would have her will,
And said, 'Nay, we are seven!'[5]

What features of the analysis tell us that the poem describes the interaction between an adult and a child? What does the matching tell us about the philosophical conflict between the child and the narrator? Whose is the more consistent position? (Look carefully at the matching within the child's first answer before answering this question; also compare verses 9 and 16.)

Notes: Chapter 7

1 The text is taken from *Poetical Works of John Donne*, ed. Sir H. Grierson (London: Oxford University Press, 1933).
2 New English Bible translation.
3 Taken from *Poetry and Prose of William Blake*, ed. G. Keynes (London: Nonesuch, 1961), pp. 76–7.
4 Taken from *Keats: Poetical Works*, ed. H. W. Garrod (London: Oxford University Press, 1973), pp. 350–1.
5 Taken from Wordsworth and Coleridge, *Lyrical Ballads 1805*, ed. D. Roper, 2nd edn (London: Macdonald & Evans, 1976), pp. 72–4.

References: Chapter 7

Hoey, M. (1979), 'Signalling in Discourse', Discourse Analysis Monographs no. 6, English Language Research, University of Birmingham.
Hoey, M. (1983), *On the Surface of Discourse* (London: Allen & Unwin).
Hoey, M., and Winter, E. O. (1981), 'Believe Me for Mine Honour: A Stylistic Analysis of the Speeches of Brutus and Mark Antony at Caesar's Funeral in Julius Caesar from the Point of View of Discourse Construction', *Language and Style*, vol. 14, no. 4, pp. 315–39.
Jordan, M. P. (1978), 'The Principal Semantics of the Nominals "This" and "That" in Contemporary English Writing', PhD. thesis, Council for National Academic Awards, London.
Jordan M. P. (1980), 'Short texts to explain Problem–Solution Structures – and Vice Versa: An Analytical Study of English Prose to Show the Relationship between Clear Writing and Clear Thinking', *Instructional Science*, vol. 9, no. 3, pp. 221–52.
Jordan, M. P. (1984), *Rhetoric of Everyday English Texts* (London: Allen & Unwin).
Milic, T. (1967), *A Quantitative Approach to the Style of Jonathan Swift* (The Hague: Mouton & Co.).
Ohmann, R. (1962), *Shaw: The Style and the Man* (Middletown Coun.: Wesleyan University Press).

Ohmann, R. (1964), 'Generative Grammars and the Concept of Literary Style', *Word*, vol. 20, pp. 424–39.

Sinclair, J., and Coulthard, R. M. (1975), *Towards an Analysis of Discourse: The English used by teachers and pupils* (London: Oxford University Press).

Winter, E. O. (1974), 'Replacement as a Function of Repetition: A Study of Some of its Principal Features in the Clause Relations of Contemporary English', PhD thesis, University of London.

Winter, E. O. (1976), 'Fundamentals of Information Structure: A Pilot Manual for Further Development according to Student Need', mimeo, Hatfield Polytechnic.

Winter, E. O. (1977), 'A Clause-relational Approach to English Texts: A Study of Some Predictive Lexical Items in Written Discourse, *Instructional Science*, vol. 6, no. 1, pp. 1–92.

Winter, E. O. (1979), 'Replacement as a Fundamental Function of the Sentence in Context', *Forum Linguisticum*, vol. 4, no. 2, pp. 95–133.

Winter, E. O. (1983), *Towards a Contextual Grammar of English* (London: Allen & Unwin).

Introduction to Chapter 8

In this the first of three chapters which focus specifically on dialogue, Mick Short offers an overview of the ways in which discourse models may be usefully employed in the analysis of drama texts.

Short begins his chapter by arguing that the drama *text* (rather than the performance) is a valid object of study, but that the analytic apparatus required to study such texts must be radically revised. As drama dialogue conveys implied meanings which go beyond the literal meanings of the words the characters speak, then the model of analysis should be one which can account for these implied meanings. Where traditional textual analysis has failed in this respect, a discourse-oriented approach can succeed, as it focuses on the text as communication within a set of linguistic and non-linguistic conventions. As such, a discourse-stylistic analysis seeks to uncover precisely the sorts of meanings which would elude a traditional stylistic analysis.

Short continues his chapter with a demonstration of the ways in which a variety of techniques can be used fruitfully in the analysis of drama. Among the several major topics in discourse analysis which he covers are the following:

(1) speech acts
(2) presuppositions
(3) the co-operative principle in conversation
(4) terms of address.

In the course of his demonstration, Short provides numerous illustrations of how these categories may be applied to drama dialogue. In addition to this, he develops a schema which highlights the kind of discourse relations that drama exhibits, showing how, for example, one level of discourse is embedded in another.

After his illustrated demonstration, Short goes on to provide a more extended analysis of a drama text. He examines Harold Pinter's short sketch *Trouble in the Works*, drawing on various aspects of the framework he has outlined in the course of the chapter. He shows how an analysis of discourse can lead to a greater understanding of the nature of the 'absurdity' of the play, as well as allowing readers to appreciate the text without having to see it performed. Short concludes his chapter by assessing the wider pedagogical implications of his approach to the study of drama.

8 Discourse Analysis and the Analysis of Drama

MICK SHORT

I Background Remarks

It has become a commonplace of dramatic criticism over the past ten years or so to suggest that the only adequate analysis of drama must be the analysis of performance. In the first part of this chapter I argue that this view is incorrect and that critics should concentrate on dramatic texts. I also argue that this erroneous view has come about partly because of the inability of practical criticism (including traditional stylistic analysis, which has concerned itself mainly with deviation and textual pattern) to cope with the meanings which are produced by dramatic texts. During the whole of this chapter I shall be limiting myself to matters of interpretation only. Those critics who have argued over what the object of dramatic criticism should be have concerned themselves with interpretaton and effects on the audience, sometimes without discriminating sufficiently between these aspects. It is my view that the position that I argue with respect to the interpretation of plays holds good for many audience effects as well; but the substantiation of this position would require separate argumentation, something which is beyond the scope of the present chapter.

II What Should We Study – Text or Performance?

Dramatic critcism of the 1940s, 1950s and 1960s was a text-based study which treated plays rather like poems, analysing metaphors, strands of imagery and so on, often lifting parts of plays (for example, soliloquies) out of context in order to treat them more or less as poems in their own right. It is not surprising that such a criticism arose when we remember that the analysis of poetry was (and still is) the most developed of the Anglo-American critical apparatus. Until very recently there have been ways of analysing in texts what is commonly held to be the stuff of drama, namely the meanings which are said to be implied behind the words that the characters speak, and which are often made apparent to the audience in a theatre by the use of gesture, tone of voice and so on. Necessarily, therefore, these features have only been observable in performance, and this has led many recent critics to suggest that plays can only be properly understood and evaluated on the stage. Hence J. D. Styan tells us that:

> The worst difficulty in thinking about a play is simply to remember that, given words for demonstration on a stage, there is no other *completely* valid means of judging their efficiency and value except within their own terms. Leave your armchair throne of judgement, says Granville-Barker, submit for the while to be tossed to and fro in the action of the play: drama's first aim is to subdue us. (Styan, 1960: 65)

He, like many other critics, distinguished between complete appreciation, which can only go on in the theatre, and a by definition impoverished literary analysis.[1] Talking of Ibsen's *Rosmersholm* he says:

> A 'literary' analysis will tend to confine itself to comments on the theme of the play, and perhaps to a statement about Rebecca's realization of the position she has reached in her understanding of the household. On the stage Ibsen gives us a much larger statement. (Styan, 1960: 18)

The problems which bringing the theatrical experience into the realm of criticism raises are two-fold. First, plays have to be treated in a *radically* different way from other literary works. This means that there can be no coherent discipline called criticism. Second, the object of dramatic criticism becomes infinitely variable. Both meanings and value will change not just from one production to another but also from one performance of a particular production to another. There then becomes no play to criticize. Instead we will have to talk about 'X's production of *Hamlet* performed in theatre Y on the evening of Z', and critical discussion becomes impossible unless the two critics concerned have both seen and are arguing about exactly the same performance.

Luckily there are a number of considerations which suggest that the object of dramatic criticism should not be the theatrical performance:

(1) Teachers and students have traditionally read plays without necessarily seeing them performed and have still managed to understand them and argue about them.
(2) A special case of this is the dramatic producer, who must be able to read and understand a play in order to decide how to produce

it. Such a decision is also crucial because a production of a play is in effect a play plus an interpretation of it, in just the same way that a reading (performance) of a poem must select one of a number of possible interpretations.

(3) There is a logical and terminological distinction between a play and a performance of it. Coming out of the theatre, people can be heard making comments of the form 'that was a good/bad production of a good/bad play'. Morever, this distinction works not just for value judgments about plays and performances but also in terms of whether or not a particular production of a play was a *faithful* one. After a performance of *Hamlet* I once heard one academic tell another that what he had seen was 'good theatre but bad Shakespeare'. In this case, then, both the play and the performance were deemed to be good but the latter was not thought of as being an accurate rendering of the former.

All this does not suggest that critics should never go to the theatre. After all, general knowledge of theatrical conventions is part of the equipment that we have to possess in order to be able to understand this particular universe of discourse; but it does indicate that going to a performance of such and such a play is not a *necessary* condition for understanding it and responding to it sensitively. In other words, we must, as Styan and others have done, distinguish between literary and theatrical analysis but not so that one is deemed to be the poor relation of the other. Literary criticism should take the text as its object of investigation and develop techniques of textual analysis able to cope with the implied aspects of meaning mentioned earlier. Theatrical criticism on the other hand has a perfectly valid area of interest in, for example, comparing different ways of performing the same scene (*a*) in terms of its theatrical effect and (*b*) in terms of its faithfulness to the dramatic text. Literary criticism and theatre studies are distinct areas of study which have overlapping boundaries. Hence the critical analysis of a dramatic text is likely to produce suggestions for performance which would have to be tested in the theatre, and a new performance of a play might well suggest an interpretation which no critic had ever thought of but which could only be evaluated by checking it against the text.

Such a distinction entails a decision not to merge wilfully the contribution of playwright, producer and actor, as some have done. Stanley Wells, for example:

But no matter how detailed the instructions a playwright may give – let him not only be the writer of the play but also the producer, the designer of the sets and costumes, the composer of the music, the choreographer – he remains a participant in an essentially collaborative act. The hints that he gives have to be transmitted to the audience by people other than himself. Other human beings come between his creative effort and the experience of the audience. They may dull it, or they may sharpen it. They may be inefficient trans- mitters, or they may themselves bring to their roles a creative capacity, making it impossible for us to distinguish between the achievements of the writer and of the actor. (Wells, 1970: 7)

Wells produces a number of examples of the kind of merger that he is talking about. What is interesting, however, is that in describing them he is forced to do what he claims is impossible, namely to distinguish between the playwright's and the actor's contribution. For example, he analyses a contemporary account of Irving's utterance of the word 'exactly' while playing Mathias in L. Lewis's *The Bells*. While claming that the contributions of the various people involved are intermingled inextricably, he describes what is very obviously Irving's contribution alone, and concludes by saying:

When we have said that with Irving as Mathias it was successful we have acknowledged that the writer is only one of the team that is necessary to make a good play. We have admitted that Leopold Lewis wrote a script that, with a genius in the main role, provided an absorbing theatrical experience. We have not suggested that what he wrote has any literary value, or that it should have any intrinsic interest for later generations. It happened that Irving came upon a script that suited his talents peculiarly well; and the result has passed into thea- trical history. (Wells, 1970: 16–17)

It is quite apparent that the latter part of this quotation belies the first. Although it takes a team to perform a play, it takes only one person to write it.

I suspect that many readers will by now have decided that I have given the game away by my constant reference to the dramatic *text*, and that the problem with textual analysis is that it does not get at many of the meanings that people perceive in plays. No amount of textual analysis will enable one to capture the significance felt in the theatre when Hamlet produces his crushing reply to Polonius:

Polonius: What do you read, my lord?
Hamlet: Words, words, words. (II, ii, 190–1)

It is precisely this kind of meaning which must be accounted for, and it can only be done by regarding the text in a less impoverished light than that in which it has previously been held.

Much of the blame here must lie at the door of the New Critics, who have tended to make us all believe that texts are merely verbal objects.

But it should be apparent on reflection that no text can be just this. To understand the meaning of a word in a poem one needs to know its normal meaning, the significance of its particular position in its syntactic construction and so on. In other words a text can only be understood as an object embedded within a set of linguistic (and other – for example, sociological, literary) conventions. One of the most important sets of linguistic conventions for interpretation are those which govern language use. For instance, we generally assume that one should answer questions relevantly and with a degree of information appropriate to one's interlocutor. Thus, if my young daughter comes into my study while I am writing a lecture and asks me how to make butter, I might reasonably reply by telling her to put some cream into a bottle and shake it until it solidifies. If I reply 'buy a cow' I am giving insufficient and non-relevant information and will probably be interpreted as being offhand. She may well therefore conclude that I don't want to be disturbed. Similar kinds of consideration apply to the quotation from Hamlet above. Hamlet answers Polonius's question by stating the obvious. He has therefore not given the old man an appropriate reply, and, given our experience of the play so far, we are likely to conclude that Hamlet is being rude to Polonius in order to get rid of him, or that he is trying to feign madness. Further contextual considerations will then have to be taken into account to enable us to choose between the possible alternatives. This in effect means treating the text as a series of communicative acts, not just as a configuration of phonetic, syntactic and lexical patterns. This is what I suggest that the sensitive reader does when he reads a play in any case. It is only by applying such criteria that he can judge the significance of Hamlet's reply to Polonius. The important point to note is that we do not have to see the play in order to understand Hamlet's words and their significance. But what dramatic criticism does need is a way of explaining how these meanings are arrived at. And it is recent developments within discourse analysis, I would claim, that allow one to begin to do just this, hence rescuing dramatic criticism from the variability of performance analysis on the one hand and the inadequacy of traditional textual analysis on the other.

III   Discourse Analysis and its Application to Dramatic Texts

Recent developments in discourse analysis are now fairly familiar, and as the main aim of what follows is to show how that analysis can be applied to dramatic texts the description of each type of analysis will be relatively brief and informal. For those not familiar with a particular approach, references to more expanded treatments are given at appropriate points in the text.

(i)   Speech Acts

The theory of speech acts (Austin, 1962; Searle 1965, 1969) has drawn attention to the fact that when we produce various utterances we actually *do* things. Thus when A says to B 'I promise to bring it tomorrow', under normal circumstances A actually makes a promise. In this case the action is made obvious by the presence of the performative verb 'promise'. However, 'I will bring it tomorrow' can also be a promise, given the right contextual circumstances. The introduction of context is important because it is this (what Searle, 1969: Ch. 3, calls *preparatory and sincerity conditions*) which helps us to capture the important observation that the same sentence may in different circumstances perform different acts. Thus 'I will bring it tomorrow' is a promise when the action mentioned is beneficial to B and when A knows this. If it is obviously not of benefit then the speech act status changes to that of a threat or warning – where it is a court summons, for example. Given general knowledge about the world, it is often possible to deduce the speech act status from the utterance alone. Hence 'I'll kick your face in' and 'I'll bring you tea in bed' are unlikely to be thought of as having the same speech act status (although they *could*, of course, given knowledge of very special contextual circumstances). This is dramatically important at the beginnings of plays and when new characters are introduced, as it allows us immediately to grasp important social relations. Thus when Jonson's *The Alchemist* opens with:

Face:	Believ't I will.
Subtle:	Thy worst. I fart at thee.
Dol Common:	Ha' you your wits? Why, gentlemen! for love –
Face:	Sirrah, I'll strip you – (I, i, 1–4)

it is quite apparent, even without the stage direction that tells us so, that Face and Subtle are quarrelling, because they are abusing and threatening each other. On stage the actors would have to produce appropriate actions and tone of voice, which might be actualized in a number of different ways. But the intended meaning and effect are clear from the text and general knowledge (for example, that being stripped is usually unpleasant) alone. The fact that Face and Subtle are threatening each other also allows us to deduce that they are of roughly equal social status. A servant cannot, given normal circumstances, threaten a master. If he does so in play, it signals a change in their relationship.

Commands, like threats, are not accessible to all of the participants in a particular speech situation and therefore also mark clear social relationships. One of the most obvious examples is the first entrance of Lucky and Pozzo in Beckett's *Waiting for Godot*, where the master–servant relationship is marked before Pozzo even appears on the stage:

Enter Pozzo and Lucky, Pozzo drives Lucky by means of a rope passed round his neck, so that Lucky is the first to appear, followed by the rope which is long enough to allow him to reach the middle of the stage before Pozzo appears. Lucky carries a heavy bag, a folding stool, picnic basket and a greatcoat. Pozzo a whip.

Pozzo: (*Off.*) On! (*Crack of whip. Pozzo appears.*)[2]

This is also a good example of the prescribed visual and verbal aspects supporting each other to reinforce the significance of the deduction that one makes.

The felicity conditions that have been explored so far have all concerned factors prior to the speech event. But Searle notes that post-conditions also apply. Thus, if you make a promise and then fail to carry it out, you have broken that promise (unless outside circumstances have prevented you). At the end of each act of *Waiting for Godot* Vladimir and Estragon make an agreement, which on both occasions they fail to carry out:

Vladimir: Well, shall we go?
Estragon: Yes, Let's go.
              (*They do not move*) (p. 94)

It is the fact that they agree to go and then do not which the critic has to explain. Presumably they either wilfully break agreements, in which case the value of agreeing in their world is different from ours, or they are prevented from doing what they want by some unknown internal or external force. Which way one jumps interpretatively will depend upon other information. For example, the fact that Pozzo also has difficulty in leaving when he apparently intends to is likely to incline us to the second of the two types of possibility outlined above. What is important to note here is that it is our knowledge of the normal production of speech acts which allows us to deduce contextual information when that production is apparently normal and which also allows us to perceive deviant speech act production and interpret it. (For a discussion of the status of speech acts in fiction, see Searle, 1975*a*.)

(ii) Presuppositions

The work on presuppositions within both linguistics and philosophy is assuming voluminous proportions, and there is considerable dispute as to how to analyse and categorize them. See, for example, Keenan (1971), Kempson (1975) and Leech (1974). It will be noted that presuppositions often form part of the preconditions for the felicitous production of speech acts. Here I wish to discuss three overlapping kinds of presupposition: existential, linguistic and pragmatic. They are distinguished as useful categories for textual analysis rather than because they are theoretically distinct. Debate on the kinds of presupposition is still inconclusive. For Kempson (1975) and Wilson (1975), for example, all presuppositions are pragmatic.

The notion of *existential presupposition* was first developed by Strawson (1952) to cope with the philosophical question whether statements like 'The present king of France is wise' could be deemed to be true or false. He claimed that such a sentence presupposed that the king of France existed and therefore could only have a truth value when the presupposition was true. In fictions there are of course many sentences which have false presuppositions; while we experience such fictions, we conventionally assume that such presuppositions are true, and it is this convention amongst others that allows us to 'enter into' the world of the novel or play. Thus when, at the beginning of Marlow's play, Faustus says:

How I am glutted with conceit of this!
Shall I make spirits fetch me what I please,
Resolve me of all ambiguities,
Perform what desperate enterprise I will?
I'll have them fly to India for gold . . . (*Doctor Faustus*, I, i, 77–81)

we conventionally enter into a world where spirits exist, in spite of the fact that we may not believe in such things at all. 'Spirits' in this quotation can be interpreted as non-referential, as it is generic and occurs in an interrogative sentence. But 'them' in the last line of the quotation does have definite reference, and co-refers to 'spirits'.

Once the world of the play is established we expect to see and hear things consistent with that world. Inconsistencies produce a jarring which the critic is likely to explain either by ascribing demerit to the work or by changing his mind as to the kind of work in front of him. Arguably, the first obvious indication of the absurd nature of *Waiting for Godot* involves a clash between the existential presuppositions held by us and those held by one of the characters. On the first page, Vladimir turns to Estragon saying 'So there you are again', and Estragon replies by asking 'Am I?' Here Estragon challenges a presupposition, namely that he exists, that we assume he must hold.[3]

The distinction which Strawson makes between what a sentence asserts and what it presupposes is useful for explaining the communicative effect of much embedded material in English sentences. Thus the sentence 'The man that I met yesterday is ill' 'contains' two propositions:

(1)   I met a man yesterday

and
(2)   The man that I met yesterday is ill.

The sentence presupposes (1) and asserts (2). These clauses or phrases which are embedded in sentences in this manner may be said to contain *linguistic presuppositions*. There are, of course, other presuppositions in the sentence besides 'I met a man yesterday', for example, that the man exists. Indeed in theoretical terms existential presuppositions are probably best treated as a subset of linguistic presuppositions. I have treated them as a separate category above because of their interesting role in the establishment of fictions. Because the information structure of sentences is arranged so that one is invited to challenge what a sentence asserts rather than what it presupposes, writers of persuasive prose sometimes place rather dubious propositions in the presupposed parts of sentences (for example in nominalized or relative clauses) in order to dupe their audience into accepting them without thinking. In plays such presuppositions are often used to establish the world of the play, and in absurd drama much of the absurdity can come from a clash between presuppositions held by the characters and those held by the audience. Hence, in N. F. Simpson's *One Way Pendulum*, Mrs Groomkirby says:

> If you were to do your proper share of the eating between you, instead of leaving it all to me, I shouldn't have to have Mrs Gantry in anything like so often. (*Pause*) Paying out good money all the time. (*Pause*) If it weren't for your father's parking meters we just shouldn't be able to run it. Then we should *have* to get it eaten ourselves.[4]

Mrs Groomkirby's third sentence presupposes that her husband owns a string of parking meters from which he gains revenue. Her assumption goes unchallenged by the other characters and therefore is presumably shared by them. However, it is obviously at odds with the presuppositions which we as onlookers hold. In our world parking meters are only owned by town councils and the like. But perhaps the most astounding feature of this quotation is Mrs Groomkirby's remarks about eating. The noun phrase 'your proper share of the eating' presupposes that eating is a chore to be shared by the whole family. This presupposition in concert with other assumptions allows us to take part in a complex and crazy chain of inference whereby we deduce that all food has to be eaten, and that you have to pay a professional to finish up what you cannot finish. Presumably, without Mr Groomkirby's parking meters they would not have been able to buy the food that they have to get rid of, let alone pay Mrs Gantry to eat it!

The term 'pragmatic' is usually reserved for presuppositions relating to immediate context and immediate social relations. Hence a command like 'shut the door' presuppposes that the speaker is in a social relation to the hearer such that he is able to order him to do things. The preconditions for the production of the threats in the extract from *The Alchemist* discussed above are obvious examples of *pragmatic presuppositions*. Another interesting example comes from the first scene of *King Lear*, where Lear as king is in an obvious position of authority. Kent continually tries to intercede on Cordelia's behalf, thus using his status as adviser. Lear slaps him down on each occasion, forcing Kent to produce more and more obvious intercessions, ranging from mere vocatives like 'good my liege' through questions and opposing statements and finally to the very explicit commands and warnings which provoke his banishment:

> *Kent:* Revoke thy gift,
> Or, whilst I can vent clamour from my throat
> I'll tell thee thou dost evil.
> *Lear:* Hear me recreant
> . . . if, on the tenth day following
> Thy banish'd trunk be found in our dominions,
> The moment is thy death . . . (I, i, 164–78)

Each time Kent tries to protect Cordelia he is prevented. This forces him to use speech acts carrying pragmatic presuppositions (reinforced by the insulting use of *thee*) which assume social relations more and more at odds with those that in fact exist, until the role relations become apparently almost reversed. It is at this point that Lear finally banishes him.

(iii)   General Discourse Relations

The canonical form of a communicative event is one in which one person addresses and gives information to another (see Fig. 8.1).

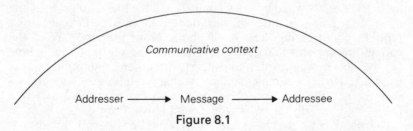

Communicative context

Addresser ⟶ Message ⟶ Addressee

Figure 8.1

In a conversation the two participants continually exchange roles, and it is easy to think of situations which deviate from this basic form in some way. For example the addresser and addressee may be the same (a diary), there might be one addresser and many addressees (a lecture), the addresser and addressees may be physically and temporally separated (a recorded party political broadcast) and so on. However, these situations are all variations in some way on the basic format. Drama shares this base form, but like many texts it has a structure whereby one level of discourse is embedded in another. Sometimes one is tempted to characterize play-going as a situation in which we 'overhear' the talk between the characters. But the situation of drama is unlike that of eavesdropping because it is arranged to be overheard on purpose (see Fig. 8.2).

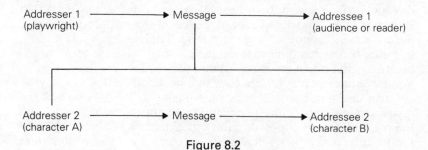

Figure 8.2

Character speaks to character, and this discourse is part of what the playwright 'tells' the audience. Any play will consist of a series of such embedded discourses, and there can be even more layers, as when one character reports to another the words of a third. But the important thing to notice is the general *embedded* nature of drama, because features which, for example, mark social relations between two people at the character level become messages *about* the characters at the level of discourse which pertains between author and reader/audience. Hence the ability of Pozzo to command Lucy is something which is taken as given between them but is important information *about* them for the critic. When relations change, as in the Kent/Lear example, there is a message conveyed between the two characters, namely that Kent is challenging Lear's authority, and this message is the same at the author/reader level. The assumptions which the characters share in *One Way Pendulum* are presumably not thought of as odd by the characters. But the fact that they clash with our assumptions in a play world which at first sight appears to be isomorphous with our own itself constitutes one of a number of accumulated messages which Simpson is giving us about the world in which his characters live. It should be apparent that this embedded model of discourse has been tacitly assumed in the discussion so far. It becomes even more obviously relevant when one examines Grice's notion of the co-operative principle.

(iv)   The Co-operative Principle in Conversation

Grice (1975) is one of the first attempts to account for meaning as it develops in conversation. To this end he distinguishes between what a sentence means and what someone means by uttering that sentence. Hence in the following possible dialogue:

A: Did you enjoy the play?
B: Well, I thought the ice creams they sold in the interval were good.

it is quite apparent that B is saying in an indirect and therefore relatively polite way that he did not enjoy the play, even though he does not actually say so. In ordinary language terms we might say that B implied that he did not like the play even though he did not say so. In order to avoid confusion over the term 'imply', which has a more technical use within philosophical logic, Grice coins the term 'implicature' for this kind of indirect, context-determined meaning. Hence, in the above example, B *implicates* that he did not enjoy the play.

Grice distinguishes first between what he calls *conventional* and *conversational* implicature. Conventional implicature has to do with the conventional as opposed to the logical meaning of certain words, particularly connectors. Hence, if someone says 'She comes from Oxford, so she must be a snob', the word *so* apparently makes an implicative relation between coming from Oxford and being a snob, in spite of the fact that when asked the speaker is hardly likely to want to say that *everyone* from Oxford is a snob.

An interesting example of the use of conventional implicature comes from Act III of Oscar Wilde's *The Importance of Being Earnest*. Jack is trying to persuade Lady Bracknell of the eligibility of Cecily Cardew:

Jack: Miss Cardew's family solicitors are Messrs. Markby, Markby and Markby.
Lady Bracknell: Markby, Markby and Markby? A firm of the very highest position in their profession. Indeed I am told that one of the Mr Markbys is occasionally to be seen at dinner parties. So far I am satisfied. (III, 139–44)

The sentence relating one of the Mr Markby's presence at dinner parties is obviously meant to be a reason for suggesting that the firm is 'of the very highest in their profession'. This is apparent from Lady Bracknell's use of the adverb 'indeed'. For *her*, someone's professional reputation can be judged by which table he sits at. However, this is unlikely to be the case for the audience and the use of 'indeed' points up the ironic contrast between us and her.

The distinction between what one says and what one means is also apparent in conversational implicature, where inferred interpretations cannot be ascribed to the conventional meanings of words like *so* and *indeed*. In explanation of this kind of meaning Grice claims that people entering into conversation with each other tacitly agree to co-operate towards mutual communicative ends, thus obeying the co-operative principle and its regulative conventions. He calls these conventions maxims, and has suggested that at least the following four obtain:

(1) *the maxim of quantity:* make your contribution as informative as is required – don't give too much or too little information;
(2) *the maxim of quality:* make your contribution one that you believe to be true;
(3) *the maxim of relation:* be relevant;
(4) *the maxim of manner*: avoid unnecessary prolixity, obscurity of expression and ambiguity, and be orderly.

Maxims are not, however, as strongly regulative as grammatical rules, and are therefore broken quite often. Grice outlines four such cases:

(i) A speaker may unostentatiously *violate* a maxim; this accounts for lies and deceits.
(ii) He may *opt out* of the co-operative principle, as, for example, members of government do when they refuse to answer questions on the ground that the information required is classified.
(iii) He may be faced with a *clash*, and will have therefore to break one maxim or another.
(iv) He may ostentatiously *flout* a maxim, so that it is apparent to his interlocutors.

It is under the final specification that conversational implicature occurs. Hence in the dialogue between A and B cited above, where maxims (1), (3) and (4) are broken, it is quite apparent to A that B could answer directly, relevantly and more economically whether or not he enjoyed the play. A assumes that B is still obeying the co-operative principle and that B knows that he will assume this. Given this set of assumptions, A then works out the implicature, namely that B did not enjoy the play but does not want to say so in a direct and relatively impolite way.

At this stage in the development of the theory it is by no means clear how much conversational meaning can be accounted for in this way, or how it fits in exactly with linguistic theory as a whole. Searle's (1975b) suggestion that the rules for conversational implicature form merely a subset of a set of rules and procedures for the specification of what he calls 'indirect speech acts' looks promising. Both Grice and Searle insist that implicatures must be derivable from an informal set of step-by-step inferences, and there appears to be much conversational meaning which cannot yet be adequately accounted for in this way. But it should be apparent that even the initial work in this area has considerable relevance for the study of literary texts in general and dramatic texts in particular (for other initial suggestions in this area see Tanaka, 1972; Pratt, 1977 chs 4, 5). Hamlet's reply of 'Words, words, words' to Polonius is an obvious flouting of the maxim of quantity, as it merely gives Polonius information which he patently already possesses. The flouting of the maxim of quantity often seems to be rude, as can be seen from the first scene of *Romeo and Juliet*, where Gregory and Sampson are picking a quarrel with Abraham and Balthasar:

> Abraham: Do you bite your thumb at us, sir?
> Sampson: I do bite my thumb, sir. (I, i, 43–4)

It is arguable that Sampson's reply breaks the maxim of relation as well, and the repetition and parallelism also help mark the aggression. But what is important to notice here is that Shakespeare exploits the co-operative principle to help establish very quickly indeed the state of near war between the Capulets and Montagues. Incidentally, Shakespeare uses a similar tactic later on in the scene to mark the offhand way in which Romeo treats Benvolio's anxious inquiries about him:

> Benvolio: Tell me in sadness, who is it that you love
> Romeo   In sadness cousin, I do love a woman. (I, i, 203, 207)

As Grice (1975: 52) himself says, one obvious kind of example of the breaking of the maxim of quality is the phenomenon of metaphor:

> Romeo: If I profane with my unworthiest hand
>   This holy shrine, the gentle sin is this:
>   My lips, two blushing pilgrims, ready stand
>   To smooth that rough touch with a tender kiss. (I, v, 95–8)

Juliet's hand is self-evidently not a holy shrine; but, by stating that it is, Romeo can implicate his respect and devotion. Similarly his lips are not two blushing pilgrims, but Juliet and the audience can easily infer his intention to reinforce his statement of quasi-religious love.

An example of the breaking of the maxim of relation can be seen in Tom Stoppard's *Enter a Free Man*:

> Riley: (sharply)   Give me that tape.
> Brown: I haven't got one!
> Riley: My patience is not inexhaustible![5]

Brown explicitly rejects the presupposition contained in Riley's first utterance that he has got a tape. Riley interprets this as being an avoidance strategy, and in effect threatens him when he says: 'My patience is not inexhaustible'. We infer that this is a threat because Riley's statement about his patience, although not strictly relevant to the conversation at this point, can be interpreted as an indication that an important pre-condition for violent action on his part, namely the losing of his temper, is about to be fulfilled. Riley's statement also breaks the maxim of manner because of its indirect, double negative form. Interestingly enough, if the *indeed* was removed from the Oscar Wilde example quoted above, the ironic contrast between the workings of our world and Lady Bracknell's would still be apparent. It is thus possible that Grice's category of conventional implicature is really a special, explicit case of the maxim of relation. This maxim is also problematical in other ways, because it is sometimes difficult to determine if it is broken when a speaker tries to change the topic of a conversation. Consider, for example, the following interchange in Act I of Robert Bolt's *A Man For All Seasons*. More and his daughter are talking just after the exit of Roper:

> Margaret: You're very gay. Did he talk about the divorce?
> More: Mm? You know I think we've been on the wrong track with Will – It's no good arguing with a Roper –
> Margaret: Father, did he?
> More: *Old* Roper was just the same. Now let him think he's going *with* the swim and he'll turn around and start swimming in the opposite direction . . .[6]

It is quite apparent that More wants to change the subject in order not to talk about the royal divorce and hence refuses to answer Margaret's questions. She, on the other hand, is anxious to know what happened, and therefore makes her second question unrelatable to his utterance by echoing her first question. More avoids it. Do implicatures pass *between the characters* here, are they just ignoring each other's contribution in order to gain topic control, or are both of these things happening? The possible ambiguity arises partly because of the embedded nature of dramatic discourse. What is an implicature for us, the audience is not necessarily one for More's addressee. Does More want Margaret to realize his intention or not? Conversational structures where one or more participants more or less ignore each other's contributions have been noted by Sacks, for example. In the extract below, Roger and Jim are battling for control of the topic of conversation by relating their utterances not to the immediately previous one but to the last but one. It is not at all obvious, in spite of the fact that some of the utterances are not relevant to the previous one, that implicatures are being passed:

> *Roger:*   Isn't the New Pike depressing?
> *Ken:*   Hh. The Pike?
> *Roger:*   Yeah! Oh the place is disgusting. ⌈Any day of the week
> *Jim:*   ⌊I think that
>   P.O.P. is ⌈depressing it's just –
> *Roger:*   ⌊But you go – you go – take
> *Jim:*   Those guys are losing money.
> *Roger:*   But you go down-dow, down to the New Pike . . . (quoted by
>   Coulthard, 1977: 78)

This phenomenon, which it is claimed is fairly common in ordinary conversation, has been termed 'skip connecting' (see Coulthard, 1977: 78–9).

For some reason it is fairly difficult to find clear examples of the flouting of the maxim of manner, especially in isolation. Another extract from *A Man For All Seasons* is particularly interesting, however. Norfolk is quizzing Rich in Act II about the cup which More gave to Rich in Act I, and which Cromwell wants to use as evidence of More accepting bribes:

> *Norfolk:*   When did Thomas give you this thing?
> *Rich:*   I don't exactly remember.
> *Norfolk:*   Well, make an effort. Wait! I can tell you! I can tell you – it
>   was that Spring – it was that night we were together. You
>   had a cup with you when we left; was that it?
>   (*Rich looks to Cromwell for guidance but gets none.*)
> *Rich:*   It may have been.
> *Norfolk:*   Did he often give you cups?
> *Rich:*   I don't suppose so, Your Grace. (p. 60)

First, it should be noted that this text contains examples of someone unostentatiously breaking the maxim of quality. Rich does not want to admit the details of the gift to Norfolk. But his replies are also more indirect than they need be. The modification of 'I don't remember' by 'exactly' and the use of 'I don't suppose so' are obvious examples. Rich's purpose in breaking the maxim of manner is not to convey implicatures to Norfolk. Quite the contrary. But at the higher level of discourse Bolt demonstrates to his audience/reader Rich's discomfiture in attempting to conceal the truth.

(v)   More General Discourse Relations

A number of categories discussed so far (for example, speech acts and pragmatic presuppositions) are relevant to the explication of social relations, which is of much importance to the study of drama. Another fruitful area is the sociolinguistic study of status and terms of address. As is pointed out in Brown and Gilman (1960: 253–60), the 'T/V distinction' (for example, *tu/vous* in French) is used not just to account for singular and plural but also to indicate nearness or remoteness in social relations. This then gives rise to the possibility of productive stylistic use of such categories to indicate swift variation of attitude along the closeness/remoteness scale. Interesting early examples of the discussion of such variation (using *thee* and *thou*) in Shakespeare can be found in Mulholland (1967) and Quirk (1974).

Closely related to the use of the pronoun system is the exploitation of the naming system. The sociolinguistic use of terms of address in American English has been ably described by Ervin-Tripp (1969). The rules for British English are slightly different and just as complex. But some simple examples will suffice here. Title plus last name and *Sir* plus first name can be used by people of inferior status when addressing social superiors. Last name alone is used by close equals or by people of superior status to well known inferiors. In fact the situation is rather more complex than the above description suggests, but this general level of analysis will be sufficient to show how the social relations between More and the steward are marked at the beginning of *A Man For All Seasons:*

> *More:* The wine, please, Matthew.
> *Steward:* It's there, Sir Thomas. (p. 2)

It is also interesting to note in this respect that Lady Britomart, when talking to her son at the beginning of Shaw's *Major Barbara*, uses the first-name vocative 'Stephen' in eight out of her first nine utterances and 'my dear boy' in the other. This consistent usage in conjunction with other features, such as the frequent use of commands, demonstrates the complete dominance of Lady Britomart over her son, and contributes markedly to the comedy when she says a few lines later 'Stephen, may I ask you how soon you intend to realise that you are a grown-up man, and that I am only a woman?'[7] Other factors which indicate the dominance relation at the beginning of *Major Barbara* are who speaks first, and hence initiates the exchanges, and who speaks the most.

One strange use of the pronoun system in English is the reference to people present in the speech situation by the third-person pronoun. This occurs where it is assumed by the interlocutors that some other person is of such an inferior status as to debar him from making a reasonable contribution. One example is the way in which many parents talk over their children; another is where interlocutors talk about people with disabilities as if they were not there, even in situations where the disability involved may not actually impair the ability to contribute to the conversation at all. This rather bizarre usage has been ably demonstrated by the ironic title of a radio series for the blind on BBC Radio 4, *Does He Take Sugar*? Productive use of this kind of feature is also made in *Romeo and Juliet*, when Capulet indicates his anger at his daughter's refusal to marry Paris by asking questions about her as if she were not there:

> Capulet: Soft! Take me with you, take me with you, wife.
> How will she none? Doth she not give us thanks?
> Is she not proud? Doth she not count her blest,
> Unworthy as she is, that we have wrought
> So worthy a gentleman to be her bridegroom? (III, v, 141–5)

An interesting preliminary attempt to apply general discourse analysis to Shakespeare is Coulthard's discussion (1977: 170–81) of *Othello*.

IV   'Trouble in the Works'

So far in this chapter I have given illustrative examples of the ways in which discourse analysis can help explain meanings which we intuitively perceive in dramatic texts. However, a better sense of its use can be gained from a more extended analysis. To this end I now turn to an examination of a complete short text, a sketch by Harold Pinter called *Trouble in the Works*. For ease of reference the full text is given below along with sentence numbering. Given the limitations of space, my treatment of the text can only be relatively superficial. A full analysis would have to be more systematic than that which appears below, and would need to be supplemented by a full stylistic analysis of the more traditional kind.

> (*An office in a factory.*(1) *Mr Fibbs at the desk.*(2) *A knock at the door.*(3) *Enter Mr Wills.*(4))

> Fibbs: Ah, Wills.(5) Good.(6) Come in.(7) Sit down will you?(8)
> Wills: Thanks, Mr Fibbs.(9)
> Fibbs: You got my message?(10)
> Wills: I just got it.(11)
> Fibbs: Good.(12) Good.(13)
> (*Pause.*(14))
> Good.(15) Well now . . .(16) Have a cigar?(17)
> Wills: No, thanks, not for me, Mr Fibbs.(18)
> Fibbs: Well, now, Wills, I hear there's been a little trouble in the factory.(19)
> Wills: Yes, I . . . I suppose you could call it that, Mr Fibbs.(20)
> Fibbs: Well, what in heaven's name is it all about?(21)
> Wills: Well, I don't exactly know how to put it, Mr Fibbs.(22)
> Fibbs: Now come on, Wills. I've got to know what it is, before I can do anything about it.(23)

Wills: Well, Mr Fibbs, it's simply a matter that the men have . . . well, they seem to have taken a turn against some of the products.(24)

Fibbs: Taken a turn?(25)

Wills: They just don't seem to like them much any more.(26)

Fibbs: Don't like them?(27) But we've got the reputation of having the finest machine part turnover in the country.(28) They're the best paid men in the industry.(29) We've got the cheapest canteen in Yorkshire.(30) No two menus are alike.(31) We've got a billiard hall, haven't we, on the premises, we've got a swimming pool for the use of staff.(32) And what about the long-playing record room?(33) And you tell me they're dissatisfied?(34)

Wills: Oh, the men are very grateful for all the amenities, sir.(35) They just don't like the products.(36)

Fibbs: But they're beautiful products.(37) I've been in the business a lifetime.(38) I've never seen such beautiful products.(39)

Wills: There it is, sir.(40)

Fibbs: Which ones don't they like?(41)

Wills: Well, there's the brass pet cock, for instance.(42)

Fibbs: The brass pet cock?(43) What's the matter with the brass pet cock?(44)

Wills: They just don't seem to like it any more.(45)

Fibbs: But what exactly don't they like about it?(46)

Wills: Perhaps it's just the look of it.(47)

Fibbs: That brass pet cock?(48) But I tell you it's perfection.(49) Nothing short of perfection.(50)

Wills: They've just gone right off it.(51)

Fibbs: Well, I'm flabbergasted.(52)

Wills: It's not only the brass pet cock, Mr Fibbs.(53)

Fibbs: What else?(54)

Wills: There's the hemi unibal spherical rod end.(55)

Fibbs: The hemi unibal spherical rod end?(56) But where could you find a finer rod end?(57)

Wills: There are rod ends and rod ends, Mr Fibbs.(58)

Fibbs: I know there are rod ends and rod ends.(59) But where could you find a finer hemi unibal spherical rod end?(60)

Wills: They just don't want to have anything more to do with it.(61)

Fibbs: This is shattering.(62) Shattering.(63) What else?(64) Come on Wills.(65) There's no point in hiding anything from me.(66)

Wills: Well, I hate to say it, but they've gone very vicious about the high speed taper shank spiral flute reamers.(67)

Fibbs: The high speed taper shank spiral flute reamers!(68) But that's absolutely ridiculous!(69) What could they possibly have against the high speed taper shank spiral flute reamers?(70)

Wills: All I can say is they're in a state of very bad agitation about them.(71) And then there's the gunmetal side outlet relief with handwheel.(72)

Fibbs: What!(73)
Wills: There's the nippled connector and the nippled adapter and the vertical mechanical comparator.(74)
Fibbs: No!(75)
Wills: And the one they can't speak about without trembling is the jaw for Jacob's chuck for use on portable drill.(76)
Fibbs: My own Jacob's chuck?(77) Not my very own Jacob's chuck?(78)
Wills: They've just taken a turn against the whole lot of them, I tell you.(79) Male elbow adaptors, tubing nuts, grub screws, internal fan washers, dog points, half dog points, white metal bushes – (80)
Fibbs: But not, surely not, my lovely parallel male stud couplings.(81)
Wills: They hate and detest your lovely parallel male stud couplings, and the straight flange pump connectors, and back nuts, and front nuts, *and* the bronzedraw off cock with handwheel and the bronzedraw off cock without handwheel!(82)
Fibbs: Not the bronzedraw off cock with handwheel?(83)
Wills: And without handwheel.(84)
Fibbs: Without handwheel?(85)
Wills.   And with handwheel.(86)
Fibbs: Not with handwheel?(87)
Wills: And without handwheel.(88)
Fibbs: Without handwheel?(89)
Wills: With handwheel *and* without handwheel.(90)
Fibbs: With handwheel *and* without handwheel?(91)
Wills: With or without!(92)
          (*Pause.*(93))
Fibbs: (*Broken*) Tell me.(94) What do they want to make in its place?(95)
Wills: Brandy balls.(96)[8]

I once saw this sketch performed by a student group. At the beginning of the scene Fibbs, the manager, was seated in a swivel chair at a large desk on a raised dais and dressed in a three piece suit. When Wills sat down it was on a small chair in front of the desk and below the dais. As the sketch progressed the two men got up and moved clockwise round the desk, so that at the end Fibbs was in Wills's seat and vice versa. This aspect of the staging was obviously designed to bring out one of the sketch's main characteristics, namely that by the end the role relations which have been established at the beginning of the piece, and which normally pertain between employer and worker, have been reversed. This in turn contributes to the second characteristic which I intend to explicate, the sketch's patently absurd nature.

The role relations of the two characters will be marked on stage by their dress, seating position etc. But even on a reading of the sketch, they are easily perceived from the beginning. First, they are indicated by the vocatives. Fibbs always uses last name only, whereas Wills uses either title plus last name or 'sir'. In the first part of the sketch Fibbs speaks first and initiates the conversational exchanges (see Coulthard, 1977: 95–6). He also uses the speech acts of commanding and questioning, which correlate with the pragmatic presupposition that he is socially superior to Wills. Wills, for his part, at the beginning of the piece answers the questions exactly, producing no extra comments of his own, uses lexical items introduced by Fibbs rather than bringing in his own, and does not initiate new topics (cf. the pregnant pause (14)).

When Fibbs asks Wills the cause of the trouble it is quite apparent that Wills is distinctly uneasy about telling his boss:

> *Fibbs:* Well, now, Wills, I hear there's been a little trouble in the factory.(19)
> *Wills:* Yes, I . . . I suppose you could call it that, Mr Fibbs.(20)
> *Fibbs:* Well, what in heaven's name is it all about?(21)
> *Wills:* Well, I don't exactly know how to put it, Mr Fibbs.(22)
> *Fibbs:* Now come on, Wills, I've got to know what it is, before I can do anything about it.(23)
> *Wills:* Well, Mr Fibbs, it's simply a matter that the men have . . . well, they seem to have taken a turn against some of the products.(24)

Will's unease is indicated largely by his flouting of the maxim of manner. In sentence 20 he might have replied with 'Yes', but that would have broken the maxim of quality, as there has obviously been more than a little trouble. Instead, he uses the modal verb 'could' (which allows the possibility of *couldn't*) embedded under the non-factive 'suppose'. In 22 he breaks both manner and relation. In 24 he hesitates and has to reformulate his sentence, and then gives the essential information that the men have 'taken a turn' against some of the products, embedded under another non-factive, 'seem'. This circumlocution allied to the use of 'seem' is also used in 26 and 45.

The turn-around in relations in the sketch occurs as Fibbs discovers how intransigent the men are towards the products he is so attached to. This takes place gradually in the middle of the sketch. I therefore want to suggest a division of the text into three main sections, corresponding approximately to the following sentence numbers: I = 1–35; II = 36–71; III = 72–96. In terms of numbers of sentences these sections are roughly equal. The first shows Fibbs dominant over Wills and exhibits all of the features outlined above, the third shows Wills dominant over Fibbs, and the second provides the mediation for the change. I have selected sentence 36 as the hinge point between sections I and II because it is here that Wills initiates a conversational exchange for the first time in the sketch. First he replies to Fibbs's question and then he adds a new comment, taking the subject back to that of his previous utterance(26). In so doing, he also denies the presupposition in Fibbs's question, namely that employees cannot be dissatisfied if they have good amenities. Section II shows the two men exchanging control of the conversation. Fibbs takes back the initiative in 41, Wills attempts to take control in 53, Fibbs takes it back in 54, and so on. Section III, on the other hand, is marked by the fact that from the point at which Wills takes back the initiative in 72 he never loses it. As the sketch progresses through this last section Wills's lexis also becomes dominant, so that at the end, in the sequence about the bronzedraw off cock with and without handwheel, Fibbs, in his disbelief, merely repeats the main part of Wills's previous utterance. The last section is also completely denuded of vocatives marking their 'official' status relations. If we compare the density of status-marking vocatives in sections I and II we find that in section I there are five instances of 'Mr Fibbs', one occasion where Wills calls Fibbs 'sir', and three occasions where Fibbs uses 'Wills' – i.e. there is a status-marking vocative once very three and a half sentences. In section II there are two instances of 'Mr Fibbs', one of 'sir' and none of 'Wills' – i.e. one every ten sentences. Section III has none at all. We have already noticed that the conversational initiative changes hands relatively often only in the middle section. Hence there is a fairly gradual change in the relations exhibited between the two men. It is also interesting to note in this respect that as the middle section develops Wills breaks the maxim of manner less and less, becoming more and more direct in his replies. The battle for dominance can be neatly illustrated in sentences 55–61.

Wills:	There's the hemi unibal spherical rod end.(55)
Fibbs:	The hemi unibal spherical rod end?(56) Where could you find a finer rod end?(57)
Wills:	There are rod ends and rod ends, Mr Fibbs.(58)
Fibbs:	I know there are rod ends and rod ends.(59) But where could you find a finer hemi unibal spherical rod end?(60)
Wills:	They just don't want to have anything more to do with it.(61)

In 58 Wills breaks the maxim of relation by not directly answering Fibbs's question, and the maxim of quantity by producing a near tautology. The implicature is that Fibbs's rod ends are not superior after all. Fibbs still keeps the initiative in the conversation with his next question, but Wills immediately counters by breaking the relation maxim in 61.

By now the linguistic basis for the turn-around in the situation should be clear. This leads to the absurd position whereby the manager at the end of the sketch is at the mercy of his shop steward. But this is not the only thing which makes the sketch unreal. It is also the case that there is a series of existential presuppositional clashes between characters and audience. Wills and Fibbs spend their time discussing items about whose existence we must have considerable doubt. A good example is 'high speed taper shank spiral flute reamers'. Like the other products in the sketch they are referred to partly by the use of a noun–noun sequence, this time an extremely long one. Noun–noun sequences in English are difficult for foreign learners because they exhibit few surface relational markers but can cover a wide range of semantic relations:

> *bath mat* – mat for being placed by the side of a bath
> *armchair* – chair with arms to it
> *desk drawer* – drawer in a desk
> *can opener* – product designed to open cans.

Because of the wide range of semantic relations associated with such sequences, the longer they get the more uninterpretable they become. Even 'spiral flute reamer' would present problems. Is it something spiral which reams flutes, or a reamer with a spiral flute? And so on. This problem of interpretability is made worse by the use of technical terms like 'comparator', 'flange' and 'bronzedraw', and the fact that a good few of the words and phrases carry overt sexual connotations, for example, 'parallel male stud couplings', 'off cock', 'pet cock'. Given the difficulty of interpreting the sequences and their bizarre connotations, I suggest that most people would infer that Pinter had made them up (in fact I am informed that they all exist; it would be interesting in this respect to know whether a group of workers from appropriate factories would find the sketch so absurd). We thus have a situation where the two men are becoming very heated over items whose existence we doubt. This is made even worse by the fact that both men presuppose that these objects are to be evaluated not in terms of utility but aesthetically and emotionally (cf. 'beautiful products' (37, 39), 'perfection' (49, 50), 'lovely parallel male stud couplings' (81, 82) and 'my . . . own Jacob's chuck' (77, 80) and Wills's explanation that 'perhaps its just the look of it' (47)).

This analysis has not used all of the categories outlined in the previous section of this chapter. It is, after all, only tentative and incomplete, and in any case it is unlikely that one short sketch would exhibit all the features discussed earlier. But it should be apparent that discourse analysis can be usefully applied in this example to account for much of the sketch's absurdity and 'dramatic' nature, a quality which is quite apparent even if one has never seen the piece enacted.

V   Conclusion

There are of course problems in using the kind of analyses outlined above.[9] Not least is the fact that the linguistic theory used for analysis is still open to discussion and modification. In spite of initial work by Searle (1975*b*) it is by no means clear how conversational implicature fits in exactly with the more general notion of indirect speech acts. Moreover, because the original categorization, although not as informal as my treatment, is still relatively informal, it is difficult in some cases to know whether a particular maxim is broken or not (cf. the discussion in subsection III (iv) above of the relation maxim), or whether a 'meaning' of which one is intuitively aware can be explained by the implicature theory. A related problem is that of the relative uncontrollability of speaker intention in what has sometimes been called a communication-intention theory of meaning. A speaker might break the maxim of manner, for example, either to implicate something or to try to disguise something from his interlocutor, as Rich does in the example from *A Man For All Seasons* in subsection III (iv) above. A complete theory will need to determine which case applies where. The maxim of quality often appears to be broken in casual conversation, where people quite frequently repeat what has already been said in another form. But the 'meaning' of such behaviour is more likely to be part of the general expression of social cohesion than implicature-like in type. Ordinary conversation is also more meandering than the strict application of the maxim of relation would allow. These two features of 'man-in-the-street-speak' can be observed in some dramatic dialogues, for example Pinter's sketch, *Last To Go* (for discussion of this work in sociolinguistic terms see Burton 1980: ch. 1), where the implicatures that arise pass not from character to character but from Pinter to his audience. The problem as to what level of discourse implicatures operate at is a good indication of the need for a fuller and more formal account; and to count as a reasonable and observable analysis almost all the passages I have looked at would require more detailed and explicit treatment. Another question which arises is 'How many maxims are there?' Grice suggests the possibility of a politeness maxim, for example, a notion which has been expanded in Leech (1983: *passim*), and which I have not really touched on at all, although more attention will be given to the general principles of politeness in the following chapter.

What holds for implicatures also often applies to speech acts and presuppositions. It is not clear how many speech acts there are, or if they can be defined so that each is distinguishable from one another, particularly when we seem to be able to subdivide within speech act types – cf. requesting, begging, pleading etc. Do all speech acts have to have names already existing in our vocabulary? What speech act is performed by the normal utterance of 'Here's your tea, dear'? There are also problems in distinguishing presupposition from logical implication, and the types of presupposition that I have discussed do not seem to be discrete categories any more than those for speech act analysis are. But in a sense these are questions which always dog the stylistician. There will always be arguments over how detailed and explicit critical analysis should be. And as no area of linguistic analysis can ever really be said to be complete, the stylistician has always to take the analysis he applies partly on trust. Otherwise he would never begin his work at all.

Suggestions for Further Work: Chapter 8

1   Read the following extract from the beginning of Shaw's *Major Barbara*.

> *(It is after dinner in January 1906, in the library in Lady Britomart Undershaft's house in Wilton Crescent. A large and comfortable settee is in the middle of the room, upholstered in dark leather. A person sitting on it (it is vacant at present) would have, on his right, Lady Britomart's writing table, with the lady herself busy at it; a smaller writing table behind him on his left; the door behind him on Lady Britomart's side; and a window with a window seat directly on his left. Near the window is an armchair.*
>
> *Lady Britomart is a woman of fifty or thereabouts, well dressed and yet careless of her dress, well bred and quite reckless of her breeding, well mannered and yet appallingly outspoken and indifferent to the opinion of her interlocutors, amiable and yet peremptory, arbitrary, and high-tempered to the last bearable degree, and withal a very typical managing matron of the upper class, treated as a naughty child until she grew into a scolding mother, and finally settling down with plenty of practical ability and worldly experience, limited in the oddest way with domestic and class limitations, conceiving the universe exactly as if it were a large house in Wilton Crescent though handling her corner of it very effectively on that assumption, and being quite enlightened and liberal as to the books in the library, the pictures on the walls, the music in the portfolios, and the articles in the papers.*
>
> *Her son, Stephen, comes in. He is a gravely correct young man under 25, taking himself very seriously, but still in some awe of his mother, from childish habit and bachelor shyness rather than from any weakness of character.)*

Stephen:	What's the matter?
Lady Britomart:	Presently, Stephen.
	(Stephen submissively walks to the settee and sits down. He takes up a Liberal weekly called The Speaker.)
Lady Britomart:	Don't begin to read, Stephen. I shall require all your attention.
Stephen:	It was only while I was waiting –

5

Lady Britomart:	Don't make excuses, Stephen. (*He puts down* The Speaker.) Now! (*She finishes her* 10 *writing; rises; and comes to the settee.*) I have not kept you waiting very long, I think.
Stephen:	Not at all, mother.
Lady Britomart:	Bring me my cushion. (*He takes the cushion from the chair at the desk and arranges it for* 15 *her as she sits down on the settee.*) Sit down. (*He sits down and fingers his tie nervously.*) Don't fiddle with your tie, Stephen; there is nothing the matter with it.
Stephen:	I beg your pardon. (*He fiddles with his watch* 20 *chain instead.*)
Lady Britomart:	Now are you attending to me, Stephen?
Stephen:	Of course, mother
Lady Britomart:	No: it's not of course. I want something much more than your everyday matter-of- 25 course attention. I am going to speak to you very seriously, Stephen. I wish you would let that watch-chain alone.
Stephen:	(*Hastily relinquishing the chain.*) Have I done anything to annoy you mother? If so, it was 30 quite unintentional.
Lady Britomart:	(*Astonished.*) Nonsense! (*With some remorse*). My poor boy, did you think I was angry with you?
Stephen:	What is it then, mother? You are making me 35 very uneasy.
Lady Britomart:	(*Squaring herself at him rather aggressively.*) Stephen may I ask how soon you intend to realize that you are a grown-up man, and that I am only a woman? 40
Stephen:	(*Amazed.*) Only a –
Lady Britomart:	Don't repeat my words, please: it is a most aggravating habit. You must learn to face life seriously, Stephen. I really cannot bear the whole burden of our family affairs any 45 longer. You must advise me: you must assume the responsibility.
Stephen:	I!
Lady Britomart:	Yes, you, of course. You were 24 last June. You've been at Harrow and Cambridge. 50 You've been to India and Japan. You must know a lot of things, now; unless you have wasted your time most scandalously. Well, advise me.
Stephen:	(*Much perplexed.*) You know I have never 55 interfered in the household –
Lady Britomart:	No: I should think not. I don't want you to order the dinner.

Stephen:	I mean in our family affairs.	
Lady Britomart:	Well, you must interfere now; for they are getting quite beyond me.	60
Stephen:	(*Troubled.*) I have thought sometimes that perhaps I ought; but, really, mother, I know so little about them; and what I do know is so painful! It is so impossible to mention some things to you — [*He stops, ashamed.*)	65
Lady Britomart:	I suppose you mean your father.	
Stephen:	(*Almost inaudibly.*) Yes.	
Lady Britomart:	My dear: we can't go on all our lives not mentioning him. Of course you were quite right not to open the subject until I asked you to; but you are old enough now to be taken into my confidence, and to help me deal with him about the girls.	70
Stephen:	But the girls are all right. They are engaged.	75
Lady Britomart:	(*Complacently.*) Yes: I have made a very good match for Sarah. Charles Lomax will be a millionaire at 35. But that is ten years ahead; and in the meantime his trustees cannot under the terms of his father's will allow him more than £800 a year.	80
Stephen:	But the will also says that if he increases his income by his own exertions, they may double the increase.	
Lady Britomart:	Charles Lomax's exertions are much more likely to decrease his income than to increase it . . .	85

(i) How would you describe the character of each of the two participants? Note down the evidence in what each of them says which suggests your characterization.

(ii) How is the relationship between the two characters revealed in the ways in which they interact? In support of your response to this question, you might wish to analyse the following aspects of dialogue: (*a*) *Speech acts*. What *kinds* of speech acts are used by the characters? Is there a consistent pattern in the distribution of speech acts? If so, what does this pattern reveal about the social relationship of the characters? What do the speech acts *implicate* to the reader/audience? (The material covered in subsections III (i) and III (iv) of the chapter should be relevant here.) (*b*) *Turn-taking, turn length* and *interruptions* (see subsection III (iv)). (*c*) *Vocatives* (see subsection III (v) and section IV). (*d*) *Personal style*. The discussion of *modality* and *modulation* in Chapter 5 of this book is particularly relevant here. Look at how, for instance, high-value modulation is used by Lady

Britomart in lines 42–6, but note also the comparative oddity of her remarks in lines 39–40.

(iii)   Using your description of the discourse structure of the passage, write a set of instructions for actors performing the piece. Your instructions might include information on gestures; facial expressions; intonation; and paralinguistic features, such as loudness, pitch and voice quality.

2   The following short extract is from N. F. Simpson's *One Way Pendulum*.

Mrs Gantry:	You heard about Mr Gridlake?
Mrs Groomkirby:	No?
Mrs Gantry:	I thought you might have heard. Had an accident on his skis.
Mrs G'Kirby:	Serious?
Mrs Gantry:	Killed himself.
Mrs G'Kirby:	No!
Mrs Gantry:	Straight into the jaws of death, so Mrs Honeyblock was saying. (*Pause.*)
Mrs G'Kirby:	What on earth did he expect to find in there, for goodness sake?
Mrs Gantry:	Showing off, I suppose. (*Pause.*)
Mrs G'Kirby:	You think he'd have had more sense. (*Pause.*)
Mrs Gantry:	He hadn't intended staying there, of course. (*Pause.*)
Mrs G'Kirby:	In one side and out the other, I suppose.
Mrs Gantry:	That's why he had his skis on sideways, according to Mrs Honeyblock. (*Pause.*)
Mrs G'Kirby:	I can't think what possessed him. (pp. 32–3)

There is clearly something odd going on in this dialogue. Drawing on your knowledge of discourse analysis, can you explain why? The discussion of *presupposition* in subsection III (ii) may help here.

3   Refer back to the schema representing the embedded nature of drama discourse (subsection III (iii)). How would the text of Tom Stoppard's *The Real Inspector Hound* slot into such a schema? Would you have to modify the schema, or build in additional embedded layers? How would you attempt to construct a similar schema for novelistic discourse? What, primarily, would be the causes of any difficulties in such an attempt? Could a schema be developed which would adequately account for complex, multi-layered narratives, such as Emily Bronte's *Wuthering Heights*?

Notes: Chapter 8

1   In fact the text v. performance controversy is a long-standing one, going back to at least Renaissance times (cf. Dessen, 1977).
2   Samuel Beckett, *Waiting for Godot* (London: Faber, 1965), 2nd edn, pp. 21–2.
3   It is possible to treat Estragon's question as having to do with location rather than existence; but existence presumably depends upon spatio-temporal location in any case. Either way, Estragon's question is absurd.
4   N. F. Simpson, *One Way Pendulum* (London: Faber, 1960), p. 24.
5   Tom Stoppard, *Enter a Free Man* (London: Faber, 1968), p. 26.
6   Robert Bolt, *A Man for All Seasons*, with notes by E. R. Wood (London: Heinemann Educational, 1960), p. 18.
7   Penguin edn (Harmondsworth, 1965), p. 52. The beginning of this play is reproduced in 'Suggestions for Further Work', exercise 1, at the end of the chapter.
8   'Trouble in the Works', in Harold Pinter, *Plays: Two* (London: Methuen, 1977), pp. 241–3.
9   For an 'opening out' of many of the above questions from within the domain of semiotics, see Elam (1981).
10 Many people have read this chapter for me. In particular I should like to thank Malcolm Coulthard, Geoffrey Leech, John Sinclair, Katie Wales, Richard Dutton and Henry Widdowson for their helpful comments.

References: Chapter 8

Austin, J. L. (1962), *How to Do Things With Words* (Oxford: Oxford University Press).

Brown, R, and Gilman, A. (1960), 'The Pronouns of Power and Solidarity', in T. A. Sebeok (ed.), *Style in Language* (Cambridge, Mass.: Massachusetts Institute of Technology Press), pp. 253–76.

Burton, D. (1980), *Dialogue and Discourse: A Sociolinguistic Approach to Modern Drama Dialogue and Naturally Occurring Conversation* (London; Routledge & Kegan Paul).

Coulthard, R. M. (1977), *An Introduction to Discourse Analysis* (London: Longman).

Dessen, A. C. (1977), *Elizabethan Drama and the Viewer's Eye* (Chapel Hill, NC: North Carolina University Press).

Elam, K. (1981), *The Semiotics of Theatre and Drama* (London: Methuen).

Ervin-Tripp, S. M. (1969), 'Sociolinguistic Rules of Address', in L. Berkowitz (ed.), *Advances in Experimental Social Psychology* (New York: Academic Press), vol 4, pp. 93–107.

Grice, H. P. (1975), 'Logic and Conversation', in P. Cole and J. Morgan (eds), *Syntax and Semantics*, vol. 3, *Speech Acts* (New York: Academic Press), pp. 41–58.

Keenan, E. L. (1971), 'Two Kinds of Presupposition in Natural Language', in C. J. Fillmore and D. T. Langendoen (eds), *Studies in Linguistic Semantics* (New York: Holt Rinehart & Winston), pp. 45–54.

Kempson, R. M. (1975), *Presupposition and the Delimitation of Semantics* (Cambridge: Cambridge University Press).

Leech, G. N. (1974), *Semantics* (Harmondsworth: Penguin).

Leech, G. N. (1983), *Principles of Pragmatics* (London: Longman).

Mulholland, J. (1967), ' "Thou" and "You" in Shakespeare: A Study in the Second Person Pronoun', *English Studies*, vol. 48, pp. 34–43.

Pratt, M. L. (1977), *Toward A Speech Act Theory of Literary Discourse* (Bloomington, Ind.: Indiana University Press).

Quirk, R. (1974), 'Shakespeare and the English Language', in Quirk, (ed.), *The Linguist and the English Language* (London: Edward Arnold), pp. 46–64.

Searle, J. R. (1965), 'What is a Speech Act?', in M. Black (ed.) *Philosophy in America* (London: Allen & Unwin), pp. 221–39.

Searle, J. R. (1969), *Speech Acts: An Essay in the Philosophy of Language* (Cambridge: Cambridge University Press).

Searle, J. R. (1975a), 'The Logical Status of Fictional Discourse', *New Literary History*, vol. 6, pp. 319–32.

Searle, J. R. (1975b), 'Indirect Speech Acts', in P. Cole and J. Morgan (eds), *Syntax and Semantics*, vol. 3, *Speech Acts* (New York: Academic Press), pp. 59–82.

Strawson, P. (1952), *Introduction to Logical Theory* (London: Methuen).

Styan, J. L. (1960), *The Elements of Drama* (Cambridge: Cambridge University Press).

Tanaka, R. (1972), 'Action and Meaning in Literary Theory', *Journal of Literary Semantics* vol. 1, pp. 41–56.

Wells, S. (1970), *Literature and Drama* (London: Routledge & Kegan Paul).

Wilson, D. (1975), *Presuppositions and Non-Truth-Conditional Semantics* (London: Academic Press).

Introduction to Chapter 9

This is the second of three chapters which explore the ways in which discourse models can be usefully employed in the analysis of literary dialogue. Here, Paul Simpson focuses on the linguistic strategies of politeness used by the characters in Ionesco's play *The Lesson*.

Simpson begins by summarizing some of the important work of Brown and Levinson on politeness phenomena. Introducing relevant terms and categories from the Brown and Levinson model, he outlines the different sorts of strategies that speakers may use in a variety of verbal acts, ranging from commands and complaints to compliments and offers. He also explains how the choice of a particular strategy – whether it is polite or impolite – is constrained by important contextual factors relating to both speaker and hearer. These contextual factors include the relative power of the interactants, the relative social distance of the interactants and the attitude of the interactants to one another. In the case of more 'encroaching' types of acts (such as requests, complaints and questions) the precise nature of the imposition being made will also form an important constraint. With respect to such cases, the general axiom is: the greater the imposition, the greater the use of politeness strategies.

Having outlined the relevant components of the Brown and Levinson model, Simpson proceeds with his analysis of *The Lesson*. He demonstrates how the complete reversal in the interactive roles of the two main characters is signalled, during the course of the play, by a gradual change in their linguistic behaviour. One character, for instance, uses abundant hedges and elaborate deference phenomena at the start of the play, yet by the end has switched to unmitigated impoliteness. Simpson uses his analysis both as a means of displaying the oddity and absurdity of the play's dialogue, and as a way of assessing the peculiar relationship of the characters to one another. He also proposes a wider application of the politeness model in order to account for interaction between, for example, the implied authors and readers of texts – a theme which is carried over into the further work section at the end of the chapter.

9 Politeness Phenomena in Ionesco's *The Lesson*

PAUL SIMPSON

I General Framework

In the final section of the previous chapter, Mick Short, following the philosopher Grice, suggests that there is an important *politeness maxim* in conversation. Grice himself points out that there are, in addition to the four sets of conversational maxims he proposes, all sorts of other maxims, such as 'Be polite', which are normally observed by participants in talk exchanges. (Grice 1975: 47). Politeness may thus be seen as a departure from 'maximally efficient' conversation, drawing, as it frequently does, on hints and indirections. However, the strategies of politeness are not arbitrarily chosen by speakers in interaction. On the contrary, their choice is constrained by important contextual features, such as the relative power of the speakers, the social distance of the speakers and what the speakers happen to be negotiating at the time. Short, again, touches on this in the previous chapter when he comments on how interactive rights are not always shared equally by participants in interaction. He notes, for instance, that

> A servant cannot, given normal circumstances, threaten a master. If he does so in a play, it signals a change in their relationship.
>   Commands, like threats, are not accessible to all of the participants in a particular speech situation and therefore mark clear social relationships. (p. 144)

In this chapter, to contrast with the more eclectic approach adopted by Short, I intend to narrow the analytic focus by concentrating solely on the linguistic strategies of politeness as represented in a drama text. The text chosen for analysis is Ionesco's *The Lesson* – a play which, on an initial intuitive reading, would be amenable to and, indeed, would virtually demand a politeness-based analysis. The discourse model which has been selected for the analysis is one which should enable me to explore, in a systematic way, the relation between language use and the social relationship of the speakers. This model will be outlined shortly.

In keeping with most of the chapters in this book, the present study will examine literary text data from a discourse-oriented perspective. This is not intended to deny the validity of syntactically, lexically or phonologically based approaches to stylistic analysis, but, given that the subject of the analysis is drama dialogue, these types of approaches are clearly less appropriate than a discourse-oriented one. The choice of a discourse model is further justified when one notes that the drama dialogue selected for analysis represents a particular kind of discourse situation: a lesson. However, this is not only a question of adapting the appropriate framework to the particular need. A discourse-stylistic analysis of the sort to be undertaken should open the way for wider discussion of the text as interaction on several levels. As well as examining the interaction between the fictional characters in the play, it should encompass the interaction between writer/playwright and reader/audience. This echoes Short's observations on the *embedded* nature of drama discourse. Finally, a discourse-stylistic analysis should highlight the roles of writer and reader as conversationalists in real-time speech events, pointing particularly to the former's ability to exploit the conventions of language use for stylistic effect and the latter's ability to recognize these exploitations and the motivations behind them.

II Outline of the Analytic Model

It was stressed in section I that a discourse framework which was capable of describing the quality of social relationships between individuals would be suited to a stylistic analysis of Ionesco's *The Lesson*. One such framework, which specifically sets out to integrate a description of language use with an account of the social relations of the interactants, is that developed by P. Brown and S. Levinson in their impressive monograph-length paper (Brown and Levinson, 1978; see also Brown and Levinson, 1987). Brown and Levinson seek to uncover the principles which underlie polite usage. They contend that message construction – or 'ways of putting things' – is part of the expression of social relationships. By isolating the central motive of *politeness* (which they define in considerable depth) they develop a comprehensive framework of the analysis of this aspect of verbal interaction. What follows is a simplified account of this framework.

Central to the Brown and Levinson notion of politeness phenomena, is the concept of *face*. Face is seen as a kind of public 'self-image' which speakers in a society claim for themselves. It consists of two related aspects, called *positive* and *negative* face. Negative face refers to any speaker's basic claim to territories, personal preserves and the right to non-distraction: in other words, that speaker's freedom of action and freedom from imposition. Positive face, on the other hand, refers to the positive consistent self-image or 'personality' claimed by interactants, including the desire that this image should be appreciated and approved of by others. These components of face may be condensed into the following two concise definitions:

(1) *negative face* – the desire of every speaker that his actions should be unimpeded by others;

(2) *positive face* – the desire of every speaker that his wants should be desirable to at least some others.

Now, speakers often perform acts which may be said to 'threaten' the face of the addressee. For instance, asking someone for the loan of their car, or requesting a similar service, is clearly an impingement on that person. Such requests specifically threaten the *negative* face of the addressee, encroaching on their desire to be free from imposition. Other acts, such as the use of insults and terms of abuse, pose a different kind of threat to the interlocutor. Calling someone a 'damn fool' or 'silly ass' clearly demonstrates an unfavourable evaluation by the speaker of the addressee's public self-image, and can thus be regarded as a threat to the latter's *positive* face. Such acts, which pose a threat to either the positive or the negative face of the addressee are known as *face threatening acts* (hereafter abbreviated to FTAs).

There are various ways of performing FTAs, depending on, amongst other things, the context of interaction, the social relationship of the speakers and the amount of imposition which the FTA entails. This may be explained by taking a hypothetical example. Imagine a situation where one interactant wishes another to close a door. Although not serious, this request will pose some threat to the negative face of the addressee. To carry out this FTA, the speaker may select one from a number of strategies. For instance, he may choose a direct – although somewhat impolite – form such as:

(*a*) Close the door.

This type of FTA has been done *baldly, without redress*. The use of such a strategy makes the act clear, unambiguous and concise. In fact, a bald, non-redressive act is one which adheres faithfully to Grice's four conversational maxims (see p. 151 above). It is maximally efficient in so far as it is non-spurious (*quality*), it does not say more or less than is required (*quantity*), it is relevant (*relation*) and it avoids ambiguity and obscurity (*manner*). It is also significant that in performing such an act, a speaker shows little concern for the hearer's *face*. This explains why many bald non-redressive FTAs occur where the speaker holds high relative power and fears no threat to his own face from the addressee.

There are (thank goodness) a number of alternatives to performing an FTA baldly, without redress. A rather radical solution would be not to perform the FTA at all, but then the request would never be made. Another solution would be to perform the FTA using an indirect strategy. For instance, one might request the addressee to close a door in the following way:

  (*b*) It's a bit draughty in here.

This FTA has been performed *off-record*. By choosing to go off record, speakers adopt a strategy in which the utterance often takes the form of a declarative sentence containing no direct lexical link to the goods and services implicitly demanded of the addressee. In example (*b*), by selecting this particular declarative form, the speaker can appear not to be coercive and can thereby avoid the responsibility for a potentially face-damaging interpretation. Brown and Levinson elaborate on this idea using a similar example:

if I say 'It's hot in here' and you say 'Oh, I'll open the window then', you may get credit for being generous and co-operative, and I avoid the potential threat of ordering you around. (Brown and Levinson, 1978: 76)

In general, linguistic realizations of *off-record* strategies include metaphor and irony, rhetorical questions, understatement, tautologies and all kinds of indirect hints as to what a speaker wants or means to communicate.

Assuming, however, that a speaker opts not to go *off-record* in the performance of an FTA, he will then, by imputation, go *on record*. By going on record, the speaker makes clear to the addressee what communicative intention led him to perform the FTA. For instance, if he states 'I hereby promise to come tomorrow', then the other participants will normally concur that the speaker has expressed the intention of committing himself to that future act. Therefore, in making such a promise, a speaker will have been seen to go *on record*.

But by going *on record*, a speaker is faced with a further choice. He may choose – as has already been demonstrated – to perform the FTA baldly, without redress. On the other hand, he may choose to perform the FTA with redressive action. Redressive action basically means action that 'gives face' to the addressee. By giving face to the hearer and by recognizing his wants, the speaker can thereby indicate that no threat to face was intended.

Thus, if the speaker wishes the addressee to close a door, he may select a redressive FTA like one of the following:

(c) Could you close the door.
(d) Would you mind closing the door.
(e) I wonder if you could close the door.

These hypothetical redressive FTAs can be contrasted with, on the one hand, the bald, non-redressive FTA of example (a), and, on the other, the off-record FTA of example (b). Although, examples (c) to (e) do not allow the addressee the same options of refusal as does (b), they are clearly more polite than example (a). This is because they give redress to the hearer's desire for self-determination and freedom from imposition in a way that an utterance like 'Close the door' does not. As examples (c) to (e) specifically redress the hearer's negative face they can be said to be instances of *negative politeness*. This particular form of politeness is essentially 'avoidance-based' and, according to Brown and Levinson, consists of:

> assurances that the speaker recognizes and respects the addressee's negative face wants and will not (or will only minimally) interfere with the addressee's freedom of action. Hence, negative politeness is characterized by self-effacement, formality and restraint, with attention to very restricted aspects of (the hearer's) self-image, centring on his want to be unimpeded. (Brown and Levinson, 1978: 75)

At this stage it might be worth condensing the possible strategies for performing FTAs into a basic schema, following Brown and Levinson (1978: 74). (See Fig. 9.1.) Each strategy on the schema is numbered, the general principle being that the higher the number the more polite the strategy. Clearly, strategy (5) – which avoids the FTA altogether – represents no imposition at all on the addressee. Strategy (4) is the off the record ploy exemplified by example (b). Because the intended function of the FTA is obscured, considerable choice of interpretation is given to the addressee, and the speaker can appear uncoercive and unintrusive. Strategy (1), which is maximally direct, incorporates no politeness markers at all (see example (a)) and unless the imposition carried by the FTA is very small, the use of such a strategy would normally carry unpleasant sociological implications. Of course, there are some situations in which speakers use bald, non-redressive FTAs. One is where a speaker holds a position of high relative power over the addressee and fears no serious interactive consequences from using such a strategy. Other situations are emergencies where the demands of politeness may be suspended in the interests of expediency and

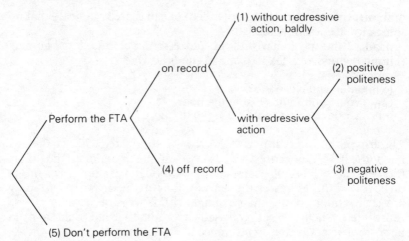

(1) without redressive
action, baldly

on record

(2) positive
politeness

Perform the FTA

with redressive
action

(4) off record

(3) negative
politeness

(5) Don't perform the FTA

Figure 9.1

urgency. Strategies (2) and (3) on the schema represents ways of performing FTAs which cater for the face wants of the addressee. Strategy (3), where the FTA is performed with redress to the hearer's negative face, realizes *negative politeness*. This aspect of politeness phenomena was illustrated by examples (*c*) to (*e*), and will be explained in more detail shortly. Strategy (2), which redresses the positive face of the addressee, realizes *positive politeness*. Bearing in mind the scope of this chapter, I have chosen not to deal with positive politeness in detail at this stage. Instead, this particular feature has been reserved for the further work section at the end of the chapter.

III The Strategies of Negative Politeness

Brown and Levinson go into considerable detail in their discussion of negative politeness, providing a comprehensive description of the various strategies that speakers have at their disposal. What follows is a summary of seven of these negative politeness strategies:

(i) Hedge

Hedges are items which soften or weaken the impact of an FTA. Good examples are phrases like 'sort of', 'by any chance' and 'as it were'. Whilst these phrases frequently supply no extra information, they do function as mitigation markers, making more tentative the assumptions and commitments implicit in the FTA. Hedges are also achieved through the use of hypothetical modal verbs such as 'could', 'would', 'might' and 'should'. (Note the use of 'would' and 'could' in examples (*c*) to (*e*) above). Other ways of achieving hedges include deliberate mumbling and hesitations, and the use of particles such as 'ahh' and 'umm', not to mention non-verbal strategies such as averted eyes or a lowered head.

(ii) Indicate Pessimism

This strategy draws attention to the speaker's doubt about the success of an FTA. Such 'polite pessimism' is often encoded in requests like:

> (*f*)   I don't suppose I could hand this in on Friday.
> (*g*)   Perhaps you could take this now.

It is worth noting the superficial indirectness of these forms with respect to the particular task requested. The following example, taken literally, is actually a statement concerning the addressee's inability to lend the goods in question:

> (*h*)   You couldn't possibly lend me your rod and reel for this afternoon.

(iii) Minimize the Imposition

By adopting this strategy, speakers suggest that the intrinsic serious-ness of the imposition is not great. This can be achieved by a number of expressions, all of which attempt to minimize the potential threat to the addressee. In the following examples, the emphasized items fulfil such a function.

> (*j*)   Could you *just* extend the thing for a *couple of days*.
> (*k*)   Could I *borrow* a *tiny wee bit* of paper.

In fact, this particular negative politeness strategy is one often employed by vagrants in their requests for money from strangers. In a recent personal encounter, the (successful) opening gambit went as follows:

> (*l*)   Would you . . . ah . . . just a couple of pence, sir . . .

Here the intended imposition is minimized so that the threat to the negative face of the addressee is reduced. Of course, the speaker in this case would have probably been offended to receive the *actual* amount specified in the request.

(iv)   Indicate Deference

Deference is often communicated by *honorifics*, i.e. terms of address which reflect the relative social status of the participants in interaction. The use of 'sir' in example (*l*) above is a good illustration of this. However, deference may also extend to humbling one's self, capacities and possessions. For example:

(*m*)   I'm ashamed to have to ask you this favour.

(Humbling one's self)

(*n*)   It's not much of a meal, but it'll fill our stomachs.

(Humbling one's capacities)

(*o*)   We could all go in my rustmobile.

(Humbling one's possessions)

(v)   Apologize

By apologizing for performing an FTA, a speaker can communicate reluctance to impinge on the hearer's negative face, thereby partially redressing that impingement. In fact, Brown and Levinson identify four substrategies here. These are:

(i)   *admit the impingement*
e.g.   I know this is a bore but . . .
I'd like to ask you a big favour . . .

(ii)   *indicate reluctance*
e.g.   I don't want to intrude . . .
I hate to have to ask you this . . .

(iii)   *give overwhelming reasons* – here the speaker claims compelling reasons for performing the FTA, implying that he normally would not even consider impinging on the hearer
e.g.   There just wasn't enough time to complete this.
I've been very busy lately, so could you help me with this?

(iv)   *beg forgiveness*
e.g.   Please forgive me if . . .
Excuse me, but . . .
Sorry, but . . .

(vi)   Impersonalize

By adopting this strategy, speakers can indicate their desire not to impose personally on the addressee, by dissociating themselves from the FTA. Frequently this involves the omission of the pronouns *I* and *you*. For example, the sequence 'It would be desirable . . .' might be substituted for the more personal 'I want . . .'. On the other hand, a plural form might be used to convey impersonalization, as in 'We regret to inform you. . .'. The *impersonalize* strategy is evident in hyper-formal utterances like 'Her majesty is not amused'.

(vii)   Acknowledge the Debt

Through this strategy, a speaker can mitigate the FTA by explicitly claiming indebtedness to the hearer. This is manifest in expressions like:

(p)   I'd be eternally grateful if you would . . .
(q)   I'll never be able to repay you if you . . .
(r)   This must put you out terribly . . .

This is only a brief summary of seven of the major negative politeness strategies, and those readers who wish to obtain a more comprehensive picture should refer directly to the original Brown and Levinson (1978) article.

Before we proceed to the analysis of drama dialogue using this politeness model, one final comment is necessary. This concerns the relationship of mitigating elements (i.e. hedges, apologies, deference, indirectness etc.) to the actual face threatening act. In general, the number of mitigating elements in an FTA is in direct proportion to the amount of intended imposition on the addressee's face. In other words, where the danger to the hearer's face is very small, it is more likely that the FTA will be done baldly, without redress. If, however, the FTA is done with redressive action (when the threat to the hearer's face is very small), then the amount of mitigating elements, such as hedges, apologies or signs of deference, will be minimal. Alternatively, FTAs which pose a considerable threat to the addressee are more likely to be supplemented with such softening devices. Perhaps the best way of illustrating the relationship between the number of mitigating elements in an FTA and the amount of danger to the hearer's face is by a kind of 'mismatched' example:

(s)   I'm sorry to trouble you – I know it's an awful imposition – but could I possibly impose upon you and ask you if you could tell me what time it is.

In this case, the amount of intended imposition on the addressee's negative face is negligible – yet the number of mitigating elements in the FTA suggests that the speaker is making a great demand upon the hearer. Such a mismatch will certainly be heard as striking, and would probably be interpreted as an expression of humour, irony or sarcasm.

The following section will attempt to apply the theoretical framework outlined above to some sequences of dialogue from *The Lesson*.

IV   The Analysis

The Lesson is – as is consistent with Eugene Ionesco – an extra-ordinary play. The central event is a private lesson involving an ageing Professor and an eighteen-year-old Pupil. The specific aims of the lesson are never made clear: the Pupil, it seems, wishes to undertake 'all the Doctorates',[1] yet the Professor directs most of his pedagogical energy towards ridiculously elementary arithmetic. At the start of the play the Professor is nervous and diffident, whilst the Pupil is vivacious and dynamic. However, the Professor gradually loses his timidity, becoming increasingly domineering and aggressive, whereas the Pupil grows more and more passive. Eventually, in a storm of verbal abuse, the Professor murders the Pupil with what can only be described as an imaginary knife. The play concludes with the revelation that not only is this the Professor's fortieth victim of the day but he has planned subsequent 'lessons' of a similar nature.

The Professor's transition from diffidence to dominance, and the Pupil's decline into passivity, is, during the course of the play, a gradual, almost imperceptible process. The shift in the interactive roles of the two characters is reflected by subtle changes in their linguistic behaviour. To account for this, three short extracts have been taken from key stages in the play's development.

The first extract comprises the opening encounter between the Professor and the Pupil.

(1) *Professor:*   Good morning, good morning ... You are ... er ... I suppose you really are ... er ... the new pupil?
(The Pupil turns round briskly and easily, very much the young lady: she gets up and goes towards the Professor, holding out her hand.)

Pupil: Yes, Sir. Good morning, Sir. You see I came at the right time. I didn't want to be late.

Professor: Good. Yes, that's very good. Thank you. But you shouldn't have hurried too much, you know. I don't know quite how to apologize to you for having kept you waiting ... I was just finishing ... you understand, I was just ... er ... I do beg your pardon ... I hope you will forgive me ...

Pupil: Oh, but you mustn't, Sir. It's perfectly all right, Sir.

Professor: My apologies ... (pp. 183–4)

The Professor's first remarks are clearly *phatic*.[2] It is noticeable, however, that he *repeats* the token 'Good morning', possibly revealing some anxiety in the early stages of the encounter. The Professor then goes on to make the first face threatening act of the interaction: he requests information concerning the identity of his interlocutor. The way in which he performs this FTA is interesting. First, he begins with a declarative sentence which will function as a request for confirmation from the Pupil. However, this strategy is aborted after only two words and is immediately followed by a hedging particle:

> You are . . . er . . .

Having, it seems, decided that this strategy is too direct an imposition on the negative face of his interlocutor, the Professor reformulates his request. The second attempt is more heavily mitigated and contains hedges of various sorts:

> I suppose you really are . . . er . . . the new pupil?

In addition to the particle 'er', hedges are achieved by the phrases 'I suppose' and 'really'. The use of 'I suppose' makes more tentative the assumptions in the Professor's request, whilst 'really' – although contributing no extra information – functions to weaken the force of the request. In short, the Professor's opening gambit is a good example of negative politeness phenomena.

The pupil's response to this is interesting. Where her use of the honorific 'sir' communicates deference, her additional linguistic strategies convey confidence and self-determination. For instance, she is eager to claim merit for her punctuality ('You see. I came at the right time'), not letting this positive feature of her behaviour escape her interlocutor. Furthermore, her response to the Professor's earlier phatic initiation is calm and equanimous. The Pupil's non-verbal behaviour here is also significant in that she rises and moves towards the Professor in a gesture which displays considerable confidence on her part.

The Professor's second speech begins with some positive feedback concerning the Pupil's punctuality, but then moves into an extraordinary sequence of negative politeness. It should be noted that the Professor has kept the Pupil waiting for no more than a few seconds. Yet it is clear from his elaborate politeness strategies that he considers himself to have made some immense imposition on his interlocutor. Take, for instance, the following sequence:

> I don't know quite how to apologize to you for having kept you waiting . . .

This utterance actually realizes two negative politeness strategies. First, the Professor indicates *deference*, by explicitly humbling his own capacities (i.e. 'I *don't know* quite how . . .'). Secondly, he draws on the *apologize* strategy – or rather, claims his inability to apologize. He further supplements this by utilizing a specific substrategy of *apologize*: he *admits the impingement*, by explicitly referring to the imposition caused to the addressee (i.e. '. . . for having *kept you waiting*').

After some hesitation, the Professor proceeds with more negative politeness, most of which draws on different aspects of the *apologize* strategy. In his next remark, he attempts to state the *overwhelming reasons* which lead him to perform the FTA:

I was just finishing . . .

After this incomplete effort, the Professor attempts a more hedged version of the same substrategy, with a comparable lack of success

you understand, I was just . . . er . . .

Having abandoned the *give overwhelming reasons* strategy, the Professor then moves on to the *beg forgiveness* strategy

I do beg your pardon . . .

This is immediately followed by a variation on the same strategy, which also incorporates the *be pessimistic* strategy in its use of 'I hope':

I hope you will forgive me . . .

In order to give an overall picture of the Professor's politeness strategies, it might be worth providing a visual summary of this stretch of dialogue:

Utterance	Strategy Employed
I don't know quite how to apologize to you for having kept you waiting . . .	(1) Indicate deference (2) Apologize: admit the impingement
I was just finishing . . .	(1) Apologize: give overwhelming reasons
you understand, I was just . . . er . . .	(1) Apologize: give overwhelming reason (2) Hedge
I do beg your pardon . . .	(1) Apologize: beg forgiveness
I hope you will forgive me . . .	(1) Apologize: beg forgiveness (2) Indicate pessimism

It should be remembered that this elaborate display of politeness strategies is directed towards what is, in reality, a relatively trivial imposition. The Professor has only minimally impinged on the negative face of the addressee, yet he persists with a gratuitous build-up of repair strategies as if he has encroached seriously on his interlocutor. There is, in effect, a kind of pragmatic 'mismatch' here, which is not unlike that exemplified by the hypothetical example (s) given in the previous section. This might help support the claim that the Professor is *excessively* polite at this stage of the play: the politeness strategies he uses are vastly out of proportion to the actual imposition he makes on the hearer.

The Pupil's interjection is well timed, as there seems to be no imminent conclusion to the Professor's series of apologies. (In any case, he continues with further supplication after her remarks.) What is more significant, however, is that the Pupil grants the forgiveness requested by the Professor with her remark 'It's perfectly all right, Sir'. Indeed, on the basis of this exchange, it looks as if it is the Pupil, and not the Professor, who is the more powerful of the two interactants. The Pupil is not only the one who receives deference and apologies but also in a position to issue reassurances to her interlocutor. This makes her persistent use of the honorific 'Sir' all the more incongruous.

I want now to examine a second short extract, taken from an episode later in the play:

(2) *Professor:* What is four? Greater or smaller than three?
     Pupil: Smaller . . . no greater.
     Professor: Excellent answer. How many units are missing between three and four? . . . or between four and three, if you'd rather?
     Pupil: There aren't any units, Sir, between three and four. Four comes immediately after three; there is nothing at all between three and four!
     Professor: I can't have made myself understood properly. It's doubtless my own fault. I haven't been clear enough.
     Pupil: Oh, no, Sir. The fault is entirely mine.
     Professor: Listen. Here are three matches. And here is another one. That makes four. Now, watch carefully . . .
     (p. 192)

The 'lesson' is clearly well under way at this point. In fact, the passage begins with a good example of a *teaching exchange*. The Professor *initiates* the exchange by asking a question, to which the Pupil provides a somewhat hesitant *response* ('Smaller . . . no, greater). The third part of the exchange is realized by the Professor's inordinately positive *feedback* on the Pupil's response ('Excellent answer'). The Professor's next initiation, however, is problematic, and the result is a breakdown in the teaching framework. The way in which the characters attempt to repair this breakdown is significant, as it sheds some light on their changing interactive relationship. The Professor begins the repair with a display of *deference*.

> I can't have made myself understood properly. It's doubtless my own fault. I haven't been clear enough.

Here, the Professor indicates deference by explicitly humbling himself and his capacities. However, the Pupil immediately counters this with a similar display:

> Oh, no, Sir, the fault is entirely mine.

In fact, the two characters are competing with one another in their use of negative politeness strategies. Each claims to be the guilty party in having been responsible for the previous communicative breakdown. This 'trade' in deference phenomena would suggest that a more symmetrical power relationship exists between the two characters at this point in the play.

However, such equality in interactive rights is short-lived when one considers the Professor's final remarks of the extract. As he attempts to reformulate his earlier question, he draws on a linguistic strategy, which he has not previously used. Consider how he phrases his two commands for attention:

> Listen . . . Now, watch carefully . . .

These FTAs, which impose upon the negative face of the addressee by demanding a particular service, have been done *baldly, without redress* (see example (*a*) in the section II above). Although clear and concise, they are impolite – drawing on none of the politeness strategies available for mitigating such FTAs. Indeed, these bald, non-redressive FTAs are the first suggestion that the Professor is becoming not only more powerful but less concerned with being polite to his interlocutor. It is also noticeable that nowhere in this extract does the Professor employ his hedging particle 'er', which was used so frequently in the first extract. In short, there is a change in the Professor's general linguistic behaviour. Although some of the dialogue in the extract reflects interaction between near-equals (see, for example, the 'trade' in deference phenomena), there are signs that the Professor is beginning to assume a position of high relative power.

The third and final extract chosen for analysis is taken from near the end of the play. It comprises an episode which occurs shortly before the Professor murders the Pupil with the invisible knife – an act which might be considered the ultimate face threatening act!

(3) *Professor:* Every language, Mademoiselle – note this carefully, and remember it *till the day you die* . . .

Pupil: Oh! yes, Sir, till the day I die . . . Yes, Sir . . .

Professor: . . . and again, this is another fundamental principle, every language is in fact only a manner of speaking, which inevitably implies that it is made up of sounds, or . . .

Pupil: Phonemes . . .

Professor: I was just about to say so. Don't show off, airing your knowledge! You'd better just listen.

Pupil: Very well, Sir. Yes, Sir.

Professor: Sounds, Mademoiselle, should be caught in flight by their wings so that they do not fall on deaf ears. Consequently, when you have made up your mind to articulate, you are recommended, in so far as possible, to stretch your neck and your chin well up, and stand right on the tips of your toes, look now, like this, you see . . .

Pupil: Yes, Sir.

Professor: Be quiet. Sit where you are. Don't interrupt . . . (p. 200)

At this point in the play, the 'lesson' has collapsed into an extended nonsensical monologue from the Professor. This is punctuated by warnings and threats to the Pupil, who has now clearly assumed a role of subservience. Take, for example, the Professor's opening speech, which is the beginning of a disoriented proclamation on language. Not only is this supplemented with a bald, non-redressive FTA demanding careful attention from the Pupil ('note this carefully') but there is a sinister threatening quality to this FTA ('remember it *till the day you die* . . .'). The Pupil's reaction to this is a display of genuine deference. Her use of the honorific 'Sir' is not incongruous, as it was in the first extract, but is now the term of address used by an inferior to an acknowledged superior. Nevertheless the Pupil is still eager to participate in the interaction, and consequently volunteers some information ('Phonemes . . .'). This however, draws only admonition from the Professor in the form of another threatening, bald, non-redressive FTA ('You'd better just listen').

It takes little at this stage to produce a rebuke from the Professor, as the Pupil discovers when she interjects a simple 'Yes, Sir' into his manifestly ludicrous explanation of articulation. This comment, which really only confirms that the pupil is paying the attention that the Professor has been so anxious to elicit, is enough to invoke a string of bald, non-redressive FTAs:

Be quiet. Sit where you are. Don't interrupt . . .

These are, in effect, three unmitigated commands, which illustrate how the Professor's politeness strategies have completely vanished. It is significant also that one of these FTAs is intended to restrict the physical movement of the addressee ('Sit where you are'). Thus, the Pupil, who in the first extract was able to move confidently and freely towards the Professor, is now confined powerless to her chair.

V   Concluding Remarks

The three passages from *The Lesson*, when compared with one another, show a marked reversal in the interactive relationship of the two characters. During the course of the play this reversal is gradually achieved and it is difficult to isolate a specific point at which a character gains or loses power. One thing that is clear, however, is that the transition in interactive roles is signalled by subtle variations in the linguistic strategies which these characters use to one another. In the first extract, the Professor appears timid, diffident and self-effacing, using elaborate negative politeness strategies to his younger, more confident interlocutor. So abundant are these strategies that they suggest that the Professor is actually the inferior member of the interaction. In the second extract, the situation is somewhat different. The interactants 'trade' deference with one another, suggesting that a more symmetrical power relationship exists between them at this stage. However, there are signs of incipient aggression in the Professor as he begins to select strategies from the least polite end of the politeness continuum. By the final extract, there is evidence of a clear power differential between the interlocutors, as the Professor issues a series of bald, non-redressive FTAs to the Pupil. Whilst the Pupil has become deferential and placid, the Professor has lost his earlier timidity and does not fear any serious interactive consequences as a result of his rudeness. The change in roles is summarized below:

	Less Powerful Interactant	*More Powerful Interactant*
Extract (1)	The Professor (using elaborate negative politeness strategies such as hedges, apologies, pessimism and deference)	The Pupil (confidently granting forgiveness requested by interlocutor)
Extract (2)		The Pupil/The Professor (symmetrical trading in deference phenomena – although Professor beginning to draw on less polite strategies)

Less Powerful Interactant	More Powerful Interactant
Extract (3) The Pupil (displaying deference; verbal and non-verbal behaviour restricted by commands of interlocutor; using honorific *Sir* as indicator of genuine status differential)	The Professor (issuing bald, non-redressive FTAs, paying no attention to the face wants of interlocutor)

I hope that this analysis will have gone some way towards demonstrating how the bizarre and essentially unmotivated role reversals in *The Lesson* are reflected by changes in the linguistic behaviour of its characters. The underlying motive of *politeness* has provided the framework for assessing the peculiar quality of the social relationships which are the very essence of the play. Indeed, as with many of Ionesco's works, the title of the play is a red herring: the actual 'lesson' is, in this case, only of peripheral importance to the more central concerns of character development.

Suggestions for Further Work: Chapter 9

1 The following sequence of dialogue is taken from the early stages of *The Lesson*. It occurs just after extract (1) (see section IV above), and, amongst other things, it comprises the Professor's first attempt to initiate the lesson proper:

Professor: But if you allow me, could you perhaps tell me . . .   1
Paris, now, is the chief town of . . . er. . . ?
(*The Pupil searches for a moment, then, pleased to know the answer.*)
Pupil: Paris is the chief town of . . . France?
Professor: But yes, of course, yes! Bravo! That's fine! That's excellent! I congratulate you. You have the   5
geography of your country at your finger-tips. Your chief towns.
Pupil: Oh, I don't know them all yet, Sir. It's not so easy as that, its quite difficult to learn them.
Professor: It will come in time . . . take heart, Mademoiselle   10
. . . I beg your pardon . . . a little patience . . . quietly, quietly does it . . . you'll see, it will come.
. . . Beautiful weather we're having . . . or perhaps not so . . . er . . . but after all why not? At least it's not too bad and that's the main thing . . . er . . . er   15
. . . it's not raining . . . in fact it's not snowing, either.
Pupil: That would be rather surprising in the summer.

> *Professor:* Forgive me, Mademoiselle, I was just going to say
> that . . . but you will learn that one has to be
> prepared for anything. 20
> *Pupil:* Yes, Sir. Naturally.
> *Professor:* In this world of ours, Mademoiselle, one can
> never be sure of anything.
> *Pupil:* Snow falls in the winter. Winter is one of the four
> seasons. The other three are . . . er . . . sp . . . 25
> *Professor:* Yes, yes?
> *Pupil:* Spring . . . and then summer . . . and er . . .
> *Professor:* It begins like automobile, Mademoiselle.
> *Pupil:* Ah, yes! Autumn . . .
> *Professor:* That's quite right, Mademoiselle. A very good 30
> answer. Excellent indeed. (pp. 184–5)

(i)   Examine the opening *exchange* between the Professor and
the Pupil (i.e. lines 1–7). What can you say about the Profess-
or's teaching strategies, on the basis of (*a*) his opening elicitation, and (*b*) his evaluation of the Pupil's response to this
elicitation?

(ii) Provide an analysis of the discourse structure of the
remainder of the passage, concentrating particularly on the
Professor's change of topic in line 13 and subsequent development of this new topic by the characters. (NB the material
covered in Chapter 2 of this book may be useful here.)

2   It was stressed throughout this chapter that speakers have at their
disposal various strategies for performing FTAs. In the analysis of
extract (3) from *The Lesson*, it was noted that the Professor chose
to use the *bald, non-redressive* strategy for performing FTAs. At
one point, he issued the following string of commands to his
interlocutor:

Be quiet. Sit where you are. Don't interrupt . . .

Rewrite these examples as more 'polite' requests, by performing
the FTAs:

(i)   with redressive action;

(ii) using the *off-record* strategy

(examples (*b*), (*c*), (*d*) and (*e*) in section II of the chapter should
provide helpful illustrations).

3   Positive *face*, it may be recalled, refers to an interactant's positive
consistent self-image, and his desire that this self-image be appreciated and approved of by others. It follows, then, that *positive
politeness* is specifically concerned with redressing the positive face
of the hearer. It will include, amongst other things, offers,

compliments, claims to common ground and displays of interest and approval of each other's personality. Where negative politeness is 'avoidance-based', positive politeness is 'approach-based', extending more widely to generally 'polite' behaviour. Here are some examples of positive politeness:

(a) What a beautiful vase this is! Where did you get it from?
(b) How's it going, luv?
(c) Your blouse is nice; did you make it yourself?
(d) That was a lovely party!

Positive politeness can also be used in conjunction with other politeness strategies. The following example is a *hybrid* FTA, where positive politeness, in the form of a compliment, is used as a kind of pre-sequence to a negative politeness FTA:

(e) Goodness, you cut your hair. How lovely! . . . By the way, could I borrow a tiny bit of sugar?

Finally, positive politeness may be realized by certain terms of address which redress the positive face of the hearer. Brown and Levinson (1978: 112) refer to such terms as *in-group identity markers*. Here speakers use 'endearments' (items like 'mate', 'honey', 'luv', 'dear', 'pal') to express approval of the addressee's personality and positive self-image.

As a contrast to displays of politeness phenomena, Brown and Levinson (1978) give a list of acts which can threaten or *damage the positive face* of the hearer. These acts fall into two categories: (*a*) acts indicating that the speaker has a negative *evaluation* of the addressee's positive face (include expressions of disapproval, criticism, contempt, or ridicule, complaints and reprimands, accusations, insults); (*b*) acts indicating that the speaker *does not care* about the addressee's positive face (include irreverence, mention of taboo topics, including those that are inappropriate in the context, expressions of violent emotions).

In the light of the definitions above, re-examine the extract from *The Lesson* cited in exercise 1, paying particular attention to the Professor's use of positive politeness strategies. Follow this up with a comparable analysis of extract (3) (discussed in section IV of this chapter) and attempt to assess any significant differences in the linguistic behaviour of the characters.

4 Another potentially interesting area of study, using the positive politeness aspect of the model, concerns a higher level of literary organization. This is where authors allow a fictional speaker to direct comments towards the implied reader of a text. Frequently

terms of address are used which reveal the predisposition and attitudes of the fictional speaker towards his or her intended readership. Such terms of address are often an important feature of the overall style and tone of the text. In the following examples, which all contain comments made directly to the implied reader, the narrators emerge in different lights; some are deferential and self-effacing, whilst others are cajoling or even downright insulting. The first extract is from Charlotte Bronte's *Jane Eyre*.

> When I got there, I was forced to sit to rest me under the hedge; and while I sat, I heard wheels, and saw a coach come on. I stood up and lifted my hand; it stopped. I asked where it was going: the driver named a place a long way off, and where I was sure Mr. Rochester had no connexions. I asked for what sum he would take me there; he said thirty shillings; I answered I had but twenty: well, he would try to make it do. He further gave me leave to get into the inside, as the vehicle was empty: I entered, was shut in, and it rolled on its way.
> Gentle reader, may you never feel what I then felt! May your eyes never shed such stormy, scalding, heart-wrung tears as poured from mine. May you never appeal to Heaven in prayers so hopeless and agonized as in that hour left my lips: for never may you, like me dread to be the instrument of evil to what you wholly love.[3]

The next two extracts are from Henry Fielding's *Tom Jones*. In the first, the narrator is introducing the theme of his story. The second is taken from much later in the novel.

> The Provision then which we have here made is no other than Human Nature. Nor do I fear that my sensible reader, though most luxurious in his taste, will start, cavil, or be offended, because I have named but one article.

> Another caution we would give thee, my good reptile, is, that thou dost not find out too near a resemblance between certain characters here introduced; as for instance, between the land-lady who appears in the seventh book, and her in the ninth. Thou art to know, friend, that there are certain characteristics, in which most individuals of every profession and occupation agree. To be able to preserve these characteristics, and at the same time to diversify their operations, is one talent of a good writer.[4]

The following extract is from Byron's *Don Juan*.

> But for the present, gentle reader! and
>   Still gentler purchaser! the bard – that's I –
> Must, with permission, shake you by the hand,
>   And so your humble servant, and goodbye!

> We meet again, if we should understand
>   Each other; and if not, I shall not try
> Your patience further than by this short sample –
> 'Twere well if others follow'd my example.[5]

The last extract is from Samuel Beckett's novella *First Love*. In this episode the unnamed narrator, who spends most of the time lying prostrate on a park bench, begins to feel his privacy threatened by the visitations of a woman to the same bench.

> And the next day (what is more) I abandoned the bench, less I must confess on her account than on its, for the site no longer answered my requirements, modest though they were, now that the air was beginning to strike chill, and for other reasons best not wasted on cunts like you, and took refuge in a deserted cowshed marked on one of my forays.[6]

(i)   Examine the positive politeness strategies used by the speakers in the above extracts, focusing especially on the terms of address which reflect the attitude of the narrator towards the reader.

(ii) Can you identify any acts which explicitly *damage* positive face?

(iii) Can you detect any *irony* in the way that politeness strategies are used in any of the extracts?

(iv) To what degrees do the various narrators invite reader *participation*?

5   Edward Albee's play *Who's Afraid of Virginia Woolf?* is particularly amenable to a stylistic analysis using the politeness phenomena model. It centres on a fractious couple, Martha and George, who quarrel almost incessantly throughout the play. Their clash of personalities is aggravated not only by their drunkenness but by the fact that they have invited a younger couple, Honey and Nick, to share their evening. In the presence of this second couple, the quarrels of Martha and George become all the more pathetic and embarrassing. The first extract takes place just before the arrival of Martha and George's guests and is a good indication of the considerable friction that exists between them.

> *George:* Well, just stay on your feet, that's all . . . These people are your guests, you know, and . . .
> *Martha:* I can't even see you . . . I haven't been able to see you for years . . .
> *George:* . . . if you pass out, or throw up, or something . . .
> *Martha:* . . . I mean, you're a blank, a cipher . . .

> George: ... and try to keep your clothes on, too. There aren't many more sickening sights than you with a couple of drinks in you and your skirt up over your head, you know ...
> Martha: ... a zero ...
> George: ... your *heads*, I should say ... (*The front door-bell chimes.*)
> Martha: Party! Party!
> George: (*murderously.*) I'm really looking forward to this, Martha ...
> Martha: (*same.*) Go answer the door.
> George: (*not moving.*) You answer it.
> Martha: Get to that door, you. (*He does not move.*) I'll fix you, you ...
> George: (*fake-spits.*) ... to you ... (*Door chimes again.*)
> Martha: (*Shouting ... to the door.*) C'MON IN (*To George between her teeth.*) I said, get over there!
> George: (*moves a little towards the door, smiling slightly.*) All right, love ... whatever love wants.

(i)   Give an account of the acts each character uses which damage the *positive* face of the other.

(ii) After the doorbell chimes, the characters argue over who should answer the door. What kind of strategies do they use to one another, and can you formulate more 'polite' versions? Does anyone gain the upper hand in this linguistic battle?

(iii) What does an analysis of politeness phenomena reveal about the relationship between Martha and George?

The second extract takes place after the arrival of Nick and Honey. Note, particularly, Honey's politeness strategies.

> Honey: (*rising quickly*). I wonder if you could show me where the ... (*Her voice trails off.*)
> George: (*to Martha, indicating Honey.*) Martha ...
> Nick: (*To Honey.*) Are you all right?
> Honey: Of course, dear. I want to ... put some powder on my nose.
> George: (*As Martha is not getting up.*) Martha won't you show her where we keep the ... euphemism?
> Martha: Huh? What? Oh! Sure! (*Rises.*) I'm sorry, c'mon. I want to show you the house.
> Honey: I think I'd like to ...
> Martha: ... wash up? Sure ... c'mon with me. (*Takes Honey by the arm.*)[7]

(i)   Give an account of Honey's politeness strategies. Can you think of any more *direct* strategies that speakers might use in such a situation?

(ii) What do Honey's strategies reveal about her character and her relationship to her interlocutors?

6 Re-examine the Pinter play *Trouble in the Works* quoted in Chapter 8, section IV, of this book, using the politeness model. Is there any noticeable pattern to the exchange of politeness phenomena? Is the 'role reversal' referred to by Mick Short signalled by a parallel reversal (whether complete or partial) in the politeness strategies used by the characters?

Notes: Chapter 9

1 p. 186; quotations are from Donald Watson's translation, in Ionesco, *Rhinoceros, The Chairs, The Lesson* (Harmondsworth: Penguin, 1962). The play was first published in 1954.
2 For a discussion of this term, see Chapter 2 above.
3 Bronte sisters, *Four Novels* (London: Spring Books, 1976), pp. 271–2 (ch. 27).
4 Penguin edn (Harmondsworth, 1983), pp. 51–2 (bk 1, ch. 1), 467 (bk 10, ch. 1).
5 Verse 221, canto 1; taken from *The Poetical Works of Lord Byron* (London: Henry Fawde, 1904), p. 650. Readers interested in the study of politeness in the context of narration in poetry may like to consult material in Sell (1985a and b).
6 Beckett, *The Expelled and Other Novellas* (Harmondsworth: Penguin, 1980), p. 17.
7 Penguin edn (Harmondsworth, 1979), pp. 18, 24.

References: Chapter 9

Brown. P., and Levinson, S. (1978), 'Universals in Language Usage: Politeness Phenomena', in E. N. Goody (ed.), *Questions and Politeness: Strategies in Social Interaction* (Cambridge: Cambridge University Press), pp. 56–289.
Brown, P., and Levinson, S. (1987), *Politeness* (Cambridge: Cambridge University Press).
Grice, H. P. (1975), 'Logic and Conversation', in P. I. Cole and J. Morgan (eds), *Syntax and Semantics*, vol. 3, *Speech Acts* (New York: Academic Press), pp. 41–58.
Sell, R. (1985a) 'Tellability and Politeness in *The Miller's Tale*: First Steps in Literary Pragmatics', *English Studies*, 66.
Sell, R. (1985b) 'Politeness in Chaucer: Suggestions Towards a Methodology for Pragmatic Stylistics', *Studia Neophilologica*, 57.

Introduction to Chapter 10

Michael Toolan's is the last of the three chapters which explore the ways in which discourse models can be used in the analysis of fictional dialogue. In this chapter, Toolan directs his analysis towards sequences of conversation from the Christmas dinner scene in Joyce's *Portrait of the Artist as a Young Man*. He focuses particularly on how the initial restrained and conventional talk between the characters is disrupted and replaced by, what he terms, conversational 'turbulence'. This turbulence leads eventually to a breakdown in the discourse.

Toolan begins his analysis by drawing on the Birmingham model of discourse, and makes particular use of descriptive categories proposed by Deirdre Burton (1980) and discussed in the introduction to this book. Burton's framework takes the form of a Hallidayan hierarchy of discourse units: all interactions comprise (one or more) *transactions*, which are made up of *exchanges*, which comprise *moves*, which in turn are realized by the smallest discourse unit, *acts*. It is at the latter three unit levels that most interest has been directed.

Michael Toolan concentrates particularly on the interactive unit of the *move*. The move is a key level in discourse, as it is normally coterminous with speaker change, is the primary level for the propulsion of talk, and marks the transition points at which subsequent speakers are drawn to respond. Of the seven different types of moves, three are particularly important:

(1) *opening moves* – essentially topic-carrying items which are recognizably 'new' in terms of the immediately preceding talk;
(2) *supporting moves* – occurring after any other type of move and involving items that concur with the initiatory moves they are supporting;
(3) *challenging moves* – functioning to hold up the progress of a topic or the introduction of a topic in some way.

Through his analysis of the distribution of moves, Toolan highlights the different strategies used by Joyce's characters in conversation. He observes how, for instance, the widespread distribution of challenging moves signals the continued dispute between the participants over how the conversation should proceed.

Toolan supplements his analysis of discourse structure by introducing some of the concepts developed in CA. He also draws on Labov's work on natural narrative in order to deal with a story told by one of the conversationalists. Through using a variety of sociolinguistic sources, he demonstrates how the fictional conversation is structured and developed, and how the characters manipulate the broad collaborative principles of conversation for antagonistic and anti-collaborative purposes.

Toolan's analysis of discoursal patterning also enables him to account for the developing power relations depicted in the course of the conversation. He uses his detailed analysis to enable him to comment on the broader sociolinguistic and socio-cultural situation at this junction in the novel, and to relate such observations to some underlying themes of the novel, such as the tyrannies of nationalism, religion and family to which the hero, Stephen Dedalus, is subjected. Toolan demonstrates the ways in which an explicit, detailed and analytically retrievable treatment of a scene can provide a convincing basis for discussion of larger patterns of significance.

10 Analysing Conversation in Fiction: an Example from Joyce's *Portrait*

MICHAEL TOOLAN

In this chapter I propose to demonstrate some of the ways in which the theories and principles developed by linguists and conversational analysts for the systematic study of discourse and natural conversation may be applied illuminatedly in the stylistic and structural study of a fictional conversation within a literary text (the Christmas dinner scene in James Joyce's *Portrait of the Artist as a Young Man*).[1] I acknowledge at the outset that natural and fictional conversation differ in many ways. It is not merely that in fiction the talk is 'tidied up', that there are relatively few unclear utterances, overlaps, false starts, hesitations, and repetitions: there are also literary conventions at work governing the fictional representations of talk, so that the rendered text is quite other than a faithful transcription of a natural conversation. However, certain structural and functional principles govern fictional dialogue, as they do natural dialogue, and in the former case as in the latter any witness (a reader or hearer) must recognize and attend to those principles in order to comprehend the dialogue.

A reader's initial reaction to the early conversation might well be to note the conventionality of the early talk, evidenced by the stretches of phatic communion, the politeness phenomena[2] and various ritualized utterances, such as the sequence of formal invitations to the guests from Mr Dedalus to come and sit at the table and Stephen's recitation of the grace. The conventionality of much of this early talk should not blind us to its functionality in establishing greater speaking and acting rights for Mr Dedalus in relation to the other diners. Mr Dedalus is head of the house and head of the table, dispenser of drinks, turkey and sauce, the provider, and the talk on pp. 28–9 gives him ample opportunity to establish his roles not merely as master of ceremonies but in addition as master of the talk. Dante, as we shall see, overtly challenges the latter role, and is even notably negative in her compliance with Mr Dedalus adopting the former role: she answers his first question to her with a frowning 'No', and rejects his belated offer of sauce.

But on p. 31 the restrained and conventional talk is disrupted, supplanted by a situation in which, typically, each speaker's contribution is a critical and antagonistic response to the immediately preceding speaker's turn: in short, a row develops. Principles of consensus, co-operation, tact and all the other paraphernalia of bland, self-censoring social interaction are discarded in favour of an exhilarating confrontation of fundamental convictions.

The earliest stage of the confrontation (p. 31 to the end of p. 32) is marked by what I shall call conversational turbulence. The turbulence is due not merely to the open and divisive clash of views about politics-in-religion but also to the latent dispute or negotiation over quite what the topic of contentious talk should be. Christmas Day falls in the shadow of Parnell's recent death, and it seems that the men – Dedalus and Casey – wish to talk specifically of Parnell when denouncing Church interference in politics, while Dante does not wish to talk about Parnell particularly, unless driven to it, but does wish to defend the Catholic Church. Note that in this initial dispute (p. 31, l. 10, to p. 32, l. 18) there is no specific mention of Parnell, and the disagreement is over generalized principles, more abstract and less 'engaged' than it will be later – all of which is reflected in the swapping of generic sentences, the debating-contest style:

> We go to the house of God ... to pray and not to hear election addresses.
> They [the priests] must direct their flocks.

At p. 32, l. 19, however, the conversation quite clearly enters a new stage with the sudden and startling focusing of talk on Parnell. He is designated on first mention by the personal pronoun, thus emphasizing that, as a topic of discourse, he was already conversationally 'in play', already in the minds of the participants, and only we the readers are perplexed (temporarily) by the absence of explicit antecedent:

> – Let them leave politics alone, said Mr Casey, or the people may leave their church alone.
> – You hear? said Dante, turning to Mrs Dedalus.
> – Mr Casey! Simon! said Mrs Dedalus, let it end now.
> – Too bad! Too bad! said uncle Charles.
> – What? cried Mr Dedalus. Were we to desert him at the bidding of the English people?
> – He was no longer worthy to lead, said Dante.

The overt focusing on Parnell – and his treatment by clergy and faithful – as discourse topic, prompts an increasing mutual vehemence and intolerance in the opposed parties, and a mutually incited working towards extremes of viewpoint and language. In fact there is a repeated pattern to these confrontations, in which successive climaxes of denunciation and vituperation (often accompanied by the shocked remonstrations of the peace-loving disengaged observers, Mrs Dedalus and uncle Charles), effect breakdowns in the conversation. These occur in the first half of p. 33, and – more subtly concealed – in the exchanges from p. 34, l. 29, to p. 35, l. 20, whilst a final and clearly irreparable breakdown is reported at the bottom of p. 39. Embedded in this series of conversational clashes is a personal narrative, Mr Casey's story of 'the famous spit', which merits close analysis both in its own right and in terms of its relation to the surrounding conversation.

At the core of this scene are destructive incompatibility and violence – of the sort Stephen flies from at the close of the novel. Regardless of the considerable epicurean distractions on this, perhaps the most special day of the year for Stephen, it is the familiar Joycean tyrannical menaces of nationalism, religion and family which consume the energies of the adults. But the reader, like Stephen, is an external observer. A more *internal* perspective might assess the row in the light of the conversational analyst's view of conversation as 'a means of getting work done'. From such a perspective, we may see the flare-up as therapeutic and cathartic, an opportunity for the three main talkers to express (publicly) their intense feelings of anger, or grief, or disgust, concerning Parnell's life and death. In addition, we can see the whole argument as a negotiated dispute arriving, eventually, at a conclusion not public and articulated at the outset.

I have already said something about power relations between speakers in the scene. Nominally at one extreme, with no speaking rights, is Stephen (his reception and evaluation of events is rendered copiously in free indirect style). While Mr Dedalus occupies the dominant position in the party, and is thus likely to enjoy superior speaking rights, note that Dante has the relatively lowly status of the dependent female relative, the maiden aunt, and so may be assumed (by other participants) to have lesser speaking rights here. In addition, as a respectable middle-class woman in that society at that time, she is also constrained by tacit rules as to the language she may use and the topics she may discuss (one consequence is that she probably receives the men's vulgarities of language and topic as – calculated or inadvertent? – insults). But from a socio-cultural perspective there is an unexpected vehemence in much of Dante's talk, an unexpected frequency in the number of conversational turns she takes and a noticeable refusal to suffer the men's options in silence. Her views may be unattractively puritanical, naively submissive to the authority of the Church, but her behaviour within this scene is one of Stephen's earliest witnessings of the diabolical message of liberation, *non serviam* (I will not serve).

And that breaking of the social rules on her part is no doubt partial explanation for the vigour and violence of the men's responses, what seems to be their 'ganging-up' on Dante: her behaviour is an incitement.

In more immediate structural terms, we should note that the dinner scene is essentially a three-party conversation, with three almost wholly silent witnesses: Mrs Dedalus, uncle Charles and Stephen. As Sacks, Schegloff and Jefferson (1974) intimate, three-party conversation is problematic and transitional: in two-party conversation there is no difficulty whatsoever in identifying the next-turn speaker, if the current speaker does not self-select. And with four or more participants, 'there are mechanisms for the schism of one conversation into more than one conversation' (Sacks, Schegloff and Jefferson, 1974: 713). This possibility of four-participant interaction dividing into two conversations is frequently a valuable 'safety-valve', whereby an open and embarrassing clash of opinions is avoided by participants (often *consciously*) regrouping themselves into distinct, simultaneous interactions. In a three-party conversation, clearly, 'last as next' bias may potentially exclude the third speaker, who in addition has no recourse to a 'separate conversation' strategy. What Sacks, Schegloff and Jefferson (1974) call 'differential distribution of turns' is, in such circumstances, highly relevant, and Dante is victim of it on several occasions.

I should like now to turn to a preliminary discourse analysis of the dispute, applying the descriptive model proposed in Deirdre Burton (1980). The model is presented in the chapter of the book entitled 'Towards an Analysis of Casual Conversation'. Burton's scheme is an adaptation and revision of the discourse analysis model proposed by Sinclair and Coulthard (1975). Sinclair and Coulthard's model is a systematic descriptive framework for analysing spoken discourse but is geared specifically for the analysis of formal classroom interaction. Burton has modified this model to make it more suitable for analysing casual conversation, but, in contrast to much work within the tradition of conversation analysis (CA), she retains Sinclair and Coulthard's emphasis on there being a framework underlying the interaction. This emphasis leads Burton to propose that an extended sequence of conversational turns can be analysed, and that the model is therefore particularly suited to the analysis of dialogue in drama and novels.

I have particularly focused on what seems to me to be the key interactive level of *move* (loosely akin to the conversation analysts' unit of *turn*), the 'minimal free interactive unit' (Burton, 1980: 124). Moves – and types of moves – seem to be the key level since they are usually coterminous with speaker change; they are the primary level for the propulsion of talk, and mark the transition-points at which subsequent speakers are chiefly drawn to respond. By contrast, focus on the lower level of *act* is often too delicate a description, for which there may be several *acts* (for example, summons + starter + informative + comment) comprising a single *move* (for example, opening move); it is that composite unit, a speech act of *opening* a conversational exchange, which is the more determining of other participants' behaviour.

Identifying higher-level units here is more problematic: the structuring of moves or turns into clearly marked exchanges is largely absent – not surprisingly, since the format, the purposes and the distribution of rights and knowledge are so different from those in classroom or doctor–patient interaction. However, a single higher level, here labelled *transaction*, seems identifiable and sometimes relevant.

In her own analyses, Burton has identified seven types of move – two explicitly marking transaction boundaries (framing and focusing), and five which are properly 'conversational'. The five types of *conversation move* are listed below with some brief definitions.

(1) *Opening moves* – essentially topic-carrying items which are recognizably 'new' in terms of the immediately preceding talk;
(2) *supporting moves* – may occur after any type of move and involve items that concur with the initiatory moves they are supporting;
(3) *challenging moves* – function to hold up the progress of a topic or the introduction of a topic in some way;
(4) *bound-opening moves* – occur after a preceding opening move has been supported; they enlarge and extend the topic of the original opening move;
(5) *re-opening moves* – occur after a preceding opening move has been challenged; they reinstate the topic that the challenge has either diverted or delayed.

Working with these five conversational moves (the explicit transaction boundary moves are not common here), it is possible to achieve a preliminary characterization of the development of the Christmas dinner talk in move terms. In particular, I believe close examination of the dispute confirms that Burton's introduction of supporting and challenging moves is a valuable recognition that conversations are often power struggles between participants who adopt various strategies for dissent in pursuit of the objective that the conversational outcome should be consonant with their own conversational goal.[3]

In my analysis of the data, from p. 31, l. 10 to the bottom of p. 39, I found a quite remarkable frequency of challenging moves within the talk. There are 50 of these in the nine pages of talk, compared with 24 opening, bound opening, or re-opening moves taken as a group, and only 17 supporting moves. Such figures are in themselves strong evidence of the inappropriateness of an analytical framework oriented towards collaborative consensus in interaction (the Sinclair and Coulthard 1975 model) for the description of natural – or even fictional

– conversation. Significantly, as Table 10.1 indicates, Dante is conspicuous by her abundant contribution of challenging moves (she never offers a support!), while Mr Dedalus is the chief source of types of opening moves and of supporting moves.

Table 10.1   *Distribution of Move Types*

Challenging		Supporting		Opening*	
Dante	23	Mr Dedalus	10	Mr Dedalus	15
Casey	11	Uncle Charles	4	Casey	7
Mr Dedalus	6	Casey	2	Dante	1
Mrs Dedalus	7	Mrs Dedalus	1	Mrs Dedalus	1
Uncle Charles	1				
Total	50	Total	17	Total	24

*includes re-opening and bound opening

Typical of much of the manner of the conversation is the following extract from p. 32, to which I append a move and act description. I classify the first move here as one opening a new transaction since it ignores Mr Dedalus's preceding turn, 'Now then, who's for more turkey?', and opens a new segment of talk (although closely tied to the earlier dispute over respect for priests). That opening move is followed by a series of challenging moves, as each successive contribution disputes the justness of the content of the immediately preceding move. Burton (1980) presents challenges as obligatorily having an informative, elicitation, directive, or accusation act as head. But as my description suggests, it is not easy to assign such descriptive labels to the heads of these challenging moves without doubts remaining. That is because these are a subtle kind of challenge, a controlled and indirect dissent – rather than direct contradiction – overlaid by a veneer of politeness.

Move	Act	Dialogue
Opening	inf./acc.?	– Nice language for any Catholic to use!
Challenging	el./dir.?	– Mrs Riordan, I appeal to you, said Mrs Dedalus, to let the matter drop now. Dante turned on her and said:
Challenging	el./acc.?	– Am I to sit here and listen to the pastors of my church being flouted?
Challenging	inf./dir.?	– Nobody is saying a word against them, said Mr Dedalus, so long as they don't meddle in politics.
Challenging	inf./dir.?	– The bishops and priests of Ireland have spoken, said Dante, and they must be obeyed.

Move	Act	Dialogue
Challenging	inf./dir.?	– Let them leave politics alone, said Mr Casey, or the people may leave their church alone.
Challenging	el./acc.?	– You hear? said Dante, turning to Mrs Dedalus.

Note that in each case of uncertainty over act description, the choice of description is between a more neutral act of eliciting or informing (in Hallidayan 1970, terms, primarily 'ideational' acts) and a more marked, oppositional act of directing or accusing (in Hallidayan terms, primarily 'interpersonal' acts). I believe a description in terms of the two more neutral Acts might arise from a superficial, non-interpretative 'reading' of these moves, but that a consideration of the speaker's intention in these moves leads us to recognize the presence of the marked or oppositional acts.

The issue of how to characterize or classify challenging moves also remains problematical. Burton (1980) has proposed classifying challenges as a 'breach of discourse framework', a breach of topic-development requirements, or a breach of appropriate preconditions (the last two types of breach being subclassified in some detail). Here, the vast majority of challenges apparently fall within the insufficiently examined domain of breach of discourse framework. A valuable preliminary means of understanding the behavioural conventions subsumed under discourse framework may be to return to an aspect of conversation already covered in Chapter 8 of this book. This is the *co-operative principle* proposed by Grice (1975: 45):

Make your conversational contribution such as is required, at the stage at which it occurs, by the accepted purpose or direction of the talk exchange in which you are engaged.

For what is repeatedly apparent, as challenge succeeds challenge, is that there is a continual dispute between participants in regard to their judgements as to what type of talk 'is required', as to when it should occur and as to what 'the accepted purpose or direction of the talk exchange' is or should be.

My subjective impression is that, in addition to occasional conventional breaches of the discourse framework, the many challenging moves here are predominantly *indirect* accusations or directives (sometimes masquerading as informatives or elicitations). The indirectness represents the conversationalists' grudging recognition that they are 'polite society', that this is Christmas and that neutral observers (especially the child, Stephen) are present. The indirectness is not always immediately apparent, such is the aggressiveness of the language, but note how rarely the 'direct address' pronouns, *I* and *you*, appear in the challenge moves, and how relatively commonly, instead, sentential subjects are third-person plural, or dummy *it*, or 'existential' *there*. When first- or second-person pronouns do occur they not surprisingly mark points at which speakers feel acute personal outrage:

> – I will not say nothing. I will defend my church and my religion when it is insulted and spit upon by renegade catholics. (p. 34, l. 25)

> – And may I tell you, ma'am, that I, if you mean me, am no renegade catholic. I am a catholic as my father was and his father before him and his father before him again, when we gave up our lives rather than sell our faith. (p. 35, l. 1)

Interestingly, first-person pronouns are adopted at the climactic close of the row, by both adversaries, who also often opt for the plural form (as if to undercut any charge of personal eccentricity or position by implying that their position represents that of an indefinitely large group). Thus Mr Casey asserts 'We have had too much God in Ireland', and 'Away with God, I will', while Dante, when not screaming the directest of direct accusations at Mr Casey – for example, 'Blasphemer! Devil! . . . Devil out of hell!' – declares 'We won! We crushed him to death!'

To return to the more conventional breaches of discourse framework within the scene, the dialogue on p. 33 merits attention:

TRANSACTION	
Opening	– There's a tasty bit here as you call the pope's nose. If any lady or gentleman . . .
Challenging	He held a piece of fowl up on the prong of his carving-fork. Nobody spoke. He put it on his own plate, saying:
Re-opening	– Well, you can't say but you were asked. I think I had better eat it myself because I'm not well in the health lately.
	He winked at Stephen and, replacing the dish-cover, began to eat again.
Challenging	There was a silence while he ate. Then he said:
TRANS.	– Well now, the day kept up fine after all.
Opening	There were plenty of strangers down too.
Challenging	Nobody spoke. He said again:
Re-opening	– I think there were more strangers down than last Christmas.
Challenging	He looked round at the others whose faces were
TRANS.	bent towards their plates and, receiving no reply, waited for a moment and said bitterly:
Opening	– Well, my Christmas dinner has been spoiled anyhow.

Challenging	– There could be neither luck nor grace, Dante said, in a house where there is no respect for the pastors of the church.
	Mr Dedalus threw his knife and fork noisily on his plate.
Challenging	– Respect! he said . . .

What we witness is a series of failed transactions, initiated by Mr Dedalus in a rather pedestrian attempt both to terminate discussion of Parnell and religion and to redirect talk towards uncontentious topics. The four challenges which answer his four opening or re-opening Moves share common characteristics which Joyce has explicitly encoded in the text. Chiefly, they are all acts of reply through hostile – or at least non-compliant – silence. In conversation analysis terms, Mr Dedalus's repeated offerings to the floor are ignored and rejected by all other participants, and 'noticeable absences' occur.[4] Some constraint on self-selection is at work, presumably created by a judgement to the main protagonists, Dante and Mr Casey, that while the recent violent and disrespectful language is unpleasant and unsuitable for Stephen's ears, nevertheless the topic itself has not been satisfactorily finished with. As a result, we witness Mr Dedalus struggling to transform the gaps that develop after his moves (the silent replies) into intra-turn pauses, but finally forced to concede (p. 33, l. 21) that a lapse has developed, that current talk has failed.[5] Again, that progression is subtly encoded linguistically, since the (possibly) neutral silences reported by 'Nobody spoke' and 'There was a silence' are superseded by the almost certainly recalcitrant and oppositional silence reported by 'receiving no reply'.

I have mentioned that the other speakers' silence here is partly due to their implicit reluctance to leave the previous conversational topic. This is not at all surprising since the topic has only recently come to focus on Parnell in particular, rather than politics-and-religion in general. As we see, Mr Dedalus's strategies fail, and all three disputants are soon at it again hammer and tongs. But Mr Dedalus's efforts at topic redirection are only a more extended version of other moves, by Mrs Dedalus and uncle Charles, to close (i.e., foreclose) the persistent heated discussion. Those moves, too, are signal failures, because the main speakers have *not* agreed that they have arrived at a point of completion. One speaker's silence *is* still occasion for another's talk, and the responding speaker here (Dante, 'red in the face', p. 32) well knows that the men's silence is a 'being silent' enforced by others. She chooses to override that injunction to closure by resuming: 'There could be neither luck nor grace . . . .'.

Mr Dedalus's topic redirection, and Mrs Dedalus's and uncle Charles's attempts to compel topic closure, are then instances of a pervasive source of tension and asymmetry in the conversational structure: attempted topic suppression. I have found surprisingly little mention of topic suppression in the conversation analysis and discourse analysis literature, yet it seems to be a major determinant of the flow of conversation in the dinner scene. It first appears towards the bottom of p. 31:

> Mrs Dedalus laid down her knife and fork, saying:
> – For pity sake and for pity sake let us have no political discussion on this day of all days in the year.
> – Quite right, ma'am, said uncle Charles. Now, Simon, that's quite enough now. Not another word now.

Mr Dedalus complies here – 'Yes, yes' – but Dante is less malleable: when Mr Dedalus proceeds to offer more turkey, Dante breaks the ensuing silence and, in defiance of Mrs Dedalus's appeals, the topic of conflict is resumed (p. 32, l. 4). Soon Mrs Dedalus and uncle Charles again join forces to close the talk (p. 32, ll. 17 ff.), but are still unsuccessful. Finally, uncle Charles alludes to Stephen's presence in order to restrain Mr Dedalus. The latter, relenting a little, then takes it upon himself to reorient and reinitiate the talk but, as we have seen, fails dismally. The next major attempts at topic suppression occur midway through p. 34, soon after a particularly abusive outburst from Mr Dedalus. Once more the attempt at suppression fails. But notice that uncle Charles's contribution here is rather different from his earlier ones: he is no longer attempting to suppress the topic but simply wishing to have it discussed more temperately. I shall return later to this apparent shifting in his attitude. (Incidentally, a stylistic correlative of the relative lifelessness and blandness of the contributions made by Mrs Dedalus and uncle Charles are, arguably, the many clumsy lexical repetitions within their speech.)

At the point we have reached in the conversation – midway down p. 34 – it might appear that voluntary topic suppression occurs, since Mr Casey now introduces the story of the famous spit. But this is only a pseudo-suppression and a pseudo-redirection on Mr Casey's part, since the tale itself is very much about Parnell and his treatment by the ordinary people, and can be related directly to the framing conversational situation. The story is interesting also since it brings to an end the overt attempts at topic suppression: later, the more detached witnesses will be limited to efforts to *restrain* the adversaries (in particular, to restrain Mr Casey physically!).

In fact Mr Casey's story can be usefully subjected to a Labovian narrative-constituent analysis.[6] Labov's model is specifically drawn from analyses of oral narratives of personal experience, into which category Mr Casey's tale clearly falls.

I have space here to mention only a few patterns highlighted by a Labovian analysis. One concerns manipulation of the *orientation*. No effective story can proceed without a well understood orientation section (giving the 'who, when, what and where'). And Mr Casey shows himself quite adept at using the orientation section to further his *own* conversational goals as well as to tell the story adequately – even though this involves stating his basic orientation three times.

Thus Mr Casey provides the basic orientation, specifying the time and place: 'It happened not long ago in the county Wicklow where we are now'. But instead of proceeding to satisfy his attentive audience with the expected *complicating action* (or further orientation), he exploits his narrator's rights in order to resume his verbal battle with Dante: he breaks off his story to reject her insinuation that he is a 'renegade catholic'. It is a taking of advantage which, typically, Dante does not submit to, although her two challenging moves here, being in a sense a violation of the storytelling proprieties, mean that in the light of discourse-structural conventions she may be felt to be guilty of discourteous interruption.

When Casey now restates his orientation, he appends the evaluative comment 'May God have mercy on him!' This, too, would seem to be an incitement to further unmannerly interruption from Dante, but instead comes the first of a series of comments inserted by Mr Dedalus. Nominally challenging moves, they are in effect only pseudo-challenges, covertly supporting Mr Casey, filling pauses and providing positive feedback. The chief effect of Mr Dedalus's contribution is to enable Mr Casey to state once more, for a third time, his basic orientation.

The story provides abundant evidence that it is the polished production of an accomplished teller – as is reflected in the many and varied *evaluation* devices Mr Casey supplies. Almost every one of Labov's subtypes of evaluation techniques is represented. At the story's close comes a flurry of evaluations: laughter from Casey and Dedalus, a significant silent rocking from uncle Charles, anger and sarcasm from Dante, and a mixed response from Stephen. But one Labovian narrative constituent is conspicuous by its absence: there is no true *coda* to the story, no verbalized effort by Mr Casey to supply a conversational bridge or transition to the argumentative conversation in which the story is embedded. But then no such verbalized coda is needed, the unspoken one is clear enough, and is previewed in the story's resolution: the best response (in Mr Casey's view) to those (including Dante) who have turned on Parnell and now abuse his shade is a good spit. In addition to being the story's coda, this implicit relating of the spit to Dante may also be seen as a silent evaluation – if, as Labov states, evaluation is the means used by the narrator to indicate the point of the narrative, its *raison d'être*: why it was told and what the narrator's getting at. (Labov, 1972: 366)

And this in turn points to the likely non-discrete nature of Labovian narrative constituents in more complex personal narratives.

The general effects of Mr Casey's story, within the larger conversational framework include (*a*) earning recognition (for example, from any neutral observer) as a good talker, a source of wit and entertainment, and (*b*) causing a neutral observer to have a lessened regard for Dante, who is *apparently* an impolite co-conversationalist (interrupting Casey's narrative turn) and conspicuous by her hostile and humourless reception of the story.

The *particular* effect of the story is one which I suspect has often been overlooked in traditional critical readings of this scene, an effect which has subtle but important consequences for the dynamics of this conversational conflict. This is the shift in attitude revealed in uncle Charles. Hitherto he has been, with Mrs Dedalus, a sober, impartial peacemaker, struggling to divert the talk from the contentious topic of Parnell and the Church. Just before Mr Casey's story – as I noted earlier – we find uncle Charles offering *modified* support to Mrs Dedalus. Now, at the story's close, while Mr Dedalus laughs loudly, the narrative reports, in minimalist fashion, that 'uncle Charles swayed his head to and fro' (p. 37). But this indication is silent (and suppressed?) laughter is enough: it is taking of sides. No longer is uncle Charles a 'neutral' topic suppressor, fostering consensual conversation. The five adult conversationalists have now separated into two wholly unequal camps (interestingly, the demarcation correlates with sex). Confirmation that uncle Charles, however attenuatedly, now aligns himself with Casey and Dedalus comes soon (pp. 37–8)

Opening	– Ah, John, he said. It is true for them. We are an unfortunate priest-ridden race and always were and always will be till the end of the chapter. Uncle Charles shook his head, saying:
Supporting	– A bad business! A bad business! Mr Dedalus repeated:
Bound-opening	– A Priest-ridden Godforsaken race!

Despite a brief impression that uncle Charles's move here is a challenging one, deploring Mr Dedalus's language, it immediately becomes clear that he is *supporting* Dedalus, not censuring him, and that Mr Dedalus's next move is thus a *bound*-opening, not a re-opening.

Within this new configuration of allegiances, it is all the more likely that the confrontation should become uncontrolled. Note the 'degeneration' in the turns of pp. 38 and 39, away from the earlier controlled though opposed statements in declarative form, to an abundance of abrupt exclamations. Most of these imprecations are addressed to the subject matter:

A traitor to his country!
Another apple of God's eye!
No God for Ireland!

But finally, reflecting total conversational breakdown, Dante uses them directly of Mr Casey:

Blasphemer! Devil! . . . Devil out of hell! (p. 39)

On the way to this violent termination, note that Mr Casey – clearly the most accomplished exploiter of conversational techniques here – employs a series of aggressive marked-polarity rhetorical questions directed at Dante (p. 38). These have the appearance of permitting Dante equal rights to a full reply, even as they deny them.

I hope to have shown some of the ways in which the Christmas dinner conversation is structured and developed, using a variety of sociolinguistic sources in my discussion. What is most noticeable is the abundant manipulation of the broad principles of *recipient design* and conversational co-operation. By recipient design, Sacks, Schelgoff and Jefferson (1974: 724) mean speakers' shaping of conversation 'in ways which display an orientation and sensitivity to . . . the co-participants'. Speakers here *are* attentive and sensitive to the many features of recipient design I have discussed, they *are* aware of their co-conversationalists' orientations and goals, but that sensitivity is skilfully harnessed to antagonistic, anti-collaborative purposes.

Suggestions for Further Work: Chapter 10

1 The following passage is from the final stages of the Christmas dinner scene in *Portrait of the Artist as a Young Man* (pp. 38–9), and it charts the gradual conversational breakdown between, in particular, Dante and Mr Casey.

    – God, and religion, before everything! Dante cried. God and religion before the world.
    Mr Casey raised his clenched fist and brought it down on the table with a crash.
    – Very well then, he shouted, hoarsely, if it comes to that, no God for Ireland!

– John! John! cried Mr Dedalus, seizing his guest by the coat sleeve.

Dante stared across the table, her cheeks shaking . . .

– Blasphemer! Devil! screamed Dante, starting to her feet and almost spitting in his face.

Uncle Charles and Mr Dedalus pulled Mr Casey back into his chair again, talking to him from both sides reasonably. He stared before him out of his dark flaming eyes, repeating:

– Away with God, I say!

Dante shoved her chair violently aside and left the table . . . At the door she turned round violently and shouted down the room, her cheeks flushed and quivering with rage:

– Devil out of hell! We won! We crushed him to death! Fiend!

The door slammed behind her.

Mr Casey, freeing his arms from his holders, suddenly bowed his head on his hands with a sob of pain.

– Poor Parnell! he cried loudly. My dead king!

(i) Using the framework outlined in the chapter, provide an analysis of the discourse structure of this passage. You might wish to pay particular attention to the distribution of *moves* and consider how many of these moves are *supported* (in the more technical sense) by other participants in the interaction. Can you use your analysis to help explain the breakdown in conversational structure?

(ii) Supplement your analysis of the passage with an examination of politeness phenomena. The outline of *positive politeness* in exercise 3 of the further work section of Chapter 9 may be of help here, especially the section which deals with acts which *damage positive face*.

2 Re-examine Harold Pinter's *Trouble in the Works* (cited in Chapter 8, section iv) using the discourse model described by Michael Toolan. Concentrate particularly on how conversational exchanges are initiated. One means of doing this is to examine the distribution of *opening moves* (including *bound-opening* and *re-opening moves*) between the two characters, Fibbs and Wills. Does this distribution suggest that one of the characters has an interactive prerogative in initiating exchanges? Is there a shift in opening move distribution in the course of the play?

3 *Supports, challenges and face*. As has been argued in this Chapter, models such as those of Burton (1980) and Labov (1972) may well be compatible with, and complementary to, analysis of discourse from other perspectives. In particular, it might be illuminating to re-analyse the talk in the Christmas dinner scene in relation to the theory of *face*, and of *negative and positive politeness*, presented in Chapter 9. Compare and contrast the politeness behaviour

between Mr Casey and Dante on the one hand, with that between Mr Casey and Mr Dedalus. Are there are any off record face-threatening acts in the scene? Is there any sort of shift, amongst the on-record acts, away from or towards acts of the non-redressed kind? Consider also the mutiplicity of faces involved as the row develops; the clash is not simply between Dante and Mr Casey but includes Parnell and the Church too. Thus, when Mr Casey remarks 'We go to the house of God . . . in all humility to pray to our Maker and not to hear election addresses', this not merely contradicts Dante's adjacent remarks, and so threatens her Face, but is a more indirect threat to the face of the clergy who preach in the house of God.

4 *Dialogue and power*. Any fictional dialogue that has to do with the coercions and accommodations between speakers should be ame-nable to a move and act analysis along the lines of Burton's (1980) model. One of the central themes of Joyce's *Dubliners* (1914) is, arguably, power: the power of perceived circumstances (including other people) over these miserable, timid, self-deceiving, entrap-ped, 'partly-living' characters. Sometimes the power of the domi-nant in these stories is exercised discoursally, through directive, interruptive and dismissive language: in short, talk where powerful individuals order and challenge weaker ones (the world of *Dubliners* is no egalitarian community of mutual support and respect). The discoursal exercise is especially visible in 'Counter-parts', the story of an impoverished middle-aged clerk named Farrington, who is maddened by his humiliating work as a copyist, and by his craving for drink, and who feels himself diminished and ridiculed by everything around him. Analyse the exchanges between Farrington and his sarcastic and increasingly infuriated boss, Mr Alleyne. (The exchanges climax with a hilariously impertinent rejoinder from Farrington, which merits special con-sideration as a well constructed and 'invited' face-threatening act.)

5 *Dialogue and free indirect thought*. One obvious neglected factor in the analysis of the Christmas dinner scene in this chapter is the free indirect thought reactions of the young boy, Stephen, as he 'silently' witnesses the confrontation between the adults. (Those unfamiliar with the device of free indirect thought are referred to M. H. Short's useful (1982) discussion. Obviously, Stephen is not truly 'silent', since his internal reflections are a large contribution to the text, though not to the dialogue: they are his dialogue with the dialogue. Examine Stephen's turns at private, self-addressed talk in relation to some of the characteristics of public talk pre-sented in this chapter – namely, talk as a managed negotiation; talk as in part a mutual working at communication but in part a struggle for advancement of one's own needs and interests; talk as designed

and oriented so as to respond cogently to preceding speakers' turns; talk as typically co-operative, with tactful 'self-editing', and so on. In what ways do free indirect thought 'turns' emerge as different from the direct speech turns considered in the chapter? In what respects do we have to take Stephen's commentary on what he and we witness as being at a different level or of different status from the reported conversation itself?

6   The fictional dialogues are legion in which analysis according to Burton's (1980) or Labov's (1972) models will highlight interesting features of the structure and dynamic of the talk. But the reader could begin with two dialogues reprinted in the companion to this volume: the dialogue in Hemingway's 'Cat in the Rain' story (Carter, 1982: 65–7) and the dialogue in the extract from Lawrence's 'Daughters of the Vicar' story (Carter, 1982: 116–7). A relevant related essay, which makes reference to the dialogue in 'Cat in the Rain' and contains an extended discussion of a key dialogic scene in Melville's *Bartleby*, is Toolan (1985).

Notes: Chapter 10

1   All references are to the Penguin edition (Harmondsworth, 1960). (The novel was first published in 1916.) Readers are advised to acquaint themselves with the Christmas dinner scene in the novel, as this scene is too extensive to be quoted in its entirety here.
2   For descriptions of 'phatic communion' and 'politeness phenomena', see Chapters 2 and 9 above respectively.
3   The terminology of purposes, goals and outcomes is taken from Hymes (1972).
4   The notion of 'noticeable absences' is taken from Schegloff (1968).
5   See Sacks, Schegloff and Jefferson (1974: 715).
6   On the sociolinguistic analysis of narratives and storytelling, see Labov and Waletzky (1967), Labov (1972), and Pratt (1977).

References: Chapter 10

Burton, D. (1980), *Dialogue and Discourse: A Sociolinguistic Approach to Modern Drama and Naturally Occurring Conversation* (London: Routledge & Kegan Paul).

Carter, R. (ed.) (1982), *Language and Literature: An Introductory Reader in Stylistics* (London: Allen & Unwin).

Grice, H. P. (1975), 'Logic and Conversation', in P. Cole and J. Morgan (eds), *Syntax and Semantics*, vol. 3, *Speech Acts* (New York: Academic Press), pp. 41–58.

Halliday, M. A. K. (1970), 'Language Structure and Language Function', in J. Lyons (ed.) *New Horizons in Linguistics* (Harmondsworth: Penguin), pp. 140–65.

Hymes, D. (1972), 'Models of the Interaction of Language and Social Life', in J. J. Gumperz and D. Hymes (eds) *Directions in Sociolinguistics* (New York: Holt, Rinehart & Winston), pp 35–72.

Labov, W. (1972), 'The Transformation of Experience in Narrative Syntax', in Labov, *Language in the Inner City* (Philadelphia, Penn.: University of Pennsylvania Press), pp. 354–96.

Labov, W., and Waletzky, J. (1967), 'Narrative Analysis: Oral Versions of Personal Experience', in J. Helm (ed.) *Essays on the Verbal and Visual Arts* (Seattle, Wash.: University of Washington Press), pp. 12–44.

Pratt, M. L. (1977), *Toward a Speech Act Theory of Literary Discourse* (Bloomington, Ind.: University of Indiana Press).

Sacks, H., Schegloff, E., and Jefferson, G. (1974), 'A Simplest Systematics for the Organisation of Turn-Taking for Conversation', *Language,* vol. 50, no. 4, pp. 596–735.

Schegloff, E. (1968), 'Sequencing in Conversational Openings', *American Anthropologist,* vol. 70, pp. 1075–95.

Short, M. H. (1982), 'Stylistics and the Teachings of Literature: With an Example from James Joyce's *Portrait of the Artist as a Young Man*', in Carter (1982), pp. 179–92.

Sinclair, J. M., and Coulthard, R. M. (1975), *Towards an Analysis of Discourse: The English used by Teachers and Pupils* (London: Oxford University Press).

Toolan, M. (1985), 'Analysing Fictional Dialogue', *Language and Communication,* vol. 5, no. 3, pp. 193–206.

Introduction to Chapter 11

In the remaining three Chapters, a range of issues in *literary theory* are directly engaged as central to a formulation of discourse stylistics. In this chapter, Vimala Herman addresses some complex theoretical issues concerning the construction of the subject in poetry. Taking as her main example a first-person poem by Gerard Manley Hopkins, Dr Herman examines not simply the grammatical dimensions of the first-person subject but also the wider contextual relations contracted by the multi-levelled ways in which the 'I' is discoursally produced in the poem. As far as analysis of language is concerned, this leads into consideration of how the 'I' participates in interactive contexts where certain roles and acts are motivated by special social practices.

Herman argues that the subject of the poem is constructed in a primarily dramatic, dialogic mode, and that it is necessary to regard the 'I' in the poem not as a singular or unitary entity but rather as a series of selves. In their relation to God in the poem, these selves alternate during the course of the text from vassal to friend, from powerless supplicant to intimate associate and confidant; and the God imaged in the poem is likewise pluralized through a range of situational contexts in which the dramatized God is displaced between alternating power roles. Herman concludes that the poem works as a kind of drama in which unequal and contradictory relations are enacted, and a powerful sense of unstable and fractured subjectivities is produced.

In terms of linguistic description, Vimala Herman mounts a strong case for analysis which goes beyond a single level of analytical attention. Further, it is essential to unlock not just syntactic or semantic but also pragmatic and sociolinguistic meanings. For this, a discourse-based approach to the direct and indirect speech acts of the poem, the said and the unsaid, in which much of the power of the poem resides, is an essential step.

11 Subject Construction as Stylistic Strategy in Gerard Manley Hopkins

VIMALA HERMAN

First-person poems of the kind of Hopkins's 'Thou art indeed just, Lord . . .' are of special interest for stylistic analysis since the persona, the subject of the discourse of the poem, is basically a linguistic creation, a product of the strategies used in the poem. The fact is sometimes obscured in traditional literary-critical practices, which have generally conflated the 'I' of a poem with the person of the author. Such a move has meant, in effect, that critical activity has tended to focus on the real-world author's thoughts, feelings, mental states, experiences, as the true object of criticism and source of meaning. That real-world authors have thoughts, feelings etc. nobody would deny, and that aspects of experience motivate the writing of poems can also be seen to be empirically valid. What is at stake, however, is the legitimacy for literary-critical practice of equating the personality of the author with the meaning or value that a reader derives from the reading of a poem.[1]

The conflation has resulted in certain critical procedures which either attempt to view a 'subject of life' behind the text or attempt to map a subjectivity derived from the prose works, assumed to be the subject of life, on to the subject of discourse of the poem. That the subjectivity of the real-world author may exceed all the subjectivities posited by its different discourses is generally not attended to, nor is the fact that the subject of discourse, the 'self' we encounter in the reading of a poem, has its own textual modes of existence, its own specificities of production within a poem as a linguistic and fictional construct. The naming of such a fictional, imaginary construct as the author is done through a process of inference, but such a move also has costs, as the whole debate about its merits and demerits, from the Russian formalists and New Critics onwards, makes clear (see Robey and Jefferson, 1986). On the one hand, it down-grades the textual modes of production of meaning by which a text functions as text; in this, its verbal and linguistic status is primary, which is sacrificed to considerations of text as symptom of personality. On the other hand, the differences in subjectivity constitution between a real-world subject and a fictional one are erased. In other words, there is a 'gap' between the two subjectivities of the author as empirical author and the fictional subject in poetic discourse, and the dynamism involved in the interpretative process as interaction between text and reader is neglected in the interests of paraphrase and simple mappings in which one subjectivity or 'self' is read as synonymous with the other. Understanding in neither project is favoured by the conflation – since the subjectivity of the author as much as the subject of the text is simplified by such a procedure. There has, of course, been some movement away from such practices in literary criticism of this orientation in the use of notions like 'persona' to characterize the speaking subject of discourse, but usually the 'persona' is related to the subject of the author as being the author in a more expressive mode or frame of mind than usual.

If critical interpretation cannot be reduced to a form of transparency in which the language of the poem functions as a window through which we view the author's personality, a major critical problem for first-person poems, in particular, is 'Who speaks?' Different answers to this question have been proposed within the scope of different literary theories[2], but our concern in this study is with its significance for stylistics and with the importance of insights and modes of analysis derived from the field of modern linguistics in enabling us to answer it.[3] The claim basically is that the subject is not one that is given a priori, outside the interaction between text and reader in the reading; it is no entity of any kind which may be verified, but is the product of work done by the reader in his or her engagement with the text in acts of interpretation. The text provides the cues for such subject production in its motivated organization as discourse, but the specific realization of the subject in any one reading is also dependent on reading decisions and reader inference. Thus, the subject is produced discursively, textually, in the poem, but known as effect in the reading. The linguistic choices of which the discourse of the text is composed should, therefore, be regarded as stylistic strategies enabling the process of subject production. Analysis would enable us to make explicit the modes of construction of such subjectivity as effected in the reading, within the terms set by the poem. But such an analysis is fundamentally dependent on knowledge of and attention to the poem's linguistic functioning.

It was the linguist Emile Benveniste who focused attention on the mediation of language in the construction of the subject. In his analysis of pronouns and subjectivity (1971) he declares that the pronoun *I*, unlike referential nouns in the system, could refer to no class of objects, since each instance of its use signals a unique referent, the one who has appropriated the pronoun in the act of speech. The appropriation is the act by which a speaker is designated as subject in the 'instance of discourse' in which *I* is used. Thus, it is the use of language which designates the subject, not the other way round. To quote Benveniste:

> *I* refers to the act of individual discourse in which it is pronounced, and by this it designates the speaker. It is a term that cannot be identified except in what we have called elsewhere 'an instance of discourse', and that has only a momentary reference. The reality to which it refers is the reality of discourse. It is in the instance of discourse in which *I* designates the speaker that the speaker proclaims himself as the 'subject'. And so it is literally true that the basis of subjectivity is in the exercise of language. If one really thinks about it, one will see that there is no other objective testimony to the identity of the subject except that which he himself gives about himself. (Benveniste, 1971: 226)

And later on, in the same article, extending the scope of this insight, he declares:

> Language is accordingly the possibility of subjectivity because it always contains the linguistic forms appropriate to the expression of subjectivity, and discourse provokes the emergence of subjectivity because it consists of discrete instances. In some way language puts forth 'empty' forms which each speaker, in the exercise of discourse, appropriates to himself and which he relates to his 'person' at the same time defining himself as 'I' and a partner as 'you'. The instance of discourse is thus constitutive of all the coordinates that define the subject . . . (Benveniste, 1971: 227)

The use of the pronoun, therefore, casts the individual who has so appropriated it in the 'role' of speaker, but, more than this, discrete instances of discourse are the means by which subjectivity is exercised. Each instance of discourse affords the possibility for the exercise of subjectivity, in Benveniste, and thus, it is the linguistic options used which provide us with the means for inferring the kind of subjectivity exercised in any instance. It is discourse, therefore, which posits the subject appropriate to it.

The exercise of language affords more complex possibilities for the display of subjectivity than the 'role' of speaker which Benveniste has analysed. Sociolinguistic and speech act determinations of linguistic forms in contexts of use provide complexities of function and 'role' which constrain the exercise of subjectivity accordingly. Variables of power, social status, solidarity, formality etc. in the sociolinguistic dimension of language use complicate the notion of 'role' that a subject may occupy. The performative dimension of language use, too, affords other 'roles' for the speaker, in the 'actional' possibilities available in the speech acts which may be performed in the saying and which have the properties not only of describing an existing state of affairs but of bringing others into being. Language, therefore, mediates. Whatever the nature of the interior 'self', it may only be known to another not as interior essence but through its displacements into modes of 'objective', constrained, public and social presentations. The presence of a speaker in face-to-face interaction, and the continuity of the speaking subject afforded by such a contingency, sometimes hides the fact that discrete 'role play' of this kind is engaged even in conversation, as Erving Goffman has pointed out. Goffman's (1982) study reveals how deeply constrained is the exercise of selfhood in the most habitual of interactional contexts. The impression given of a 'self' as well as the expression of one are seen to be dependent on mediations of 'performance' in the 'roles' established and the 'routines' employed. Amongst other things in Goffman's study, it is clear that the self in interaction is not an extension of essential internality directly into either language or action but is subject to necessities or 'projection' – an activity which is socially constrained, which the self as social actor delivers and which may, in turn, be interpreted by participants. The different ways by which a social actor's 'selves' are managed through the employment of a repertoire of sign activity in interaction, in response to social pressures and communicative needs, is a large part of the interest of Goffman's book.

In poetry where the use of *I* signals a speaker, but no speaker is given, questions of subjectivity – of 'Who speaks?' and of the nature of the 'self' posited by such use – actually involve attention to the dispersal of 'roles' – discrete performances of subjectivity – across the discourse of the poem, in the play of which the 'subject' is produced. In this attempt, the reader works 'backwards', so to speak, by inference, using overall linguistic knowledge to contextualize the sentences of the text as utterances, and attending to act, role, context, as appropriate to such usage. Such attentiveness to language functioning is the means by which, in our interaction with the text as readers, we create, in imagination, the subject in its complex constitution as afforded by the poem (see Herman, 1986). The subject thus produced has no existence except in its complex discoursal determinations and only within the space of reading.

Linguistic choices which construct the discourse of the poem, therefore, could be analysed not only along grammatical lines but along other dimensions involved in language use. Considerations of context, role, act and social practices, as relevant, are thus also brought into the reckoning. Apart from patternings of grammatical forms, which stylisticians have analysed as foregrounded cues to interpretation, there is the pragmatic level of a poem's functioning as appropriate to speech act analysis (see Austin, 1962; Searle, 1969, 1979). Moreover, in discourse 'more' could be meant than is 'said', in the 'implicatures' generated by utterances, as Paul Grice (1975) has pointed out, which are not encoded in the propositions of the sentences of the text but may be 'worked out' by processes of inference (see also Levinson, 1983: 97–162). Sociolinguistic variation, too, in a text can signal systematically social relations as appropriate among participants – of power, distance, formality, equality etc. – while the concept of discourse overall signifies a meaningful unit, motivated in its organization as discourse, to be interpreted. Given that instances of discourse are the means for the exercise of subjectivity, the linguistic choices of which the text is composed could be examined as stylistic strategies functioning in multi-levelled fashion, to enable the production of the subject in its various contextualized predicaments in the reading.

The dispersal of roles in the poem ensures that subjectivity is not a static or unitary affair but a series of displacements in which the dramas of selfhood are displayed. And it is the dramatic and dialogic mode of subject construction that is offered in the use of the first-person singular pronoun. As Lyons has pointed out:

> The grammatical category of person depends upon the notion of participant-roles and upon their grammaticalization in particular languages. The origin of the traditional terms 'first person', 'second person' and 'third person' is illuminating in this connexion. The Latin word 'persona' (meaning 'mask') was used to translate the Greek word for 'dramatic character' or 'role', and the use of this term by grammarians derives from their metaphorical conception of a language-event as a drama in which the principal role is played by the first person, the role subsidiary to his by the second person, and all other roles by the third person. It is important to note, however, that only the speaker and the addressee are actually participating in the drama. The term 'third person' is negatively defined with respect to 'first person' and 'second person': it does not correlate with any positive participant role. (Lyons, 1977: 638)

The answer to 'Who speaks?', therefore, involves complexity of engagement on the part of the reader with the language of the text, and responses to the strategies for subject production which the text makes available. Since the subject of discourse can only be known through its dramas or selfhood, it is the process itself which is of primary concern to the reader. In other words, the means of effecting subjectivity which the strategies of the poem make available generate effects of selfhood which are open to analysis by the reader.

In the analysis of the poem to follow, the question of the subject of discourse is confronted through attention to its mode of construction in the text. Since the subject of the poem is discursively produced, analysis is directed towards the different levels of discoursal functioning by which the effect of a 'Self' is created. The analysis will involve different levels – grammatical, sociolinguistic, pragmatic, as appropriate, and the consequences of such a mode of construction for the meaning of the poem will be considered. Although insights about language use from the field of linguistics are used, reader decisions between the options available in interpretation are also involved. There is no claim, therefore, that all possibilities for interpretation have been exhausted in this enterprise; only that an attempt is made to explore what may be gained in understanding literary texts when activated linguistic knowledge is brought to bear on a language artefact like a poem.

Justus quidem tu es, Domine, si disputem tecum; verumtamen justa loquar ad te: Quare via impiorum prosperatur? &c.

THOU art indeed just, Lord, if I contend
With thee; but, sir, so what I plead is just.
Why do sinners' ways prosper? and why must
Disappointment all I endeavour end?

Wert thou my enemy, O thou my friend,
How wouldst thou worse, I wonder, than thou dost
Defeat, thwart me? Oh, the sots and thralls of lust
Do in spare hours more thrive than I that spend,

Sir, life upon thy cause. See, banks and brakes
Now, leaved how thick! laced they are again
With fretty chervil, look and fresh wind shakes

Them; birds build – but not I build; no, but strain,
Time's eunuch, and not breed one work that wakes.
Mine, O thou lord of life, send my roots rain.

The poem is one of those written by Hopkins in Dublin in 1889, the last year of his life. In terms of issues confronted, the poem shares much with the 'Dark Sonnets' written earlier, and critics have varied in their judgments as to whether the poem shows similar depths of desolation as the earlier sonnets or whether it could be read as revealing signs of recovery (see Mariani, 1970). Debates of this kind about how to interpret the poem reveal, too, the importance of this religious subject posited in the poem and the nature of its subjectivity. The exploration of its internal mode of construction is, consequently, relevant.

The poem is written in the first person, but includes the addressee, the second person, a 'Thou', in its discourse. Grammatically, as we have seen, the first-person singular pronoun conventionally refers to the person speaking in a context of utterance who uses the term, but in fictional texts, no 'real' speaker being available, the imaginative process of subject creation is initiated by the reader assigning a referent as required by such usage, which initiates, too, the process of interaction between text and reader that constitutes literary reading. The use of second-person forms in the poem posit an addressee, and thus the discourse is structured as interaction of a self with an other, and the strategies used to construct the terms of this interaction are the means by which the subject of discourse is effected within the drama of its interactional predicaments.

The use of 'I' and 'Thou' enables us to infer that these places in discourse have been appropriated, but we are interested not in 'what' speaks to 'what' but in 'who' to 'whom', and why – since any speaker may appropriate the pronoun and address any other. The specificities of subject production are thus dependent on other aspects of the language used, and in the relations that such usage posits between 'I', and 'Thou'.

Significantly the poem begins with 'Thou', in an act of address, a one-way address, to the other by the speaking persona. Address forms are, in fact, foregrounded in this poem by their repetitive use, but modes of address vary. 'Thou' is designated sociolinguistically as within a special register, namely within religious discourse, and hence practices appropriate to that domain are brought into play. The inter-action is thus located as a religious one – in which a self communes with its God, in acts of address. The role for the speaker, it would seem, is thus one of deference or worship in prayer, as appropriate to this domain.

This inference, however, cannot be sustained in its entirety as the poem proceeds. In the first place, the address form 'Thou' is supple-mented by other address forms – titles like 'Lord', 'Sir', 'Lord of Life' and another vocative, 'my friend', which are optional in usage. Since these forms need not be used, they are marked by their inclusion in the poem. This supplementary mode of address signals the existence of other domains than the private one of prayer. The interaction is held in tension with these other, more public, domains, and the course of prayer is constructed along the interactions of this more public and formal dimension. The consequence is that the subject of discourse is split in its construction along private and public domains accordingly.

Pronouns of address, as Brown and Gilman (1960) have shown, can be analysed along an axis of 'solidarity' and an axis of 'power', in which interpersonal relations of reciprocity or non-reciprocity can be gauged. The semantics of such pronouns can be understood as the 'co-variance between the pronouns used and the objective relationship existing between addresser and addressee' (Brown and Gilman, 1960: 253). Pronouns of power signal social contexts of the exercise of power and predicate asymmetrical relationships, while those of soli-darity signal more equal, symmetrical ones, in which rights are more equally distributed. Titles, like pronouns of power, signal asymmetrical relationships in the social contexts of their usage, and thus their appearance in the poem posits inequality, asymmetry of power and obligation between the participants in the poem. But terms of address also provide what Paul Friedrich (1972) has called 'an expressive function' within relationships. Second-person pronouns, in particular, 'link abstract properties of basic grammatical paradigms to a second matrix of culturally specific components and are of major emotional and social significance'. Thus 'cognitive aspects of culture' can be inferred from their usage, as well as 'sentiments of feeling', especially in their deviation. The deviant use of a familiar term between interactants where a formal one would be expected, or vice versa, can signify some extra emotional load – contempt, surprise etc. This holds good for other forms of address as well.

In the poem, apart from 'my friend', all the address forms signal roles of power and authority for 'Thou' – 'Lord', 'Sir', 'Lord of Life'. The interactions of the poem are thus distributed along a scale of formality and familiarity, distance and closeness. Each such usage retroactively designates a role for the speaker, of inferiority or equality, and interpersonal distance is manipulated. Formality and deference predominate, with the one reciprocal form, 'my friend', foregrounded by deviation as a consequence.

The interactions of the poem are constructed basically as 'unequal encounters' between a self placed as 'inferior' and an other as 'superior', an other of power. But even this is not stable. Roles of power are in turn specified as practised within different social domains: terms like 'Thou' are appropriate to a Christian deity; so also is 'Lord', which signifies both Christian and feudal contexts of use. 'Sir' is a secular term which in contexts of secular practice designates appropriate interactions of power and authority – a child to a schoolmaster, the non-privileged to the privileged, and so on. Such utterances place the speaker in profound postures of deference, of humility, of smallness of power, of inexperience, with respect to the other. But this strategy of specifying the self in deference, humility, inexperience, unworthiness, is also undercut by the one address form of equality, 'my friend', when the speaker is awarded a role of equality, and rights of equality, which destabilize its dominant mode of construction.

God is consequently known in two contradictory roles in this poem – the one in majesty and power, in lordship over the persona; the other, within the trust and closeness of friendship. The speaker is posited in equivalently antithetical roles, as vassal and as friend. The deviation signals optionality – the possibility of another reality of interaction, expressed with emotional force, as deviation of this kind signals, within the dominant power structure of Lord and vassal which structures the interaction. Deference and humility are both expected and given, but the existence of an option, in the use of 'my friend', signalling another status, another mode of interaction, its reduced and minimal usage, all raise questions of interpretation for the reader.

The question of power invested in the other in such interactions raises, too, the question of rights, services due, responsibilities and contractual obligations between the two interactants. The projection of a mode of equality into the poem in this way raises a crucial moment of inconsistency in which the smooth distributions of power and the functioning of contractual roles is disturbed. One mode of 'bondage' is thus held against another – in the role of vassal against friend. Contractual relations also oscillate, the one focuses on the speaker's obligations within the bond of service and obedience to 'Lord', 'Sir'; the other, on reciprocal obligations between the two within the freer and closer bonds of 'my friend'.

The instabilities generated by such variation in usage create an axis on which turns the whole question of rights, services rendered and returns due between 'I' and 'thou' in their various subroles. On the one hand, the positioning of the speaker in inferiority and inequality in the exchange places the subject within a situation of non-reciprocity in which the authority of the other is supreme, and the sway of that authority may not be questioned. The mode of subjectivity open to it is one of unquestioning service and obedience to the will of the other, in this one-way exercise of rights, in which the question of returns is inappropriate. On the other hand, there is an optional mode of subjectivity – in reciprocity, in exchange for obligations, with the expectation of returns built in. The subject of prayer is thus caught in this dialectic of reciprocity and non-reciprocity that constructs its situation. The speech appropriate to its situation, the utterances that compose the poem, is conditioned, too, by what it may say as friend and what it may not say as vassal. The management of this dialectic is, in turn, dependent on the assumption of other roles, as it performs, dramatizes, in its specificities, the impossible terms of its constitution and its consequences.

Speech act and grammatical choices reveal similar tensions and conflicts at work. Given that, overall, the sociolinguistic forms create a framework of participation of unequally matched participants, with power distributed and disrupted within the poem, speech acts analysis provides another perspective on the process of subject creation, since the subject so constituted within such contradictory power relations with its God, may yet respond in specific ways to its situation. Thus, the performative aspect of language functioning – the consideration of what is being 'done' in the 'saying' – enables the subject to be known in the specificities of its engagement with its predicament. The displacements of its acts and roles along the utterances of the poem, and the contexts and conditions of felicitous performance that they evoke, are yet another level of analysis in which the processes of subject production may be known.

The poem opens with an act of assertion,[5] an assertion of a fact, 'Thou art indeed just, Lord . . .' in a posture of deference. The propositional content of the assertion, the posture assumed and the speech act performed place the speaker as the prototypic religious subject. This assertive opening and posture is immediately undercut by the following if-clause, which is also a non-assertive clause, 'if I contend with thee'. In speech act terms, what began as a straight assertion, ends up as an explicit speech act of contention.[6] The final part of this utterance, 'but, sir, so what I plead is just', introduces yet another speech act, named in the saying as one of pleading, with the contrasting conjunction 'but' creating a rhetorical balance between the two contrasting parts of the utterance. Thus the first clause posits the speaker in a role of affirmation of a truth about the other – 'thou' as 'just' – but the second and third clauses place it as contending with, and on the basis of, that truth and pleading its case before God.

The act of contention signifies sub-acts of dispute, struggle and strife, and evokes a context of conflict and even of competition between the two participants. 'Contend' is appropriate, too, to another context in which rights are disputed, a context of Law.[7] So is 'plead', so that the act of pleading falls under the scope of the act of contention, since one may plead one's case while contesting another's. Contention could be termed a negative act – one of conflict and not of co-operation. So what is in dispute? The rhetorical balance of the syntax of the utterance places the two aspects of the dispute in symmetrical relation – 'Thou art . . . just'/'what I plead is just' – the same complement ending both clauses. It is justice which is at stake here. A wrong, some injustice, has been committed, and within the scope of law redress may be sought and justice done. The ambivalance in this scenario, that it is God whose justice is being questioned, against the standards of divine justice, makes God both the accused and the judge – the persona pleading its case before a divinity which is also its adversary, split in its role. In its pleading, accordingly, the persona is not only an advocate for its own cause, but also a supplicant.

Two modes of subjectivity are predicated for the persona. One, as supplicant, with a personal voice within the context of religion; the other, as advocate, with an institutional one, calling God to book, seemingly outside such a context. The role of contender affords a stance of equality, provisionally, with God, even if with deference, and the course of this voice, and its claims to justice and equality, is to be seen in the change in address forms used in this section of the poem. Instead of the religious 'Lord', which is used only at the beginning and the end of the poem, we get secular forms of address – 'Sir', 'my friend', or none at all – during the course of the contention. What is being contended is as much the claims of the flesh within the difficult terms of its religious bondage as the justness of God's justice overall. Equality and inequality are paradoxically and simultaneously present in this interaction, but in a kind of turbulent equilibrium.

The role of contender, with its disruptive secular voice, is not, in fact, outside the possibilities of religious subjectivity, since this drama of contention, and the threatened dislocation, is placed firmly within the tradition of religion itself: these lines are a translation of a passage from the Book of Jeremiah,[8] and hence disputation of this kind remains a religious act, the persona borrowing another role, another discourse, in which to embed its own. But the very fact of such a choice is significant, and, although the control of religious tradition holds the equivocations temporarily in place, such an appropriation has other consequences, since the speaker in the Book of Jeremiah addresses an Old Testament God, known in the Christian tradition for stringency of law. The calling on such a God in fact intensifies the dispute about justice that structures the discourse of the poem, and intensifies, too, the emotional force of the contending voice.

The rest of the poem except for the final line dramatizes the act of contention, with the speaker pleading his own case in both roles, advocate and supplicant. The skill of the advocate is to be found in the rhetorical strategies – especially in the patternings of co-ordinate clauses in the syntax, such clauses being linked by *and, but, than* etc. Such strategies create the possibility of balance – of contrast, conditionality, comparison etc. – through which the case is presented. The use of conditionals in presenting hypotheses, the repetition of questions, the direct and urgent illustrations of the speaker's point with contrasting examples from nature, all serve to create a speaker who is at one level a skilful public orator examining the workings of justice. But ghosting these manoeuvres is also the emotional force of the supplicant, a deep but unstated sense of injustice surfacing only by implication in the descriptions given of the workings of justice. The unsaid personal force of the personal predicament surfaces in the semantic load of the terms of the antithesis that construct the poem. The roles adopted and the manner of disputation in the public performances have ulterior purposes, at one level, in the fictional context of the poem, as arguments or disputations to persuade the addressee of the rights of the speaker's case; but the underside of this performance reveals a private, deeply afflicted subject, whose silent, private pleading, in its personal extremity, is for relief from the situation presented. The overall, implicit and unstated illocutionary force of this section, mediated by many other acts and roles and modes of interaction displaying the workings of the justice known, is a profoundly felt assertion of injustice – 'This is unfair'.

Speech act strategies are reinforced by grammatical strategies: the organization of syntax functions in its repeated balance like the equilibrium of the scales of justice, but the semantics of the forms used provide sharp contrasts between the two ends of the balance constructed by the syntax. Two states of affairs are posited, and contrasted or compared, but within the purview of God's justice but since the states of affairs presented are mutually contradictory with respect to any normal understanding of right and wrong, just and unjust, God's justice itself is put into crisis. The balance of the syntax provides the stance of reasonableness, of presenting the truths of the case, of stating things as they are. But the terms of the contrast are dire enough for the whole question of justice for a religious subject to be starkly dramatized within the competing terms of the contention.

This second section, which spans three stanzas, initiates the 'contention' with two parallel questions:

> Why do sinners' ways prosper? and why must
> Disappointment all I endeavour end?

In both questions the persona is cast in the role of interrogator attempting to elicit reasons, answers to the questions posed. The use of the interrogative in context, of course, signals a speaker who does not know the information to be elicited. But what is known is the two states of affairs posited in the propositions contained in these two questions – that sinners' ways prosper, and that disappointment in all his endeavours is the lot of the speaker. The syntactic parallelism of these forms also contains sharp semantic contrasts which separate the ways of sinners in their prosperity from the paucity of the speaker's lot. The questions ask for clarification, but simultaneously assert a paradoxical state of affairs in which, contrary to expectations of religious justice, 'sinners' prosper, while the other term in the opposition, 'I', not a sinner, by definition, in this opposition, fails in its endeavours and does not prosper. The public stance is still deferential, the speaker does not openly accuse or indict, merely asks for clarification, but by such a strategy opens up for consideration the question of how just is justice of this kind, for God and for the reader. Given that the state of affairs posited would normally not be regarded as fair or just, the overall illocutionary force of these speech acts is one of disavowal by any fair-minded person of the justice known in this state of affairs. Yet, another unspoken possibility also surfaces: if this is fair, what mode of religious subjectivity is open to a speaker who is placed in a situation of alienation to which not even sinners are subjected? And what mode of divine justice is this?

The stance of the speaker has been seemingly neutral, wanting to know the answers to the questions asked, in the assumption of the public role of interrogator, but the personal force of the speaking voice can be known in the repetitions expressed, since they function also, far less neutrally, as an act of lament. 'Why . . .? why . . .?': the questioning signals, too, the speaker's own bafflement at this state of affairs. The deference of the speaker posited in the address forms at the beginning is slightly suspended here, since no address forms are used, and the interaction is more direct. But the speaker's speech is still embedded in that of the Book of Jeremiah – the more secular claim to known standards of human justice, within which God is called to account, still held in place against the claims of God's justice in the working of religious law.

The second stanza opens with another complex form, in which an interrogative is embedded in a conditional. Both clauses are, of course, non-assertive forms again. Nothing is asserted as yet. The contending continues with a hypothesis which is presented for God's and the reader's consideration:

> Wert thou my enemy, O thou my friend,
> How wouldst thou worse, I wonder, than thou dost
> Defeat, thwart me?

The rational stance of the speaker as contender, in the syntax, – *if this, then how this?'* – invites both God and reader to reason through to its conclusion the hypothesis presented, but intensified contrasts are available at other levels of this utterance. The hypothesis is *if God were enemy, could worse be done*, but addressed to God, 'my friend'. The polarity of the contrasting designations of God as my enemy/my friend, one as seemingly hypothetical possibility, the other as seemingly realized fact, and the comparator in the interrogative 'how would'st thou worse . . .?', which compares the outcome of a hypothesis with the outcome of a fact, provide the continuing balance in this presentation of one state of affairs with respect to another. The simultaneous move into the informal register, signalling the other possibility – of closeness and bonds of friendship – makes the contrast stark. If God had been an enemy rather than a friend would worse accrue than the defeating and thwarting which has been done? The speech act of questioning, predicating a state of not-knowing, in fact contains an overall speech act of assertion – that it could not be worse. The presentation of the question within a hypothesis directs the reader to argue through the possibility given the facts – *would enemies do worse than friends of this kind do?* – which puts the question-mark again over the justice of God.

The 'pleading' has been conducted in the formal balance of contrasting two states of affairs. But the personal sense of 'pleading' also emerges in the use of exclamatory particles – 'O', 'Oh' which make overt in their use emotional intensities of various kinds on the part of the formal contender. In the rest of the poem, this aspect of 'pleading' surfaces often enough, not only in the use of particles of this kind but also in the use of exclamatory structures, to affect the formal balance of the other mode of pleading, to intensify the urgency in the whole undertaking. This personal, emotionally charged voice, out of place on the whole within the formal role of contender, posits its own addressee, the unused option of the other face of the deity – a personal confidant, a God of charity not law, to whom, within the bonds of friendship and the privacy of prayer, the force of the emotional charge and cost, nowhere stated as such in the disputations of the poem, may also be communicated.

The rest of the poem alternates two sets of strategies in order to build up to the climax of the last line. Declaratives alternate with imperatives, and on the face of it, a description of a state of affairs is followed by a directive to the addressee that something should be done. This initial balance of construction, however, is complicated by the internal semantic contrasts, polar and stark in their expression, within the declaratives, while the imperatives function not only as directives but also indirectly as expressives, which usually signal psychological states within the speaker. The rhetorical force of the semantic contrasts together with the indirect force of the expressives serve to construct the personal force of the 'plea' for change in the existing balance of the scales of justice. The structure of the syntax in the declaratives continues to provide the terms of the contentious workings of God's justice; the formality of the context of utterance re-emerges with the address forms used. While the context of formal pleading places the speaker still within the role of contender, disputing the terms of God's justice, this role is systematically fractured by the personal intensities that emerge, disrupting the formal role undertaken, so that the game of the contention and equality of rights ends with a cry of need to 'Lord', who is 'mine', in whose gift lies redress. The poem ends, therefore, with the speaker in a role of dependence, at the point where the terms of the dispute presented and the skill of the disputation appear to have tipped the balance in the speaker's favour.

The first declarative sentence, functioning as an assertive, states the 'facts', setting out a comparison, again, between two states of affairs – seemingly a description, but emotionally charged with the exclamatory 'Oh'. One set of affairs pertains to 'sots and thralls of lust', the other to the speaker. The opposition in these terms links back to the first opposition presented between 'sinners' and 'I', and a semantic field of opposition to 'I' is created, in a world under divine providence in which sinners prosper and the excesses of lust thrive in their carelessness to divine dictat, as opposed to 'I', who does not, in spite of his commitment to God's cause. The presentation of the two sets of facts is initiated by an exclamation, and the emotional investment signalled here is intensified by the rhetorical force of the antithesis in the contrast of time. The sots and thralls thrive more 'in spare hours' for their own ends than 'I', who does not in spite of spending 'life upon thy cause'. The unfairness of such justice is left implicit, with a force that may only be inferred, since what is shown to us as the truth of the case can be matched against standards of what is and is not fair only by the reader, who assesses the speaker's dire predicament. The starkness of the contrast between the two sets of beneficiaries of divine justice intensifies the sense of unfairness, implicit in such a presentation, the irony of the situation and the need for redress, an unstated need left open to scrutiny by a God acknowledged as the ultimate dispenser of justice.

This is followed by two imperatives – 'See', 'Look' – in which the personal urgency and emotional intensity completely disrupt the general formality of address which has been in force up till now. The directive in the imperative enjoins the addressees – God and also the reader – to turn their gaze into the world of natural fertility and the natural rhythm of regeneration and growth, to the leaved and laced chervil lush on banks and breaks, in natural movement in the wind. It also functions as yet another strategy to provide contrast – from the natural world this time – to illustrate the workings of God's justice. The expressive force of these forms, in the urgency of the imperatives, signals again emotional intensity on the part of the speaker. A three-way contrast is now set up between the diseased fertility of 'the sots and thralls of lust', the natural and seasonal fertility of the lush chervil and, in this opposition, the infertility of the speaker. A complex series of ambiguities are also brought into play on this theme of fertility – since the fertility open to 'I', who spends 'life upon thy cause' can only be metaphorical, in spiritual service, which involves the disavowal or sacrifice of both natural fertility and the fertility of lust. Moreover, it is not clear whether the contrast is, in effect, three way, or binary – nature being included among the 'sots and thralls of lust' or not. The interpretation of a three-way contrast is favoured, since it places the speaker in a complex series of exclusions and oppositions, heir to no form of regeneration, no natural and hence seasonal cycle of the regeneration of spring following upon the deaths of winter, no human mode of regeneration either, with or without the sanction of God. These symbols of barrenness, as pertinent to 'I' within the chosen life of commitment to God, pose the question of justice yet again, with deep emotional force. The urgency of the imperatives directs the addressee to focus – 'see', 'look' – and, as the beauty of the naturally fertile world swings into view, so does the contrast, with the one who is excluded in the antitheses of the poem from any such possibility. As the force of the pleading intensifies, the case for redress gets stronger.

The next clause, within the final stanza, is a declarative with the speech act of assertion and functions yet again as a strategy to intensify contrast. The assertion asserts the 'truth' of the situation presented in bare dichotomies, explicitly, within the balance of the connective 'but', which foregrounds contrast. The contrast is further emphasized by the repetitions of the negative – which create stark, explicit polarities which construct the impossible negations of the speaker's lot within the justice of God.

> ... birds build – but not I build; no, but strain,
> Time's eunuch, and not breed one work that wakes.

The force of the antithesis is in one simple parallelism of form – *birds build/but not I build*. Within the second term of the antithesis are further patternings of contrastive conjunctions and negatives which construct the state of affairs appropriate to the speaker. Everything appropriate to the 'I' side of the opposition is built in negativity – frustration and sterility. The contrast with the building of the birds carries forward the theme of barrenness in the previous stanza. Birds build nests for the young – connotations of new life, nurture, fertility, life, new beginnings of cycles of life, surface again in this simple image, none of which are open to the speaker. Instead, we get the image of sexual castration, the eunuch bonded in the service of time, straining endlessly and uselessly, fundamentally bereft of any possibility of fertility or regeneration – of one violated. The force of the speaker's complaint is left implicit. The statement of his position in these terms as 'truth', as becomes an assertive, brings to a climax the case against the dispensation of justice that has been presented in the discourse of the poem. It signals too, all the intensities of emotion which may be inferred of speakers in such a predicament, none of which is articulated. *Which just God*, we are forced to ask, *would permit such a state of affairs and such suffering to continue*? – which is the question that the rhetoric of the speaker's discourse is posing to the addressee.

The contender has presented his case, within the terms of his justice, to God, who, it has been acknowledged, is also just. In the attempt, the imbalance between the two modes of justice has been made available chiefly in the presentation of states of affairs which contradict the notion of a just working of justice. The poem ends as it began, with the address to 'lord', now further designated as 'lord of life'. Casting off the role of contender, and the equality of his rightful claims, and switching away from the secular address forms used in the central part of the poem, the speaker again assumes the deference of religious subjectivity adopted at the beginning in the address to 'Lord'. The final speech act in imperative form is one of urgent supplication – 'send my roots rain'. The utterance is in the imperative, and hence a directive to the addressee, but we may infer, too, expressive force, a powerful expression of need for such a response given the dualities that are operative. The force of the pleading thus ends with a plea in prayer, from the depths of the speaker's 'roots', as he bends the knee again in service, confirming his dependence on a God in whose power, and within whose arbitrary justice, lies the redress and relief of 'rain'.

The subject of the poem has been effected, therefore, through the stylistic strategies employed, through which a reader has come to know the deeply conflicting terms of its subjectivity. Stylistic choices, in the address forms used, the speech acts performed, the grammatical patternings and semantic contrasts employed, have been analysed as strategies to effect the kind of subject posited in the poem. In the effort, the subject has been split along dual modes of realization, known only in the exercise of such options as provided by the discourse of the poem, chiefly in the plurality of roles that the stylistic choices have made available.

The overall role for the subject has been that of supplicant to God, in a posture of prayer. But within this role, context and posture other subroles have been adopted that have deeply complicated the nature of the praying subject of the poem's opening. The assumption of the role of contender has ensured that the content of prayer will be the issue of God's justice in the life of the religious. The enactment of this role has involved the role of 'pleader', dual in its constitution. It has involved, too, rhetorical strategies of balance and contrast through which the claims of a justice on human terms has been seen to be at odds with a justice on divine terms. Within the contention addressed to a God of law have been seen traces of appeal to a God of love – a subjectivity of desire for God's charity simultaneously operative in a subjectivity constructed in knowledge of God's justice. The poem ends on a note of acceptance, the supplicant role to the fore again, but the issues of justice raised remain unclosed, as the workings of God's justice remain hard, dark and obscure. It is in the workings of such fissured subjectivity that the power of the poem lies. The underlying conflicts of its construction ensure that two modes of subjectivity are simultaneously in process. Consequently, the unsaid functions against the question of love, the rational skill of contender is underwritten by the emotional force of the supplicant, and, overall, the possibility of a subject of innocence in God's charity is held against the possibility of one of guilt in law. The complexity of the subject, therefore, has been known through the dramas of its discourse, language creating the subject in this instance, which has been analysed through attention to the poem's linguistic functioning.

Thus what we have engaged with is language: the cognitive and evocative power of the poem, a product of the linguistic system and its functions. Whatever Hopkins 'really' experienced in his private self in relation to the issues raised in the poem, we suspect, remains inviolate in spite of appearances. What we have is not transparence or some kind of 'realism', but a displaced projection – the presentation of an imaginative drama, structured as poetry and realized as art, within the shared and public medium of language.

Suggestions for Further Work: Chapter 11

1 (i) Using the modes of analysis of the 'subject' adopted in this chapter, examine the poem by Donne, 'A Hymne to God the Father', discussed by Michael Hoey in Chapter 7. How would you describe the relative nature of the interactive context in the two poems?

   (ii) Conversely, examine this poem by Hopkins with reference to the problem – solution and matching relations analysed by Hoey in his chapter. What, if any, are the extra dimensions which your analysis of 'Thou art indeed just, Lord. . .' acquires?

2 Explore *one* other of Hopkins's 'Dark Sonnets' using these modes of discourse-based analysis. Good examples might be: 'Not, I'll not, carrion comfort . . .', or 'I wake and feel the fell of dark . . .'.

3 Examine the following poem of George Herbert:

Love (III)

Love bad me welcome: yet my soul drew back,
      Guiltie of dust and sinne.
But quick-ey'd Love, observing me grow slack
      From my first entrance in,
Drew nearer to me, sweetly questioning,
      If I lack'd any thing.

A guest, I answer'd, worthy to be here:
      Love said, you shall be he.
I the unkinde, ungratefull? Ah my deare,
      I cannot look on thee.
Love took my hand, and smiling did reply,
      Who made the eyes but I?

Truth Lord, but I have marr'd them: let my shame
      Go where it doth deserve.
And know you not, sayes Love, who bore the blame?
      My deare, then I will serve.
You must sit down, sayes Love, and taste my meat:
      So I did sit and eat.[9]

In your analysis consider some of the following linguistic features of the text: direct v. reported speech; the different forms of address; the functions of interrogative and assertive (or declarative) speech acts; the relations between refusal and acceptance; the relevance of the situational context of a feast or supper.

4   An interesting article to be read alongside this chapter, and to complement the texts suggested here for further study is Wadman (1983). The article also usefully complements Chapter 9 above.

Notes: Chapter 11

1   This problem has a long history. Overviews of the issues involved from different modern literary-critical perspectives are to be found in Robey and Jefferson (1986).
2   The most influential exploration of this issue in literary theory is to be found in the work of literary critics with a psychoanalytic orientation derived from the work of Jacques Lacan. Recent explorations of the issues involved are available in the following: Belsey (1980); Easthope (1983); see also, Lacan (1977); Lemaire (1977). Recent issues on 'Psychopoetics', *Poetics* , vol. 13 (1984), and *Style*, vol. 18, no. 3 (1984), are also relevant. Although I acknowledge the value of Lacan's insights into the nature of subjectivity from the psychoanalytic point of view, my own interest in the question is from a different perspective, via the linguistic processes involved in 'subject creation', which bring into the analysis work done chiefly in the field of Anglo-American linguistics and generally not attend to, or attended to rather inadequately, by Lacanian literary critics. My orientation is different, too, in that my primary concern is not with exploring, promoting, or questioning Lacan's theories and their application to literature. It is not clear to me which notion of the 'unconscious' literary critics are arguing over – the author's, the reader's, or some, as yet, undeveloped notion of a textual unconscious, when Lacan's model is transferred to the field of literary studies. Nor am I entirely free from the suspicion that there is sometimes a reversal in literary studies of Lacan's insight that the unconscious is structured like a language into a belief that language is structured like the unconscious, which is in danger of making the enterprise into a rather circular affair.
3   'Modern linguistics' includes in its scope not only the study of the grammar but also the area of 'language-in-use' – the fields of pragmatics, sociolinguistics, discourse analysis. cf. Levinson (1983), Crystal and Davy (1969), Hudson (1980), Brown and Yule (1983), which are relevant, if selective, publications in this vast area of study. See also Herman (1983) for a more detailed exposition of the relevance of these areas to language used in literature. My view of the relationship of linguistics to literature, therefore, differs considerably from the more formalistic, non-contextualized view of this relationship in the work of those who have concentrated primarily on syntax and phonology.
4   *Poems of Gerard Manley Hopkins*, ed. W. H. Gardiner and N. H. Mackenzie (London: Oxford University Press, 1967), p. 106.
5   The speech act categories of assertives, directives, expressives, commissives, declarations, are taken from Searle (1979: 1–29).
6   See Caffi (1984: 440–67) for an account of the use of explicit performatives of this kind in discourse.
7   Literary critics have noted the intrusion of this context into the poem, but

have done so in passing, and have failed to develop its significance. See, for instance, Heuser (1958) and Gardiner (1958: 364–5). The context of law, and the issues of justice, guilt and innocence that it raises, appear in other poems of this period, and appear important in questions of religious subjectivity (cf. Herman, 1986).

8   cf. Mariani (1970: 301). The relevant verses cited by Mariani are Jer. 12: 1–3.

> Thou indeed, O Lord, art just if I plead with thee, but yet I will speak what is just to thee: why doth the way of the wicked prosper: why is it well with all them that transgress, and do wickedly? Thou hast planted them, and they have taken root: they prosper and bring forth fruit: thou art near in their mouth and far from their reins. And thou, O Lord hast known me, thou hast seen me, and proved my heart with thee.

9   Taken from *The Works of George Herbert*, ed. F. E. Hutchinson (Oxford: Clarendon Press, 1967).

References: Chapter 11

Austin, J. L. (1962), *How to Do Things With Words* (Oxford: Oxford University Press).

Belsey, C. (1980), *Critical Practice* (London: Methuen).

Benveniste, E. (1971), 'The Nature of Pronouns' and 'Subjectivity and Language', in Benveniste *Problems in General Linguistics* trans. M. E. Meek (Miami: University of Miami Press), pp. 217–22, 223–32.

Brown, G., and Yule, G. (1983), *Discourse Analysis* (Cambridge: Cambridge University Press).

Brown, R., and Gilman, A. (1960), 'The Pronouns of Power and Solidarity' in T. A. Sebeok (ed.), *Style in Language* (Cambridge, Mass.: Massachusetts Institute of Technology Press), pp. 253–76.

Ciaffi, C. (1984), 'Some remarks on Illocution and Metacommunication', *Journal of Pragmatics* vol. 8, pp. 440–67.

Crystal, D., and Davy, D. (1969), *Investigating English Style* (London: Longman).

Easthope, A. (1983), *Poetry as Discourse* (London: Methuen).

Friedrich, P. (1972), 'Social Context and Semantic Feature: The Russian Pronominal Usage', in T. Gumperz (ed.), *Directions in Sociolinguistics* (New York: Holt, Rinehart & Winston), pp. 294–8.

Gardiner, W. H. (1969), *Gerard Manley Hopkins (1844–1889): A Study of Poetic Idiosyncracy in Relation to the Poetic Tradition*, vol. 2 (London: Oxford University Press).

Goffman, E. (1982), *The Presentation of Self in Everyday Life* (Harmondsworth: Penguin).

Grice, H. P. (1975), 'Logic and Conversation', in P. Cole and J. Morgan (eds), *Syntax and Semantics*, vol. 3, *Speech Acts* (New York: Academic Press), pp. 41–58.

Herman, V. (1983), 'Literariness and Linguistics: An Introduction', *Prose Studies* vol. 6, no. 2, pp. 99–122.

Herman, V. (1986), 'Acts and Contexts in G. M. Hopkins' "I wake and feel the fell of dark . . ."', in T. D'Haen (ed.), *Linguistic Contributions to the Study of Literature* (Amsterdam: Rodopi), pp. 89–111.

Heuser, A. (1958), *The Shaping Vision of Gerard Manley Hopkins*, (London: Oxford University Press).

Hudson, R. A. (1980), *Sociolinguistics* (Cambridge: Cambridge University Press).

Lacan, J. (1977), *Ecrits: A Selection*, trans. A. Sheridan (London: Hogarth).

Lemaire, A. (1977), *Jacques Lacan*, trans. D. Macey (London: Routledge & Kegan Paul).

Levinson, S. (1983), *Pragmatics* (Cambridge: Cambridge University Press).

Lyons, J. (1977), *Semantics* vol. 2 (Cambridge: Cambridge University press).

Mariani, P. L. (1970), *A Commentary on the Complete Poems of Gerard Manley Hopkins* (Ithaca, NY: Cornell University Press), pp. 298–303.

Robey, D., and Jefferson, A. (eds) (1986), *Modern Literary Theory; A Comparative Introduction* (London: Batsford).

Searle, J. R. (1969), *Speech Acts: An Essay in the Philosophy of Language* (Cambridge: Cambridge University Press).

Searle, J. R. (1979), 'A Taxonomy of Illocutionary Acts' and 'Indirect Speech Acts', in *Expression and Meaning* (Cambridge: Cambridge University Press), pp. 1–29, 30–57.

Wadman, K. L. (1983), 'Private Ejaculations: Politeness Strategies in George Herbert's Poems Directed to God', *Language and Style*, vol. 61, no. 1, pp. 87–105.

Introduction to Chapter 12

In this chapter John Haynes calls for a more fully integrated descriptive model for the phonology of texts. His
main argument is that the analysis of metre and of the
textual meanings of particular phonological schemes is
best undertaken with reference to other levels of language organization, and to this end he makes particular
use of a systematic functional model of language. This
model compels consideration of the social functions of
language, and in this respect the functions of metre
cannot be discounted. Metre is not an intra-textual
property, describable solely in terms of its aesthetic functions; it works simultaneously within a 'higher-order'
social semiotic of choice, which signals something of the
user's own ideological preferences. Haynes mounts a
convincing case that the choice of metrical scheme is in
many ways an ideological choice, and explores the
complex connection between traditional metres in
English and the mediation of ideology with particular
reference both to the poem 'Book Ends' by the contemporary British poet Tony Harrison and to the linguistic
level of discourse.

Haynes posits seven main 'types' of metre, and
analyses them as realizations of *ideational, interpersonal*
and *textual* discourse functions. The 'intertextual' and
'ideological' types, which allude to other metrical texts,
are among the most complex. They set up problems of
both textual and interpersonal relations within which
expressions of ideology can be sited. The suggestions for
further work appended to this chapter contain a particularly rich set of opportunities for exploring Haynes's
analytical procedures with reference to a diverse range of
texts.

12 Metre and Discourse

JOHN HAYNES

There is a temptation to see metre wholly in terms of phonological schemes, i.e. as a matter of how many stresses and syllables are permitted in a line of verse.[1] Although writers on metre do raise the question of the function of metre,[2] on the whole their comments are not set within a framework which relates metre as a phonological expression to other *levels* of language which it expresses. I suggest that we can understand the point or 'meaning' of metre more clearly if we see its phonology in a way that is comparable with the way we look at other aspects of the phonology of texts, i.e. as the expression of something. This will be discussed in terms of the systemic model of language, in which the relation amongst three *levels* or *strata* is central (see Halliday, 1985). Although systemicists have discussed metre, they too have concentrated on its phonological realization, rather than seeing it in relation to other levels of language.[3]

The following text, a poem by Tony Harrison, will serve as a basis for the discussion of metre which follows:

Book ends

Baked the day she suddenly dropped dead	1
we chew it slowly that last apple pie.	2
Shocked into sleeplessness you're scared of bed	3
We never could talk much, and now don't try.	4
You're like book ends, the pair of you, she'd say.	5
Hog that grate, say nothing, sit, sleep, stare . . .	6
The 'scholar' me, you, worn out on poor pay,	7
only our silence made us seem a pair.	8
Not as good for staring in, blue gas	9
too regular, each bug, each yellow spike.	10
A night you need my company to pass	11
and she not here to tell us we're alike!	12
Your life's all shattered into smithereens.	13
Back on our silences and sullen looks,	14
for all the scotch we drink, what's still between's	15
not the thirty or so years, but books, books, books.[4]	16

I   Linguistic Levels

In systemic functional linguistics three broad levels are distinguished. These are:

(1)   *the level of discourse* – the content, attitudes and human presences which speakers exchange;

(2)   *the level of form* – the grammar and vocabulary specific to a particular language, or a particular style, which carries or *realizes* discourse;

(3)   *the level of substances* – the speech noises or written marks which manifest the other two levels.

The level of discourse is subdivided into three broad *functions*, carried and manifested by the other two. These are

(i)   *the interpersonal function* – language used to fulfil a role and to perform acts such as promising, narrating, requesting, regretting and so on;

(ii)   *ideational function* – language used to *represent* or categorize something in a speaker's mind or surroundings;

(iii) *textual function* – language used to organize a text which has coherence, emphasis and a 'thread' of continuity.

The level of discourse is encoded in the grammar and vocabulary of a particular language and style at the level of *form*, which in turn is made public and physical at the level of *substance*, either through speech sounds or through written symbols.

In Harrison's poem, the level of discourse can be described in these three ways. From the point of view of the interpersonal function, the poem is an act in that it carries the author's role of poet and also performs particular verbal acts of narrating, regretting, asserting and so on. From the ideational point of view, the poem represents a scene with himself and his father looking into the gas fire, not speaking, and so on. The poem as a whole, looked at from the point of view of the textual function, is coherent and has a thread of meaning running through it.

At the level of form, it is made up of a series of grammatical structures and vocabulary; and phonologically, at the level of substance, it is made up of speech sounds, including rhythm, which, when stylized, we call metre.

With one exception, the points made about the text so far are similar to those which would be made about a remark or conversational anecdote. What makes it a poem is that Harrison is playing the role of poet at the level of discourse, and constructs his text so as to *realize* or implement this role. In doing this, he also adheres to a discourse *code*, i.e. the way he and his audience 'take' a text they know to be intended as a poem. A fundamental aspect of this code and its implementation is that our attention should go to the way the text is produced, to the act of uttering itself.[5] One means of procuring this kind of attention, but by no means the only one, is to use metre and rhyme.

The discussion of levels and functions is summed up in relation to Harrison's poem in Fig. 12.1. The arrows after Discourse and Form, mean 'realized by'. This refers to the way in which higher levels form the content of lower ones, and the lower ones encode these meanings. The substance of a text, then, carries and in a sense 'contains' the complex of information shown in the higher level. Harrison's adoption of a discourse role is *realized* down through the levels; it is embodied in his selection of grammatical forms and vocabulary, and in his phonology, one part of which, the metre, is what we are concerned with here.

Level	Function	Description
Discourse	Interpersonal	Role of poet – highlighting language Role of 'I' in the poem – regretting, recollecting etc.
	Ideational	Representation The scenes depicted and recalled Ideas about class, education etc.
	Textual	Thread, development emphasis etc.
Form		Grammar and vocabulary
Substance		Performed speech sounds or print on page

Figure 12.1

One of the meanings of metre, then, is actional. Its presence marks the role the utterer is taking, which involves both the speech acts of regretting, remembering and so on (as the character 'I' in the world of the poem) and the codal speech act of putting his text on display as a text, his relation through the poem to an audience. Before we can give any further substance to these notions and say *how* metre highlights textuality as such, we need to look more closely at how it works.

II Metre and Rhythm

Metre is related to rhythm, and rhythm is an aspect of intonation, which falls under the textual function of language. English intonation can be studied in three *ranks*. The first of these is the *tone group*, which marks out the text into units of information based on what the speaker judges will be news to the hearer. The most important points in the text are given emphasis or focus by being made the site of a semantically significant pitch movement, or tone, where the voice rises or falls in such a way as to affect attitude and/or express emotion. For example, in

(a)   //we chew it SLOWly//

the focus falls on the first syllable of 'slowly', which is most likely to carry a falling tone, the most appropriate one for the slightly ironic regret being expressed interpersonally.

Most discussions of metre, however, concentrate on the next unit down in the rank scale, the *foot*. The foot is a pulse, or stress, falling on one syllable in words which are important from the point of view of content. In (*b*) the foot boundaries are shown by single slashes. The double slashes indicate both tone group boundaries and foot boundaries.

(b)   //.we/chew it/slowly//

The ⌃ at the beginning marks a silent stress, a pause equivalent to a stressed syllable. This is needed because each foot is defined as beginning with a stress, and the silent stress corresponds to the pause which often occurs between the lines of a poem, or between the title and the first line. A foot may have any number of unstressed syllables, but usually these do not exceed five or so. The rhythm of English is based on the distinction between stressed and unstressed syllables, even though there are different degrees of prominence in a foot.[6] Roughly speaking, the feet all take the same time to utter, so that those with more (unstressed) syllables in them require each syllable to be spoken faster, and to be made relatively shorter, than those with few syllables or just one syllable in them. This type of equivalence is a matter not primarily of stress (which we tend to hear as loudness) but of length (duration of sound).

In the commonest type of metre in English, this approximate length equivalence is reinforced and regularized by a requirement that the feet should be not just roughly equivalent in length but equal in number of syllables per foot, each foot now having but two syllables. This is opposed to the open choice that exists in other texts.

This does not mean that all feet have the same structure from the point of view of length, because stressed syllables are not necessarily long, or vice versa. A poet can adhere to the alternating rhythm while varying the temporal constitution of his syllables considerably.

There are, of course, other kinds of metre. Metre may be based on stress alone, having so many stresses per line; or it may be based on syllable numbers per line. In some languages, metre is based on the patterning of phonemic tone. Also, it must be born in mind that the notion of metre generally depends on that of line, since the line is the unit within which a particular number of feet or syllables (or high tones) have to fit. This is itself a kind of stylization, since in conversation we do not usually speak in equivalent lines, marking off their ends by a pause or a rhyme.

The stress pattern of English realizes information breakdown, in the sense that the words on one of whose syllables stress normally falls are the ones which are important from the point of view of content. These are the so-called *lexical* items which linguists contrast to *grammatical* items, words such as *is, but* and *the*. As their function is more centrally structural, grammatical items are stressed only for special contrastive emphasis. The problem of the poet writing in metre is to manage his vocabulary and syntax so that they naturally fit into the stylized pattern of the metre. Yet what this pattern is and its status are much debated.

Harrison's metre is the commonest in English poetry. It contains ten syllables as a norm, and these are alternately stressed and unstressed. Traditional scansions begin with an unstressed syllable, but in my descriptions the lines tend to begin with a pause, or silent stress. This means that 'regular' lines will have six feet, beginning usually with a foot in which a silent stress is followed by an unstressed syllable, and ending with a foot with just one, stressed syllable. Conventionally, the metre allows variation at these two points, sometimes omission of the first syllable altogether, at other times adding an unstressed syllable to the last. Sometimes, where there is no end-of-line pause, the last syllable of one line and the first of the next make a foot. A typical metrical line is the fourth line of Harrison's poem:

(c)   /ˌwe/never/could talk/much and/now don't/try/

Tone group boundaries have been left out of account here. In this poem, there is a strong tendency for six of such feet to occur in a line which strongly tends to end on a one-syllable foot followed by a pause and to begin with a silent stress. This, I emphasize, is a tendency. The pattern does not occur all the time. When we talk about a poem being written in this or that metre, we do not mean that every line is exactly 'regular' or conforms to the pattern of syllables which make its norm.

In (c), however, the conversational rhythm fits naturally into the alternating rhythmic pattern. But in line 7, for example, we have:

(d)   /ˌthe/scholar/me/you/worn/out on/poor/pay

This is one natural rendering. There are other possibilities which reflect different interpretations of the meaning of the line, i.e. different *realizations* of the level of discourse.

The fact that poems are almost never totally 'regular' metrically, that metricality is a tendency, has lead to a good deal of controversy about the status of the metre itself and the kind of reality it has. Some readers will make an attempt to modify or adapt the natural rhythm so as to fit it into an alternating pattern. In its most extreme form, this line of thinking would produce an unnatural:

(e) /.the/scholar/me you/worn out/on poor/pay/

Other readers will recite (*d*) but bear the structure of (*e*) in mind as, in the transformational-generative terminology, its *deep structure* or, more generally, as the abstract metrical scheme (or norm) which (*d*) is a variation upon. A third viewpoint would be to take account of degrees of stress and see the rhythm as relatively alternating; this will not work here, but an extension of this view would be to claim that the words which 'required' metrical stress should be given not full stress but more stress than they might ordinarily gain. Another view, which has some historical justification, is that this metre may be seen as a matter only of the number of syllables in a line.

A rendering such as (*e*) is problematic, primarily because it is sustained by a performer without there being any motivation for it at the level of discourse. It does not realize any textual function, the rhythms cutting across the informational sense of the line – which is why it sounds unnatural. There is room for disagreement here, and certainly the view that something such as (*e*) 'underlies' (*d*) in some way is widely held. But the sense of an expected rhythmical beat can be explained just as easily by pointing to the tendency of this regular beat to occur throughout the text and establish itself as a statistical norm.

For reference, my reading of the poem as a whole is given below. Here I have given what seems the most natural rendering as the realization of discourse, in other words, as an interpretation of the written script, without trying to be metrical. Different renderings are obviously possible. It may be felt that the interpretation as expressed in rhythm is insensitive, or could be improved, and the overall naturalistic style could be altered to one in which a conscious attempt was made to accommodate natural rhythm to metrical stylization; in other words, the performance itself could be stylized. In the analyis no account has been taken of information focusing or pitch movements. These on the whole do not affect metre, though they may be relevant to the *cadences* in free verse (see Crystal, 1975). Aspects of the performance could, of course, reinforce the demonstrative element in the poem by drawing attention to metricality through enunciation; or the poem might be read in Harrison's Yorkshire accent as a means of underlining traditional 'high' art norms with working-class production. This rendering is suggested by the pronunciation required to make 'pass' rhyme with 'gas' in lines 9 and 11.

1	/./**baked the**/day she/**suddenly**/**dropped**/dead	6/9/4
2	/ˆ**we**/**chew it**/**slowly**/ˆthat/last/**apple**/**pie**	6/10/5
3	/./shocked into/sleeplessness/ˆyou're/**scared of**/**bad**	6/10/3
4	/ˆ**we**/**never**/**could talk**/**much and**/**now don't**/**try**	6/10/6
5	/ˆ**you're**/like/book ends the/**pair of**/**you she'd**/**say**	6/10/4
6	/./**hog that**/grate/say/**nothing**/sit/sleep/**stare**	8/9/4
7	/ˆ**the**/**scholar**/me/you/worn/**out on**/poor/**pay**	8/10/4
8	/./only our/**silence**/**made us**/**seem a**/**pair**	6/10/5
9	/./**not as**/**good for**/staring in/blue//**gas**	6/9/4
10	/./too/regular/each/bud/ˆ each/**yellow**/**spike**	8/10/3
11	/ˆ**a**/**night you**/**need my**/company to/**pass**	5/10/4–
12	**and/she be**/**not**/**here to**/**tell us**/**we're a**/**like**	5/10/5+
13	/ˆ**your**/**life's all**/shattered into smithe/**reens**	4/10/3
14	/./back in our/silences and/**sullen**/**looks**	5/10/3
15	/ˆ**for**/**all the**/**scotch we**/**drink what's**/**still be**/**tween's**	6/10/6
16	/**not the**/thirty or so/**years but**/books/books/**books**/	6/11/3

/   Foot boundary. A rhythmical pulse falls on the syllable following it. Tone group boundaries are not shown.

ˆ   Silent stress, or pause, equivalent to a stressed syllable.

Bold print   Indicates a metrical 'regular' foot on this particular performance of the poem. A 'regular' foot is defined as (i) a foot containing two syllables only; or (ii) a foot containing one syllable if this occurs at the end of a line; or (iii) a foot beginning with a silent stress and followed either by one syllable or no further syllables, if this occurs at the beginning of a line. This last type accounts for the interlinear pause.

6/10/6 etc.   Number of feet/number of syllables/number of 'regular' feet in a line.

A 'normal' line is one with six feet, each containing two syllables except for the first and the last. The last contains one syllable, and the first is taken up with a silent stress with or without a syllable following it. In Harrison's poem there are 98 feet. Of these 66 are 'regular' in the sense defined in the key above. Eight of the lines contain the regular six feet, and all but four lines contain ten syllables. Only lines four and fifteen have six regular feet and so are regular on all counts.

The last foot in line 11 runs over into line 12. To show this line 11 is shown as having less than the full four feet (4–) and line 12 as having more (5+). This comes about because, on my reading, there is no interlinear pause here. Line 11 could have been shown as containing three and a 'half' feet, and line 12 five and a 'half'.

There are other ways of assessing metricality. For example we might gauge it by counting the number of 'regular' feet occurring in an unbroken sequence.

III The Functions of Metre

In general terms, then, metre draws attention to textmaking as such, just as does the use of other typical poetic devices such as striking metaphor, onomatopoeia, unexpected transitions and so on. In drawing attention to textuality, the metre realizes the interpersonal discourse role of the poet. The way in which it does this can be subdivided into seven broad categories, although these categories are not intended to be exclusive or indeed exhaustive.

(i) Mnemonic

From a historical point of view, the function of metre is practical. For a society without writing, metre is a means of memorizing and acts as an aid to composition. It is obviously easier to remember a text if it has rhymes running through it, and a countable number of syllables and/or stresses. A missing rhyme or syllable alerts us to missing words, and missing information. The pulse of the metre is also commonly related to music and song. The relation between metre and music is complex, and many songs have much looser metres than written poems; and song in many cultures allows us to take much greater liberties with natural speech rhythms than written poetry does.

Once a poet writes he has time to revise and redraft his composition, and the demands on his memory are reduced. The written page itself takes over this earlier function of metre. But in English literature written poetry had continued for centuries before poets began to wonder whether metre was still necessary. By this time it had assumed a different status. This can be looked at from the point of view of composition. Metre poses difficulties, and so acts as a preliminary kind of test which a poet must pass to show that he can handle his language deftly. Part of the enjoyment of poetry has always been the enjoyment of verbal skill, of the poet's role as verbal acrobat. He gains his applause this way, and through it promotes an art in which the savouring of a common language is valued. Poetry becomes a way of drawing attention to acts of human utterance, just as the acrobat's feats draw attention to the human body. The demonstration of skill is particularly important in Harrison's poetry, and many of his poems are devoted to the theme of articulacy, or 'eloquence', as he calls it. Most of his poems very consciously display skill.

(ii) Deictic

The display of skill is connected to a deeper concept, namely, that through metre the poet highlights the process by which utterances are produced. It thus has a deictic or attention-getting function. Poetry is deictic in this rather special sense in a number of ways, through striking metaphors, through onomatopoeia, and so on. But generally metre is pervasive in a poem, while these other features are not, and occur more readily in other texts. In order to see just how metre highlights basic speech acts, we will need to consider 'linguistic level' a little more closely.

Harrison's rhythm (though metrically stylized) does not encode information structure any differently from the way in which the distribution of stresses ordinarily does. The poet has managed things so that the ordinary norms of rhythm apply. This is one measure of his competence. The turning of his sentences must not seem contrived just to satisfy the metre. The structure of the first two lines is untypical of English clauses in that it is more usual to mention something first and then refer to it as 'it'. But it does not look as if Harrison was forced into this by the need for rhymes or metre. Had he written something more typical, at the level of form, such as:

(f) We slowly chew that final apple pie
    she baked the day she suddenly dropped dead

which was the same tendency towards alternating stress as his original line, he would still have been able to use the same rhymes. The structure he actually presents is motivated independently. In Harrison's

(g) We chew it slowly, that last apple pie

not only is the grammar different from (f), the information structure is, too. He breaks the line up grammatically into two, which strongly suggests that the performer gives intonational focus to the first syllable of 'slowly', and to 'pie'. The use of 'it' before mention of what it stands for, makes such a rendering almost mandatory, whereas (f) is much less commital, and (g) suggests an accompanying thinking ('chewing') over.[7] The information structure of (g) has to do with tone group structure, which is, of course, an aspect of phonology; but it is not directly relevant to this metre, and is independently motivated.

This first bound (or dependent) clause also holds us in suspense for the resolution in the second one, what it is that was baked, what happened on that day. In calculating these effects at the level of form (grammar and vocabulary), the poet writing in metre has also to glance 'ahead' in the realizational scale to see what their consequences will be for the rhythm (at the rank of foot). In conversation we do not do this. We allow the rhythm to come out almost any way without restricting our choice of vocabulary.

Fig. 12.2 shows in simple terms the realizational chain, the relations between discourse, form, and phonology or substance. In ordinary conversation phonology can be regarded as the expression, or output, of form and/or discourse. But in metrical poetry it is not only expression but also input.[8]

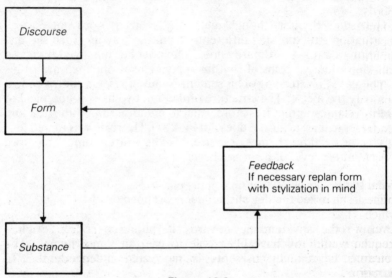

Figure 12.2

The requirement that the poet checks, and if necessary replans, his choice of vocabulary and/or grammar has the effect of highlighting the process of producing speech, the relations between levels and the fact of stratification in language. Fig. 12.2 shows this between the levels of substance and form only; but metre-oriented feedback also has implications all the way up the realizational chain. It is this sense of 'glancing ahead' at the phonological consequences of grammatical choices that gives poetry its air of carefully and often self-consciously chosen words and structures, a point which Philip Sydney made a long time ago.[9]

(iii)   Cohesive

One way in which the textual function is realized is through cohesion. This is normally studied at the level of form. The thread of meaning which runs through a text can be followed because the reader or hearer can trace back what he is presently reading or hearing to what has gone before. He does this through noticing repetitions and/or replacements of meaning. For example, in Harrison's poem the word 'she' is repeated a number of times, so is 'you'. Then, in line 12 the word 'alike' recalls 'pair' in line 5, a repetition not of words (at the level of form) but of aspects of meaning (discourse). And in line 16 the word 'books' recalls 'book ends' in line 5 and the title, and also 'scholar' in line 7.

But notice that metre and rhyme have a similar function. The word 'books' in line 16 rhymes with 'looks' in line 14, and thus serves to remind the reader that he has just heard it two lines earlier. The repetition is now of sound, at the level of substance. Metre itself is repetitive and cumulative, and so also bears comparison with cohesion.

This cohesion-like function is obviously connected to the mnemonic one, since anything which reinforces the coherence of the text is an aid to memory, and cohesion itself (like rhyme) depends upon the reader's recalling what he has read earlier in the text.

(iv) Mimetic

What has been said about metre and cohesion could be put in terms of mimesis, that the rhythm of the text is made to mime the coherence which is more firmly established by the vocabulary and grammar at the level of form. It produces a sense of textual 'inevitability' which is frequently used in oratory. Here the overall cadence of the speaker's voice can express conclusiveness in such a way as to enhance the purported conclusiveness of his reasoning at the level of discourse. This is primarily a matter of pitch, but rhythm is also involved. It can be seen in the decisiveness of these lines by Dryden:

In squandering wealth was his peculiar art:
Nothing went unrewarded, but desert[10]

Metre may be mimetic in a more straightforward way when it mimes some aspect of the topic being written about. When Pope writes

When Ajax strives some rock's vast weight to throw   1
The line too labours and the words move slow: 2
Not so, when swift Camilla scours the plain.   3
Flies o'er the unbending corn, and skims along the main[11]   4

he refers to physical movements, the effort in throwing a heavy rock, and the swift movement of Camilla. The metre is 'the same' in both, in the sense that it approximates to the traditional alternating ten syllable line, like Harrison's. But against that framework Pope has managed to make lines 1 and 2 sound laboured, and 3 and 4 swift. This is achieved by making the third line alternating, except for the first foot, while the first and the second lines are hardly alternating at all. They contain many more one-syllable feet, and so a greater proportion of the syllables are stressed, or 'heavy', which means each foot is relatively longer or 'slower'. Line 3 contains more unstressed syllables because of the greater number of two-syllable feet; then line 4 strays from the regular alternating pattern in the opposite direction from 1 and 2, by now having feet of more than two syllables, the first and fourth each having four on my rendering. It thus has, proportionally, a much greater number of unstressed or 'light' syllables. A natural reading of the lines would be:

/،when/ajax/strives some/rock's/vast/**weight to**/**throw**	7/10/5
/،the/line/too/**labours**/،and the/words/move/**slow**	8/10/3
/not/**so when**/**swift** ca/**milla**/**scours the**/**plain**	6/10/5
/flies o'er the un/**bending**/**corn and**/skims along the/**main**	5/13/3

The numbers on the right show the number of feet/number of syllables/number of 'regular' feet in the line (i.e. either two-syllable feet or one-syllable feet at the beginning or end), in my rendering.

Poets have often employed this type of mimesis, inviting a comparison of linguistic time and speed with the time and speed being described. It may be connected to the wider idea that in metrical poetry the metre should 'fit' the subject matter. Some metres seem to be intrinsically comic, others dignified. This may perhaps be related to music, and to the kind of human gait musical and verbal rhythms suggest. In 'Book Ends', the last line is mimetic in the contrastive sense and the poet breaks with the alternating norm.

(*n*)   /not the/thirty or so/years/، but/books/books/books

The three single-syllable feet at the end make a decisive break in the two-syllable foot norm, or metrical tendency, of the poem as a whole, and may be interpreted as 'emotional' in the sense that the breaking out of metrical control mimes a breaking out of ordinary everyday conversational constraint, an outburst, and a helpless reiteration of the source of an insoluble problem of communication – a resort, in fact, to inarticulacy as a way of 'articulating' the impasse. Again, this must be taken with the theme of articulacy and inarticulacy in relation to the English working class that recurs in so much of Harrison's work. The mimesis here is oriented towards the interpersonal function, to speech acts, rather than to representation in the manner of Pope.

A similar piece of mimesis, oriented towards ideation now, occurs in line 13, the metrical norm being 'shattered' also.

The referential kind of mimesis is often prominent in the practice of free verse, where the poet uses his rhythm in a completely mimetic way, and no longer bothers about stylization. This can be seen in the quotation from Ezra Pound in the suggestions for further work section. Composers of free verse tend to have problems when they do not use rhythm in a mimetic way, miming either the emotional speech acts (interpersonal) or the natural rhythms/stillness of a scene (ideational). Then they approximate to prose in the sense that the full rhythmical resources of the language are not exploited in a comparable way to metrical composition or rhythmical mimesis.

(v) Intertextual

This term will be developed more fully in section (vii), but for the present purposes it will be taken to mean roughly the same as *allusion*. It is used by writers on discourse and texts to emphasize the interrelatedness of all texts, how all texts implicitly allude to others. The very use of metre by a poet constitutes an allusion to this type of text as it has occurred at other times, and the particular metre (for example, Spenserian stanza, Elizabethan sonnet) connects the poem to particular poets or poetic movements or eras. Harrison's decisive rhythms often suggest Dryden's work, for example, and in their application to naturalistic description Crabbe's.

Since this metre has been so common in English poetry, a poet writing now may allude to it, as a metre, in a poem which is otherwise much less regular than Harrison's poem. The alternating line is so familiar that it is likely to be picked up, partly as allusion and partly because the stylization itself gives it a distinctive, perhaps 'striding' resonance.

(vi) Compositional

This function is given separate mention here, although it is closely connected with the deictic and mnemonic functions already sketched. It should be remembered that metre and/or rhyme can help a poet in the act of composition, though this function may not be apparent to a hearer or reader, especially if based just on a count of syllables. The need to fit words and clauses into a pattern forces the poet himself to turn over his words carefully, to look for economies and sometimes figurative expressions (or to find a difficult rhyme). It is sometimes imagined that free verse makes things easier for the poet. But it does so only at a cost. It is, of course, easier to produce *something* without using metre, but it is very probably harder (if indeed these things can be graded like this) to produce a satisfactory poem without metre than with it. Having a metre for a composition can be compared to a carpenter's having a vice, which holds the raw material 'still' so that he can work on it. Metre, then, is not just a mnemonic support but also a compositional one. This is closely connected to the kind of deixis metre produces, making the poet fully aware of the stratifiedness of his text, of the act of utterance.

(vii)   Ideological

The ideological function of metre is also intertextual, and although treated separately here for convenience is really an extension of what has been said about intertextual allusion.

Poets learn from each other, and develop their techniques through imitation and development of the methods of forebears. They also define what they are doing by departure from such methods. Writers such as Ezra Pound and Vladimir Mayakovsky defined the kind of poetry they were writing against the mainly still accepted techniques of rhyme, metre and conventional cohesion. Both of these poets, for widely different reasons, wanted to write an anti-capitalist, anti-bourgeois kind of verse, symptomatic of the time in which the 'languages' of science, music, art, philosophy and mathematics were all being revolutionized.

Pound's work,[12] as one of its meanings, subverted traditional notions of what can follow what, of textual and other kinds of time, of the interdependence of texts, and of the multi-dimensional meanings a single 'image' may have. In this, he anticipated ideas which are still much discussed among artists, semioticians, physicists and philosophers. The techniques of Pound and similar writers became associated with the 'modern' experience, with linguistic perception; and this was defined, mainly, against metricality. The 'meaning' of free verse, then, is in part a matter of association with new ideas in politics and science. And it also developed a traditional concept that poetry as a genre need not be identified with metrical writing. As we saw, metre is like cohesion, and mimes the thread of a text, thus reinforcing linearity and conventional notions of time. Pound's free verse (though not all free verse) was linked to psychoanalysis and ideas of explosive emanations of meaning, rather than cumulation. Poetry was thought of as the emission of verbal energy. Metre can clearly also be associated with conscious control and the rational. And the classic metricists in English poetry, Dryden and Pope, reinforced this idea, associated as both were with Newtonian physics.

Harrison's work has to be read as a turning away from the Poundian, perhaps also American, way of composing, and a return to the mainstream of English versification, like that of Auden in the 1930s and the Movement poets in the 1950s.

In an interesting argument, Easthope (1983) has claimed that the particular type of metre Harrison's poem alludes to is connected to the ruling class, to the bourgeois culture which has dominated most written English poetry, the 'high art' to be distinguished from traditional ballads and folksongs. He claims that in free verse or traditional ballad metres, the performer does not have to hesitate about poetic rhythm, since there is no numerical restriction of feet, of the kind we have noticed. He assumes, questionably in my view, that the performer of an 'iambic' poem has to bear an abstract metrical scheme in mind as he performs, and must accommodate the actual natural rhythms to it, though he gives very little demonstration of this, and some of his examples are invalid.[13] He argues that the need for this accommodation orients the poem towards an individual speaker, and against the communality of the ballad, and so fits in with the bourgeois conception of the autonomous individual 'subject'. His discussion is too complex to do justice to here, but there seem to be problems with it, both from the point of view of its conception of alternating metre and from the point of view of the inferences he draws.

Easthope cites the very clearly bourgeois poet, Philip Larkin, as an illustration of his thesis. But Harrison is as clearly a working-class poet. His use of traditional metres is, in one aspect, ironical. He demonstrates to a bourgeois tradition that he, the working-class boy, can not only match bourgeois poets at their own game but beat them. The demonstration of skill, in his work, has this bitter, Caliban-like edge. And it is a demonstration of a wider point, which Easthope, as a Marxist, might have considered: that one of the ways in which the working class gains power is by taking over techniques and institutions first created by capitalism. Revolutionaries use print and rifles, so why not metre?

On the other hand, it may be argued that Harrison's manifestly poetic and emphatic style reflects the received working-class notion that a poem is a rhyme, that it ought to be comprehensible, and so on, a down-to-earthness which is also typical of English working-class scepticism, bluntness and perhaps also conservatism as to what is real.[14] Against this it might be said that even though Harrison's work does have a working-class boldness of form, still it is directed towards a middle-class literary audience, rather than towards typical workers. But, if this is so, it is not because he writes metrically. Then again, Harrison might argue that the view that the alternating metre and naturalistic representation of experience are bourgeois is itself an idea formulated by middle-class intellectuals. He could cite the metrical conservatism of Mao, too.

(vii)   Conclusion

I have suggested seven broad 'meanings' of metre as realizations of aspects of poetic discourse, poetic discourse being thought of primarily as the highlighting of textual production itself through the realizational chain from discourse through form to substance. The ways in which metre realizes discourse differ as to the functions to which different aspects of it are connected. Table 12.1 summarizes the types and their connection to broad discourse functions.

Table 12.1   *The Functions of Metre Seen as Realization of the Level of Discourse*

Type		Description	Function it relates to
(i)	Mnemonic	Makes text memorizable or memorable	Textual
(ii)	Deictic	Draws attention to textual stratification	Interpersonal
(iii)	Cohesive	Reinforces formal cohesion	Textual
(iv)	Mimetic	Mimes aspects of the topic	Ideational
(v)	Intertextual	Alludes to other metrical texts	Textual and interpersonal
(vi)	Compositional	Orients poet to economy etc.	Ideational, interpersonal and textual
(vii)	Ideological	Extension of (v)	

Suggestions for Further Work: Chapter 12

1   In this poem, Harrison seems particularly fond of structures in which the subject of a clause or sentence is delayed. Make a note of all the examples you can find. Try rewriting the clauses concerned in a more typical sequence.

2   Comment on the motivations for his grammar, relating it both to metre and to information structure. Is he miming conversations? Is he delaying the resolution of sentences or clauses for rhetorical or 'dramatic' effect? Would you accept the criticism that he overuses this device and sounds too slick?

3   What would be gained, and what would be lost, in your view, if

'Book Ends' were rewritten in free verse, i.e. so that it no longer tended towards the alternating rhythm? Try the experiment of making minimal changes to a few lines so that the alternating rhythm is no longer the norm. Is consistent avoidance of alternation a kind of (anti-) metre? Would the reader need to be particularly sophisticated to respond to it?

4   The text reproduced as Fig. 12.3 is that of a folksong, in which the rhythm is indicated by the lengths of the notes. The black note without a tail (crotchet) has a value of one beat, the note with a hole in it (minim) two beats, and the note with a tail (which may join it to others) (quaver) is a half beat. In the last line, the first of the two notes accompanying the word 'forced', has a dot which makes it one and a half beats.[15]

A natural spoken rendering of the lines might run:

/ₐas I/walked over/salisbury/plain
/ₐoh/there I/met a/scamping young/blade
/ₐhe/kissed me and en/ticed me/so
/ₐtill a/long with him I was/forced to/go

In what ways, if any, would you say that the rhythm of the spoken version relates to the musical rhythm? And on what basis, if any, would you say that the spoken version was metrical? What makes it possible for the singer to make one syllable take more than one beat, while the speaker cannot? What general points about relating metre to song does the example raise?

5   In the following rendering of the beginning of Gerard Manley Hopkins's poem 'Windhover', I have deliberately forced myself to keep to a fixed number of feet per line, and in doing so have produced an unnatural effect from the point of view of ordinary conversational speech, particularly in reducing normally stressed syllables to unstressed status.

/The Windhover/

/ₐ/ₐ/ₐI/caught this/morning/morning's/minion/king-
    dom of/daylight's/dauphin/dapple/dawn-drawn falcon in his/riding
    of the/rolling/level under/neath him/steady/air and/striding
/high there/how he/rung upon the/rein of a/wimpling/wing
in his/ecstasy/ₐthen/off/off/forth on/swing
as a/skate's heel sweeps/smooth on a/bow/bend the/hurl and/gliding
re/buffed the/big/wind/ₐmy/heart in/hiding
/stirred for a /bird . . .[16]

How far is this rendering justified from the point of view of mimesis? Try to explain what the relation is between the verbal rhythm and the bird's flight. Discuss the ways in which this metre differs from the one used by Harrison, and how it constitutes a metre as opposed to being just ordinary English analysed into feet.

SALISBURY PLAIN

Sung by Mr and Mrs Verrall, Horsham, Sussex (R.V.W. 1904)

As I walked o-ver Salis-bur-y Plain, Oh, there I met a

scamp-ing young blade. He kissed me and en-tic-ed me

so Till a-long with him I was forced for to go.

Some versions have (a) and (b) (c)

Verse 5 begins:

Ear-ly next morn-ing my love he a-rose, And so

nim-bly he put on his clothes.

As I walked over Salisbury Plain,
Oh, there I met a scamping young blade.
He kissed me and enticed me so
Till along with him I was forced for to go.

We came unto a public house at last.
And there for man and wife we did pass.
He called for ale and wine and strong
   beer.
Till at length we both to bed did repair.

'Undress yourself, my darling,' says he.
'Undress yourself, and come to bed with
   me.'
'Oh yes, that I will,' then says she,
'If you'll keep all those flash girls away.'

'Those flash girls you need not fear,
For you'll be safe-guarded, my dear.
I'll maintain you as some lady so gay,
For I'll go a-robbing on the highway.'

Early next morning my love he arose,
And so nimbly he put on his clothes.
Straight to the highway he set sail,
And 'twas there he robbed the
   coaches of the mail.

Oh, it's now my love in Newgate Jail
   do lie,
Expecting every moment to die.
The Lord have mercy on his poor soul,
For I think I hear the death-bell for to
   toll.

Figure 12.3

6   Quotation (*a*) below is the first stanza of a poem by
    Wordsworth, usually grouped among the 'Lucy' poems. In it
    Wordsworth makes use of the metre commonly found in
    traditional English ballads, illustrated by the second quotation
    (*b*) from the traditional ballad 'The Wife of Usher's Well'.

> (*a*)   She dwelt among the untrodden ways
>   Beside the springs of Dove,
>   A Maid whom there were none to praise
>   And very few to love.[17]

> (*b*)   There lived a wife at Usher's Well,
>   And a wealthy wife was she;
>   She had three stout and stalwart sons,
>   And sent them o'er the sea.[18]

Compare the rhythm of the two poems. Would you say they were
metrical in the same ways? Based on what you know or can find out
about Wordsworth's conception of poetry, suggest why he used this
particular metre. Wordsworth aimed at a poetry which was the
natural outpouring of strong feelings. How far can metrical poetry
be like this? Relate your comments to what you can find out about
Wordsworth's own idea of the function of metre as explained in the
preface to *Lyrical Ballads* (1801).

7   The following passage is from Ezra Pound's 'Canto XLIX':

> For the seven lakes, and by no man these verses:
> Rain: empty river; a voyage,
> Fire from frozen cloud, heavy rain in the twilight
> Under the cabin roof was one lantern.
> The reeds are heavy; bent;
> and the bamboos speak as if weeping.

> Autumn moon; hills rise about lakes
> against sunset
> Evening is like curtain of cloud,
> a blurr above ripples; and through it
> sharp long spikes of the cinnamon
> a cold tune amid reeds.
> Behind hill the monk's bell
> borne on the wind.
> Sail passed here in April; may return in October
> Boat fades in silver, slowly;
> Sun blaze alone on the river.[19]

This is not metrical, but it is poetry. In what ways does the poet's
language, including his rhythm, function similarly to metre?
Discuss the ways in which time and space are treated in the passage,
and how the rhythms Pound uses might be regarded as mimetic.

8   What kinds of connections do you see between Harrison's use of
traditional metres and his working-class background? In what way,
or ways, may a poet's choice of metre be ideological?

Notes: Chapter 12

1   A partial exception is David Crystal's (1975) treatment of metre in terms
of intonation and informational 'weight'. The following accounts are well
worth reading: Zirmunskij (1966); Chatman (1965). A convenient
summary of the influential theory of Samuel Keyser and Morris Halle can
be found in Wimsatt (1971); Halle and Keyser's most succinct statement
of their theory is 'Chaucer and the Study of Prosody' in Freeman (1970:
366–426). The most interesting treatment of free verse is Crystal's 'Intonation and Metrical Theory' in Crystal (1975: 137–253. Yuri Lotman's
(1976) work attempts to relate prose, verse and free verse in a broad way.
A good general overview of the metres of different languages is Wimsatt
(1974).
2   See, again, Chatman (1965: 184–224) and Zirmunskij (1966). Also see
Epstein (1978: 25–57). Keyser and Halle discuss metre in terms of a
transformational-generative deep structure which is itself phonological,
though connected ultimately to syntax; see also Paul Fussell's historically
oriented discussion of eighteenth century versification in Wimsatt (1974:
191–203).
3   Abercrombie (1965: 16–25) gives an account of the phonological
framework I make use of here. Halliday (1978) gives a fuller account of his
theory of intonation, and includes some detailed discussion of rhythm and
some analyses of renderings of poems, without discussing metre as such.
4   From Harrison, *The School of Eloquence and Other Poems* (London: Rex
Collings, 1978), p. 24.
5   This is true of all poetry. The fact that the act of utterance is a recurring
theme in Harrison's poetry is, in principle, a separate point. The conventional attention to text as such need not be interpreted in an 'intellectual'
or solemn way. It occurs in comic rhymes such as limericks also.
6   Attempts have been made to incorporate degrees of stress into descriptions of metre, usually following the theory outlined by Trager and Smith
(1951). This allows for four degrees of stress, so secondary and tertiary
stress can be promoted or demoted to metrical stress or unstress, as the
scheme of the metre requires. But the phonological theory behind Smith
and Trager is often questioned nowadays.
7   In some other ways, Harrison's grammar is a little odd. The strict English
teacher may notice that 'baked' might be adjudged to be 'dangling', since
a perversely literal interpretation would have 'we' as the item baked, not
the pie.
8   This representation should not be taken to suggest that in the actual
production of speech a person maintains a strict sequence of events down
the realizational scale. Things happen simultaneously. The diagram
merely shows how metre requires an extra feedback 'circuit'.
9   Seymour Chatman (1965: 208) quotes this passage from Sidney: 'The
senate of poets hath chosen verse as their fittest raiment, meaning as in

matter they passed all in all, so in manner to go beyond them: *not speaking* (table-talk fashion, or like men in a dream) *words as they chanceably fall from the mouth, but peyzing each syllable of each word* by just proportion according to the dignity of the subject.' (Emphasis added.)

10   John Dryden, 'Absalom and Achitophel', from *The Penguin Book of English Verse*, ed. J. Hayward (Harmondsworth: Penguin, 1956), p. 179.

11   From 'An Essay on Criticism', *The Poems of Alexander Pope*, ed. J. Butt (London: Methuen, 1963), p. 155.

12   Pound was not, of course, alone. He is cited here as an example. Very similar points could be made by reference to the work of other poets, and writers such as Joyce and Beckett. Free verse had been discussed and experimented with by French poets in the nineteenth century, and by earlier poets such as Hölderlin, Blake and Whitman.

13   In his analysis of *Three Ravens*, Easthope (1983: 88) departs from natural rhythm when he scans:

> There *were* three ravens sat on a tree
> They *were* as black as *they* might be
> The one of *them* said *to* his mate
> 'Where shall *we* our breakfast take'

The words which are italicized are all unnaturally stressed. What Easthope has done here is to assume a communal type of reading where sense is subordinated to ritual. But Harrison's poem can be read in this way too, as example (*d*) shows. Easthope also assumes that poetry can be described as writing in 'lines'. But this fails to account for prose poetry, and more damagingly for lined texts such as shopping lists, football results and Euclidean theorems.

14   Harrison writes in the English realist tradition of Crabbe, a tradition which has been championed along socialist realist lines. More recent ideas about language, realism and the notion of cultural and artistic hegemony have, to my mind, cast some doubt on the realist position. It is now often argued that naturalistic representation of experience is, in a covert way, reinforcement of the order of things which suits the ruling class, who manage to persuade the rest of the society that their world view is the 'natural' one.

15   Text and music reproduced from R. Vaughan Williams and A. L. Lloyd (eds), *The Penguin Book of English Folksongs* (Harmondsworth: Penguin, 1959), p. 95.

16   Taken from J. Hayward (ed.), *The Penguin Book of English Verse* (Harmondsworth: Penguin, 1956), p. 387.

17   Taken from Hayward, *Penguin Book of English Verse*, p. 261.

18   Taken from M. Hodgart (ed.), *The Faber Book of Ballads* (London: Faber, 1965), p. 58.

19   *The Cantos of Ezra Pound* (London: Faber, 1964), p. 255.

References: Chapter 12

Abercrombie, D. (1965), *Studies in Phonetics and Linguistics* (London: Oxford University Press).
Chatman, S. (1965), *A Theory of Meter* (The Hague: Mouton).
Crystal, D. (1975), *The English Tone of Voice* (London: Edward Arnold).
Easthope, A. (1983), *Poetry as Discourse* (London: Methuen).
Epstein, E. L. (1978), *Language and Style* (London: Methuen).
Freeman, D. C. (ed.) (1970), *Linguistics and Literary Style* (New York: Holt, Rinehart & Winston).
Halliday, M. A. K. (1970), *A Course in Spoken English: Intonation* (London: Oxford University Press).
Halliday, M. A. K. (1985), *An Introduction to Functional Grammar* (London: Edward Arnold).
Lotman, Y. (1976), *Analysis of the Poetic Text* (Michigan: Ann Arbor).
Trager, G. L., and Smith Jr, H. L. (1951), *An Outline of English Structure* (Oklahoma: Norman).
Wimsatt, W. K. (1971), 'The Rule and the Norm: Halle and Keyser on Chaucer's Meter', in S. Chatman (ed.), *Literary Style: A Symposium* (New York: Oxford University Press) pp. 197–220.
Wimsatt, W. K. (ed.) (1974), *Versification: Major Language Types* (New York: New York University Press).
Zirmunskij, V. (1966), *Introduction to Metrics*, ed. and intr. E. Stankiewicz and W. N. Vickery (The Hague: Mouton).

Introduction to Chapter 13

This contribution by David Birch comes fittingly as a final chapter to this introductory reader, for in it he provides positive and well-argued proposals for the development of discourse stylistics, and, at the same time, suggests some possible limitations to the descriptive concerns of linguists working on literary texts. His paper thus parallels that of Deirdre Burton in the companion volume (Carter, 1982) in aiming to construct a challenging and provocative basis from which, it is hoped, readers will want to explore further their own analytical and interpretative priorities at the interface of language, discourse and literature.

David Birch expresses strong reservations about a stylistics which is text-immanent and insufficiently intertextual in orientation; he argues against analyses of meaning which assume that meanings are located on the page and not in the subjective readings of the reader/analyst. He also has reservations about interpretations of stylistic effects which assume a neat fit between linguistic forms and literary meanings. For Birch, the reader is part of a social and historical context. This context invariably determines the knowledge and value systems of the reader and influences the nature of the reader's interpretations. Thus an analysis of the relationship between language and meaning is never neutral and objective. Birch argues instead, that linguistic analysis, as applied and used in the analysis of literary texts, has to be *intertextual, interdisciplinary* and above all *reader-oriented*. And, furthermore, he argues strongly that literature is 'in the reader', and that we cannot foreclose on what is of value in literature by assuming a canon of texts from which we automatically draw when undertaking stylistic analysis.

Birch exemplifies these arguments with an analysis of several texts, both poetic and critical, centring on the work of the Singaporean poet Edwin Thumboo. Thumboo's work is not 'canonical' outside Singapore and the context of what is termed 'commonwealth' literature, but Birch's systematic and detailed account of its textual properties is closely related to his own experience and 'readings' of Singapore, especially the texts which he has read as an analyst. In this account, Birch enhances our own appreciation of Thumboo's work through an analysis which cannot be separated from Birch's own 'intertext' of socio-political, cultural and ideological positions.

13 'Working Effects with Words' – Whose Words?: Stylistics and Reader Intertextuality

DAVID BIRCH

The starting point for interpretation processes has to be the language of the text. The question, of course, is 'Whose language? Whose words?' The writer's? The reader's? Can we, as readers, 'access' a text – any text– if we are concerned only with the language of the writer? Can we 'get' to that language without using 'our own'? Can we 'get' to the text without constructing it with our own intertextuality? When we talk about style and stylistic effects, whose are they? 'Ours' as readers, or 'theirs' as writers? Neither literary nor stylistic analysis (if indeed one can make that separation at all) is just a matter of discussing such effects of language in a text, but is, as Deirdre Burton and others have suggested, 'a powerful method for understanding the ways in which all sorts of *realities* are constructed through language' (Burton, 1982: 201). But what realities? Whose realities? The writers' or the readers'? Or that of the worlds they variously belong to – including the academic? Statements made by the critic only gain significance when the forms of the text are related to textual functions in one or more of those (and other) contexts. Understanding and articulating that context, I would suggest, requires rather close attention to be paid to the reader's intertextuality.

Deirdre Burton has posed the following question:

> And where do you go from here? You've taken some poem or conve-niently sized piece of prose. You've spent time and effort mastering a sensible descriptive grammar of English. You've meshed understand-ing and knowledge of both to produce a rigorous analysis of the language used to construct your text, together with a relevant sensi-tive interpretation. You have talked about 'effects', 'foregrounded features,' 'overall impressions', and so on. Very nice. Very satisfying. But what are you going to *do* with it. What now? (Burton, 1982: 195)

The question, I would suggest, is the wrong way round. The analysis should not come *before* the question 'where do you go from here?'; the *where* needs to be determined by the *why?* and *so what?* of the analysis. And that is determined, it seems to me, by readers, and articulated *through* their recognition of what it is that makes them read a text in a particular way, i.e. *intertextuality*. Analysis therefore provides the means for you as reader to relate the text to your own experience of language and reality by actually constructing the text through and with your intertextual experiences.

But is that all? I would suggest not. We need to add that that construction and consequent articulation of your understanding *how* and *why* you read in the way you did cannot be done in a non-committed, apolitical, neutral way. 'Language use is not merely an effect or reflex of social organisation and processes, it is a *part* of social process. It constitutes social meanings and thus social practices' (Fowler *et al.*, 1979: 2). All language use is value-laden, but the quest for scientificness of language study has resulted in a discipline that is not prepared to make any judgements about its results, nor prepared to apply those judgements to the society in which the so-called 'science' operates.

Linguistic structures can and are used to 'systematise, transform and often obscure analyses of reality; to regulate the ideas and behaviour of others; to classify and rank people, events and objects in order to assert institutional or personal status' (Fowler, *et al.*, 1979: 2). It is naive to suppose that literature is any different from any other language in use in this respect. A critical linguistics, in this light, is therefore an alternative to a mainstream linguistics which has failed to 'serve as a tool for the reformation of society' (Jonz, 1982: 176). As part of this politicizing of linguistic stylistics, linguistic analysis and the experiences of the reader should *determine* the analysis and interpretation from the very beginning.

The Cartesian legacy of self, free from context, is no longer tenable in linguistics (see Quinn, 1982: 34). And the myth of 'self' as writer, and 'self' as reader functioning as separate, unrelated entities becomes equally untenable.

Linguistic structure is not arbitrary (see Pêcheux, 1982). It is determined by the functions it performs. Linguistics, for whatever use, must therefore be reoriented. This is happening, and, as it happens, more and more information is going to be made available for mapping the networks of meaning and significance which mediate between the structure and representations of reality. Probably one of the most common reactions to the earlier Jakobsonian analyses of texts', and their reluctance to engage in such discussions of meaning, has been a stylistics which is close to traditional literary analysis and concerns, and, of course, to traditional literary ideologies about the status of the text and its language within the canon.

Where discussions of meaning have been drawn from linguistics, the emphasis has tended to rest almost exclusively at an ideational level, resulting in a stylistics that seeks more and more to relate literary effect to linguistic forms within a *single* text. Rarely does this stylistics move beyond the boundaries of this text. The result, tends, then, to be little more than a linguistically oriented practical criticism, with the ideologies of a literature discipline determining the theoretical direction of the stylistics (and all that means in terms of a privileging discourse and critical elite) and not the ideologies of a linguistic discipline that sees, for example, language as social semiotic.

But too much work has been done, it seems to me, in both literary and linguistic theory for stylistics to continue, as it seems to be doing, underpinned with a theoretical assumption that the text is sufficient unto itself. Single-text analyses dominate almost exclusively (but see Threadgold, 1987). Intertextuality – the consequent alternative to analyses determined by a 'text in itself' ideology – has never been effectively tackled within literary stylistics, not that it has actually moved very far from its theoretical base into practical literary studies either. The consequence of this inactivity is a stylistics which continues to support the primacy of the writer and to interpret the linguistic struggles of the writer, not the struggles of readers, to produce dynamic meanings. A stylistics predominantly concerned with static interpretation spends its time *recovering* meaning by close analysis of interrelated linguistic levels. This is an argument in support of maintaining the primacy of the writer (and the mythical static meaning supposedly encoded into the text by the writer), and as a consequence, in support of the whole literature discipline and literature machinery that judges what should and should not be read (but see Hyland, 1986). Such a stylistics produces some valuable insights, but they are insights related to a theoretical base which is, for me at any rate, wholly unsatisfactory. I prefer to work with a stylistics that is more focused on the semiotics of the production of meanings in social discourse, of which a text, determined by whatever means to be literary, is just a part, not the whole; a stylistics, then, which is rather more concerned with reading processes; a stylistics which is intertextual, instead of treating the text as an autonomous artefact labelled as intrinsically special by literary ideologues. This does not mean that this stylistics is simply a study of register, but that it is concerned with understanding literariness and intertextuality as *a process of reading*, and with demythologizing notions of autonomy of text and 'poetic language' and that language, style, literary form and critic are innocent, disinterested and transparent vehicles for the expressing of meaning.

As a way of moving towards that, I look here at a tiny segment of the literary work of Edwin Thumboo, Professor of English Literature in the National University of Singapore, critic, academic, 'blooded' dissenter against British colonial rule in the 1950s, and now member of one of the higher echelons of the Singapore establishment. These are important things to mention, because this knowledge and the fact that I worked with him for four and a half years determine the way I read his work, both poetry and criticism.

I am interested here in a short poem called 'Steel', written very early in Thumboo's career as a poet (1954), and published in his first collection of poems *Rib of the Earth* (Thumboo, 1956).

Steel

They gave me subterraneous thoughts
How to work effects with words; for sauce
I gamed with alphabet,
Marshalling sense into the line
Till cunning showed beneath the verbs, cunningly.

Till mind, my mind, grew slanting
With habitations of the past.
Bowels of the soul congested, cough
In a current of fixed sounds.
How can others know my tongue-fire
Agony deprived of action?

O Abel, Rima's chords are lost:
The serpent bites,
Green Mansions, a scarecrow of steel
To hang our automatic greetings.

I chose this poem because it struck me as being an interesting statement about the dilemma faced by a writer as a radical under colonial domination (Singapore gained independence in 1965) – a dilemma which stands at odds with my image of Edwin Thumboo as a conservative, establishment figure in contemporary Singapore. This analysis is a way of me trying to sort out these different images I have as a reader of Edwin Thumboo. To get that far I have made certain assumptions: (*a*) that the 'me' of the poem is a writer, Edwin Thumboo, (*b*) that the 'they' of the poem represents a colonial presence; and (*c*) that the relation between these two creates a dilemma for one, but not necessarily for the other.

Beginning, then, with the first line, I immediately need to know who the 'they' are and who the 'me' is. What I know is that the 'they' gave 'subterraneous thoughts' to the 'me'. I wonder immediately about what is happening here. Can thoughts actually be given from one agent to another? The nominal 'subterraneous thoughts' is a surface realization for an underlying relational. That relational is a judgemental statement. What I do not know, though, is who is making that judgement. Is it the 'they' or is it the 'me'? The answer is important because,

as 'subterraneous' denotes something underground, and possibly connotes 'dissent' when collocated with 'thoughts', who determines the
dissent is presumably of importance. If it is the 'they' who are the
cause of the dissent, then the 'they' might well refer to some organization intent on dissent. If it is the 'me', then presumably the dissent
rests with the individual, and it is dissent quite possibly against the
'they'. The nominal does not tell me, but looking at it in this way can
raise some interesting questions and more importantly fix the stylistics
into an analytic methodology that questions every underlying assumption – a methodology that never assumes we have a shared vocabulary
and understanding of texts. Is the 'me' the subject of the following verb
group 'to work effects', or is it the 'they'? If it is the 'me', and the 'me' is
the source of the dissent, then presumably the working of effects with
words is tangible evidence of the dissent. One cannot work an effect
without making the words public. I do not know, of course, whether
the words are made public, what those words are even. If it is dissent
that is being talked about here, though, it is tentative, uncommitted. I
read it like that because of the following clause: 'sauce' connotes for
me, in tandem with the idea of dissent, a sort of 'cheekiness' that may
dissent but does so in a sort of tag-game way, a brief touch, not a
full-blooded grasp and dissent against an issue. The verb 'gamed'
seems to support this reading; it connotes, for me, the idea of playing,
of toying with something. What that something is is the alphabet. What
alphabet it is the poem does not reveal – is it for English? Malay? It is
not Chinese. Is it the language of the 'they' as well as the 'me'?
Presumably it is the language of the people that effects are being
worked for, but whether that is the same as the 'they' is not given. This,
presumably, would be needed information if I were reading 'dissent' as
one of the meanings in this poem. The 'me' is presumably the subject
of the following verb 'marshalling', which connotes an opposite for me
of the idea of playing. But just how does one marshal sense into a line?
The image is military, it seems to me, one of bringing language under
control, on the one hand, and of bringing, perhaps, people in a line
under control as well. It may be different, of course, for other readers.
Perhaps a reading that would contrast the control of the 'me' by the
'they' with the control of the language by the 'me' might work for me
here? But of course I have made quite a large assumption in doing that.
'Sense' denotes both the idea of meaning and the idea of common-
sense. Perhaps this refers to both the sense required to argue against
control by someone and the sense required to recognize that one
should dissent against such control. Either way, the manner in which
such sense can be marshalled is not tackled, but a result is given which
suggests that 'cunning showed beneath the verbs cunningly'. 'Cunning'
connotes for me both the idea of dissent and the idea of knowledge.
Both suggest the idea of power. Whose power, and what type of

power, is not given. What is the agent for the verb 'showed'? 'Cunning' is the subject, but someone – an agent – needed to put it where it was so that it could be seen. The agent is not made clear here, and as a consequence the activity looks rather mysterious, as if it just happens naturally. Things, of course, do not work like that.

What I am reading here is a set of assumptions. One is that language can be controlled as an instrument of dissent, another is that the agent of that dissent is somehow 'outside' that language once meaning or sense has been marshalled into a line; 'cunning' shows all by itself, but it was put there 'cunningly', in other words 'knowingly' as one reading of 'cunning', and as a sort of sleight of hand, as another way of reading 'cunning'. The 'sleight of hand' reading would seem to be supported by 'sauce', 'gamed' and indeed 'alphabet', with its connotations of the nursery/playroom. The 'knowingly' reading would seem to be supported by the 'to work effects' and 'marshalling', where material supervention processes connote a rather more serious agentive control, one that looks outside the playroom and into the big nasty world where dissent is a political and dangerous activity. I do not think, though, that it is an either/or reading here. Agentive control is exercised both in playing a game and in controlling dissent. The question here is 'Who is the agent, and who put that agent into this position?' The nursery/playroom image is useful here, I think, in helping me understand my reading. Nurseries are where minds are shaped by people – usually parents or guardians. Perhaps that is what is actually happening here. The following line suggests this, 'Till mind, my mind, grew slanting'. Of course 'my mind' may be a grammatical subject of the verb 'grew slanting', but it is certainly not the agent. Who or what is? 'Slanting' connotes both deviation and conformity. Deviation from what? Conformity to what? Whatever the 'what' is, the supervention process suggests a mysteriousness, as if it is perfectly natural for minds to grow in a particular direction. But of course this is not the case. Someone or something determines that direction. Presumably the 'they' of this poem. If it is the 'they', then the 'they' are the nursery guardians, to keep that image going for the moment, and the 'me' the occupant of that nursery. In other words the 'me' is under the control of the 'they', not just in an ability to put words together in a particular way but controlled to the extent that thinking processes are controlled; they have been slanted with 'habitations of the past'. This is not such an innocent nominal as might at first appear. I would suggest that it is a complicated realization of several processes conflated together, the result of which is to make unclear whose habitations are being talked about, and whose past is being talked about. The chances are it is the habitation of the 'they', the guardians, and the past of the 'they' as well. In other words the 'me' is shaped and directed towards a particular way of thinking, and that thinking is located in a past that belongs not to the 'me' but to an unnamed 'they'.

My reading so far is that someone, the 'me', is under control. That control is in the hands of a 'they' who do not simply control innocent activity but also determine thought. That thought is the early, shaping, cultural thought of early life, and also a thought that recognizes this determinism as an activity unescapable though undesirable. The effect, I would suggest, is a dilemma of identity. People are what they are, yet, given certain changing circumstances, what they are may not be the appropriate identity. The result: one uses what one is, to determine what one ought to be. In the light of this poem, and the reading so far, I would suggest that this is the dilemma of the English-educated anglophile conscious of a past and an identity rooted in the colonial power but mindful of the need to break away from that colonial power and strike out on one's own. The child, if you like, is ready to break away from the family, i.e. the colonized country is ready to break away from the colonial power, but the break is difficult because emotions are pulled in both ways. The phenomenon is very interesting in a South-East Asian context, because the image of the child breaking away is a product of the colonial value-system, not the Asian one, rooted in the notion of an undivided family. This is the dilemma in 'Steel' it seems to me, written by an English-educated Thumboo in 1954 when calls for breaking away from Britain came strong and fast. It was not a dilemma that the Chinese-educated faced; the colonial power was never the guardian that shaped their thoughts in the nursery.

I have, of course, from the very beginning been reading 'beyond the text itself', and am, in effect, using the text as a surface on which to combine a variety of intertextual sources of my previous reading knowledges. So far these sources have remained unnamed. But I need to incorporate some of my reading history into my analysis of my reading of 'Steel'. Compare, for example, the following:

Singapore Writing in English:
A Need for Commitment

Despite being a residue of colonialism, English turned out to have blessings the more practical of which are too well known to repeat. At least three ASEAN nations are among the beneficiaries. Such is the rate of change nowadays that 25 years of gathering direction ought to suffice for a language to steady its literary nerves. If one had to hazard a date for so subtle a matter as a shift in attitudes to a language, I would suggest 1950 as the time by which English, which had arrived more than a century earlier, ceased to lie outside the imagination, the aesthetics of those using it. What marginally creative writing that had hitherto emerged, sporadically, remained so precisely because writers did not see themselves as Singaporean or Malayan. Their literary consciousness, the idiom they employed or approved in others were appendages of metropolitan traditions represented by England and America. They lacked an informing vision, and even were there semblance of one, fragmented and dim, its ingredients were not drawn from the real-politik of life under colonial dispensation. Borrowed visions, however potent, tempting and fructifying originally, do not take root in colonised hearts. (Thumboo, 1978: 20–1)

This is an academic article written by Professor Thumboo and published in 1978, more than twenty years, at least, after the writing of 'Steel'. It is not disinterested, it is not the innocent, neutral comments of an objective academic: such things do not exist.

There are a number of assumptions here of interest for me.

(1)   English, a residue of colonialism, has blessings.
(2)   A language can steady its literary nerves.
(3)   Before 1950 English did not lie outside the imagination of those using it.
(4)   Creative writing in English would not have been 'marginal' if the writers before 1950 had had an 'informing vision'.
(5)   A shift took place from English as a descriptive medium to English as a creative medium.
(6)   This shift was crucial to the growth of literature.
(7)   This literature was specifically Singaporean/Malayan.
(8)   The shift was created by those who rose against colonial power.

The opening clause, with its nominal 'a residue of colonialism', followed by the noun 'English' acting in apposition to the first clause and as subject of the second clause, avoids actually stating the underlying relational: 'English is a residue of colonialism'. This is a fairly bold judgemental statement about how one sees the role of English. 'Residue of colonialism' is a pejorative, and, as one half of a relational, English would presumably also be a pejorative. This is avoided by giving theme prominence to the adverbial 'despite' in the first clause, and not to 'English', which is as far away as it could possibly be from a theme position in the first clause, by using the progressive aspect of the verb; and by making 'English' the subject and theme of the second clause. 'English', which is actually understood to be a pejorative, is kept quite far away from that judgement in the surface of the text. Instead, 'English' 'turned out' to have blessings. Just what exactly is the agent of the verb 'turned'? Certainly not 'English', because English itself cannot be the agent of a material action or supervention clause. But, by making 'English' the subject of this verb and giving it thematic prominence, the writer makes it look as if 'English' is actually the agent as well. What does not actually get said is who did the turning. In other words just who exactly is it who decided that 'English' 'turned out' to have blessings? It certainly did not happen by itself, though it is made to look as if this was a perfectly natural phenomon.

I then read that it has 'blessings' which, following the clausal patterning of the first and second clause, has an appositional nominal following – 'the more practical of which' – which acts as subject and theme of the third clause. What happens here is that the nominal actually realizes conflated relationals: 'there are blessings'; 'some blessings are practical'; 'some blessings are not practical'. Thematic prominence is given to the 'practical' not the unpractical blessings. In other words the emphasis is again on the positive side of English, even though it is a residue of colonialism. That positive side is reflected in the use of the nominal 'beneficiaries', which realizes something like 'X receives benefits'. The nominal actually conceals the process involved in the idea of receiving benefits – someone gives the benefits. The nomimal here focuses attention away from that 'someone'. The 'someone' presumably would be the 'owners' of English, i.e. the colonial power, but the nominal makes it appear as if receiving benefits is just something that happens naturally, or, because the theme position in the clause is taken up by the nominal 'At least three ASEAN nations', that it is actually these nations and not the colonial power who are the agents beneath the nominal 'beneficiaries'.

Information that I am lacking at the moment, then, is just what are the blessings and who actually discovered them?

Being told that 'they are too well known to repeat' begs the question. Who are they too well known to? The readers of a journal devoted to English literature and thus with a vested interest in ensuring that English as a residue of colonialism is made to appear valuable in a country that actually rejected that colonialism and is made up of a population very few of whom could claim English as a mother tongue?

I get into the third sentence with a number of assumptions already made about the status of English, though none of them adequately explained. The explanation for accepting this 'residue of colonialism' starts to be made in this third sentence. The explanation rests on the nominal 'the rate of change', which assumes that the rate at which things change is a natural activity, that no one is actually responsible for that rate of change, yet is a realisation of a verbal process that would require there to be an agent. Using the nominal removes the agent and hence the people responsible for the act of change. This is true also of the following nominal '25 years of gathering direction'. The verbal process of directing is removed by using the nominal. Who determines the direction? What exactly is that direction? Directions do not 'gather' on their own. People are behind this– who are these people? Who controls the rate at which the direction 'gathers'? Who decides how fast or slow it goes? The nominal makes it look as if directions just 'gather' mysteriously on their own, but this is not the reality. The reality is that there are people with vested interests in the direction something takes. In this case, that something is the status of a language which is the 'residue of colonialism'. Hence, the people with the vested interests are the people who wish to keep that residue of colonialism, rather than rejecting it with the rest of colonialism.

The distancing of these agents continues in this same sentence. What is the 'real' agent behind the process of the language steadying its literary nerves? Languages do not steady. People steady. So who are these people who have decided that twenty-five years is a long enough time for English to 'steady its literary nerves'? Because it certainly is not a natural process, as it is made to appear here. Likewise the nominal in the following sentence, 'a shift in attitudes to a language'. Here I seem to have moved from a point where time was the myster-ious and innocent agent involved in making English acceptable, to a position where it is assumed that time created the shift in attitudes. I do not read who the agents are of the process realized by the nominal 'a shift', yet shift implies a supervention process which in turn requires an agent. It is not given, and again the whole process of accepting English is seen to be one without agents; without people with vested interests involved; as if it is simply a natural, uncontrollable event. It is not.

I read that 1950 might usefully be suggested as the time when English 'ceased to lie outside the imagination, the aesthetics of those using it'. The point of pinpointing the actual date is to show at which time the 'literary nerves' of English had settled. Again, the verbal process realized by the nominal 'literary nerves' (a relational) is disguised in the nominal, and as a consequence so are the agents of that process. The relational, 'nerves are literary' or some such equivalent, is a judgement made by someone, not a natural phenomenon. In other words 1950 is a point in time when someone made a judgement about the ability of English to be used for writing literature. But what had it been used for before then? Was it incapable of producing literature before 1950? Well, it was a residue of colonialism, so presumably before 1950, when it was not capable of literature, it was capable of colonialism. In other words English equals colonialism but not litera-ture before 1950, and because it can be used for literature after 1950 it is no longer equatable with colonialism. The logic involved here seems to be a little skewed towards a vested interest in maintaining English as a language for writing in, even though it represents in 'real' terms – though not in the terms of Thumboo's article – colonialism. It could be used for literature after 1950 because before then it did 'lie outside the imagination, the aesthetics of those using it' but by 1950, because of the *mysterious* agency of time, it did not.

Just what does this mean? First of all it looks as if one of the blessings that English had was that it could lie outside the imagination. But of course this makes it appear as if 'English' could cease of its own volition to lie outside the imagination, when in fact there had to be agents involved in that process. Who are the agents who decided that English could cease to lie outside the imagination?

Obviously, in these terms, one of the 'practical blessings' of English is therefore its ability to cease to lie outside the imagination, and thus be usable for writing literature. But of course this is a decision that has been made by an agent, not by language or time, as is made to appear the case here. In other words by an agent with a vested interest in promulgating English as a vehicle for writing literature in a country that had rejected colonialism, and all that that meant for the status of writing in English.

The next nominal to follow is 'what marginally creative writing', which is a conflated nominal for a series of processes something like: 'there is creative writing'; 'creative writing is marginal'; 'creative writing is not marginal'. In other words in the relationals underlying this nominal a judgement is being made; this judgement is not something that is 'natural', something that is innocent, it is a judgement made by an agent. Again, I do not read who that agent is in this text. It appears as if everything here is part of the natural, not culturally created, order. Further, the notion of marginal is not something that is related to the natural order of things. Again, someone has to decide what marginal means, what it is relative to. I read that marginal is relative to whether or not the writer was a Singaporean or Malayan. In other words creative writing was marginal before 1950 because it was produced with a language that was colonial and by writers for whom the language did not lie outside their imagination and aesthetic. In other words those writers who did not identify themselves as anti-colonial produced marginally creative writing in English. Those who claimed themselves to be anti-colonial in and after 1950 produced non-marginally creative writing – presumably.

I further read with another nominal, that, 'the literary consciousness' etc. of these writers who did not proclaim themselves as anti-colonial were 'appendages of metropolitan traditions'. The traditions belonged to England or America, and so therefore did the consciousness of the writer who had not declared an anti-colonial interest. How then did that consciousness become Singaporean or Malayan? I read this in another nominal – with 'an informing vision'. Of course, the nominal realizes an underlying process, the agent of which is not clearly seen or stated in this article. Who decides on what constitutes 'informing'? Who does this actual informing? It is assumed, again, that it is a natural, innocent operation. It is not, of course; people with vested interests are the agents. What I read is that the informing vision would come 'from the real-politik of life under colonial dispensation' – in other words, unpacking the nominal and the processes it realizes, *dissent* would inform the vision. Those visions which are borrowed from colonialism 'do not take root', but visions cannot take root, they can be put into place, though, by people.

What I have tried to show so far is that the position Edwin Thumboo takes up in this article informs the way I read his poem 'Steel'. It does not mean, of course, that this is at all relevant to Edwin Thumboo's reading of this poem. I am not trying to psychologize readings for Thumboo; I am not trying to uncover meanings in the poem that say anything about him. It is *my* reading I am trying to understand and explain, not Thumboos's intended meanings.

I suggested in that reading that identity was a central issue for me. The critical article supports my reading to the extent of showing that a writer like Edwin Thumboo inevitably has a vested interest in his English-educated roots, though this needed to be unpacked in this article. Further understanding might perhaps be had by comparing two other poems by Thumboo, 'May 1954', a poem written, as far as I can tell, at pretty much the same time as 'Steel', and 'Fifteen Years After', dedicated to Shamus Frazer, Edwin Thumboo's English literature teacher in Singapore and written many years after 'Steel'.

May 1954

We do not merely ask
No more, no less, this much:
That you white man,
Boasting of many parts,
Some talk of Alexander, some of Hercules
Some broken not long ago
By little yellow soldiers
Out of the Rising Sun . . .
We ask you see
The bitter, curving tide of history,
See well enough relinquish,
Restore this place, this sun
To us . . . and the waiting generations.

Depart white man.

Your minions riot among
Our young in Penang Road
Their officers, un-Britannic,
Full of service, look
Angry and short of breath.

You whored on milk and honey.
Tried our spirit, spent our muscle,
Extracted from our earth;
Gave yourselves superior ways
At our expense, in our midst.

Depart:
You knew when to come;
Surely know when to go.

Do not ignore, dismiss,
Pretending we are foolish;
Harbour contempt in eloquence.
We know your language.

My father felt his master's voice,
Obeyed but hid his grievous, wounded self.
I have learnt:
There is an Asian tide
That sings such power
Into my dreaming side:
My father's anger turns my cause.

Gently, with ceremony;
We may still be friends,
Even love you . . . from a distance.

Fifteen years after

That day when you left,
Taking for the safe keeping of us,
My figure from Bali,
Smooth, beckoning goddess
Urged to serenity by the lotus she stood on,
You too were poised in the brittle afternoon . . .
That day of incense I have kept to this.

You died recently. They say you died.

But no matter,
Image and breath persist,
Grow as I grow, would not suffer the mind's quip.
Your beard, dubious, smelling of cheese and beer,
Affectionate, still presides; your voice pursues,
Sweet or harsh, but ever itself.
Many sit in their rooms, remembering how
You took us through Christabel, Sohrab and Rustum,
Death's Jest-Book, The Raven,
Brought new worlds to meet our own.
You lived – beautiful, precarious
Feeding us irrevocably on your self
While other gods shed their skin, withdrew,
Taking their notes with them.

But teacher and friend, white man,
What are they doing to you.
They, who come after?

Smaller, paler, full of themselves,
Suave, sideburned, tousled? Setting up trade
In principle, freedom, intellectual honesties?

They are eloquent,
These revivers of cliches, these late comers,
Who strike a neat phrase, write letters to the press.

Old Shamus,
Your image and breath slip.
You are dying now,
When I need you most to live.

'May 1954' shows mostly in the modals and the qualifications, the dilemma that exists between the 'they' and 'me' of 'Steel', i.e., in my reading, between the colonial and the English-educated 'anti-colonist' torn between independence of nation and independence (or lack of it) of thought. The contrast in 'May 1954' is expressed as existing between the 'we' and the 'you white man'. Dissent is open: the moods of the verbs are imperatives; the agent of those imperatives is the 'we', the goal the 'white man'. The language is no longer seen as belonging to the 'we', as it was in 'Steel' and as it was in the critical article; here it belongs to the white man. What belongs to the 'we' is the land, 'this place', 'the sun', peaceful streets, natural resources, self-respect, national identity, Asian identity. The only thing that belongs to the white man is the language. 'May 1954' represents one side of that dilemma, then: the need to demonstrate solidarity with a cause against colonialism. The modal 'may' in the line near the end of the poem 'We may still be friends' could well be expressing a willingness to remain friends, or it may well be a way of showing that the power now rests in the hands of the 'we' not the 'white man'. The modal shows that a decision has to be taken, and that decision lies in the hands of the ones ordering the white man to leave. Identity in this poem, though, rests with a return to non-colonial roots, in other words the ones not talked about in 'Steel'. The nominal 'waiting generation' is a realization for an underlying relational which is a judgement based on an assumption that future generations are (a) waiting to be born and (b) waiting for the white man to depart. The contrast is made throughout between the 'we' and the 'white man'; it is 'your minions' versus 'our young', 'our spirit', 'our earth', 'our expense', 'our midst'; and it is these that will be the heritage of those 'waiting generations', not the colonials who whore, who are short of breath, who riot, who adversely influence the young by such rioting, who try the spirits of others, who make their muscles tired, who extract things from the earth that is not theirs, who give themselves superior ways. The agents are out in the open, and it is clear, it seems to me, that identity in this case rests not so much in a positive vision of the future – that occurs nowhere in my reading of this text – but in a rejection of what is considered to be negative.

The other side of the dilemma, it seems to me, can be read in Thumboo's poem 'Fifteen Years After'. Here the actual heritage is a heritage rooted not in a father's anger 'turning a cause', as in 'May 1954', but in an English education which shaped a young mind. This mind expresses itself in a language which, if indigenized, could create a literature within which a national identity could be located. Potentially, it is a language which, if Singaporeanized, would be a mark of colonialism no longer. But the roots go deep. The English literature teacher – a white man, a colonist – is not treated as the white men of 'May 1954' are. It is interesting that 'Fifteen Years After' was not included in *Rib of Earth*, Edwin Thumboo's collection of poems which was dedicated to Shamus Frazer and contained 'Steel'. The white man of 'Fifteen Years After' is compared, like the anti-colonialists and the 'white man' of 'May 1954', with the new white men of post-colonial Singapore – the expatriates who 'come after'. I note the agent deletion here: the expatriates do not mysteriously 'come' to Singapore, they are invited and paid for doing a job, which, if it could be, would be done by a Singaporean. These expatriates, like the colonials in 'May 1954', are negatively contrasted in the poem. Shamus Frazer had a sweet voice, not harsh, 'ever itself', which connotes for me the idea of honesty. He 'brought new worlds', he 'lived – beautiful, precarious', he fed his students with his self. He was a teacher and friend; he was also a colonialist and all that meant in 'May 1954', but none of this is mentioned. Shamus Frazer belongs to the nursery; he is one of the guardians I posited in my reading of 'Steel', who helped to slant the mind, to shape the subterraneous thoughts, to show how to work effects with words, to marshal sense into a line. He was part of the 'habitations of the past', and he is uncriticized in 'Fifteen Years After'. He, I would suggest, is the other half of the identity dilemma. The expatriates in 'Fifteen Years After' are the necessary scapegoat for the sycophantic presentation of English education in the poem. They are used to offer a post-colonial, ideologically acceptable view of a Singaporean identity which in 'May 1954' came with a rejection of the colonials, and which in the critical article came with what looked like a rejection of colonialism but, once unpacked stylistically, turned out to be an embrace of it. The expatriates in this poem are like the colonials in 'May 1954'; they are small, pale, 'full of themselves', which I presume to connote 'arrogance'; they are suave, sideburned and tousled. They revive cliches and write letters to the press. In other words they show themselves to be disrespectful of the new order; they upset the kindly face of English colonialist humanism which was held so dear in 'Steel', in the critical article and in the figure of Shamus Frazer in 'Fifteen Years After', whose image is dying and being damaged by the white men who came 'after'.

The dilemma is very apparent. English, the residue of colonialism, was what shaped the 'me' of 'Steel'; it belonged to kindly old men like Shamus Frazer, who helped to shape the mind of the 'me' in 'Steel'. English as a language shaped the heritage of the 'me'; that heritage is inescapable and cannot be lost or shaken off, neither could the actual languages, the critical article made clear. Solution: suggest arguments about national identity and so on that are based on the reshaping of English as the property no longer of the colonial but now of the Singaporean/Malayan. The second paragraph of the critical article opens with the following line:

The shift from descriptive to creative modes, which turned English into an instrument meeting the expanding psyches, themselves evolving, was crucial to the growth of literature. (Thumboo, 1978)

What caused this shift? This is not mentioned. Shifts do not happen by themselves, they are created and controlled by people – people with vested interests. If your heritage, your mind, was shaped by English, as suggested in 'Steel', then you have a vested interest. If you are a Professor of English Literature in a country that rejected colonialism and have been writing only in English, you have a vested interest. If you have argued that English is now a property of Singaporean identity, then you are going to condemn expatriates who come to Singapore and use that language to 'revive cliches' and write letters to the press, because you are disturbing the carefully constructed order that has been designed (it did not happen naturally) by the people with the vested interests in maintaining the controlling power of English.

This, then, is the sort of analysis I would offer in an alternative, intertextual stylistics designed to explain readings. It is not disinterested; it is motivated from a position that is interested in understanding a text as a surface upon which meanings can be produced – meanings created by readers, not meanings supposedly encoded in a text by a writer. Whether they are 'in there' is not the issue. Something has 'allowed' me to read 'Steel' in that way, and I have tried to show some of the ways in which that has happened. I have tried to understand some of the relations that I feel obtain amongst my readings of a number of texts (a very limited number for the purposes of this chapter). More delicate analyses could take place amongst these texts and more stylistic comparisons be made at more sophisticated, more detailed levels than I have undertaken here. Further texts could be added.[1] My message is that an interested, intertextual reader's stylistics will necessarily be open-ended; it will be discursive and will not be specifically designed to articulate, as its sole purpose, connections between linguistic levels and literary effects, but will be as concerned with the reader's connections amongst texts as well. Intertextual approaches argue against seeing a text as an end in itself, and argue against explanations of reactions and responses to texts by intralinguistic means only.[2]

Suggestions for Further Work: Chapter 13

1 In this chapter, David Birch covers several important theoretical issues, one of which is his discussion of the methodological weaknesses of traditional stylistic analysis. Traditional stylistics, he claims, rarely moves beyond the boundaries of a particular text, and as a result, tends to be 'little more than a linguistically oriented practical criticism, with the ideologies of a literature discipline determining the theoretical direction of the stylistics'.
How do the numerous *discourse stylistic* analyses undertaken in the course of this book stand in the light of this criticism? Are they simply an extension of traditional practical stylistics? Or do they not fit into this category at all? Whichever conclusion you reach, try to support it with explanations of what you see to be the aims and scope of discourse stylistics.

2 Consider the extent to which a stylistic analysis you have recently undertaken has been affected by the following factors:

   (i)   *gender*
   (ii)   *social class*
   (iii) *politics*
   (iv)   *culture*
   (v)   *education*
   (vi)   *racial group.*

These factors overlap, of course, but which are the most powerful determining influences on your position as an analyst of texts? Which of these factors are most responsible for your understanding of the term literature? When you analysed the text, were you aware of any recent reading which accounted for the way in which you analysed the text and the interpretations of it which you may have made? What knowledge of what other texts may have affected the nature of your interpretation?

3 Particularly valuable sources for further reading in this area are Alexander (1982), Durkin (1983), Fowler (1975, 1980), Hodge (1977), Norris (1976) and, especially, Threadgold (1986, 1987). For further texts by Thumboo, see Thumboo (1970, 1973, 1976, 1977, 1979).

Notes: Chapter 13

1 In this paper I concentrate on the criticism and poetry of Edwin Thumboo,

but see Birch (1986: 171–90) for a much wider selection of texts by other writers which form a part of my reading intertextuality for 'Steel'.
2   A version of this essay was delivered to the 23rd AULLA Congress, Melbourne, February, 1985, and appeared as Birch (1986). I have also included some of Birch (1984), given the difficulty of obtaining that volume.

References: Chapter 13

Alexander, G. (1982), 'Politics of the Pronoun in the Literature of the English Revolution', in Carter (1982), pp. 217–35.

Birch, D. (1984), 'Style, Structure and Criticism: Introduction', *Indian Journal of Applied Linguistics*, special issue, vol. 20, nos 1–2, pp. 1–8.

Birch, D. (1986), 'Cunning Beneath the Verbs: Demythologising Singapore English Poetry', in Hyland (1986), pp. 147–90.

Burton, D. (1982), 'Through Glass Darkly: Through Dark Glasses', in Carter (1982), pp. 195–214.

Carter, R. (ed.) (1982), *Language and Literature: An Introductory Reader in Stylistics* London: Allen & Unwin.

Durkin, K. (1983), Review of Kress and Hodge (1979), *Journal of Pragmatics*, vol. 7, no 1, pp. 101–4.

Fowler, R. (ed.) (1975), *Style and Structure in Literature: Essays in the New Stylistics* (Oxford: Blackwell).

Fowler, R. (1980), 'Linguistic Criticism', *UEA Papers in Linguistics*, vol. 11, pp. 1–26.

Fowler, R. *et al.* (1979), *Language and Control* (London: Routledge & Kegan Paul).

Hodge, R. (1977), 'Literacy and Society: Some Consequences of Linguistic Modes of Production', *UEA Papers in Linguistics*, vol. 4, pp. 1–17.

Hodge, R., and Kress, G. (1974), 'Transformations, Models, and Processes: Towards a More Usable Linguistics', *Journal of Literary Semantics*, vol. 3, no. 1, pp. 5–21.

Hyland, P. (ed.) (1986), *Discharging the Canon: Cross-Cultural Readings in Literature* (Singapore: Singapore University Press).

Jonz, J. (1982), Review of Fowler *et al.* (1979), *Applied Linguistics*, vol. 3, no. 3, pp. 176–8.

Norris, C. (1976), 'Theory of Language and the Language of Literature', *Journal of Literary Semantics*, vol. 5, pp. 90–7.

Pêcheux, M. (1982), *Language, Semantics, Ideology,* trans. H. Nagpal (London: Macmillan).

Quinn, Jr. C. J. (1982), '"Literary" Language: Is it Different?', *University of Michigan Papers in Linguistics*, vol. 4, no. 1, pp. 29–56.

Threadgold, T. (1986), 'Introduction' to Threadgold *et al.* (eds), *Language, Semiotics, Ideology*, Sydney Studies in Society and Culture No. 3 (Sydney: University of Sydney), pp. 15–60.

Threadgold, T. (1987), 'Stories of Race and Gender: An Unbounded Discourse', in D. Birch and M. O'Toole (eds), *Functions of Style* (London: Frances Pinter).

Thumboo, E. (1956), *Rib of Earth* (Singapore: privately published).

Thumboo, E. (ed.) (1970), *The Flowering Tree* (Singapore: Educational Publication Bureau).

Thumboo, E. (1973), *Seven Poets: Singapore and Malaysia* (Singapore: Singapore University Press).

Thumboo, E. (1976), *The Second Tongue: An Anthology of Poetry from Malaysia and Singapore* (Singapore: Heinemann).

Thumboo, E. (1977), *Gods Can Die* (Singapore: Heinemann).

Thumboo, E. (1978), 'Singapore Writing in English: A Need for Commitment', *Commentary* (Singapore), vol. 2, no. 4, pp. 20–5.

Thumboo, E. (1979), *Ulysses by the Merlion* (Singapore: Heinemann).

Glossary

This is a glossary of the main and most frequently used discourse and stylistic terms in the book. However, definitions of this kind can be dangerous, glossing, as they frequently do, over complex theoretical issues. In this respect, the cited sources should be consulted wherever possible. A few of the technical terms used in the book are not included in the glossary as they have been defined, expanded and applied within individual chapters. Examples of this kind are *phatic communion* (Chapter 2), *logico-deductive* and *associative relations* (Chapter 6), *presupposition* (Chapter 8), *face-threatening acts* (Chapter 9), *intertextuality* (Chapter 13). Shorter, more crude definitions of such terms in a glossary would be of limited value.

Act
The act is the smallest unit on the discourse rank scale, occurring below that of the *move*. Some acts can be used independently (e.g. elicitations, directives and informatives), although some (e.g. starters) must be bound to other acts. See **elicitation**, **directive**, **informative** and **starter**. See also **move**.

Alethic (system)
One of the four modal systems proposed by L. Dolezel for the analysis of narrative texts. An alethic system consists of the concepts of possibility, impossibility and necessity. Alethic stories often explore 'alternative possible worlds'. For instance, narrative agents impossible in the real world (gods, spirits etc.) are assigned properties and perform actions in the fictional world. Agents from one narrative world may also intervene in the events of another world – Lewis Carroll's *Alice's Adventures in Wonderland* providing a paradigm example of this type of alethic story. See Dolezel (1976). See also **axiological**, **deontic** and **epistemic** systems.

Apposition
Elements of language which have equal grammatical status or which are co-referential are said to be in apposition:

   I gave John, my brother, a book.

Here 'John' and 'my brother' are in apposition. To remove one or the other element does not affect the grammar or meaning of the sentence.

Axiological (system)
One of the four modal systems proposed by L. Dolezel for the analysis of narrative texts. An axiological system is constituted of concepts of goodness, badness and indifference. Axiological stories are those in which narrative

agents desire certain values and are consequently prompted into initiating action that will lead to an attainment of those values. The underlying structure of the most popular type of axiological story is the *quest*, which provides the modal base for 'a host of narratives, ranging from the expedition of the Argonauts to typical erotic narratives' (Dolezel 1976: 8). See also **deontic**, **epistemic** and **alethic** systems.

Coda
A narrative component which signals that a story has been ended. A coda brings the listener back to the point at which he or she entered the narrative and is often realized by a general observation which is timeless in character. For example:

And I see that man now and again . . .
And ever since that time I feel paranoid about riding in a car.

See Labov (1972).

Comment
A discourse act which functions to expand, justify and provide additional information to a preceding **informative** (or comment). For example:

A: I think I'll go into town . . . (*informative*)
    After all, it shouldn't be too busy . . . (*comment*)
    mind you, it might rain . . .(*comment*)

See **informative**.

Complicating action
An important narrative category which provides the 'what happened?' element of a story. Complicating action is realized by *narrative clauses* which normally have a verb in the simple past. These clauses are also temporally ordered, so that a change in their sequence will also result in a significant change in the order of the events of the story. For example:

. . . we ate at the bistro and then we got on a bus and went to the museum . . .

See Labov (1972).

Constative
Constatives were originally distinguished from *performative* utterances by the philosopher J. L. Austin as statements, assertions, or descriptions of states of affairs. Examples are:

(*a*)   The cat is on the mat.
(*b*)   I'm sorry.
(*c*)   There is a bull behind you.

They were thus viewed as utterances which *say* things rather than *do* things. Furthermore, they could be true or false:

A: I'm sorry
B: No you're not!

Austin himself acknowledged that there were problems with the performative/ constative dichotomy. For instance, in response to example (*c*), B may reply 'Thank you for your warning'. This suggests that an ostensibly constative utterance (i.e. a description of a state of affairs) may have a performative function (i.e. a warning) and is thus quite similar in its consequences to an explicit performative like 'I warn you that there is a bull behind you'. On the basis of this and other more complex arguments, the distinction between constatives and performatives was eventually collapsed in favour of a more general theory of *speech acts*. See **speech act** and **performative**.

Conventional Implicature

Conventional implicatures are derived from conventional – as opposed to strictly logical – meanings of certain words. Particularly important are *connectives* (such as *therefore*, *so*, *but*, *besides* etc.), which do not contribute to the truth conditions of the expressions they occur in, but nevertheless convey 'meaning'. For instance, the use of 'but' in

He arrived on Thursday, but left on Sunday

conventionally implicates that there is some kind of contrast between the two conjuncts. This contrast cannot be adequately recovered by reference to truth conditions alone. Levinson (1983) contends that a great many expressions have conventional implicatures associated with them. The use of terms of address is one such case. For example, in the utterance

Could I go home, sir?

the item 'sir' conventionally implicates that the addressee is male and is socially higher in rank.

Conversation(al) Analysis

Conversation analysis (CA) refers almost exclusively to the work on conversational structure undertaken by the ethnomethodologists (notably, that of H. Sacks, E. Schegloff and G. Jefferson). It is an approach which stresses speakers' own interpretations of the structure of interaction and it attempts to account for the ways in which utterances are *sequenced* in conversation. (Hence the development in the literature of terms such as *side-sequence*, *insertion-sequence*, *pre-sequence*, *misapprehension-sequence* and so on.) Being strongly data-oriented, work in CA often uses detailed transcriptions of actual talk as a means of gaining insights into the recurrent patterns and sequential organization of naturally occurring conversation. Levinson (1983: ch. 6) provides a useful overview of conversation analysis. See also **ethnomethodology**.

Conversational Implicature

Conversational implicature accounts for the inferences that are drawn when speakers flout one or more of the four conversational maxims. For instance, if A writes the following as a reference for a candidate who has applied for a post in philosophy

Mr X's command of English is excellent, and his attendance has been regular then the maximum of *quantity* has been flouted. (A has given less information than would have been required). This *implicates* that A thinks that Mr X is unsuitable for the post. In the following example

A: You failed your exam.
B: Terrific!

B's remark flouts the maxim of *quality* (it is not literally truthful) and hence *implicates* the opposite of what is actually stated. In the following

Johnny: Hey, let's play marbles.
Mother: How's your homework progressing?

the maxim of *relation* is flouted. The *implicature* generated by this is regulative in function, as the mother attempts to modify the behaviour of Johnny. See the important article by Grice (1975) for a fuller account of conversational implicature. See also **conversational maxim**.

Conversational Maxim

Grice (1975) contends that speakers observe the co-operative principle in conversation by adhering to four sets of conversational maxims. These maxims are general principles which underlie an optimally efficient, co-operative use of language. The four categories are:

(1) *quantity:* make your contribution as informative as is required for the current purposes of the exchange –don't say too much or too little;
(2) *quality:* try to make your contribution one that is true;
(3) *relation*: be relevant;
(4) *manner:* be perspicuous – avoid unnecessary obscurity and ambiguity.

Grice formulates these maxims on the assumption that the purpose of the conversation is a maximally efficient exchange of information, and he notes that speakers, through their need for indirection, tact, politeness and so on, do not always obey these maxims in conversation. He outlines four typical cases where speakers fail to fulfil maxims:

(i) They may unostentatiously *violate* a maxim, which in some cases will lead to lies and deceit.
(ii) They may *opt out* of fulfilling the maxim (e.g. 'I cannot say more, my lips are sealed').
(iii) They may be faced with a *clash*, being unable to fulfil one maxim without breaking another.
(iv) They may *flout* a maxim, by blatantly failing to fulfil it. This is the situation which characteristically gives rise to *conversational implicatures*. See **co-operative principle** and **conversational implicature**.

Co-operative Principle

The notion of the co-operative principle has been developed by the natural language philosopher H. P. Grice, who contends that conversations normally exhibit some degree of coherence and continuity. This suggests that participants are observing a general principle of co-operation. Grice formulates this co-operative principle in the following way:

Make your conversational contribution such as is required, at the stage at which it occurs, by the accepted purpose or direction of the talk exchange in which you are engaged. (1975: 45)

See **conversational maxim**.

Declarative

The sentence structure standardly used to make statements:

The cat is in the garden
He seems ill.

In declarative sentences the subject comes before the verb. See **imperative** and **interrogative**.

Deixis

This may loosely be characterized as the 'orientational features of language'. It comprises the elements of language which locate an utterance in relation to a speaker's viewpoint, whether in space (e.g. *these/those*), time (e.g. *now/then*) or interpersonal relations (e.g. *we/you*). The individual words are called *deictics*.

Deontic (system)

One of the four modal systems proposed by L. Dolezel for the analysis of narrative texts. A deontic system is formed by the concepts of permission, prohibition and obligation. Thus a story in which a deontic modality predominates will be one which concerns moral and legal constraints and involves narrative concepts such as *prohibition, punishment, reward* and *test*. In a deontic narrative, the courses of possible actions that are open to characters will be governed by some sort of norms. See Dolezel (1976). See also **alethic**, **axiological** and **epistemic** systems.

Directive

A discourse act which is realized by a command and functions to request a non-linguistic response. The appropriate non-linguistic response to a directive is known as a *react*. Hence:

A: Pick up that coat! (*directive*)
B: *picks up coat.* (*react*)

See Burton (1980) for a fuller discussion.

Elicitation

A discourse act which is normally realized by a question and functions to request a linguistic response.

A: Fancy a drink?
B: Fine.

In this exchange, A's utterance is an elicitation. B's utterance is a *reply*, functioning to provide the appropriate linguistic response. See Burton (1980) for a fuller discussion.

Epistemic (system)
One of the four modal systems proposed by L. Dolezel for the analysis of narrative texts. An epistemic system is represented by concepts of knowledge, ignorance and belief. The modal base of the epistemic narrative is the *mystery* or *secret*, from which develops the transformation of ignorance into knowledge. Epistemic modality underlies a wide variety of texts, ranging from detective stories to more 'literary' narratives, such as Dickens's *Little Dorrit* and Conrad's *Heart of Darkness*. See Dolezel (1976). See also **alethic, axiological** and **deontic** systems.

Ethnomethodology
Ethnomethodology is the subdiscipline of sociology that has been pioneered by Harold Garfinkel and developed in the work of his followers (notably, H. Sacks, E. Schegloff and G. Jefferson). Ethnomethodology focuses on the 'commonsense knowledge' and 'practical reasoning' used by members of a culture, and seeks to explain how these members interpret the world around them and interact with that world. Ethnomethodologists are concerned with the interpretative processes which underlie verbal (and non-verbal) acts, and how speakers employ certain techniques to make sense of interaction. Hence the choice of the term **ethnomethodology** – the methodology employed by speakers themselves in interpreting social interaction. Ethnomethodologists do not undertake large-scale quantitative surveys of social behaviour, but instead develop their theoretical constructs from detailed analyses of data obtained from 'everyday activities'; and, as much of human interaction is *verbal* interaction, a great deal of attention has been directed towards *conversation analysis*. Two collections which contain several important ethnomethodological studies are Sudnow (1972) and Gumperz and Hymes (1972). See also **conversation analysis**.

Evaluation
An important element in natural narrative, which functions to make 'the point' of a story clear. Evaluation is marked by a number of linguistic forms, including, amongst other things, expressive phonology, ritual utterances, explications, and evaluative commentary which is directly addressed to the listener and is external to the events of the narrative proper.

Exchange. See **Move**

Exophora
Exophoric reference is reference *outside* the text to the immediate context of situation. For instance, in the command

   Close that window!

the item 'window' can be understood by reference to the immediate situation, without prior introduction in the discourse. The term *homophora* is reserved for a special kind of 'fixed' exophoric reference, where the entities referred to are stable fixed phenomena. For example:

   The octopus is a delicacy in Greece.

Here, the interpretation of 'octopus' does not depend on the immediate context of interaction.

Felicity Conditions
A set of conditions which must be satisfied if a performative utterance is to be successful. For instance, in the case of the performative

I now pronounce you man and wife

the speaker must be the appropriate institutional figure and the words must be uttered in the presence of the relevant parties. In the case of naming a ship, the speaker must be the appointed namer and the ship must not already be named differently; only if these and other felicity conditions are met can the act of naming be successful. If felicity conditions are not satisfied, then the resulting peformative will be *unhappy* or *infelicitous*. Thus, the performative

I bequeath my watch to you

will be infelicitous if the speaker possesses no watch, whilst

I hereby sentence you to death

will be infelicitous if the speaker has not been appointed to carry out such a procedure.
See **performative**.

Generic sentence
A sentence which has generalized reference and proclaims a univeral truth, for example:

Lions are dangerous.

Note that 'lions' here is generic, since it denotes the class *lion* without any specific reference to a particular lion. A famous (ironic) generic sentence is the opening of Jane Austen's *Pride and Prejudice*:

It is a truth universally acknowledged, that a single man in possession of a good fortune, must be in want of a wife.

Grammetrics
Grammetrical relations in poetry are those affecting the congruence of grammar and metrics. For example, a grammetrical account of a poem might explore, amongst other things, the interrelationship between clause structure, lines in a poem and its metrical and stanzaic organization.

Idiolect
An idiolect is the language of an individual speaker.

Illocutionary Act. See Speech Act

Imperative
The sentence structure standardly used to issue commands, for example:

Close the door.
Leave the room!

Structurally, imperative sentences do not contain a grammatical subject, nor do they permit distinctions of tense. See **interrogative** and **declarative**.

Implicature. See **Conventional Implicature** and **Conversational Implicature**

Indirect Speech Act
Examples of indirect speech acts are:

(*a*) Could you leave now? (*as command*)
(*b*) It would be helpful if you mended it. (*as command*)
(*c*) You're going home now? (*as question*)

In general, indirect speech acts *do not* (i) contain an explicit performative verb indicating illocutionary force (i.e. 'I order you . . .', 'I hereby declare . . .' etc.), (ii) use the three major sentence types in the roles normally associated with them (i.e. imperatives for commanding, interrogatives for questioning, declaratives for stating). Note that, in the indirect speech acts above, (*a*) commands through the use of an interrogative and (*b*) through the use of a declarative, whilst (*c*) questions through the use of a declarative. Clearly indirect speech acts are a widespread feature of language usage. See Searle (1975). See also **speech act**.

Information structure
Information structure is the ordering of a text (independently of its grammatical structure) into units of information. These units of information fall into two general categories: the *given* (what the speaker treats as information recoverable to the hearer) and the *new* (what the speaker treats as non-recoverable).

Informative
A discourse act which functions solely to provide information. The appropriate response to an informative is an *acknowledge*, which signals attention and understanding. Hence:

A: I think I'll go into town. (*informative*)
B: OK. (*acknowledge*)

See Burton (1980) for a fuller discussion.

Interrogative
The sentence structure which is frequently (although not always) used to ask questions:

Is the cat in the garden?
Do you live around here?

Interrogatives are normally characterized by the positioning of the first element of the verb phrase at the start of the sentence. Interrogative sentences are often used as *indirect speech acts*, as in

Could you pass the salt?

where the communicative function is a request for action rather than information. See **declarative**, **imperative** and **indirect speech act**.

Locutionary Act. See **Speech Act**

Material process
This is where the process expounded by the verb in a clause is one of *doing*. A material process has two inherent participant roles associated with it which are *actor* (obligatory) and *goal* (optional). Thus:

> The farmer / chased / the animal
> *actor*   *process*   *goal*

> The bomb / exploded
> *actor*   *process*

Berry (1975) makes some useful distinctions between different types of material processes. For instance, they may be *action* processes (performed by animate actors) or *event* processes (where the actor is inanimate). Action processes may themselves be further subdivided into *intention* processes (performed voluntarily) and *supervention* processes (where the process just happens). Thus, the system network for material processes displays the set of options shown in Fig. 14.1.

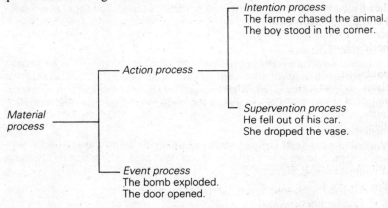

Figure 14.1

See Berry (1975) and Halliday (1985) for a fuller discussion. See also **transitivity** and **relational process**.

Maxim. See **Conversational Maxim**

Membership Categorization Device
A termed coined by Harvey Sacks to explain how communication often works through sets of shared assumptions and associations. He provides the following example, which comprises the first two sentences of a child's story:

> The baby cried. The mommy picked it up.

Sacks seeks to explain how we know that the 'mommy' of the second sentence is the mother of the 'baby' in the first – even though there are no syntactic or lexical links between the two. He contends that 'baby' and 'mommy' are *categories* from the same *collection*. This collection (which could also include the category 'daddy') has a *device* called 'family'. Thus, if the first person has been categorized as 'baby', then further persons may be referred to by other categories from the same collection (e.g. 'mommy', 'daddy', but not, say, 'adult'). 'Family' will therefore be the membership categorization device which allows us to read 'the mommy' as 'the mommy of the baby' in the example above. See Sacks (1972*a*, 1972*b*).

Modality

Modality refers to the means by which speakers express judgements on the truth of the propositions they utter. It encompasses the degrees of

(1) probability (*possibly*, *probably*, *certainly*)
(2) usuality (*sometimes*, *usually*, *always*)

that speakers attach to propositions. There are various forms of modal expressions. Particularly important are modal verbs which express varying degrees of commitment ranging from low-value modality (*could*, *might*) through median-value modality (*would*, *should*) to high-value modality (*must*, *need*, *has to*). Other forms of modal expression are sentence adverbs (see examples under (1) and (2)), evaluative adverbs (*luckily*, *fortunately*, *sadly*) and *generic sentences*. See Halliday (1985) for a fuller definition. See also **modulation** and **generic sentences**.

Modulation

Related to **modality**, modulation refers to the degree of *obligation* and *inclination* that speakers attach to the propositions they utter. In commands, the intermediate points between positive and negative represent degrees of obligation:

You're allowed to / supposed to / required to leave the room.

In offers, the intermediate points represent degrees of inclination:

I'm willing to / anxious to / determined to help.

See Halliday (1985) for a fuller explanation.

Mood

This is the general term used to describe different types of sentence. The major mood categories are **imperative**, **interrogative** and **declarative**. These, however, are **grammatical** categories and they do not form a one-to-one correspondence with the *discourse* categories of command, question and statement. Any one mood type may, in fact, have a variety of communicative functions.

Move

The move is the minimal interactive unit in discourse. It has an internal structure of its own, consisting of one or more *acts*. Moves themselves go to make up *exchanges* – the unit next up on the discourse hierarchy. Thus, the following example is a *single* conversational exchange which is made up of *two* moves:

A: John! Have you got the time? (*opening move*)

B: Four o'clock (*supporting move*)

The opening move here itself consists of two discourse acts: a *summons* ('John!') and an *elicitation* ('Have you got the time?'); whilst the supporting move consists of a single act: a *reply*. Discourse analysts have offered different classifications of move types, but see Burton (1980) and Sinclair and Coulthard (1975) for important definitions. See also **summons** and **elicitation**.

Nominal Group

A nominal group is a phrase which contains a noun as *headword*. The headword of a nominal group may be *modified* by items which precede it, or *qualified* by items which follow it. For example,

the large houses nearby
is a nominal group of which 'houses' is the headword, 'the' and 'large' are modifiers and 'nearby' is a qualifier.

Orientation

One of the categories identified by Labov in his work on natural narrative. The orientation component provides information concerning the *who*, *what*, *when* and *where* of a story, thereby helping the listener to identify the relevant time, place, persons and situation. Orientation is frequently characterized by past-progressive verbs and adverbs of time, manner and place. For example:

We were living in Sheffield that year and both of us were working at the time.

Performative

Originally distinguished from *constatives* by the natural language philosopher J. L. Austin. Performatives are utterances which perform an action, rather than just describing or asserting something. Examples are:

(*a*)   I name this ship the King John.
(*b*)   I declare war on X.
(*c*)   I bequeath you my gold watch.
(*d*)   I warn you that there is a bull behind you.

Utterances (*a*) to (*d*) perform the actions of naming, declaring, bequeathing and warning respectively. Austin suggests that the insertion of the adverb 'hereby' is a useful test for performative utterances ('I hereby name this ship . . .'; 'I hereby declare war . . .'). Furthermore, performatives cannot be considered true or false, as in

A: I hereby sentence you to death.
B: ?That's false.

although they may be *troubled* or *infelicitous*. See **constative** and **felicity conditions**.

Perlocutionary Act. See Speech Act

Pragmatics

Pragmatics is the study of the use and meaning of utterances in context. It attempts to account for those aspects of meaning which cannot be recovered by straightforward references to the semantic properties of the sentences uttered. See Levinson (1983) and Leech (1983).

Recipient Design
Recipient design refers to how speakers in conversation construct their talk in ways which display an orientation and sensitivity to other conversationalists. Recipient design has an important bearing on topic selection and it also functions to regulate the size and distribution of speaker *turns*. See Sacks, Schegloff and Jefferson (1974: 727). See also **turn.**

Register
A rather imprecise term which describes the kind of language use appropriate to a particular function in a situational context. For example, a legal register or a register of advertisements. Features of language are selected in accordance with content, purpose, the relation of the language user to an audience etc.

Relational process
This is a process of 'being' and it represents relationships that exist between elements in a clause. These relationships may be intensive (as in 'John is wise'), circumstantial (as in 'John is at home') or possessive ('John owns a piano'). See Halliday (1985: ch. 5) for a comprehensive definition. See also **transitivity** and **material process**.

Resolution
A narrative component which recapitulates the final events of a story. The resolution normally contains the last of the narrative clauses which began the complicating action. For example:

... and when all was said and done the plane landed safely.

See **complicating action.**

Skip connecting
Whereas a speaker's utterance normally relates to the previous utterance (of another speaker), skip connecting occurs where a speaker relates back to the last-but-one utterance (i.e. his or her own). For example:

A: You've lived in this area a long while?
B: ... they used to be coming up the hill ...
A: I mean, in Belfast?
B: ... the army ...

Here, A and B decline to talk about the previous speaker's topic and reassert their own. Skip connecting is fairly common in conversations. See Coulthard (1977: 78) for further examples.

Sociolect
A sociolect is a social-class dialect. Sociolects are not defined according to region (as in regional dialects) but according to social group. The sociolect used by a particular social group will differ from those used by other groups from the same area. However, the term itself is rather loose.

Sociolinguistics

Sociolinguistics is the study of language and society. It examines the ways in which language varies systematically in relation to the social characteristics of its speakers. These social characteristics include, among other things, social class, social network, ethnic group, race, religion, age, gender.

Speech Act

The term speech act refers to what is *done* when something is said (e.g. requesting, stating, declaring, warning, threatening etc.). Utterances may thus be viewed as performing specific actions as well as providing a particular 'meaning'. It is important to note, however, that the speech act status of an utterance is not always recoverable by reference to the form of the sentence used. For instance, the interrogative sentence 'Could you close the door?' will often be interpreted as a request for action (and not a question), whilst the imperative sentence 'Have some cake' will often be interpreted as an offer (and not a command). Austin (1962) argues that in producing a speech act a speaker performs three kinds of act simultaneously. These are:

(1)   *locutionary act* – the act of saying (i.e. uttering a meaningful grammatical utterance in the given language);
(2)   *illocutionary act* – the act performed in saying something (i.e. making a statement, request, declaration etc.);
(3)   *perlocutionary act* – the act performed by saying something (i.e. the effects on the hearer produced by the illocutionary act – e.g. frightening, convincing, persuading etc.).

Thus, the utterance 'Shoot him!' is, in a *locutionary* sense, a meaningful imperative sentence. It may perform the various *illocutionary acts* of ordering, urging or advising, which may have the *perlocutionary* effects of forcing, persuading, or frightening the addressee into carrying out the shooting. A sentence may have different illocutionary *force* depending on the context in which it is uttered. For instance, the utterance 'Go!' may, in different situations, have the illocutionary forces of (i) ordering; (ii) giving advice (e.g. as a response to the question 'Should I go to the party tonight?'); (iii) granting permission (e.g. as a response, in friendly tones, to 'Can I have the afternoon off?'). For some of the original work on speech acts, see Austin (1962) and Searle (1969); for useful discussions in the general area, see Stubbs (1983), Levinson (1983) and Coulthard (1977); for a specific application of speech act theory to literary discourse, see Pratt (1977).

Starter

A discourse act which directs attention towards an area, in order to ensure the successful uptake of a following initiation. For example:

Listen to this!

See Burton (1980) for a fuller discussion.

Summons

A discourse act which functions to mark a boundary in discourse and indicate that the producer of the summons has a topic to introduce. Summonses are normally realized by reference to the name of another participant. See Burton (1980) for a fuller discussion. See also **vocative**.

Suprasentential
The organization of language *above* the level of the sentence.

Theme
The theme of a clause is the element which comes first and signals what the clause is going to be about. It introduces the topic which will be developed in the remainder of the clause (the *rheme*). Hence:

The old man / ate the fish slowly
theme   rheme

When the theme of a clause is coincidental with its grammatical subject (as in the example above) it is said to be *unmarked*. When the theme is not the subject, it is *marked*, as in:

Slowly / the old man ate the fish
theme   rheme

See Halliday (1985) for a comprehensive definition.

Transaction
A larger discourse unit, the transaction occurs above the *exchange* and below *interaction* in the discourse hierarchy. Burton (1980) proposes the following discourse rank scale:

(1)   interaction
(2)   transaction
(3)   exchange
(4)   move
(5)   act

A transaction will thus be made up of one or more exchanges, all of which should relate to the same general topic. See **move** and **act**.

Transitivity
In systemic-functional linguistics, transitivity concerns the representation of meaning in the clause and features the different types of *process* that are recognized in the language. Transitivity is an important component of any language as it shows how speakers encode in their language their mental picture of reality and how they account for their experience of the world around them. Halliday (1985: 101) points out that speakers' most powerful conception of reality is that it consists of 'goings-on' (of doing, happening, feeling, being) and that these goings-on are 'sorted out in the semantic system of the language and expressed through the grammar of the clause'. The semantic processes expressed by the clause have potentially three components. These are:

(1)   the *process* itself – typically realized by the verbal group;
(2)   the *participants* in the process – typically realized by nominal groups;

(3)   the *circumstances* associated with the process – typically expressed by adverbial and prepositional groups.

The following example exhibits all three components:

The farmer / chased / the duck / through the yard
participant   process   participant   circumstances

See Halliday (1985: ch. 5) for a comprehensive account of transitivity. See also **material process** and **relational process**.

Turn

The turn is the basic analytic unit in *conversation analysis*. Speaker turns may vary in length, ranging from a minimal one-word utterance to extended talk for many minutes. The following example is a two-turn sequence:

A: You've been here before, haven't you?
B: Yeah.

Note that A's tag question ('haven't you?') signals that the first turn has been completed, inviting the second party to speak next. Much attention has been paid to the organization of *turn-taking* in conversation. See, for example, Sacks, Schegloff and Jefferson (1974). See also **conversation analysis**.

Vocative

Vocatives are items such as *summonses* and *address forms* which refer directly to the addressee. These items are not part of the main body of the sentence which accompanies them. The italicized items in the following examples are vocatives:

Hey, give us a break!
What's the time, *Joe*?
I think, *sir*, that you should leave.

See Levinson (1983: ch. 2) for a fuller discussion. See also **summons**.

References: Glossary

Austin, J. L. (1962), *How to Do Things with Words* (Oxford: Oxford University Press).

Berry, M. (1975), *Introduction to Systemic Linguistics*, vol. 1 (London: Batsford).

Burton, D. (1980), *Dialogue and Discourse: A Sociolinguistic Approach to Modern Drama Dialogue and Naturally Occurring Conversation* (London: Routledge & Kegan Paul).

Cole, P., and Morgan, J. (eds) (1975), *Syntax and Semantics*, vol. 3, *Speech Acts* (New York: Academic Press).

Coulthard, R. M. (1977), *An Introduction to Discourse Analysis* (London: Longman).

Dolezel, L. (1976), 'Narrative Modalities', *Journal of Literary Semantics*, vol. 5, pp. 5–14.

Grice, H. P. (1975), 'Logic and Conversation', in Cole and Morgan (1975), pp. 41–58.

Gumperz, J. J., and Hymes, D. (eds) (1972), *Directions in Sociolinguistics* (New York: Holt, Rinehart & Winston).

Halliday, M. A. K. (1985), *An Introduction to Functional Grammar* (London: Edward Arnold).

Labov, W. (1972), *Language in the Inner City* (Philadelphia, Penn: University of Philadelphia Press).

Leech, G. N. (1983), *Principles of Pragmatics* (London: Longman).

Levinson, S. (1983), *Pragmatics* (Cambridge: Cambridge University Press).

Pratt, M. L. (1977), *Toward a Speech Act Theory of Literary Discourse* (Bloomington, Ind.: Indiana University Press).

Sacks, H. (1972a), 'On the Analyzability of Stories by Children', in Gumperz and Hymes (1972), pp. 325–45.

Sacks, H. (1972b), 'An Initial Investigation of the Usability of Conversational Data for doing Sociology', in Sudnow (1972), pp. 31–74.

Sacks, H., Schegloff, E., and Jefferson, G. (1974), 'A Simplest Systematics for the Organization of Turn-Taking for Conversation', *Language*, vol. 50, no. 4, pp. 696–735.

Searle, J. R. (1969), *Speech Acts: An Essay in the Philosophy of Language* (Cambridge: Cambridge University Press).

Searle, J. R. (1975), 'Indirect Speech Acts', in Cole and Morgan (1975), pp. 59–82.

Sinclair, J. M. and Coulthard, R. M. (1975), *Towards an Analysis of Discourse: The English Used by Teachers and Pupils* (London: Oxford University Press).

Stubbs, M. (1983), *Discourse Analysis: The Sociolinguistic Analysis of Natural Language* (Oxford: Blackwell).

Sudnow, D. (ed.) (1972), *Studies in Social Interaction* (New York: Free Press).

Index